THE SUBVERSION OF THE APOCALYPSES IN THE BOOK OF JUBILEES

Society of Biblical Literature

Early Judaism and Its Literature

Judith H. Newman, Editor

Mark J. Boda
George J. Brooke
Esther G. Chazon
Steven D. Fraade
Martha Himmelfarb
James S. McLaren
Jacques van Ruiten

Number 34

THE SUBVERSION OF THE APOCALYPSES
IN THE BOOK OF JUBILEES

THE SUBVERSION OF THE APOCALYPSES IN THE BOOK OF JUBILEES

Todd R. Hanneken

Society of Biblical Literature
Atlanta

THE SUBVERSION OF THE APOCALYPSES
IN THE BOOK OF JUBILEES

Copyright © 2012 by the Society of Biblical Literature

All rights reserved. No part of this work may be reproduced or transmitted in any form or by any means, electronic or mechanical, including photocopying and recording, or by means of any information storage or retrieval system, except as may be expressly permitted by the 1976 Copyright Act or in writing from the publisher. Requests for permission should be addressed in writing to the Rights and Permissions Office, Society of Biblical Literature, 825 Houston Mill Road, Atlanta, GA 30329 USA.

Library of Congress Cataloging-in-Publication Data

Hanneken, Todd Russell.
  The subversion of the apocalypses in the Book of Jubilees / by Todd R. Hanneken.
     p. cm. — (Early Judaism and its literature ; no. 34)
  Includes bibliographical references and indexes.
  ISBN 978-1-58983-642-6 (paper binding : alk. paper) — ISBN 978-1-58983-643-3 (electronic format)
  1. Book of Jubilees—Criticism, Textual. 2. Apocalyptic literature—History and criticism. 3. Hebrew language—Morphology. I. Title.
  BS1830.J8H37 2012
  229'.911—dc23   2012003461

Printed on acid-free, recycled paper conforming to
ANSI/NISO Z39.48-1992 (R1997) and ISO 9706:1994
standards for paper permanence.

Contents

Preface ix
Abbreviations xiii

1. Introduction 1
   1.1. The Problem   3
      1.1.1. Overestimating the Similarity to the Apocalypses   5
      1.1.2. Underestimating the Similarity to the Apocalypses   8
   1.2. The Solution   11
      1.2.1. Distinguish Layers of Abstraction: Literary
             Morphology, Typical Ideas, and Social Context   11
      1.2.2. Define the Genre Based on Literary Morphology   16
      1.2.3. Other Layers Follow: Ideas, Social Movements,
             and Function   22
      1.2.4. Jubilees Uses the Typical Literary Morphology to
             Express Atypical Ideas   24
   1.3. Introductory Examples of Subversion   26
      1.3.1. Survey of Pervasive and Structurally Significant
             Use of the Literary Genre   26
      1.3.2. Evil, Injustice, and the Lack Thereof   31
      1.3.3. Eschatology   38
      1.3.4. Conclusion   49

2. The Spatial Axis 51
   2.1. Angels and Demons   53
      2.1.1. Before the Flood: The Origin of Evil   54
         2.1.1.1. The Enochic Apocalypses   54
         2.1.1.2. The Danielic Apocalypses   57
         2.1.1.3. Jubilees   57
      2.1.2. After the Flood: The Persistence of Demons   60
         2.1.2.1. The Early Apocalypses   61

2.1.2.2. Jubilees	61
2.1.3. Angelic Mediation	64
2.1.3.1. Evidence outside the Apocalypses	64
2.1.3.2. The Early Apocalypses	68
2.1.3.3. Jubilees	69
2.1.4. The Leader of Evil	70
2.1.4.1. Terms, Names, and Titles	71
2.1.4.2. Satan in Nonapocalypse Received Scriptures	75
2.1.4.3. The Early Apocalypses	76
2.1.4.4. Mastema in Jubilees	77
2.1.5. Angels and Demons in the Eschatological Crisis and Restoration	82
2.1.5.1. The Early Apocalypses	83
2.1.5.2. Jubilees	84
2.2. Humans	88
2.2.1. Groups	88
2.2.1.1. Third Isaiah	90
2.2.1.2. The Enochic Apocalypses	91
2.2.1.3. The Danielic Apocalypses	95
2.2.1.4. Jubilees	97
2.2.2. Violence	105
2.2.2.1. The Enochic Apocalypses	107
2.2.2.2. The Danielic Apocalypses	108
2.2.2.3. Jubilees	111
3. The Temporal Axis	119
3.1. The Decline of History	120
3.1.1. The Enochic Apocalypses	120
3.1.2. The Danielic Apocalypses and the Book of Daniel	123
3.1.3. Jubilees	125
3.2. The Final Woes	127
3.2.1. The Enochic Apocalypses	129
3.2.2. The Danielic Apocalypses	135
3.2.3. Jubilees	136
3.2.3.1. The "Final Woes" Are Just Chastisement from God as Prescribed by the Covenant	136
3.2.3.2. The "Final Woes" Have Already Been Fulfilled	138
3.2.3.3. The White Children	144
3.3. The Judgment	148

3.3.1. The Enochic Apocalypses	149
3.3.2. The Danielic Apocalypses and the Book of Daniel	151
3.3.3. Jubilees	153
3.3.3.1. Jubilees 23	154
3.3.3.2. The Judgment Discourse in Jubilees 5	157
3.3.3.3. The Role of Enoch in Judgment	158
3.3.3.4. The Judgment of Individual Nations	161
3.4. The Restoration	165
3.4.1. Third Isaiah	166
3.4.2. The Enochic Apocalypses	167
3.4.3. The Danielic Apocalypses and the Book of Daniel	170
3.4.4. Jubilees	171
3.4.4.1. The Restoration in Jubilees 23 Is Gradual and Has Already Begun	172
3.4.4.2. Jubilees 1:26–29 Identifies the Indwelling of the Sanctuary in the Restoration with the Indwelling of the Sanctuary of Aaron	174
3.4.4.3. The Law Revealed at Sinai Will Not Be Surpassed	181
3.4.4.4. The Separation of the Israelites Was Planned from the Beginning	183
3.4.4.5. The Borders of the Land of Israel Will Be Restored, Not Dissolved	187
3.4.4.6. The Eschatological Calendar Will Restore, Not Replace, the Calendar Observed in the Past and in Heaven	190
3.5. Conclusion	193
4. The View of Revelation	195
4.1. The Use and View of Received Authority	196
4.1.1. The Enochic Apocalypses	201
4.1.1.1. The Use of Enochic Traditions	202
4.1.1.2. The Use of Non-Enochic Jewish Traditions	203
4.1.2. The Danielic Apocalypses	207
4.1.2.1. The Use of Danielic Traditions	207
4.1.2.2. The Use of Non-Danielic Jewish Traditions	212
4.1.3. Jubilees	217
4.1.3.1. The Heavenly Tablets	220
4.1.3.2. Departures from Genesis and Exodus	225

4.2. The Dependence of Revelation on Wisdom	236
4.2.1. The Enochic Apocalypses	240
4.2.2. The Danielic Apocalypses	242
4.2.3. Jubilees	246
4.2.3.1. Revelation without the Elitism of Wisdom	247
4.2.3.2. Revelation Made Unambiguous and Accessible	252
5. Explanation	259
5.1. Literary Insights into the Author's Process	261
5.2. Literary Insights into the Audience's Process	266
5.3. Historical Context	272
5.4. Cultural Context	284
5.5. Conclusion	290
Bibliography	295
Index of Ancient Sources	313
Index of Modern Authors	325
Index of Subjects	329

Preface

The core idea of this book came together remarkably quickly as a seminar paper for James VanderKam's "Jubilees" seminar in the spring of 2005. Especially as I look back, I see how many people helped me leading up to that whirlwind of research and writing and in the years of development and revision since. My first course in biblical literature as an undergraduate, "The Song of Songs," with Michael Fishbane, started me in the direction of paying attention to nuance and reshaping in ancient literature. Meanwhile, a course on the sociology of Second Temple Judaism with John Collins laid the groundwork of my understanding of apocalyptic literature, thought, and movements. I wish I could remember more frequently where I learned something, but when a characterization of apocalyptic thought comes into my head with an Irish accent, I know where I first heard it.

My interest in early interpretation flourished with respect to Jubilees in several courses with my master's level adviser, James Kugel. His seminar on Pseudo-Philo provided my first entry into the diversity and rivalry of eschatological thought, particularly messianic biblical interpretation. This interest developed in a course on the Dead Sea Scrolls with Hanan Eshel, ז״ל, who continued to guide me in the following years and whom I miss greatly.

I came to Notre Dame for doctoral work with interests in the diversity of eschatological thought and the reuse of scriptural authority. There seemed to be no end to courses related to eschatology in various periods, through twentieth-century systematic theology as taught by Mary Doak. Eugene Ulrich and Hindy Najman shaped my appreciation of pluriformity and development in scriptural authority. Two courses in particular laid the groundwork for the present project. First, in Gary Anderson's "Leviticus" seminar I paid special attention to the covenant curses in Leviticus (and their relationship to Deuteronomy), which prepared me to contrast covenant curses with the typically apocalyptic "final woes." Second, James

VanderKam's "Daniel" seminar pressed me to think about the relationship between the court tales and apocalypses in Daniel, particularly the ideas and literary genre of chapters 2 and 7, as well as the penitential prayer recontextualized in Dan 9. With an interest in eschatology, apocalypses, and interpretation I started exploring a paper topic for VanderKam's "Jubilees" seminar by reading through his bibliography on Jubilees. One entry jumped off the page, "Kugel, 'The Jubilees Apocalypse.'"

I had not been thinking of Jubilees as an apocalypse. I immediately turned to Jub. 23 with an eye to the ways in which the chapter is and is not like the apocalypses. From the beginning of the chapter I noticed that "snow, frost, stomach aches" sounded more like a typical day in March than final woes, although it may have helped that I was in South Bend rather than San Antonio. I would have been content to focus on one verse, but every verse in that chapter stood out as sounding like an apocalypse, with a change in meaning. The seminar paper focused on Jub. 23. I am indebted to VanderKam for suggesting that the paper could develop into a dissertation.

I started by learning Ethiopic and returning to the early apocalypses and the rest of Jubilees. I tested whether my view of Jub. 23 held for other chapters and found that the tension appeared in several structurally significant chapters and in smaller references throughout the book. I investigated scholarship on the genre of the apocalypses and found many useful tools, but never an adequate treatment of Jubilees. I worked on the historical context of Jubilees, particularly comparison with 1 Maccabees, 2 Maccabees, Josephus, and what we know about the high priesthood from 175 to 150 B.C.E. Over my remaining three years at Notre Dame the committee for my candidacy exams and dissertation was tremendously supportive and challenging in helpful ways. I am grateful to James VanderKam, Eugene Ulrich, Gary Anderson, and Gregory Sterling. I am also grateful for the intellectually stimulating environment of my peers, especially Rhodora Beaton, D. Andrew Teeter, Molly Zahn, and J. Wesley Foreman. I was fortunate enough to have the time and resources to focus on my work and complete the basic content of the dissertation in the summer 2007 and defend it in 2008. The dissertation, "The Book of Jubilees Among the Apocalypses," is freely available online from the University of Notre Dame library.

The present work is significantly reworked from the dissertation, based on much helpful feedback and additional research. The present first and last chapters are new, drawing from chapters 1, 2, 3, and 7 from the dissertation. The present chapters 2–4 depend on the dissertation chapters 4–6 for the basic points, with changes more in the conclusions. Since the dissertation, I was aided by many readers who challenged me to refine my explanation of discord between Jubilees and the typical apocalypses of its day. Among these, I am especially grateful to several rounds of feedback from John Collins and Annette Reed and ongoing conversation with James VanderKam. In particular, I previously focused on a particular understanding of the term "irony" but have since decided that the term has too many imprecise connotations, many of which do not apply to Jubilees. Like the present work, the dissertation focused on the layers of literature and ideas as independent and logically prior to reconstructions of ideological movements. The dissertation used the term "apocalyptic worldview" to mean a cluster of ideas in which ideas of the apocalypses overlap in ways implicit in the literary genre. I have since decided that the term "worldview" too much connotes a complete system of ideology held by a person or movement and is not appropriate for the cluster of ideas typical of the apocalypses. I do not claim to have found the perfect word in "subversion" to describe the use of the apocalyptic genre in Jubilees. Simpler terms would not have conveyed the complexity of what Jubilees does with the genre. I have also tried to avoid jargon that relies too much on one theory of genre, although my thinking about genre has grown significantly since the dissertation. The present work is a study of Jubilees, first and foremost. I modestly hope that it also makes a contribution to the discussion of authorship and authority in antiquity and the use of genre in early Jewish literature, especially the apocalypses.

Abbreviations

ANTZ	Arbeiten zur neutestamentlichen Theologie und Zeitgeschichte
ArBib	The Aramaic Bible
BETL	Bibliotheca Ephemeridum theologicarum Lovaniensium
BJRL	*Bulletin of the John Rylands University Library*
BJS	Brown Judaic Studies
BO	Biblica et Orientalia
BZAW	Beihefte zur Zeitschrift für die alttestamentliche Wissenschaft
CBET	Contributions to Biblical Exegesis and Theology
CBQMS	Catholic Biblical Quarterly Monograph Series
CEJL	Commentaries on Early Jewish Literature
ConBNT	Coniectanea biblica New Testament Series
CurBR	*Currents in Biblical Research*
DSD	*Dead Sea Discoveries*
EDSS	*Encyclopedia of the Dead Sea Scrolls*. Edited by Lawrence H. Schiffman and James C. VanderKam. 2 vols. New York: Oxford University Press, 2000.
HSS	Harvard Semitic Studies
HTR	*Harvard Theological Review*
HUCA	*Hebrew Union College Annual*
IDBSup	*The Interpreter's Dictionary of the Bible: Supplementary Volume*. Edited by Keith R. Crim. Nashville: Abingdon, 1976.
JBL	*Journal of Biblical Literature*
JJS	*Journal of Jewish Studies*
JQR	*Jewish Quarterly Review*
JSJ	*Journal for the Study of Judaism*
JSJSup	Journal for the Study of Judaism Supplement Series
JSOT	*Journal for the Study of the Old Testament*

JSOTSup	Journal for the Study of the Old Testament Supplement Series
JSJ	*Journal for the Study of Judaism*
JSP	*Journal for the Study of the Pseudepigrapha*
JSS	*Journal of Semitic Studies*
JTC	*Journal for Theology and the Church*
JTS	*Journal of Theological Studies*
Neot	*Neotestamentica*
OTL	Old Testament Library
RB	*Revue biblique*
RevQ	*Revue de Qumran*
SBLEJL	Society of Biblical Literature Early Judaism and Its Literature
SBLSCS	Society of Biblical Literature Septuagint and Cognate Studies
SBLSP	Society of Biblical Literature Seminar Papers
SBLSymS	Society of Biblical Literature Symposium Series
SemeiaSt	Semeia Studies
SJT	*Scottish Journal of Theology*
STDJ	Studies on the Texts of the Desert of Judah
StPB	Studia post-biblica
SVTP	Studia in Veteris Testamenti Pseudepigrapha
TRu	*Theologische Rundschau*
TSAJ	Texte und Studien zum antiken Judentum
VT	*Vetus Testamentum*
VTSup	Supplements to Vetus Testamentum
WMANT	Wissenschaftliche Monographien zum Alten und Neuen Testament
WUNT	Wissenschaftliche Untersuchungen zum Neuen Testament
ZAW	*Zeitschrift für die alttestamentliche Wissenschaft*

1
Introduction

The book of Jubilees was written at a crossroads in Jewish history. In the wake of the Maccabean revolt, the most fundamental issues of Jewish identity, practice, and authority were fiercely debated. Over time, multiple positions emerged, none of which matched the claims of Jubilees perfectly. Those who did accept the authority of Jubilees were at the margins of the Jewish, and later Christian, intellectual worlds. Thanks mostly to the church of Ethiopia and the caves at Qumran, the book was preserved remarkably well for modern scholars. Since the nineteenth century, and increasingly in recent years, Jubilees has been a rich resource for many areas of inquiry in early Judaism. The book is unrivaled for length and coherence in the period. For example, Jubilees is almost twice the length of Sirach[1] and seems to have undergone less revision since the original composition. Among those many pages, scholars consistently find something of interest to almost any inquiry.

Among the wealth of information, Jubilees sometimes sends mixed signals. Among the diversity of scholarly perspectives, confusion sometimes results. One area of confusion was identified early in the modern study of Jubilees and remains unresolved: the relationship of Jubilees to contemporary apocalypses such as 1 Enoch and Daniel. Although some scholars do not hesitate to put Jubilees and 1 Enoch in the same category, and others study Jubilees at length without observing anything apocalyptic about it, most scholars are aware of the tenuous connection. At times Jubilees sounds very much like an apocalypse, and at other times not at all. Points of similarity and difference are often noted, but without a criti-

---

1. The comparison is based on the word count of James C. VanderKam's translation of Jubilees (48,337 words; see *The Book of Jubilees* [2 vols.; CSCO 510–511; Leuven: Peeters, 1989], vol. 2) and the NRSV translation of Sirach (without the prologue, 25,701 words).

cal standard for prioritizing one feature over another. In order to move forward, unexamined assumptions need to be examined, definitions need to be clarified, and layers of abstraction distinguished. Fortunately, the essential tools have already been established. This study will apply those tools to Jubilees, with surprising results. Out of the confusion emerges a clear and consistent pattern.

The similarities between Jubilees and the apocalypses lie at the level of the literary genre. Jubilees meets every morphological requirement of the genre as defined by *Semeia* 14.[2] The differences lie at the level of ideas, the claims made about the elements of the morphology. Jubilees radically subverts the most basic claims made by the apocalypses. The use of the literary genre raises the issues, but Jubilees rejects the typical positions on those issues. This can be seen in the three major parts of the definition of the literary genre: transcendence on the spatial axis, transcendence on the temporal axis, and the revelatory framework.

Every apocalypse, by definition, deals with transcendence on the spatial axis, such as invisible agents, instruments, and places of judgment. Jubilees talks about demons, sinful watchers, angelic princes of nations, and a cosmic figure evocative of Satan. Typically, apocalypses raise these issues because they explain the experience of evil and suffering in the visible world.[3] These agents temporarily interfere with the expected relationship between God and the righteous. In Jubilees they have no relevance for the righteous. Ancient sin has no enduring effects for Israel. Demons and angelic princes afflict other nations, but Israel has full immunity as long as it stays away from Gentiles.

Similarly, every apocalypse deals with transcendence on the temporal axis. They address themes such as protology, eschatology, or the structure and meaning of history. They often include particular motifs such as final woes, a day of judgment, and a new creation. Jubilees consistently deals with protology and the structure and meaning of history. Chapter 23 deals with eschatology most explicitly, and essential language and motifs of judgment and new creation pervade the book. Typically, the transcendent view of the temporal axis conveys the idea that the present moment

---

2. John J. Collins, "Apocalypse: The Morphology of a Genre," *Semeia* 14 (1979): 1–19. The present study follows the basic approach to morphological definition of the literary genre "apocalypse" laid out in *Semeia* 14. Clarifications, refinements, and challenges to the definition and the basic approach to genre are discussed below in §1.2.

3. See note 73 below for surveys of the ideas typical of the apocalypses.

is a surge of injustice unlike other moments in history (except, perhaps, the wickedness before the flood). The present will soon be resolved by radical divine intervention, cosmic judgment, and the beginning of a new world order that replaces structures of the status quo such as the temple, priesthood, social boundaries, and law. In Jubilees those structures of the status quo were intended from the beginning of creation and will not be revised in a new creation. Suffering is never the suspension of justice but only occurs as just punishment from God. Judgment is never delayed. The turning point is not divine intervention but human repentance. More radically, the turning point has already occurred.

Finally, every apocalypse, by definition, narrates the revelation of hidden things through otherworldly beings to a human recipient. Jubilees narrates precisely the time, place, divine orders, heavenly source, angelic dictation, and Mosaic transcription of the book. This occurs in detail in the first chapter, with frequent reminders throughout the book. Typically the revelatory framework conveys the idea that, to understand the present world, one needs revelation that is otherwise unknown (new) and esoteric or elite (requires wisdom to decipher). Jubilees fills the revelatory framework with the already-familiar, public information of Israel's received scriptures. Not only does Jubilees avoid recourse to cryptic codes and mantic revelation; it purges any such suggestion from its retelling of Genesis. The heavenly tablets were already made public and explained to all of Israel at Sinai.

Jubilees includes all the basic elements of the literary genre, more than enough to raise the inherent issues. On each issue Jubilees says the opposite of what the apocalypses typically say. Jubilees uses the literary genre of the apocalypses to subvert the typical claims of the apocalypses. The rest of this chapter will elaborate the preceding summary of the problem of Jubilees' relationship to the apocalypses, the method of the proposed solution, and a selection of summary examples. The second, third, and fourth chapters will compare Jubilees to early apocalypses in greater detail, following the three major parts of the morphological definition of the literary genre. Finally, the fifth chapter will venture to explain the subversion in literary, historical, and cultural context.

1.1. The Problem

The place of Jubilees among the apocalypses has been observed as complex but not explained. The best of what has been said thus far about Jubilees in relationship to the apocalypses is that it is a complex work with mixed affinities. On a good day, similarities and differences are noted and kept separate. August Dillmann's assessment, in the first modern study of Jubilees, is virtually unsurpassed to this day.[4]

> Both on account of its form, and also in as much as the book in several places refers to the distant, even messianic, future, it can indeed be placed with the numerous apocalyptic compositions of the last centuries before and the first after Christ; and the second name of the book, the Apocalypse of Moses, is explicable on account of this. On the other hand, however, it is, by its contents and whole nature, so different from the books which we now call apocalypses that we cannot easily give it that title.

The work of improving this assessment will be largely a matter of clarifying the contrast between "form" and "contents." The ambivalence is articulated more precisely by more recent scholars. For example, John Collins calls Jubilees a "borderline case for the apocalyptic genre," in that the generic framework is that of an apocalypse, but most of the contents differ in their "close reliance on the biblical narrative and halakic interests."[5] Attempts to explain the pattern of similarities and differences, or claim one as essential and the other as superfluous, have fallen short. Two major patterns recur. First, studies that set out to trace social or intellectual history in terms of the groups that produced texts like 1 Enoch, Jubilees, and the sectarian literature from Qumran tend to find more similarities and ignore or deemphasize the differences. Second, studies that focus on the literary study of Jubilees tend to ignore the apocalyptic elements or demote them to a secondary status. It would be easy to pile up untenable statements from scholars, especially from works that attempt to trace the history of a motif over many centuries. The problem is not so much that a prior study is incorrect but rather that there simply has never been a thorough examination of the relationship of Jubilees to the apocalypses of its day in terms of literary genre. In the absence of a clear explanation, some scholars have over- or underestimated the extent to which Jubilees fits among the apocalypses. Others intuit vaguely that Jubilees resembles the apocalypses in some ways or in some parts but cannot really be counted as a prime example of an apocalypse.

---

4. August Dillmann, "Das Buch der Jubiläen oder die kleine Genesis," *Jahrbücher der Biblischen Wissenschaft* 2–3 (1850–1851): 74, my translation.

5. John J. Collins, *The Apocalyptic Imagination: An Introduction to Jewish Apocalyptic Literature* (2nd ed.; Grand Rapids: Eerdmans, 1998), 83.

1.1.1. OVERESTIMATING THE SIMILARITY TO THE APOCALYPSES

A complete understanding of Jubilees requires understanding it in its cultural context. In the case of Jubilees, our knowledge of the book is purely literary, and our knowledge of the cultural context is primarily literary. Consequently, we must understand the literature first and build models for social and intellectual history on this foundation. Hasty recourse to social models leads either to circular reasoning, in which the social model explains the text on which the model was built in the first place, or to categories that are far too general to be useful. For example, we may indeed say the same circle produced 1 Enoch and Jubilees if we define the circle as religiously zealous intellectuals grounded in the traditions of Judaism and opposed to Hellenistic assimilation and Antiochus Epiphanes. Casual assertions that 1 Enoch and Jubilees promote the same calendar need to be reexamined,[6] but one may still find some general common ground here as well. Such a circle, however, is too large to be adequate in explicating any one text. Many contradictory ideas could exist in such a circle. The task of defining more specific circles involves determining the importance of cultural symbols and distinguishing the ideas around which groups formed. In the case of Jubilees, the foundational layers of abstraction have not been properly understood. We must understand the literary genre and the ideas conveyed thereby. Once we understand *how* Jubilees uses the literary genre typical of Enochic literature, the proposal of a common circle of composition becomes unlikely.

In several otherwise helpful studies, haste to explain Jubilees with recourse to social models has led to overestimating or overvaluing the common elements between Jubilees and the apocalypses. Friedemann Schubert, for example, enjoyed the benefit of building on the foundations of Koch, Hanson, Collins, Stegemann, and others responsible for the essential tools used in this study, and he observed some important

---

6. Jonathan Ben-Dov, "Tradition and Innovation in the Calendar of Jubilees," in *Enoch and the Mosaic Torah: The Evidence of Jubilees* (ed. Gabriele Boccaccini and Giovanni Ibba; Grand Rapids: Eerdmans, 2009), 276–93. For more ambitious theories that bring out problems and variations in the 364-day year calendars, see Leora Ravid, "The Book of Jubilees and Its Calendar—A Reexamination," *DSD* 10 (2003): 371–94; Gabriele Boccaccini, "The Solar Calendars of Daniel and Enoch," in *The Book of Daniel: Composition and Reception* (ed. John J. Collins, Peter W. Flint, and Cameron VanEpps; VT Sup 83; Leiden: Brill, 2001), 311–28.

differences thereby. In the end, however, Schubert relied on Hengel to place Jubilees on a line of tradition that includes 1 Enoch and Qumran sectarian literature.[7] Michel Testuz also notes some key differences but still concludes that Jubilees comes from the same stream associated with the Damascus Document, other sectarian literature, and Josephus's description of the Essenes.[8] Testuz exemplifies a common problem in characterizing parallels. Jubilees may have gone on to influence sectarian groups, but that does not mean that Jubilees was originally sectarian. Indeed, the views in Jubilees about the unity of Israel, the temple, and the priesthood oppose sectarianism, even if other positions such as a 364-day festival calendar later became distinctively sectarian.[9]

Paolo Sacchi includes Jubilees without qualification as an example of Enochic Judaism, taking Jubilees' use of traditions about Enoch and associated with Enoch as an endorsement of a figure who defined a distinct form of Judaism.[10] Gabriele Boccaccini continues to place a high value on Enoch as a cultural symbol and views Jubilees as theologically grounded in Enochic Judaism, but he also recognizes differences substantial enough to call Jubilees a "rapprochement" with Zadokite/Mosaic Judaism.[11] Since the figure of Enoch is not a defining element of the literary genre, the pres-

---

7. Friedemann Schubert, *Tradition und Erneuerung: Studien zum Jubiläenbuch und seinem Trägerkreis* (Europäische Hochschulschriften 3, Geschichte und ihre Hilfswissenschaften 771; Frankfurt am Main: Lang, 1998), 78–80, 263. Based on a 1996 dissertation at the University of Leipzig.

8. Michel Testuz, *Les idées religieuses du Livre des Jubilés* (Genève: Droz, 1960), 165, 179–95.

9. Martha Himmelfarb, *A Kingdom of Priests: Ancestry and Merit in Ancient Judaism* (Jewish Culture and Contexts; Philadelphia: University of Pennsylvania Press, 2006), 81; idem, "Jubilees and Sectarianism," in *Enoch and Qumran Origins: New Light on a Forgotten Connection* (ed. Gabriele Boccaccini; Grand Rapids: Eerdmans, 2005), 129–31.

10. Paolo Sacchi, *Jewish Apocalyptic and Its History* (trans. William J. Short; JSPSup 20; Sheffield: Sheffield Academic Press, 1990); idem, "The Theology of Early Enochism and Apocalyptic: The Problem of the Relation between Form and Content of the Apocalypses; The Worldview of Apocalypses," *Henoch* 24 (2002): 80.

11. Gabriele Boccaccini, *Beyond the Essene Hypothesis: The Parting of the Ways Between Qumran and Enochic Judaism* (Grand Rapids: Eerdmans, 1998), 87–89; idem, "Qumran and the Enoch Groups: Revisiting the Enochic-Essene Hypothesis," in *The Bible and the Dead Sea Scrolls: The Second Princeton Symposium on Judaism and Christian Origins* (ed. James H. Charlesworth; Waco, Tex.: Baylor University Press, 2006), 45–47; idem, "From a Movement of Dissent to a Distinct Form of Judaism: The Heav-

ent study will defer consideration of the figure of Enoch until the concluding chapter on the cultural context. By then it will be clear that whatever intellectual circle may be defined by the inclusion of the figure of Enoch must be very broad.

Others have overestimated the connection between Jubilees and other apocalypses by placing emphasis on a "movement" or "spirit" of "apocalyptic."[12] This is especially true of studies that predate or reject the distinction between the literary genre "apocalypse," the typical "apocalyptic" ideas conveyed, and the religio-social phenomenon of "apocalypticism."[13] For most of the twentieth century, the dominant assumption was that "apocalyptic" was a coherent entity in which literature, ideas, and social structures were inextricably linked.[14] Literary genre is the most objective level of abstraction available to us, and this level is precisely where Jubilees overlaps with the apocalypses. Consequently,

---

enly Tablets in Jubilees as the Foundation of a Competing Halakah," in Boccaccini and Ibba, *Enoch and the Mosaic Torah*, 193–210.

12. D. S. Russell exemplifies the reified view of "apocalyptic" with a single coherent "method and message." Russell generally treats Jubilees as a witness to that method and message but also notes important ways in which Jubilees is exceptional (*The Method and Message of Jewish Apocalyptic, 200 BC–AD 100* (OTL; Philadelphia: Westminster, 1964), 269 n. 4. Christopher Rowland rejects the stratification of literary genre, ideas, and religio-social phenomenon and continues to use "apocalyptic" as a noun to refer to a "spirit" that includes Jubilees (*The Open Heaven: A Study of Apocalyptic in Judaism and Early Christianity* [New York: Crossroad, 1982], 51–52).

13. See the following section for the development of these distinctions in the 1970s.

14. This tendency is largely a consequence of the influence of Hermann Gunkel and Martin Dibelius in developing form criticism. Gunkel did assert that formal features, ideology, and social location were intertwined, but he only asserted this with respect to small oral compositions, not long and complex literary works. Gunkel's concept of *Gattung* is very different from genre. See Hermann Gunkel, "Jesaia 33, eine prophetische Liturgie: Ein Vortrag," ZAW 42 (1924): 183; Martin Dibelius, "Zur Formgeschichte der Evangelien," *TRu* NS 1 (1929): 187; Klaus Koch, *The Growth of the Biblical Tradition: The Form-Critical Method* (trans. S. M. Cupitt; New York: Scribner, 1969); Martin J. Buss, *Biblical Form Criticism in Its Context* (JSOTSup 274; Sheffield: Sheffield Academic Press, 1999); Erhard Blum, "Formgeschichte—A Misleading Category? Some Critical Remarks," in *The Changing Face of Form Criticism for the Twenty-First Century* (ed. Ehud Ben Zvi and Marvin A. Sweeney; Grand Rapids: Eerdmans, 2003), 32–45. For a more complete discussion, see Todd R. Hanneken, "The Book of Jubilees among the Apocalypses," (Ph.D. diss., University of Notre Dame, 2008), 45–57.

the reified view of "apocalyptic" naturally led to an overestimation of the extent to which Jubilees fits. Furthermore, at a fundamental level, the use of a literary genre functions to generate reader expectations that typical literary forms will express typical ideas.[15] The present work will argue that Jubilees subverts those expectations. Jubilees uses the genre to raise a set of issues and address the expected, typical positions on those issues. Jubilees then rejects or corrects the typical positions. The differences in ideas are radical enough that the ancient audience could have been expected to catch the subversion. Nevertheless, generic reader expectation may help explain how some modern readers have missed the differences.

1.1.2. UNDERESTIMATING THE SIMILARITY TO THE APOCALYPSES

The opposite problem, underestimating the significance of the apocalyptic genre in Jubilees, occurs more frequently in studies focused on Jubilees. Usually this takes the form of neglect to mention anything apocalyptic about Jubilees.[16] One notable exception is Armin Lange's study of allegorical dreams in Jubilees, which concludes that Jubilees cannot be called apocalyptic.[17] This important observation will figure prominently in chapter 4 below, on the view of revelation. More points should be considered, and, more importantly, a distinction should be drawn between the level of

---

15. For more on how the use of literary genre generates reader expectations, see §5.2 below.

16. For example, Michael Segal's thorough study of Jubilees includes a section on the genre of Jubilees but makes no mention of the apocalyptic genre and says of chapters 1, 23, and 50 (the beginning, middle, and end of the book) that they are "formally anomalous" (*The Book of Jubilees: Rewritten Bible, Redaction, Ideology and Theology* [JSJSup 117; Leiden: Brill, 2007], 3–5). VanderKam discusses many individual points shared or not shared between Jubilees and the apocalypses but makes no pronouncements about the genre and the book as a whole (*The Book of Jubilees* [Guides to Apocrypha and Pseudepigrapha; Sheffield: Sheffield Academic Press, 2001]; idem, "The Angel Story in the Book of Jubilees," in *Pseudepigraphic Perspectives: The Apocrypha and Pseudepigrapha in Light of the Dead Sea Scrolls* [ed. Esther G. Chazon, Avital Pinnick, and Michael E. Stone; STDJ 31; Leiden: Brill, 1999], 151–70; idem, "The Demons in the *Book of Jubilees*," in *Die Dämonen: Die Dämonologie der israelitisch-jüdischen und frühchristlichen Literatur im Kontext ihrer Umwelt* [ed. Armin Lange, Hermann Lichtenberger, and Diethard Römheld; Tübingen: Mohr Siebeck, 2003], 339–64).

17. Armin Lange, "Divinatorische Träume und Apokalyptik im Jubiläenbuch," in *Studies in the Book of Jubilees* (ed. Matthias Albani, Jörg Frey, and Armin Lange; Tubingen: Mohr Siebeck, 1997), 35.

literary genre and the level of ideas. Although Jubilees does depart from apocalyptic ideas about coded or esoteric revelation, Jubilees nonetheless uses the revelatory framework of the literary genre.

The major reason studies of Jubilees tend to neglect consideration of the apocalyptic literary genre is that most of the book uses other genres. The genre appears most clearly at key locations in the book (the beginning, middle, and end), and characteristic phrases and structures appear throughout the book (day of judgment, demons, angels, heavenly tablets, heavenly liturgy, righteous plant). However, by volume, most verses do not depend on the genre. It is worth being clear that, in discussing the genre "apocalypse" in Jubilees, we are not speaking exhaustively about literary genre in the book. Prototype theory will aid the articulation that Jubilees is not completely apocalyptic or the classic case of the literary genre. Indeed, Jubilees is not prototypical in at least two ways: it uses other literary genres, and it subverts the ideas typical of apocalypses. Nevertheless, it is widely accepted that literature cannot be expected to be exclusive in the use of genres. The small proportion of the genre in Jubilees may explain, but not justify, the neglect of its study.

Another tendency in literary studies of Jubilees does not directly relate to apocalyptic genre but testifies to a deeper observation about Jubilees, namely, that it sends mixed signals. Jubilees is a complex work, and much of that complexity is not yet understood. One recurring response to the complexity is to identify multiple authors or sources behind the book as we have it. It may not be a coincidence that Gene Davenport's study of the eschatology of Jubilees led to the most ambitious attempt to divide Jubilees into layers of redaction.[18] Since then many scholars have postulated either additions to an otherwise coherent composition[19] or multiple

---

18. Gene L. Davenport, *The Eschatology of the Book of Jubilees* (StPB 20; Leiden: Brill, 1971). Although that study differs from the present study in fundamental ways, both attempt to explain the mixed signals Jubilees sends about the particularly apocalyptic issue of eschatology.

19. James L. Kugel identifies twenty-nine interpolations characterized by reference to heavenly tablets and chronological determinism based on a solar calendar ("On the Interpolations in the *Book of Jubilees*," *RevQ* 24 [2009]: 215–72). Christoph Berner identifies Jub. 1:5–28 and 23:14–31 as additions intended to extend the scope of the work past the days of Moses, but distinguished by lack of concern for heptadic chronology (*Jahre, Jahrwochen und Jubiläen: Heptadische Geschichtskonzeptionen im antiken Judentum* [BZAW 363; Berlin: de Gruyter, 2006], 239–48). Leora Ravid considers Jub. 50:6–13 an addition ("6–13 נ היובלים בספר השבת הלכות," *Tarbiz*

sources used by a final redactor.[20] The present study treats Jubilees as a coherent composition by a single author, such as authorship was in antiquity. It is valuable to recognize the complexity of the manner in which the author used authoritative traditions and attempted to reconcile traditions already in tension. It is also helpful to recognize rhetorical or stylistic seams in the composition. Of course, we can never know exactly all the oral or written sources available to the author, and we cannot rule out the possibility that two or more like-minded authors worked on the composition as we have it. The present work deals with the composition as we have it, regardless of the processes by which it came into existence. It is not the case that multiple authorship could explain the tension between apocalyptic literary morphology and nonapocalyptic ideas. The same phrases raise the issues and subvert the meanings. It is also worth noting that none of the source- or redaction-critical proposals has gained traction, and many have been refuted by argument and new evidence.[21] None of the theories

---

69 [2000]: 161–66). Menahem Kister modestly suggests that Jub. 23:12 may begin an interpolation and later supports a version of Ravid's argument with modification ("לתולדות כת האיסיים: עיונים בחזון החיות, ספר היובלים וברית דמשק," *Tarbiz* 56 [1986]: 6 n. 21; idem, "על שני מטבעות לשון בספר היובלים," *Tarbiz* 70 [2001]: 297 n. 47). Before Davenport, Michel Testuz identified 23:11–32 as an interpolation (*Les idées religieuses*, 40).

20. Michael Segal (*The Book of Jubilees*) has identified seams and tensions between different types of material in Jubilees (narrative, legal, and chronological) and argued that contradictions indicate multiple authorship. Cana Werman considers 23:9–15, 17–18, 25–30a, 31–32 to be an older source interpolated by the author ("ספר היובלים ועדת קומרן: לשאלת היחס בין השניים," *Meghillot* 2 [2004]: 43). Devorah Dimant perceives a contradiction that would indicate borrowing from a different source without attempting to reconcile contradictions ("The Biography of Enoch and the Books of Enoch," *VT* 33 [1983]: 21 n. 17). Ernest Wiesenberg attempted to identify a chronological contradiction ("The Jubilee of Jubilees," *RevQ* 9 [1961–1962]: 3–40).

21. James C. VanderKam has consistently defended the coherence of the composition, particularly refuting the arguments of Segal, Ravid, Wiesenberg, Testuz, and Davenport. See his "Review of Michael Segal, *The Book of Jubilees*," *JSP* 20 (2010): 154–57; idem, "Recent Scholarship in the Book of Jubilees," *CurBR* 6 (2008): 410–16; idem, "The End of the Matter? Jub. 50:6–13 and the Unity of the Book," in *Heavenly Tablets: Interpretation, Identity and Tradition in Ancient Judaism* (ed. Lynn LiDonnici and Andrea Lieber; JSJSup 119; Leiden: Brill, 2007), 267–84; idem, "Studies in the Chronology of the Book of Jubilees," in *From Revelation to Canon: Studies in the Hebrew Bible and Second Temple Literature* (JSJSup 62; Leiden: Brill, 2000), 522–44; idem, "The Putative Author of the Book of Jubilees," *JSS* 26 (1981): 209–17. Lutz Doering rejected Ravid's argument; see "Jub 50:6–13 als Schlussabschnitt des Jubiläenbu-

have been supported by the considerable manuscript evidence. However complex the process of composition may have been, the book as we have it is remarkably coherent, especially relative to its own day and especially for a composition that claims to reconstruct the unified source of all the revealed traditions of Israel (the heavenly tablets).

1.2. The Solution

In order to explain the ways in which Jubilees is like and not like apocalypses of its day, it will be necessary to distinguish between three layers of abstraction: literary elements, ideas conveyed, and social context. A clear and established definition of the morphology of the genre (*Semeia* 14) will confirm that Jubilees uses apocalyptic literary elements and will also suggest categories for the issues inherently raised in the use of the genre. The distinction of layers is not an end in itself, and the identification of apocalyptic literary morphology in Jubilees does not resolve the larger question of genre. Genre is not only literary morphology but the complex relationship between the various layers at which communication can use and subvert expectations. Cognitive psychology will help explain the consequence of adopting one layer of what is typically apocalyptic while rejecting another. Jubilees uses apocalyptic literary elements to raise reader expectations about certain issues. Jubilees undermines superficial expectations with contrary claims. The subversion enhances the dramatic effect.

1.2.1. Distinguish Layers of Abstraction: Literary Morphology, Typical Ideas, and Social Context

In the 1970s a whirlwind of scholarly effort attempted to bring order to the terminological and conceptual confusion in scholarship about "apocalyptic" (as a noun).[22] Although there had been suggestions of stratifying literary

---

chs—Nachtrag aus Qumran oder ursprünglicher Bestandteil des Werks?" *RevQ* 20 79 (2002): 359–87. I offer a more elaborate discussion of the coherence of the composition and theories of multiplicity of authorship in Hanneken, "The Book of Jubilees among the Apocalypses," 121–41.

22. Reviews of the history of scholarship can be found in Hanneken, "The Book of Jubilees among the Apocalypses," 30–110. Scholarship up to 1947 is covered in Johann Michael Schmidt, *Die jüdische Apokalyptik* (Neukirchen-Vluyn: Neukirchener, 1969).

features and ideas,[23] the reified view of "apocalyptic" as a monolith of literary form, ideas, social location, and social function remained dominant.[24] Klaus Koch is often credited with leading the push for systematic reevaluation of the study of "apocalyptic."[25] Michael Stone[26] and Paul Hanson[27] established the need for distinguishing layers of abstraction, which led to Hellholm's particularly thorough articulation of a hierarchy of layers of abstraction.[28] Hanson argued that distinct terms should be used for the type

---

Subsequent scholarship is reviewed in James Barr, "Jewish Apocalyptic in Recent Scholarly Study," *BJRL* 58 (1975): 9–35; John J. Collins, "Genre, Ideology, and Social Movements in Jewish Apocalypticism," in *Mysteries and Revelations: Apocalyptic Studies since the Uppsala Colloquium* (ed. John J. Collins and James H. Charlesworth; JSPSup 9; Sheffield: JSOT Press, 1991), 11–32; Lorenzo DiTommaso, "Apocalypses and Apocalypticism in Antiquity (Part I)," *CurBR* 5 (2007): 235–86; and idem, "Apocalypses and Apocalypticism in Antiquity (Part II)," *CurBR* 5 (2007): 367–432.

23. Attempts to stratify literary features and ideas were suggested as early as Schürer and Rowley (first published 1944) but did not take hold. See Emil Schürer, *Geschichte des jüdischen Volkes im Zeitalter Jesu Christi* (Leipzig: Hinrichs, 1886); and H. H. Rowley, *The Relevance of Apocalyptic: A Study of Jewish and Christian Apocalypses from Daniel to the Revelation* (3rd ed.; Greenwood, N.C.: Attic, 1980), 51.

24. Exemplified by Russell, Vielhauer, and Schmithals: Russell, *Method and Message*; Philipp Vielhauer, "Apocalypses and Related Subjects," in *New Testament Apocrypha* (ed. E. Hennecke and W. Schneemelcher; Philadelphia: Westminster, 1965), 581–607; and Walter Schmithals, *The Apocalyptic Movement, Introduction and Interpretation* (trans. John E. Steely; Nashville: Abingdon, 1975).

25. Klaus Koch, *Ratlos vor der Apokalyptik: Eine Streitschrift über ein vernachlässigtes Gebiet der Bibelwissenschaft und die schädlichen Auswirkungen auf Theologie und Philosophie* (Gütersloh: Mohn, 1970); trans. as *The Rediscovery of Apocalyptic: A Polemical Work on a Neglected Area of Biblical Studies and Its Damaging Effects on Theology and Philosophy* (trans. Margaret Kohl; Naperville, Ill.: Allenson, 1972).

26. Michael E. Stone, "Lists of Revealed Things in the Apocalyptic Literature," in *Magnalia Dei, the Mighty Acts of God: Essays on the Bible and Archaeology in Memory of G. Ernest Wright* (ed. Werner E. Lemke, Patrick D. Miller, and Frank Moore Cross; Garden City, N.Y.: Doubleday, 1976), 414–52.

27. Paul D. Hanson, "Jewish Apocalyptic against Its Near Eastern Environment," *RB* 78 (1971): 31–58; idem, *The Dawn of Apocalyptic* (Philadelphia: Fortress, 1975); idem, "Apocalypse, Genre and Apocalypticism," *IDBSup*, 27–34; idem, "Prolegomena to the Study of Jewish Apocalyptic," in Lemke, Miller, and Cross, *Magnalia Dei*, 389–413.

28. David Hellholm, "The Problem of Apocalyptic Genre and the Apocalypse of John," *Semeia* 36 (1986): 13–64. Collins has recently renewed the call for distinguishing a hierarchy of features at different levels of abstraction, taking the literary features as primary ("Epilogue: Genre Analysis and the Dead Sea Scrolls," *DSD* 17 [2010]: 420, 428–30).

of literature (apocalypse), religious perspective (apocalyptic as an adjective), and religio-social phenomenon (apocalypticism).²⁹ Some scholars went as far as to call for a complete divorce between the three layers,³⁰ while others maintained, as does this study, that there is a relationship, though not a simple relationship,³¹ namely, that the type of literature expresses a cluster of typical ideas about the literary elements. The apocalypses can have variations within that cluster, they can have other ideas besides that cluster, and the ideas in that cluster can also be found in works that do not use the literary genre. Similarly, the literary morphology can suggest, but not determine, social function or social location, as discussed below.

As we shall see, additional controversy surrounds both privileging literary morphology for defining the genre and the morphological definition itself. First, there is also controversy about the very enterprise of using genres and distinguishing layers within them. The charge of anachronism builds on the fact that the term "apocalypse" is not widely used to identify a type of literature until the second century C.E., but there are many patterns in antiquity that were not named until later.³² Criticisms

---

29. Hanson, "Apocalypse, Genre and Apocalypticism," 27–34. In effect, this was a claim that Herman Gunkel's method of treating the three elements as inseparable in small oral units does not apply to large literary works, such as the apocalypses. See also Buss, *Biblical Form Criticism*; and Koch, *The Growth of the Biblical Tradition*.

30. Hartmut Stegemann reacts to attempts to define the genre in terms of ideas and goes further than *Semeia* 14 in restricting the genre to the formal feature of the revelatory framework. Stegemann does not deny, however, that the formal features imply certain ideas ("Die Bedeutung der Qumranfunde für die Erforschung der Apokalyptik," in *Apocalypticism in the Mediterranean World and the Near East: Proceedings of the International Colloquium on Apocalypticism, Uppsala, August 12–17, 1979* [ed. David Hellholm; Tübingen: Mohr, 1983], 499–500). More radically, Jean Carmignac rejects an exclusive correspondence between a type of literature and a distinctive theology. He concludes that one cannot be defined in terms of the other ("Qu'est-ce que l'Apocalyptique: Son emploi à Qumrân," *RevQ* 10 [1979]: 19; idem, "Description du phénomène de l'Apocalyptique dans l'Ancien Testament," in Hellholm, *Apocalypticism in the Mediterranean World*, 164–65).

31. Lars Hartman, "Survey of the Problem of Apocalyptic Genre," in Hellholm, *Apocalypticism in the Mediterranean World*, 334; Hellholm, "The Problem of Apocalyptic Genre," 13–64; and Collins, "Genre, Ideology, and Social Movements," 11–32.

32. Klaus Koch uses the example of "piel" as a grammatical concept known to speakers of ancient Hebrew long before it was named as such (*The Growth of the Biblical Tradition*, 12). Still, it is worth remembering that genre study is a tool, not an end in itself. Ultimately, the validity of the tool will be established by the extent to which it

are often made of Aristotelian approaches to genre for their binary analysis of a work as in a genre, or not, and certainly not in more than one genre.[33] However, this was never true of the *Semeia* 14 approach.[34] Carol Newsom has demonstrated ways in which *Semeia* 14 anticipated or is compatible with subsequent developments in genre theory.[35] In particular, the inductive approach of *Semeia* 14 anticipates prototype theory in beginning with easily recognized examples and measuring variation according to a schema that distinguishes required, default, and optional elements (distinguishing definition and description in the "master paradigm").[36] Some have construed, often misconstrued, developments in genre theory to suggest that genre cannot be defined.[37] Genre theory has come to rec-

---

explains texts and relationships between texts. The present study should demonstrate that distinguishing genres and layers of genre leads to a more precise understanding of what is typical and atypical about Jubilees among the apocalypses.

33. George W. E. Nickelsburg has cautioned against isolating corpora and questioned the usefulness of categories in "Wisdom and Apocalypticism in Early Judaism: Some Points for Discussion," in *Conflicted Boundaries in Wisdom and Apocalypticism* (ed. Benjamin G. Wright and Lawrence M. Wills; SBLSymS 35; Atlanta: Society of Biblical Literature, 2005), 36.

34. In prior and subsequent works, Collins demonstrated classification as a tool for considering (not a means of neglecting) borderline cases, related categories, and compatible genres; see "The Court-Tales in Daniel and the Development of Apocalyptic," *JBL* 94 (1975): 218–34; idem, "Apocalypse: The Morphology of a Genre," 18; idem, "Wisdom, Apocalypticism, and Generic Compatibility," in *In Search of Wisdom: Essays in Memory of John G. Gammie* (ed. Leo G. Perdue; Philadelphia: Westminster John Knox, 1993; repr. as pages 165–85 in *Seers, Sybils and Sages in Hellenistic-Roman Judaism* (Leiden: Brill, 1997); idem, "Epilogue: Genre Analysis and the Dead Sea Scrolls," 419–21, 427–28.

35. Carol A. Newsom, "Spying Out the Land: A Report from Genology," in *Seeking Out the Wisdom of the Ancients: Essays Offered to Honor Michael V. Fox on the Occasion of His Sixty-Fifth Birthday* (ed. Ronald L. Troxel, Kelvin G. Friebel, and Dennis Robert Magary; Winona Lake, Ind.: Eisenbrauns, 2005), 437–50. Newsom's work has recently served as the foundation for studies of wisdom and pesher as genres: Benjamin G. Wright III, "Joining the Club: A Suggestion about Genre in Early Jewish Texts," *DSD* 17 (2010): 260–85; Robert Williamson Jr., "Pesher: A Cognitive Model of the Genre," *DSD* 17 (2010): 307–31. Newsom has reviewed several approaches to genre with illustration of how they might aid analysis of the Hodayot in "Pairing Research Questions and Theories of Genre: A Case Study of the Hodayot," *DSD* 17 (2010): 241–59.

36. Newsom, "Spying out the Land," 445; Collins, "Epilogue: Genre Analysis and the Dead Sea Scrolls," 423–25.

37. Alastair Fowler, *Kinds of Literature: An Introduction to the Theory of Genres*

ognize that all communication depends on the use of borrowed elements to convey meaning. A comprehensive theory of all genre is certainly elusive, and many genres are in fact very difficult to define. The family resemblance model has often been invoked to explain groups, the members of which are not all distinguished by a common element.[38] However, it hardly follows that no genre can be defined and distinguished using formal criteria.[39] The genre "sonnet" is a clear example that can be defined using morphological features alone, even as typical ideas and function may also be worthy of analysis.[40] If one does not expect a morphological definition of a literary genre to describe all that is typical about a text or body of texts, the genre "apocalypse" can and has been defined.[41] Still, alternative approaches to genres and layers of abstraction remain. Fundamentally, some of the criticisms of *Semeia* 14 discussed below, particularly those of Rowland and Matlock, build on a reluctance to constrain a genre or distinguish layers of abstraction within it.[42] Rowland, for example, speaks more broadly of a "spirit of apocalyptic" that observes no boundaries between literary features, theology, and social reality.[43]

Before turning to the morphological definition of the literary genre, clarifications, and alternatives, a set of basic examples should illustrate the three major layers of abstraction accepted by most scholars and used in this study. Words and phrases related to demons, angelic princes, and

---

and Modes (Cambridge: Harvard University Press, 1982); John Frow, *Genre* (ed. John Drakakis; The New Critical Idiom; London: Routledge, 2006).

38. Fowler, *Kinds of Literature*, 39–41.

39. See the criticisms of John Swales, *Genre Analysis: English in Academic and Research Settings* (Cambridge Applied Linguistics Series; Cambridge: Cambridge University Press, 1990), 51; David Fishelov, *Metaphors of Genre: The Role of Analogies in Genre Theory* (University Park: Pennsylvania State University Press, 1993), 54; and Collins, "Epilogue: Genre Analysis and the Dead Sea Scrolls," 422.

40. Fishelov, *Metaphors of Genre*, 8, 13–15.

41. This is strikingly so in comparison with the controversy over defining as genres "wisdom" and "rewritten scripture." See most recently, Wright, "Joining the Club," 260–85; Matthew J. Goff, "Qumran Wisdom Literature and the Problem of Genre," *DSD* 17 (2010): 286–306; and George J. Brooke, "Genre Theory, Rewritten Bible and Pesher," *DSD* 17 (2010): 332–57.

42. Rowland, *The Open Heaven*; and R. Barry Matlock, *Unveiling the Apocalyptic Paul: Paul's Interpreters and the Rhetoric of Criticism* (JSNTSup 127; Sheffield: Sheffield Academic Press, 1996), especially 198.

43. "A definition of apocalyptic should not be too restricted but attempt to do justice to all the various elements in the literature" (Rowland, *The Open Heaven*, 70).

angelic agency are typical of the apocalypses at the level of *literary morphology*. The *idea typically conveyed* through discussion of these agents is that they explain the unjust suffering of the righteous in the present and will execute justice in the future. At the level of apocalypticism we could ask if there was a *community or movement* for which belief in such cosmic agents determined their identity and practices.[44] Another distinctive phrase at the level of literary morphology is "great day of judgment." The phrase inherently lends itself to the claim that there will be a great day of judgment in the future, but meanwhile justice is not fully realized, having been deferred until a collective judgment. Again, apocalypticism would describe a group or movement for which such a belief established identity and practices, such as the belief that group members would be vindicated on the great day of judgment. Language for an elite implied audience, such as "righteous plant," lends itself to the idea that a group within Israel would have special status, which is separable from the question of whether such a group actually existed. One could go on with phrases such as "heavenly tablets" and "new creation" typically implying ideas, which may in turn have social significance. In each of these cases the level of literary morphology is objectively detectable and present in Jubilees. In each of these cases, the social context at the time of Jubilees is not known directly, and only with difficulty might be established through careful consideration of the ideas conveyed in Jubilees and other texts. Thus, the social reality is logically posterior to understanding the ideas. The present work will show that Jubilees rejects the ideas typically, almost inherently, implied in the use of the literary morphology of the genre.

1.2.2. Define the Genre Based on Literary Morphology

The Apocalypse Group of the Society of Biblical Literature Genres Project worked from 1975 to 1978 and in 1979 published in *Semeia* 14 a morphological definition of the literary genre "apocalypse."[45] The definition does

---

44. Much later Josephus tells us that the Essenes hold the names of the angels among their prized secret wisdom (*B.J.* 2.142); the War Scroll cites angelic enlistment in the army as reason for purity practices (1QM vii, 6–7; cf. Deut. 23:15); and 1 Cor 11:10 cites angels as a reason for women to wear veils.

45. Collins, "Apocalypse: The Morphology of a Genre," 1–19. In addition to John Collins, the SBL Genres Project Apocalypse Group included Harold W. Attridge, Francis T. Fallon, Anthony J. Saldarini, and Adela Yarbro Collins.

what a definition is supposed to do. Some critical evaluation can be taken as clarifications or warnings against treating the morphological definition as an end in itself. While it is worth noting that some scholars continue to call for a fundamentally different approach to the genre, most scholars today accept the definition.

> "Apocalypse" is a genre of revelatory literature with a narrative framework, in which a revelation is mediated by an otherworldly being to a human recipient, disclosing a transcendent reality which is both temporal, insofar as it envisages eschatological salvation, and spatial insofar as it involves another, supernatural world.[46]

The definition draws on the most objective elements sufficient to distinguish the literary type.[47] The definition relies on elements that are always present, not subjective evaluations of a preponderance of optional characteristics.[48] The definition does not depend upon a complete study of the genre at all levels but can contribute to it.[49] The definition does not claim to describe everything generic about the apocalypses or any one apocalypse.[50] The definition grounds the terminology of apocalyptic ideas and

---

46. Ibid., 9.

47. Stegemann, Carmignac, and Sanders sought more minimal definitions focused on the manner of revelation but failed to distinguish the apocalypses from prophetic literature or Joseph's dreams in Genesis. See Stegemann, "Die Bedeutung der Qumranfunde," 498–99; Carmignac, "Description du phénomène," 169. E. P. Sanders, "The Genre of Palestinian Jewish Apocalypses," in Hellholm, *Apocalypticism in the Mediterranean World*, 456–58; see also Collins, *Apocalyptic Imagination*, 9–10.

48. Earlier attempts at definition listed optional but indicative characteristics from multiple layers of abstraction. See Vielhauer, "Apocalypses and Related Subjects," 583–94; Koch, *The Rediscovery of Apocalyptic*, 24–33; and Russell, *Method and Message*, 105. Hanson ("Jewish Apocalyptic against Its Near Eastern Environment," 33) and Stone ("Lists of Revealed Things," 440) were particularly critical of this approach. This approach is similar to what is now called the "family resemblance model." The *Semeia* 14 definition limited discussion to literary morphology and distinguished the "always true" definition from the optional descriptors in the master paradigm (Collins, "Apocalypse: The Morphology of a Genre," 8–9). This distinction resembles the gestalt complex described by genre theorist Michael Sinding, "After Definitions: Genre, Categories, and Cognitive Science," *Genre* 35 (2002): 200.

49. See below for controversy about privileging literary morphology.

50. The 1979 Uppsala conference in particular perceived definition and description as mutually exclusive. See David Hellholm, "Introduction," in Hellholm, *Apocalypticism in the Mediterranean World*, 2. See also Eibert Tigchelaar, "More on Apoca-

apocalypticism in a set of texts but does not otherwise limit the study of what may be typical of the ideas and movements related to the apocalypses.[51] The definition provides precise terminology for describing variation and mixed relationships but does not preclude study of borderline cases and related types.[52] The definition accurately indicates a coherent pattern in ancient texts.[53] It facilitates study of the boundaries of that pattern without isolating categories of literature.[54]

The *Semeia* 14 definition has gained wide acceptance, and certainly no alternative has gained greater acceptance. Nevertheless, the definition has been the frequent object of criticism along lines ranging from clarifications and cautions to substantially different ways of thinking about the genre "apocalypse." Two particular issues merit discussion: the debate about including eschatology in the definition and the debate about privileging literary morphology for the definition rather than ideology or social context.

---

lyptic and Apocalypses," *JSJ* 18 (1987): 144. Collins has often emphasized that the definition is not a complete study of the genre or all that is borrowed in a text or body of texts ("Apocalypse: The Morphology of a Genre," 1–2).

51. In particular, works of testamentary literature, Qumran sectarian literature, and Paul can still be pertinent for comparison in ideas and social setting, even if those works cannot be called apocalypses or apocalyptic ideas defined based on them. See Richard E. Sturm, "Defining the Word 'Apocalyptic': A Problem in Biblical Criticism," in *Apocalyptic and the New Testament: Essays in Honor of J. Louis Martyn* (ed. Joel Marcus and Marion L. Soards; JSNTSup 24; Sheffield: JSOT Press, 1989), 25; and John J. Collins, "Apocalypticism and Literary Genre in the Dead Sea Scrolls," in *The Dead Sea Scrolls after Fifty Years: A Comprehensive Assessment* (ed. Peter W. Flint and James C. VanderKam; Leiden: Brill, 1998), 403–30.

52. Collins, "Genre, Ideology, and Social Movements," 19. Jubilees is an excellent example of a complex case. The aim of the definition is not simply to say that Jubilees is or is not an apocalypse but to allow precision in describing the levels at which it is or is not typical.

53. Collins describes this as "inner coherence." Although some specific features may happen to be true of several texts, *Semeia* 14 seeks to avoid the limitations of an inductive approach by providing an extensible standard; idem, "Apocalypse: The Morphology of a Genre," 10; idem, "Epilogue: Genre Analysis and the Dead Sea Scrolls," 420.

54. For more detailed discussion of the purpose of a definition of a literary genre see Hanneken, "The Book of Jubilees among the Apocalypses," 78–110.

The debate about the centrality of eschatology in the apocalypses started before *Semeia* 14.[55] Some scholars, at least superficially, had equated the theology of the apocalypses with the eschatology of the apocalypses.[56] Shortly after *Semeia* 14, Carmignac and Stegemann attempted definitions that avoided reference to eschatology, based on the lack of uniformity with which eschatology is found in the apocalypses. Carmignac in particular had trouble distinguishing the apocalypses from prophetic literature and even Joseph's dreams in Genesis.[57] Stegemann made a noble attempt to focus a definition primarily on the revelatory framework but ultimately found it necessary to go beyond the framework of revelation. *Semeia* 14 also found it necessary to go beyond the revelatory framework but appealed to relatively robust features of what is contained in the revelation, namely, transcendence on the spatial and temporal axes. Stegemann made appeal to the much more subjective features of authorial intent and original audience.[58] Stegemann's resistance to including eschatology was based on a definition of eschatology that excluded personal eschatology and realized eschatology, which Collins includes.[59] It is true that "eschatology" is a loaded term, and the kind of eschatology varies among the apocalypses. Nevertheless, a God's-eye view of the meaning or resolution of history is a distinctive element of the apocalypses. Other protests to the inclusion of "eschatology" do not so much deny that eschatology is found in the apocalypses as object that focus on eschatology distracts from what may be a more essential feature.[60] The morphological definition claims to

---

55. Graham I. Davies, "Apocalyptic and Historiography," *JSOT* 5 (1978): 15–28.

56. So, for example, Rowley, *The Relevance of Apocalyptic*, 51; Vielhauer, "Apocalypses and Related Subjects," 597–98; Hanson, "Jewish Apocalyptic against Its Near Eastern Environment," 35; idem, *The Dawn of Apocalyptic*, 7; idem, "Apocalypse, Genre and Apocalypticism," 27–34.

57. Carmignac, "Qu'est-ce que l'Apocalyptique," 11, 13, 20–21, 33; idem, "Description du phénomène," 165, 169.

58. Hartmut Stegemann, "Die Bedeutung der Qumranfunde," 498–99. See Hanneken, "The Book of Jubilees among the Apocalypses," 95–97.

59. Stegemann, "Die Bedeutung der Qumranfunde," 500; Collins, "Genre, Ideology, and Social Movements," 16; idem, *Apocalyptic Imagination*, 10–12, 16. See also David E. Aune, "The Apocalypse of John and the Problem of Genre," *Semeia* 36 (1986): 89.

60. Rowland does not so much deny the relevance of eschatology as subordinate it to the visionary/vertical dimension (*The Open Heaven*, 70–72; idem, "Review of: *The Apocalyptic Imagination: An Introduction to the Jewish Matrix of Christianity*, by John

include the most robust features necessary for distinguishing the class, not to exhaust all that may be typical, even at the level of literary morphology. Although the definition does suggest features likely to be discussed at the level of ideas, this is only a starting point. Other ideas may also be typical, but are not always easily identified at the level of literary morphology. This brings us to another area of protest against the *Semeia* 14 definition: the controversy about starting from literary morphology.

A related and more fundamental protest against the *Semeia* 14 definition surrounds the decision to define the genre in terms of literary morphology, without reference to ideology, social location, or social function. The primary argument in favor of grounding terminology in literary morphology is simply that literary morphology is the most robust feature available to us, whereas ideology and social context are reconstructed based on the literature.[61] One argument against this approach claims that focus on literary morphology misses the essence of apocalyptic thought or the putative apocalyptic movement.[62] Another argument resists excluding corpora previously held as central to the reified "apocalyptic." In particular, many scholars of "Paul and apocalyptic" suddenly felt excluded because Paul did not use the literary genre "apocalypse."[63] Similarly, the Qumran sectarian literature did not meet the definition of "apocalypse."[64] Of course, this

---

J. Collins; and *Jewish Writings of the Second Temple Period*, edited by Michael E. Stone," *JTS* 37 [1986]: 489–90). Following Rowland, several scholars in England have rejected eschatology as a major concept of the apocalypses: Matlock, *Unveiling the Apocalyptic Paul*, 284; Lester L. Grabbe, "Prophetic and Apocalyptic: Time for New Definitions— and New Thinking," in *Knowing the End from the Beginning: The Prophetic, the Apocalyptic and Their Relationships* (ed. Lester L. Grabbe and Robert D. Haak; London: T&T Clark, 2003), 114–15; Crispin Fletcher-Louis, "Jewish Apocalyptic and Apocalypticism," in *Handbook for the Study of the Historical Jesus* (ed. Tom Holmén and Stanley E. Porter; 4 vols.; Leiden: Brill, 2011), 2:1569–1607.

61. Most recently, Collins, "Epilogue: Genre Analysis and the Dead Sea Scrolls," 425–30.

62. Rowland, *The Open Heaven*; Fletcher-Louis, "Jewish Apocalyptic and Apocalypticism."

63. Richard Sturm, a scholar of Paul, prefers to approach apocalyptic as a theological concept ("Defining the Word 'Apocalyptic,'" 17–48). See also Matlock, *Unveiling the Apocalyptic Paul*.

64. Marc Philonenko calls Qumran sectarian literature apocalyptic based on the level of ideas, whereas Jean Carmignac and Hartmut Stegemann would limit the extent to which the term applies. The texts cannot be called apocalypses if they do not use the literary morphology, but the ideas can still be called apocalyptic if they are the

never meant that one could not describe the ideas in Paul or the Qumran sectarian literature as apocalyptic if those ideas are demonstrably shared with apocalypses. It does mean, and was very much intended to mean, that the terminology would be constrained by what can be grounded in texts.[65] Precision in terminology is not a barrier to study; rather, it is the only way it becomes possible to make statements such as, "the sectarians at Qumran appear to have held an apocalyptic worldview but to have produced no apocalypses of their own."[66] In addition to those who would have preferred terminology rooted in ideology, others claim an apocalyptic movement as the central point of departure.[67] Similarly, some find fault with the synchronic approach of *Semeia* 14.[68] There may indeed be a danger in letting any one approach become so dominant as to neglect other approaches.[69]

---

ideas typically found in apocalypses. See Marc Philonenko, "L'apocalyptique qoumrânienne," in Hellholm, *Apocalypticism in the Mediterranean World*, 211–18 ; Carmignac, "Qu'est-ce que l'Apocalyptique," 3–33; idem, "Description du phénomène," 163–70; and Stegemann, "Die Bedeutung der Qumranfunde," 496.

65. Koch (*The Rediscovery of Apocalyptic*) initiated the push for terminological clarity in response to the terminological chaos not only among scholars of Jewish literature but also historical Jesus scholarship and systematic theology. James Barr offered a quotation from Jürgen Moltmann as an example of the term being used in systematic theology in such a way that could hardly be verified or falsified on the basis of ancient texts, "while apocalyptic does conceive its eschatology in cosmological terms, yet that is not the end of eschatology, but the beginning of an eschatological cosmology or an eschatological ontology for which being becomes historic and the cosmos opens itself to the apocalyptic process" ("Jewish Apocalyptic in Recent Scholarly Study," 31).

66. Collins, "Apocalypticism and Literary Genre," 428. The present work relies on the same distinction, in reverse, ultimately arguing that Jubilees uses the literary morphology of the apocalypses to subvert the ideas they typically convey.

67. Paolo Sacchi focuses on apocalypticism as a social movement, even to the point of excluding the Apocalypse of John from the apocalyptic tradition as he understands it ("The Book of the Watchers as an Apocalyptic and Apocryphal Text," *Henoch* 30 [2008]: 9–11); see also Gabriele Boccaccini, "Jewish Apocalyptic Tradition: The Contribution of Italian Scholarship," in Collins and Charlesworth, *Mysteries and Revelations*, 38.

68. Florentino García Martínez ("Encore l'apocalyptique," *JSJ* 17 [1986]: 224–32) and Eibert Tigchelaar ("More on Apocalyptic and Apocalypses," 137–44) have questioned Collins's claim that literary description and identification are logically prior to study of the history and social function of the genre. Of course, a synchronic definition does not prohibit diachronic analysis. In the following chapters, comparison will focus on apocalypses from the time of Jubilees.

69. James H. Charlesworth recently expressed reservations about focusing too

Certainly for other genres, and perhaps even for the apocalypses, other approaches hold promise without reducing the legitimacy of the approach focused on literary morphology.[70]

1.2.3. Other Layers Follow: Ideas, Social Movements, and Function

The morphology of the literary genre does not depend upon or dictate exhaustively the layer of ideas, but it does suggest categories. The layer of ideas is related to the layer of morphology, with the possibility of exceptions. The transcendent agents and places on the spatial axis suggest ideas about their importance for understanding the visible world. The transcendent view of the temporal axis suggests ideas about the present world in terms of otherwise unknowable patterns and plans for history. The revelatory framework lends itself to conveying ideas about revelation. These three categories—the spatial axis, the temporal axis, and revelation—will provide the structure for chapters 2–4 of the present work. These three categories are convenient but not exhaustive. Other ideas have been suggested as important and typical of the apocalypses, including the permeation of boundaries[71] and temple cosmology.[72] None of these directions of inquiry should be excluded. Similarly, none should be elevated to exclusive importance as the definitive apocalyptic idea. A rigorous definition of the

---

much on elements in texts and isolating form from function or ideas from literary genre ("What Is an Apocalyptic Text, and How Do We Know That? Seeking the Provenience of the Book of the Watchers," *Henoch* 30 [2008]: 37–39).

70. Recently Carol Newsom has discussed a variety of approaches to genre. The Hodayot, for example, may be appropriate for analysis in terms of social function if we can assume that, unlike the apocalypses, they all originate in the same social location ("Pairing Research Questions and Theories of Genre," 241–59).

71. Frances Flannery-Dailey shows the interest of the apocalypses in overcoming ontological, spatial, and temporal boundaries; see *Dreamers, Scribes, and Priests: Jewish Dreams in the Hellenistic and Roman Eras* (JSJSup 90; Leiden: Brill, 2004), 113, 272; idem, "Lessons on Early Jewish Apocalypticism and Mysticism from Dream Literature," in *Paradise Now: Essays on Early Jewish and Christian Mysticism* (ed. April D. DeConick; SBLSymS 11; Atlanta: Society of Biblical Literature, 2006), 241–47.

72. Fletcher-Louis ("Jesus and Apocalypticism," in Holmén and Porter, *Handbook for the Study of the Historical Jesus*, 3:2877–2909), building on the work of Margaret Barker ("Beyond the Veil of the Temple: The High Priestly Origins of the Apocalypses," *SJT* 51 [1998]: 1–21), suggests that the ideas of the apocalypses are best understood from the perspective of temple cosmology.

literary genre frees us from need of an elaborate definition of apocalyptic ideas. An idea is "apocalyptic" if it is generic among all the apocalypses or an appropriately qualified subset of the apocalypses. Helpful, but not exhaustive, *descriptions* of the ideas typical of the apocalypses have been offered by Collins.[73]

Paul Hanson, who best established the threefold distinction between the literary genre "apocalypse," apocalyptic ideas, and apocalypticism, was most interested in apocalypticism. However, reconstructions of a religio-social movement that may have produced all (or at least a critical mass) of the apocalypses are particularly speculative. One might say that the social location of any one apocalypse is an instance of apocalypticism, but detailed study of a *typical* social setting of the apocalypses is a difficult matter unrelated to the present study. The three following chapters are concerned with establishing a pattern of shared literary forms expressing opposite ideas. Only the last chapter, in an effort to explain the pattern, will speculate on authorial intent and reader expectations based on historical and cultural context. Even that is not a study of apocalypticism. Similarly, the present work avoids the term "apocalyptic worldview" in as much as it may imply not just a set of ideas typically conveyed by the apocalypses but a complete and comprehensive ideological or theological system of a person or group. The latter pertains more to the layer of abstraction of apocalypticism as a religio-social phenomenon.[74]

A complete study of the genre would ultimately also include function. *Semeia* 36 addressed the aspects of function and offered several proposals for statements of the function of apocalypses.[75] The exercise demonstrated that the *Semeia* 14 definition naturally implies some categories for function, as it did for the layer of ideas. For example, the literary contents of transcendence on the spatial axis imply a function of interpreting earthly

---

73. John J. Collins, "From Prophecy to Apocalypticism: The Expectation of the End," in *the Origins of Apocalypticism in Judaism and Christianity* (vol. 1 of *The Encyclopedia of Apocalypticism*; ed. John J. Collins; New York: Continuum, 1998), 157; idem, "The Legacy of Apocalypticism," in *Encounters with Biblical Theology* (Minneapolis: Fortress, 2005), 161–62.

74. Collins sometimes refers to apocalypticism as a worldview: "Wisdom, Apocalypticism, and Generic Compatibility," 387; idem, *Apocalypticism in the Dead Sea Scrolls* (Literature of the Dead Sea Scrolls; London: Routledge, 1997), 8.

75. Adela Yarbro Collins, "Introduction," *Semeia* 36 (1986): 7; Hellholm, "The Problem of Apocalyptic Genre," 27; Aune, "The Apocalypse of John and the Problem of Genre," 87, 89–91.

circumstances in light of the supernatural world. *Semeia* 36 also demonstrated the difficulty of being more precise and still speaking for all the apocalypses. David Aune contrasted social function with literary function, but both are less objectively measurable than the morphological definition of the genre.[76] None of the statements of function aid identification or affect the classification of texts on the basis of the *Semeia* 14 definition. The most helpful insight for the present purposes was David Hellholm's description of a matrix in which form, content, and function fill one axis that intersects all three (or more) layers of abstraction (literary, conceptual, social).[77] Thus, one can speak of literary forms, literary contents, literary functions, social forms, social contents, and so on. One might add a more basic level at which any literary genre functions to create reader expectations. Further consideration of the function of the genre "apocalypse" in Jubilees is logically posterior to understanding the use of the literary morphology and the ideas conveyed but will be taken up when the final chapter seeks to explain the subversion of the genre.[78] In the meantime, Hellholm's observation of complexity in the larger structure of genre illustrates the need to put all these aspects and elements into a meaningful relationship. We need to move from distinguishing individual components back to the larger question of how genre communicated meaning to the audience.

1.2.4. Jubilees Uses the Typical Literary Morphology to Express Atypical Ideas

Cognitive psychology examines the process of determining meaning, particularly when there are mixed signals to be processed, as in the case of Jubilees.[79] The mind organizes new material through comparison with familiar models, not necessarily application of definitions. For the ideal

---

76. Aune, "The Apocalypse of John and the Problem of Genre," 89.
77. Hellholm, "The Problem of Apocalyptic Genre," 13–64.
78. Understanding literary morphology may lead to understanding social function, but we cannot expect a simple correlation between form and function. See Hanneken, "The Book of Jubilees among the Apocalypses," 104–7; Collins, "Epilogue: Genre Analysis and the Dead Sea Scrolls," 425–28.
79. Eleanor Rosch pioneered research in the cognition of categories, introducing "prototype theory" and overturning a view of taxonomy by which all members of a category are equal. See the survey in George Lakoff, *Women, Fire, and Dangerous Things: What Categories Reveal about the Mind* (Chicago: University of Chicago Press, 1987), 1–57. See also, Swales, *Genre Analysis*, 51–52. Michael Sinding ("After Definitions,"

model, or "prototype,"[80] all signals concord at all levels. For example, for a subject in North America, a robin is easily recognized as a bird. The signals of flying, laying eggs, having feathers, size, and sound all concord easily with the prototype of the category "bird." A penguin or an ostrich is not as easily classified. There is a degree of discord and conflicting signals to be sorted through. One could defend the classification of a penguin as a bird using rigorous criteria, but from a perspective of human cognition, there is more to the story.[81] Jubilees is like a penguin. Jubilees satisfies the definition of the literary genre "apocalypse" (among others),[82] but that does not end the consideration of the apocalyptic genre in Jubilees. The purpose is not to classify Jubilees but to understand how it uses the genre to convey meaning. The fact that Jubilees uses the literary morphology but rejects the ideas typically conveyed thereby demands further explanation.

Jubilees subverts the apocalyptic genre. Jubilees uses the literary morphology to raise reader expectations that typical ideas will be expressed. Literary cues such as the revelatory framework and transcendent contents suggest a preliminary meaning. The preliminary meaning is not sustained, however, in what is actually said about the issues related to the literary elements. The preliminary meaning discords with the sustained meaning. The discord enhances the contrast between the meanings. The "discovery" of the "true" meaning, at least for a certain audience, causes dramatic effect. The final chapter will explore the helpfulness of terms such as "irony" or "satire" to explain the discord. The

---

184–86) explored the implications for literary genre. Carol Newsom ("Spying out the Land," 442–45) brought these advances into conversation with the genre "apocalypse."

80. The ideal model can be called a "prototype" in the sense of fitting expectations of a type, not in the sense of historical derivation. Cf. Collins, "Apocalypse: The Morphology of a Genre," 1. Furthermore, prototypes, according to Rosch, are not fixed objects but "judgments of degree of prototypicality." The point is *not* to reduce the apocalyptic genre in Jubilees to comparison with one particular text such as the Book of the Watchers or the Animal Apocalypse (Lakoff, *Women, Fire, and Dangerous Things*, 44).

81. See also Lakoff's discussion of idealized cognitive models in *Women, Fire, and Dangerous Things*, 68–90.

82. See further discussion in the following section. Jubilees uses other genres, even more so by volume, but uses the genre "apocalypse" in all its major components at key parts of the book (the beginning, middle, and end). Others have identified Jubilees as a partial apocalypse, a borderline apocalypse, or an apocalypse with various qualifications (see above). This study aims for greater precision.

term "irony" may not be more specific than "subversion." "Satire," with the entailed intent to ridicule, is inherently more speculative. In order to approach an explanation, the final chapter will consider historical and cultural context. Meanwhile, the following three chapters will establish that apocalyptic literary morphology typically expresses certain ideas and that Jubilees uses the literary morphology while thoroughly rejecting the typical ideas. This will be accomplished through detailed analysis of Jubilees and contemporary apocalypses, with occasional reference to related material.[83] Before turning to detailed comparison, an introductory survey of three major issues will establish the broad outline of the subversion of the apocalypses in Jubilees.

1.3. Introductory Examples of Subversion

The following chapters will explore in precise detail the issues implied in specific elements of apocalyptic literary morphology. A few introductory examples will illustrate the broader picture of the issues at stake. First we will utilize the "master paradigm" description of apocalypses to illustrate the use of the genre. We will then consider the problem of evil and injustice second and eschatology third.

1.3.1. Survey of Pervasive and Structurally Significant Use of the Literary Genre

Apocalyptic literary morphology does not account for all or even most of Jubilees, if one could measure genre by volume of words and verses. Jubilees does include all the defining features of the literary genre and more elements of the *Semeia* 14 "master paradigm" than some works that are easily recognized as apocalypses.[84] The genre of a work is not simply a matter of volume or counting literary elements but structure. Jubilees concentrates apocalyptic literary elements in the beginning, middle, and end

---

83. Detailed consideration of the date and historical context of Jubilees will be presented in the last chapter. There is broad consensus that the Book of the Watchers, the Animal Apocalypse, the Apocalypse of Weeks, and the Danielic apocalypses can be treated as representatives of apocalypses available at the time of Jubilees. Some of these were certainly known to the author, some may or may not have been known, and others not known to us may have been known to the author.

84. Collins, "Apocalypse: The Morphology of a Genre," 6–8.

of the book (chs. 1, 23, and 50). Within that framework, Jubilees frequently reminds the audience of the revelatory framework and includes the requisite contents of language and issues of spatial and temporal transcendence. A brief review of the master paradigm will illustrate how Jubilees concentrates generic elements in the structural framework, while further development recurs through much of the rest of the book.

The master paradigm is not the definition of the genre, but a hierarchical description of typical morphological features in their more specific variants. Thus, while all apocalypses include a narrative framework of a revelation, the contents of which are spatially and temporally transcendent, there are a number of frequent but optional ways each can be realized in any one text. Jubilees makes at least superficial use of almost all and pervasive use of many elements of the master paradigm. The fact that Jubilees says atypical things about these elements is a different matter. In the following review, parenthetical numbers refer to the numbering in *Semeia* 14. The *medium* (1) of revelation is primarily *auditory* (1.2), with some *dialogue* (1.2.2) but mostly *discourse* (1.2.1). Jubilees 1 narrates the setting of the revelation on Mount Sinai on the sixteenth of the third month of the exodus from Egypt (Exod 24). After a conversation between God and Moses, God commands an angel of the presence to dictate the heavenly tablets to Moses and Moses to write down the dictation. Jubilees often reminds the audience of the revelatory framework with direct address of the angel (first person) to Moses (second person). In addition to the framework of auditory revelation, *visual* (1.1) revelation appears in Jub. 1:3 (Moses sees the glory of the Lord like a blazing fire); 4:19 (Enoch saw a vision); and 32:21 (Jacob reads the heavenly tablets in a vision, cf. 45:4), although in no case is the vision very graphic. The framework is not an *otherworldly journey* (1.3), other than Moses going up Sinai and God coming down. The medium of *writing* (1.4) is heavily emphasized, both in the outer framework (Jub. 1:1, 5, 7, 26; 2:1; 50:6, 12) and frequently throughout (the base "writ-" appears fifty-three times in VanderKam's translation). The *otherworldly mediator* (2) is an angel of the presence. The *human recipient* (3) is Moses, a *venerable figure from the past* (3.1), whose *reaction* (3.3) is briefly conveyed in Jub. 1:19–21, but there is no elaboration on *disposition* (3.2). *Paraenesis* (11) and *instructions to the recipient* (12) appear in the first chapter and pervasive instructions to Moses to write down the dictation and teach the Israelites. There is a very short *narrative conclusion* (13), whether we assume Jub. 50:4–5 or 50:13 is the original ending.

The temporal axis underlies the entire book in *protology* (4) and *his-*

tory (5). The eschatological crisis, judgment, and salvation (7, 8, 9) appear most clearly in Jub. 23, along with shorter allusions in Jub. 1, 50, and elsewhere. More generally, the temporal aspect of judgment appears often, especially in Jub. 5 and with every mention of figures such as Cain receiving punishment within his lifetime. *Cosmogony* (4.1, and *theogony*, if one counts the creation of the angels) and *primordial events* (4.2) are no less temporally transcendent if they are based on received scriptures. *History* (5) is mostly *explicit recollection of the past* (5.1), although at least some of the heavenly tablets are claimed to have been written well in advance of the associated events, such as the election of Jacob. Unmistakable *ex eventu prophecy* (5.2) occurs in the description of the Maccabean revolt in Jub. 23 and to a lesser degree in discussions of the Idumeans "until today"[85] (Jub. 38:14) and "predictions" that Israelites will forget laws such as circumcision and festival calendar (Jub. 1:9; 6:34; 15:33). *Semeia* 14 mentions *present salvation through knowledge* (6) in the context of later gnostic texts, but technically Jub. 23:26–27 (realized eschatology through study of the law) could be read in this way. Jubilees 23 describes an *eschatological crisis* (7) that superficially resembles Seleucid *persecution* (7.1) and *other eschatological upheavals* (7.2) of the created order, although closer examination will show the crisis to be just punishment under the terms of the covenant. Likewise, *eschatological judgment* (8.1) is certainly present in phrases such as "the great day of judgment" and "there will be a great punishment from the Lord" (Jub. 23:11, 22), even though what is said about these elements is atypical. *Sinners* (8.1) are emphatically punished in chapter 23 and elsewhere, and *the world* (8.2) is superficially punished in 23:18, "the earth will indeed be destroyed." *Otherworldly beings* (8.3) are judged in Jub. 5:6–11 (watchers) and arguably 48:18 (Mastema, probably not 10:8), although significantly there are no otherworldly agents in the eschatological scenario of Jub. 23 (other than mention of their absence). *Eschatological salvation* (9) is developed in Jub. 23:26–31 and 50:5, although we will leave to the layer of ideas whether it is brought about by supernatural intervention or, more fundamentally, human repentance. The *cosmic transformation* (9.1) is even more clear outside of Jub. 23, in statements that the properly functioning sanctuary will renew the cosmos: "All the luminaries will be renewed for (the purpose of) healing, health, and blessing for all the

---

85. Unless otherwise noted, all translations are from VanderKam, *The Book of Jubilees*, vol. 2.

elect ones (Israel)[86] and so that it may remain this way from that time throughout all the days of the earth" (Jub. 1:29; likewise 4:26 and 19:25). Human salvation is more collective than *personal* (9.2), but the increase in longevity to a thousand years constitutes a clear transformation. The issue of *resurrection* (9.2.1) or *other forms of afterlife* (9.2.2) is more tricky, but at least the superficial cues of the issue can be found in statements such as "they will rise and see great peace" and "their bones will rest in the earth and their spirits will be very happy" (Jub. 23:30–31).

The most obvious and pervasive *otherworldly elements* (10) on the spatial axis are *otherworldly beings* (10.2), although one might also mention the place of judgment (7:29; 10:5, 9, 11; 22:22), heavenly tablets (frequent), the heavenly liturgy (30:18; 31:14, similarly 2:17–21, 28; 15:27), and the holy places (4:26; 8:19). The holy places are not technically otherworldly but are compared superficially to such places in contexts of Enoch being taken there and eschatological restoration originating there. Much more frequently and thoroughly discussed are otherworldly beings, particularly demons, angels who sinned, Belial, "satans," and the heavenly accuser evocative of *ha-satan*, the Prince of Mastema. For the demons we learn their origin, raison d'être, and how to avoid them. Similarly, we learn about the Prince of Mastema in various places throughout the book. Following the distinction between literary morphology and the ideas, we must count use of these evocative terms even when an additional word such as "no" changes the meaning, "there was *no* satan or any evil one" (Jub. 23:29; 40:9; 46:2; 50:5).

Depending on how one counts superficial or fleeting mentions of elements typical of apocalyptic morphology, Jubilees includes almost everything mentioned in the master paradigm, even in the third-level subpoints. The question is how some of those superficial connections should be counted. For example, point 1.1 from the master paradigm applies to Jubilees in that Jubilees includes visionary revelation and makes distinctive claims about the legitimacy of visions, yet Jubilees is not itself a vision in its fundamental structure. Jubilees does not use the literary morphology any less if what it says about coded symbols is that they are absent from legitimate revelation. Once the apocalyptic framework is established, certain elements that would not be apocalyptic by themselves might fit into the "dialogism" between the ideas typically associated with

---

86. "All the elect ones (Israel)," literally, "all the elect ones of Israel." See §2.2.1.4 for the case for understanding this verse as nonsectarian, like the rest of the book.

the apocalypses and the ideas sustained in Jubilees. For example, if we had only a fragment that said Cain was judged and received a fitting punishment within his lifetime, we could not treat it as a subversion of the apocalyptic idea of deferred, eschatological judgment. However, once the framework is established and a critical mass of issues and terms associated with the apocalypses is reached, more points can be treated as participating in the broader comparison of ideas. Furthermore, because Jubilees follows Genesis so carefully, a conspicuous silence can be more meaningful than the common argument from silence. Again, for example, a fragment mentioning only Joseph's cup would not be called a subversion of the apocalypses, yet if the audience recalls that in Genesis Joseph's cup was a divining cup, and if the audience notices the other ways in which Jubilees rejects esoteric coded revelation, then even a passage with no explicit use of apocalyptic literary morphology can represent a confrontation with apocalypses. At the very least, Jubilees explicitly draws on typical apocalyptic morphology in the framework and particular passages throughout the work. Jubilees meets all the requirements of the definition and enough of the points of the description in the master paradigm. Arguably, almost all of them come up at least indirectly. The audience is reminded throughout the work of the revelatory framework, cosmic agents such as Mastema, and the structure of history. If one accepts further that additional elements not *exclusively* associated with apocalypses can participate in a confrontation with the apocalypses in context (once a critical mass of framework and explicit elements is reached), then apocalyptic literary elements pervade the entire book.

This is not to say that the apocalyptic genre accounts exclusively for the genre of Jubilees or that it would be possible to rank primary and secondary genres in a complex work. Nor could we end the discussion by saying Jubilees counts as an apocalypse without accounting for the deep discord at the level of ideas. Furthermore, the above survey based on the definition and description (master paradigm) of the genre in *Semeia* 14 is only an introductory discussion, to be validated with close comparison with the known apocalypses that existed around the time of Jubilees. Especially if one focuses on the early apocalypses, other issues might be added to the master paradigm, such as a reveal-conceal dialectic,[87] an esoteric

---

87. Aune, "The Apocalypse of John and the Problem of Genre," 84; Stegemann, "Die Bedeutung der Qumranfunde," 488–99.

INTRODUCTION   31

implied audience,[88] or temple cosmology.[89] The spatial axis might include ontological classification of humanity and their roles on the cosmic stage. Even with a hypothetical "complete" description it would be necessary to emphasize that evaluation of the genre relies on structures and issues more than checkboxes of distinctive phrases and elements. With that in mind, we move from a survey of affinities at the base layer of abstraction to the discord at the layer of ideas. The basic issues of the explanation of unjust suffering (evil) and eschatology will lay out the fundamental ways in which Jubilees clashes with the apocalypses. It is not that Jubilees resembles apocalypses in some places and differs in other places. It is precisely the passages that evoke the apocalypses in literary morphology that clash with the apocalypses in ideas. Sometimes it is a simple matter of the layers of terminology and syntax, sometimes it is more complex, but consistently there is a contrast between the superficial resemblances with the apocalypses and the sustained messages about the implicit issues.

1.3.2. Evil, Injustice, and the Lack Thereof

One of the fundamental issues typically, even inherently, raised by the apocalyptic literary genre is the problem of evil. More specifically, the underlying problems are the suffering of the righteous and the prosperity of sinners, with the constraint that the explanation may not challenge God's justice (theodicy). The history of philosophy and religion has complicated the issue, such that a preliminary clarification of the terms applicable in Jubilees is necessary. Jubilees uses the words "sin" and "evil" often, but they are not entities that exist outside of human choice. The nouns "sin" (ኀጢአ) and "evil" (እኪይ) never govern a verb, even metaphorically.[90] The "problem of evil," in terms appropriate to Jubilees, is the problem of injustice—unjust suffering or unpunished sin. If suffering comes from God as just punishment for bad choices, it is not evil. If individual sin is always resolved with prompt punishment, it is not a theological problem (as far as Jubilees is concerned). One might argue that Jubilees anticipates

---

88. William Adler, "Introduction," in *The Jewish Apocalyptic Heritage in Early Christianity* (ed. James C. VanderKam and William Adler; Minneapolis: Fortress, 1996), 13.

89. Fletcher-Louis, "Jewish Apocalyptic and Apocalypticism."

90. The related term "injustice" (ዐመፃ) "increases" in Jub. 5:2, based on Gen 6:5, "human wickedness increased on the earth."

an idea of ontological wickedness in its view of the nations, but not as a force in the cosmos in the dualistic sense. At least for Israel, sin is a reversible choice, not an independent entity imposed on humanity from without.

Simply put, the typical apocalypses seek to explain unjust suffering in the present, while Jubilees denies the existence of unjust suffering: "there is no injustice" (Jub. 5:13). In the typical apocalypses, injustice is larger than the visible realm. Injustice can be understood from a view outside the present (on the temporal axis) to its primordial origins and/or eschatological resolution. It can be understood from a view outside the visible world (on the spatial axis) to agents other than humans and God. Justice will eventually prevail, but not yet. In Jubilees, sin is always promptly punished. Justice is never deferred. The covenantal relationship between God and Israel is not impeded by any invisible agents. The foreign nations are in fact punished with demons and angelic bureaucracy, but only because of their sin. Israel is immune from "evil" as long as it separates from the nations and studies the law. The following chapter will compare Jubilees to the typical apocalypses through the component themes of the origin of evil, the ongoing explanation or raison d'être of evil, and the resolution of evil. By way of introduction, it will serve better to introduce some of the central passages in Jubilees with their distinctive claims.

Before coming to the passages in which Jubilees develops its claims about injustice and the lack thereof, a few conspicuous silences should be noted. Although evil in creation is not present in the contemporary apocalypses either, it has been suggested that the view of evil in Jubilees is "created dualism," comparable to the Instruction on Two Spirits at Qumran.[91] If this were the case, one would expect some hint to that effect in Jubilees' lengthy account of creation. Other than an acknowledgement that most nations will not be chosen to keep the Sabbath, there is no suggestion of dualism, corruption, opposition, or fault in creation. Similarly, Jubilees retells Gen 3 without any hint toward explanation of ongoing sin and suffering,[92] although again this point does not contrast with contem-

---

91. Segal, *The Book of Jubilees*, 323.

92. The retelling of Gen 3 in Jubilees is most remarkable for the lack of expansion along any lines, let alone the lines associated with etiology of sin. If anything, Jubilees reduces the lasting significance of the sin by emphasizing that Adam and Eve worked before the sin, "Adam and his wife spent the seven years in the Garden of Eden *working* and guarding it. We gave him *work* and were teaching him (how) to do everything

porary apocalypses. Jubilees omits the personification of sin in Gen 4:7, "sin crouches at the door craving to get you."

Jubilees develops the theme of realized justice from the beginning. First, Jubilees counters the possibility that Adam escaped God's threat of punishment by living far longer than the day on which he ate the fruit. Jubilees draws from Ps 90:4 to claim that the day meant a thousand years, reconciling Genesis with the idea of undeferred justice, "Therefore he [Adam] did not complete the years of this day because he died during it" (Jub. 4:30). Similarly, Jubilees infers that a just God must have killed Cain: "His house fell on him, and he died inside his house. He was killed by its stones for with a stone he had killed Abel and, by a just punishment, he was killed with a stone" (Jub. 4:31).

Jubilees 5 confronts the Book of the Watchers directly, although the underlying idea is no less true of the Danielic apocalypses. Jub. 5 retells the story of exogamous watchers with some glaring changes. First, Jubilees has the angels sent to earth with a good mission; only later do they sin.[93] This displaces a willful rebellion against God in heaven that imposes its consequences on earth. Jubilees also retells the story such that there are no innocent victims. The watchers sin and are punished with eternal imprisonment. The giants sin and are killed by war. Humans, except for Noah, sin and are drowned, "Every thought of all mankind's knowledge was evil like this all the time" (Jub. 5:2; utilizing Gen 6:5). A related point is subtle in Jub. 5 but consistent with a larger pattern. In the Book of the Watchers angels hear the cry of the innocent and mediate the complaint before God. In Jub. 5:3 God sees directly.

Another conflict between superficial association and sustained ideas begins with Jub. 5:10,

> Now their fathers [the fathers of the giants, the watchers] were watching, but afterwards they were tied up in the depths of the earth for the great day of judgment, so that there would be[94] condemnation on all who have corrupted their ways and their actions before the Lord. (Jub. 5:10)

---

that was appropriate for *working* (it). While he was *working*..." (Jub. 3:15–16, emphasis added). Gen 2–3 might seem to suggest that labor is a consequence of sin, not the original plan for creation.

93. It has been suggested that this change meets a chronological need. That may also be the case, but the implication for the view of evil stands nevertheless and is consistent with other details. See Segal, *The Book of Jubilees*, 132.

94. "For the great day of judgment, so that there would be," እስከ ፡ ዕለተ ፡

In the Book of the Watchers, the watchers are detained pending a final judgment in the distant future. Charles expected such an idea and thus emended the text (arguing that Hebrew converted-perfect verbs were mistaken for perfects).[95] Verse 10 teases such as association, but the rest of the passage sustains a different claim, that the watchers have already been judged and punished once and for all. The "great day of judgment" was when the watchers, giants, and humans all received their just punishments.

> 5:11 He obliterated all from their places; there remained no one of them whom he did not judge for all their wickedness. 5:12 He made a new and righteous creation for all his works[96] so that they would not sin with their whole nature until eternity. Everyone will be righteous—each according to his kind—for all time. 5:13 The judgment of them all has been ordained and written on the heavenly tablets; there is no injustice. (As for) all who transgress from their way in which it was ordained for them to go—if they do not go in it, judgment has been written down for each creature and for each kind. 5:14 There is nothing which is in heaven or on the earth, in the light, the darkness, Sheol, the deep, or in the dark place—all their judgments have been ordained, written, and inscribed. 5:15 He judges[97] each person—the great one in accord with his greatness and the small one in accord with his smallness—each one in accord with his way. (Jub. 5:11–15)

Jubilees transforms the tradition from an etiology of evil to an example of perfect justice. The typical apocalypses presume and explain the existence of evil in the sense of unpunished sin, but Jub. 5:13 rejects not just the explanation but the preliminary assumption that evil exists: "there is no injustice." Notice also that the "new and righteous creation" has already

---

ደይን ፡ ዐቢይ ፡ ለሕፀን (< εἰς ἡμέραν κρίσεως μεγάλην εἶναι < ליום המשפט הגדול להיות). VanderKam translates, "until the great day of judgment when there will be." Cf. 2 Pet 2:9; 3:7; Jude 1:6. The preposition could come from עד, which could still fit the understanding of the day of judgment as the flood. The important point is that the angel's address to Moses does *not* use any imperfect verbs for the judgment of the watchers.

95. R. H. Charles, *The Book of Jubilees: Or The Little Genesis* (London: Black, 1902), 44–45.

96. "Creation for all his works," ለኩሉ ፡ ግብሩ ፡ ፍጥረት. VanderKam translates, "nature for all his creatures." Both are possible.

97. "He judges," ይኴንን. VanderKam translates, "He will exercise judgment regarding." Grammar permits either translation, but context suggests an ongoing habit rather than a future action.

been given. The world was purified through the flood and received a fresh start. There is no permanent contagion of sin that originated with the watchers and continued past the flood, at least according to this passage. Jubilees does appropriate the idea of demons and illicit teaching, but conspicuously not until two generations after Noah, with the division of nations. Demons, angelic princes, and false wisdom exist but only apply to Gentiles. This brings us to the next major passage.

Jubilees 10 finds a place for demons (the spirits of the giants) after the flood, but not as an explanation of suffering and injustice against the righteous. Demons are assigned to the punishment of Gentiles, and the revelation of demonic activity serves as a warning to Israel to stay away from Gentiles. Consequently, Jubilees does not address the demons until it can address the nations, which begins with Noah's grandchildren.

> During the third week of this jubilee impure demons began to mislead Noah's grandchildren, to make them act foolishly, and to destroy them. (Jub. 10:1)

The striking part is how easily these demons are defeated by the righteous. Noah eliminates all of them simply by asking.

> Then our God told us to tie up each one. (Jub. 10:7)

Here, for the first time, we meet the leader of these spirits, the Prince of Mastema, or simply Mastema, whom we will introduce more in the next paragraph. Mastema makes a counterintercession to restore 10 percent of the demons, but with the clear function of punishing wickedness, not afflicting or testing the righteous.

> For they are meant for destroying and misleading before my authority because human wickedness is great. (Jub. 10:8)[98]

God then allows Mastema to use 10 percent of the demons. Jubilees is the only ancient text to describe a diminishment of demons.[99] For those who

---

98. For this understanding of the verse, see ch. 2 n. 58. VanderKam translates, "For they are meant for (the purposes of) destroying and misleading before my punishment [ቅድመ ፡ ኩነኔየ] because the evil of mankind is great."

99. VanderKam, "The Demons in the *Book of Jubilees*," 344.

obey the books of Noah, later identified as the books preserved by the Levites for Israel "until today" (Jub. 45:16), the demons have no power.[100]

> Noah wrote down in a book everything (just) as we had taught him regarding all the kinds of medicine, and the evil spirits were precluded from pursuing Noah's children. He gave all the books that he had written to his oldest son Shem because he loved him much more than all his sons. (Jub. 10:13–14)

The demons and the idolatry they inspire are reduced to impotence against the righteous, which soon equals Israel. Demons are utilized as an explanation of whatever power is perceived in foreign magic, but absolutely not an explanation of why the righteous suffer.[101]

Mastema is a good example of subversion of an idea typically associated with the apocalypses. Mastema superficially resembles a figure from an apocalypse but is denied any similar function. The name sounds like Satan but is not. Mastema evokes the role of a leader of evil forces in rebellion against God but remains in constant submission to God. Mastema explains some trouble that the righteous face but never claims any victory, only shame. As discussed at length in chapter 2, Mastema is a complex figure. Jubilees likes the idea of a figure who can proxy for the unbecoming deeds attributed to God in Exodus. There is also a complication in the extent to which "Satan" is relevant here as a particularly apocalyptic idea by the time of Jubilees. It may not be the case that portraying Mastema as a bungling variation on Satan ridicules any one apocalypse, but it does subvert the idea that God's covenantal relationship with God's people is successfully impeded by independent forces in the cosmos.

Discussion of the apocalyptic view of evil and the angelic world usually focuses on bad angels, but even good angels can account for some

---

100. What the author of Jubilees had in mind in speaking of Noah's books is a matter of great debate. See especially Michael E. Stone, Aryey Amihay, and Vered Hillel, eds., *Noah and His Book(s)* (SBLEJL 28; Atlanta: Society of Biblical Literature, 2010). It is certainly possible that the author knew or imagined books that were physically separate from the books of Moses, but Jubilees emphasizes the conceptual and legal unity of all legitimate revelation. This is most striking in Jub. 21:10, which asserts that Enoch and Noah wrote books containing a law known to us only in Lev 19:5–8.

101. As discussed in chapter 2, the same basic point is true of the other enduring consequence of antediluvian sin, illicit teaching. The teaching of the watchers does not corrupt the chosen line (Jub. 12:16–18), but only one of Noah's grandchildren (8:3).

delay, inefficiency, or imperfection of justice without impinging on God's ultimate perfection. Angelic mediation was disputed in several texts. Jubilees makes its position clear in chapter 15. God never outsources sovereignty over Israel to any intermediary.

> 15:30 For the Lord did not draw near to himself either Ishmael, his sons, his brothers, or Esau. He did not choose them (simply) because they were among Abraham's children, for he knew them. But he chose Israel to be his people. 15:31 He sanctified them and gathered (them) from all mankind. For there are many nations and many peoples and all belong to him. *He made spirits rule over all in order to lead them astray from following him. 15:32 But over Israel he made no angel or spirit rule because he alone is their ruler.* He will guard them and require them for himself from his angels, his spirits, and everyone, and all his powers so that he may guard them and bless them and so that they may be his and he theirs from now and forever. (Jub. 15:30–32, emphasis added)

The issue is not whether other nations have angelic princes; Jubilees agrees with the apocalypses that they do, although there is a twist in that the angels are there to lead them astray, not to help them. The issue is whether Israel has one or more angels who mediate God's sovereignty. The implication in the apocalypses seems to have been that the present time cannot be reconciled with the perfect justice expected from God, so there must be some other agents involved that both explain the inefficacy of justice in the present and ensure that God will soon retake the helm and intervene radically. Jubilees 15:32 makes clear that the unnamed angel of the presence is not comparable even to the good angels in the apocalypses who exercise some independent will. This is borne out by the rest of the book, since the angel of the presence appears often but only following the direct command of God. "Angelic instruction" is a concept, but the angel of the presence is often more a tutor than a revealer of hidden things, as when the angel tutors Abraham in Hebrew (Jub. 12:25–27). In other apocalypses angels interpret symbols in their own voice, but Jub. 1 establishes that the angel merely dictates. The point is emphasized elsewhere,

> For I know and from now on will inform you—not from my own mind because this is the way the book is written in front of me, and the Divisions of Times[102] are ordained on the heavenly tablets.... (Jub. 6:35)

---

102. Capitalization added, since the text itself and the Damascus Document sug-

These examples are typical of many ways in which Jubilees does not simply reject everything about apocalypses but adapts, interprets, and appropriates the literary elements while fundamentally subverting the ideas. Apocalypses typically describe invisible places and angelic agents in order to explain the suffering of the righteous and lack of punishment of the wicked in the present. The apocalypses portray earthly events as the by-product of a cosmic drama, with humans in minor roles. In Jubilees angels are the supporting cast in the story of God's exclusive relationship with Israel.

1.3.3. Eschatology

By the time the audience comes to the middle of Jubilees,[103] many typical literary elements from the apocalypses have appeared and atypical things have been said about them. The revelation of hidden things turned out to be a revelation of the publicly received traditions of Israel. The cosmic drama turned out to have only two major characters, God and Israel. "Protology" established that the separation of Israel from the nations is God's eternal plan, as are the established structures of the temple and priesthood. Early history testifies to the timelessness of law and justice, not to the introduction of some corruption. Creation and justice do not require an eschatological resolution. The groundwork has been laid for a sustained, direct confrontation with the most significant remaining literary and conceptual feature of the apocalypses: eschatology.

Apocalyptic literary elements and issues pervade Jubilees, but chapter 23 is a sustained concentration. Jubilees 23 uses all the distinctive literary elements of apocalyptic eschatology, including phrases such as "great day of judgment" and "in those days" and the structure of decline of history, final woes, judgment, and restoration. The conflict of ideas can be summarized, in modern terms, as the conflict between apocalyptic and Deuteronomistic views of history.[104] Daniel 9 also reflects this confrontation, from the other

---

gest this was understood as the title of the book we call Jubilees. Devorah Dimant has challenged the prevailing view that the Damascus Document cites Jubilees. See below, ch. 5 n. 35.

103. Jub. 23 is central in the book of Jubilees in several ways. If modern versification may be used as an approximate measure of length, the middle verse of the book is Jub. 23:23. It has been recognized that Jacob is a central figure in Jubilees, and Jub. 23 makes the narrative transition from Jacob's ancestry to Jacob himself.

104. George W. E. Nickelsburg rightly reiterates this striking observation in his

perspective.[105] The apocalyptic view is that the "present" moment is the climax of the sovereignty of evil, the nadir of history, a crisis either unprecedented or with precedent only before the flood. Just when things cannot get worse, God will intervene to judge the wicked, reward the righteous, and restore creation to the original plan. The Deuteronomistic view is that history is "determined" only in the laws of cause and effect. Human sin causes divine punishment, which causes human repentance, which causes divine restoration. Suffering is chastisement, not a temporary suspension of justice or a test to be endured until an appointed time. Although Jubilees sets up the idea of calculated history elsewhere, a fixed date outside of human choice is conspicuously lacking in the most eschatological chapter.[106] Although Jubilees deals with angels and demons at length in other chapters, they are absent in chapter 23. The enemies of Israel are not God's enemies but God's servants sent to punish sin. The sinners are not foreign nations but self-righteous Jewish zealots.[107] The restoration begins with human repentance, not divine intervention. These subversions of general principles and specific issues can be seen in the following survey of the chapter in its entirety (other than the first seven verses, which describe the death of Abraham). Chapter 3 will focus on the individual themes of the temporal axis, with close comparison of Jubilees and contemporary apocalypses. Historical allusions will be discussed in chapter 5.

> 23:8 He had lived for three jubilees and four weeks of years—175 years—when he completed his lifetime. He had grown old and (his) time was completed. 23:9 For the times of the ancients were 19 jubilees [931 years] for their lifetimes. After the flood they started to decrease

---

discussions of Jubilees: *Jewish Literature between the Bible and the Mishnah: A Historical and Literary Introduction* (2nd ed.; Minneapolis: Fortress, 2005), 73 (1981, 78); idem, "The Nature and Function of Revelation in 1 Enoch, Jubilees, and Some Qumran Fragments," in *Pseudepigraphic Perspectives: The Apocrypha and Pseudepigrapha in Light of the Dead Sea Scrolls* (ed. Esther G. Chazon, Avital Pinnick, and Michael E. Stone; STDJ 31; Leiden: Brill, 1999), 104.

105. See §4.1.2.2 below, especially John J. Collins, *Daniel: A Commentary on the Book of Daniel* (Hermeneia; Minneapolis: Fortress, 1993), 348–60.

106. See §3.1.3 below, especially Martha Himmelfarb, "Torah, Testimony, and Heavenly Tablets: The Claim to Authority of the *Book of Jubilees*," in *A Multiform Heritage: Studies on Early Judaism and Christianity in Honor of Robert A. Kraft* (ed. Benjamin G. Wright; Scholars Press Homage Series 24; Atlanta: Scholars Press, 1999), 24.

107. See §3.2.3.1 below, especially Jub. 13:16–21.

> from 19 jubilees, to be fewer with respect to jubilees, to age quickly, and to have their times be completed in view of the numerous difficulties and through the wickedness of their ways—with the exception of Abraham. 23:10 For Abraham was perfect with the Lord in everything that he did—being properly pleasing throughout all his lifetime. And yet (even) he had not completed four jubilees during his lifetime when he became old—in view of wickedness—and reached the end of his time.

Scholars who have attempted to explain the apocalypse-like elements in Jubilees as an insertion or redaction from a separate source have had trouble deciding where the apocalypse begins. Jubilees 23 starts slowly but in these three verses already picks up some elements from the apocalypses. The issue of longevity takes the form of an apocalyptic decline of history, with the variation that the decline is gradual and in no way implies a crisis in the present moment.

> 23:11 All the generations that will come into being from now until the great day of judgment will grow old quickly—before they complete two jubilees [98 years]. It will be their knowledge that will leave them because of their old age; all of their knowledge will depart.

This verse introduces the historical "prediction" and the particular temporal point called the "great day of judgment." The point, however, is shown not to be an end of history, but a turning point. Most significant, the great day of judgment comes to be portrayed as a *past* event, relative to the time of composition. Another nuance may be at work here. As discussed in chapter 4, the term "wisdom" is largely avoided. "Knowledge" may be comparable, but the comparison brings with it an inversion. In several apocalypses, knowledge, wisdom, or enlightenment arises in a certain group. Jubilees does not single out a group here for lacking knowledge, but it is striking that knowledge/wisdom/enlightenment appears in the chapter only as being absent. The restoration involves repentance to the old laws, not some new gnosis or mystery.

> 23:12 At that time, if a man lives a jubilee and one-half of years [73.5 years], it will be said about him: "He has lived for a long time". But the greater part of his time will be (characterized by) difficulties, toil, and distress without peace 23:13 because (there will be) blow upon blow, wound upon wound, distress upon distress, bad news upon bad news, disease upon disease, and every (kind of) bad punishment like this, one

with the other: disease and stomach pains; snow, hail, and frost; fever, cold, and numbness; famine, death, sword, captivity, and every (sort of) blow and difficulty. 23:14 All of this will happen to the evil generation which makes the earth commit sin through sexual impurity, contamination, and their detestable actions. 23:15 Then it will be said: "The days of the ancients were numerous—as many as 1000 years—and good. But now the days of our lives, if a man has lived for a long time, are 70 years, and, if he is strong, 80 years". All are evil and there is no peace during the days of that evil generation.

These verses introduce the "final woes" that develop more specifically in 23:16-25. Jubilees includes the generic categories of "famine, death, sword and captivity." One would not want to say that these categories are not woeful, but the twist is in the elaboration of the categories. Typically an apocalypse is both graphic and absolute, whereas Jub. 23 elaborates the categories with relatively quotidian woes. In particular, natural and quotidian problems such as stomach ache, snow, hail, frost, fever, cold, numbness, and mortality at the age of seventy or eighty years invert the idea of final woes. Not only are the woes "normal" and unwoeful relative to the apocalypses, which are evoked by the literary genre, but they are unwoeful relative to the covenant curses of Deut 28, which are evoked by language and theme. A reader expects graphic elaboration of unimaginable woes but basically learns that life as we know it is punishment relative to God's plan. The final woes typically imply a crisis of history, an unraveling of nature from normal to far worse than normal. In Jubilees, normal life is the nadir of history and is woeful only relative to an imagined ideal of utopian blessing. We will come to some exceptions that have their own subversive twist, but basically Jub. 23 takes the crisis out of the apocalyptic crisis of history by making the decline, nadir, and restoration gradual and realized in the known world. The final chapter will return to this verse with the question of whether subversion of expectations with a radical demotion of significance, in this case replacing unimaginable horrors with stomach aches and frost, constitutes humor.

23:16 During that generation the children will find fault with their fathers and elders because of sin and injustice, because of what they say and the great evils that they commit, and because of their abandoning the covenant which the Lord had made between them and himself so that they should observe and perform all his commands, ordinances, and all his laws without deviating to the left or right. 23:17 For all have acted wickedly; every mouth speaks what is sinful. Everything that they do is impure and something detestable; all their ways are (characterized by) contamination, and corruption.

It is easy for a modern reader to project expectations of typical apocalyptic contents after the introduction, "During that generation the children will…." One expects the "children" to be praised and free of sin, as in the comparable passage in the Animal Apocalypse:

And look, lambs were born of those white sheep, and they began to open their eyes and to see and to cry out to the sheep. But they did not listen to them nor attend to their words, but they were extremely deaf, and their eyes were extremely and excessively blinded. (1 En. 90:6–7, Nickelsburg)

Jubilees 23:16 is relatively ambiguous, but verse 17 is the first to suggest that "all" are at fault, confirmed later by the fact that each group commits the sin of bloodshed and God punishes all without vindicating any group. Assuming a savvy reader would have picked up on the subversion by now, verse 16 begins to turn on the apocalypses even while remaining ambiguous. After all, is it really so praiseworthy by itself for children to find fault with elders? An apocalypse such as the Animal Apocalypse praises the new movement of "the children" with a clear claim that youth were right and the elders wrong. Verse 16 evokes such an association, but one is soon caused to question, if one has not questioned already, whether "because of sin and injustice" refers to the sin and injustice of the elders or the accusers. Indeed, accusing elders could itself be a form of abandoning the covenant. Deuteronomy 21 calls on the elders to judge and kill the child who defies a parent, not to mention the Decalogue command to honor parents. Even if verse 16 is ambiguous enough to permit an assumption that the children are sinless and the elders are sinful, the subsequent verses overturn such an assumption.

"The children" is not a technical term for a particular group, but it is the case that apocalypses sometimes use such language to describe the origin of a new and separate group outside established structures.[108] The children in verse 16 are contrasted with the children in verse 26, showing that the proper action is repentance and study of the traditional laws, not accusations and bloodshed. Even if they were a particular group and the

---

108. See §§2.2.1.4 and 3.2.3.3, especially Kister, "לתולדות כת האיסיים," 8–9.

INTRODUCTION 43

same particular group in both verses (radically reformed), the course of action in verse 16 is rejected. Others had used the genre "apocalypse" to claim pretension. The author of Jubilees seems to use it to call the pretension false.

> 23:18 The earth will indeed be destroyed because of all that they do. There will be no produce from the vine and no oil because what they do (constitutes) complete disobedience. All will be destroyed together—animals, cattle, birds, and all fish of the sea—because of mankind.

This verse plays between the apocalyptic language of final catastrophic destruction of the world as we know it and the Deuteronomistic function of divine chastisement through famine. Especially in the context of the other literary elements from apocalypses, the translation "the earth will be destroyed" is appropriately suggestive of the total ecological destruction found especially in the Book of the Watchers, Enoch's First Dream Vision, or the Epistle of Enoch. The twist, however, is that life goes on in the next verse unobliterated. Especially if the audience would have understood this as the famine of 162 or 160 B.C.E., as discussed in chapter 5, the sense is more that "the bounty of the earth will be diminished." The difference between cosmic catastrophe in other apocalypses and the famine here is not just a matter of degree and finality, it is a matter of timing. The imagery evokes a final, future destruction but is applied to a *past* event. The event *sounds like* a flood of complete destruction but functions more like famine in Deuteronomy or Hosea, where similar language lacks eschatological finality.

> Thus the land dries up [תֶּאֱבַל].
> Everything that dwells on it languishes [אֻמְלַל].
> Everything among the beasts of the field and the birds of the sky,
> Even the fish of the sea are withheld. (Hos 4:3)

Along similar lines, the agency involved here is not a cosmic conflict and purgation but human sin and divine chastisement. Famine has theological significance in the Deuteronomistic perspective, but the proposed response is to repent, not to panic and imagine that the sky is falling and the whole world is coming apart. Jubilees subverts apocalyptic imagery of cosmic catastrophe.

> 23:19 One group will struggle with another—the young with the old, the old with the young; the poor with the rich, the lowly with the great; and

the needy with the ruler—regarding the law and the covenant. For they have forgotten commandment, covenant, festival, month, sabbath, jubilee, and every verdict. 23:20 They will stand up with swords and warfare in order to bring them back to the way; but they will not be brought back until much blood is shed on the earth by each group. 23:21 Those who escape will not turn from their wickedness to the right way because all of them will elevate themselves for (the purpose of) cheating and through wealth so that one takes everything that belongs to another. They will mention the great name but neither truly nor rightly. They will defile the holy of holies with the impure corruption of their contamination.

If verse 19 evokes the suggestion of a great struggle of good against evil, the persecuted breaking the bonds of persecution and establishing lasting justice,[109] the suggestion is quickly subverted. Especially in Jubilees, there is nothing glorious about "shedding much blood on the earth," and Jubilees' harsh condemnation of all forms of fratricide should likewise be considered as part of the condemnation of the civil war. The generic associations make it easy to expect that Jubilees is praising one side in the war, but on closer examination there are no militant groups here or later that escape condemnation. Chapter 5 will explore specific historical references in these verses in greater depth. The point here is that Jubilees uses literary elements that evoke the portrayals of the civil war in the Animal Apocalypse and Dan 11 but subverts the pretension of acting on behalf of God in the slaughter of other Jews.

23:22 There will be a great punishment from the Lord for the actions of that generation. He will deliver them to the sword, judgment, captivity, plundering, and devouring. 23:23 He will arouse against them the sinful nations who will have no mercy or kindness for them and who will show partiality to no one, whether old or young, or anyone at all, because they are evil and strong so that they are more evil than all mankind. They will cause chaos in Israel and sin against Jacob. Much blood will be shed on the earth, and there will be no one who gathers up (corpses) or who buries (them).

---

109. For a thorough treatment of the sociopolitical features typical of the apocalypses around the time of Jubilees, see Anathea Portier-Young, *Apocalypse against Empire: Theologies of Resistance in Early Judaism* (Grand Rapids: Eerdmans, 2011).

Jubilees here takes a break from subtlety to make clear its evaluation of the civil war and the explanation of suffering typically associated with the apocalypses. The lesser point is that the whole generation (old and young, perhaps referring to the description of the two groups in 23:19) is punished; no side is vindicated. The greater point is that the foreign occupation is viewed as punishment *from God* for the sin of the civil war. Suffering is not the result of forces of evil in the cosmos rebelling against God, persecuting the righteous, and perverting justice. Justice is fully intact, and suffering comes from God as punishment for sin.

> 23:24 At that time they will cry out and call and pray to be rescued from the power of the sinful nations, but there will be no one who rescues (them). 23:25 The children's heads will turn white with gray hair. A child who is three weeks of age will look old like one whose years are 100, and their condition will be destroyed through distress and pain.

For the most part, the present work is concerned with the abstract layers of literary genre and typically implied ideas and is less dependent on comparison of specific passages. The main argument does not argue or assume that the author of Jubilees knew the same specific apocalypses that we know. Here, however, at the hyperbolic description of the nadir of history typical of the apocalypses, it is possible to identify some specific antiparallels in imagery. First, we should consider Isa 65:20. Even though Third Isaiah does not use the apocalyptic literary genre, a conceptual relationship has long been recognized.[110] The image of an infant who looks like an old man seems to derive from distorting the syntax of Isa 65:20.

לֹא־יִהְיֶה מִשָּׁם עוֹד עוּל יָמִים וְזָקֵן אֲשֶׁר לֹא־יְמַלֵּא אֶת־יָמָיו כִּי הַנַּעַר בֶּן־מֵאָה שָׁנָה יָמוּת וְהַחוֹטֶא בֶּן־מֵאָה שָׁנָה יְקֻלָּל׃

> No more shall there be in it an infant that lives but a few days, or an old person who does not live out a lifetime; for one who dies at a hundred years will be considered a youth, and one who falls short of a hundred will be considered accursed. (Isa 65:20, NRSV)

Whereas modern translations rightly grasp the disjunction, rendering something to the effect of, "There will be neither an infant nor an old man

---

110. See especially, Hanson, *The Dawn of Apocalyptic*.

who dies prematurely," Jubilees presupposes a conjunction, "one who is both an infant and an old man." The terminology is recognizable from Third Isaiah, but Jubilees rearranges the climax of restoration into a ridiculous image of a gnome. As discussed in chapter 3, the hope of restoration in Jubilees is at odds with that imagined in Third Isaiah. It is possible that Jubilees not only asserts a differing viewpoint but slips in some spoof imagery to illustrate how ridiculous the author thinks such an agenda really is (particularly in expecting a new people with a new name, new priesthood, new heaven, and new earth).

These two verses also intersect in language with Dan 11:34–35 and contradict in meaning. The Animal Apocalypse intersects here as well. The two intersecting issues are white children and crying for help.

> When they fall they will receive a little help, but many will join them insincerely. Some of the enlightened [מַשְׂכִּילִים] will fall so as to be refined [לִצְרוֹף], purified [לְבָרֵר], and whitened [לְלַבֵּן] until the time of the end, for it is not yet the appointed time. (Dan 11:34–35)

The basic issue is whether being white is a good thing or a bad thing. In Leviticus or Numbers, a white head is a skin disease and a threat to purity (Lev 13; Num 12:10). In fact, the European association of whiteness with purity is mostly absent from the Hebrew scriptures. Daniel 11 is one of the few cases where being made white and being made pure are in parallel (likewise Dan 7:9). The Animal Apocalypse is another clear case where whiteness is a good thing (consider also the birth of Noah tradition preserved in 1 En. 106:2 and the Genesis Apocryphon). Especially if "the children" connoted reformist groups around the time of the civil war, it becomes no neutral issue whether "white children" are glorified or despised. In Jubilees, the white children are the lowest of the low, the worst of all punishments. It is not important for the present point whether this image referred to a specific group, but it is clear enough that the image subverts the imagery that the authors of contemporary apocalypses found fit for self-glorification.

We should also consider the implication of the different images of calling for help in the same passages. In the Animal Apocalypse, Judah Maccabee brings about the eschatological victory not by winning the war himself but by crying out for help while engaged in a just struggle. The angel and God hear the cry and intercede (90:11–15). Daniel differs on whether the help received in battle marks the true resolution but still seems at least vaguely comparable in language. If we are to imagine that the author or audience of Jubilees knew Dan 11 or the Animal Apocalypse well enough to make an association, it is noteworthy that no help at all comes in Jub. 23:24. Since Jubilees already identified the civil war as the sin that brought on the punishment from God, the idea that they would receive any help at all is out of the question. Jubilees relies on Deut 28:29, 31 for the idea that there will be no help against divine chastisement (אֵין מוֹשִׁיעַ), while borrowing literary elements from the apocalypses to illustrate the contradiction in specific application.

> 23:26 In those days the children will begin to study the laws, to seek out the commands, and to return to the right way.

After condemning the militant "children," we finally come to the normative response of repentance and nonviolent study. Any image of an elite group is not sustained in the immediate context and the rest of the book. The point seems to be that Israel as a whole repents. The idea that Israel's suffering can be resolved by repentance conflicts with apocalyptic ideas, particularly as contrasted in Dan 9.

> 23:27 The days will begin to become numerous and increase, and mankind as well—generation by generation and day by day until their lifetimes approach 1000 years and to more years than the number of days (had been).

Whereas the apocalyptic view of the temporal axis is characterized by radical reversal, Jubilees proposes a gradual, natural return to the original plan of creation. More important, the modest claims of restoration allow the claim that the "crisis" is already past and the restoration underway.[111]

> 23:28 There will be no old man, nor anyone who has lived out his lifetime, because all of them will be infants and children.

Although the sentiment appears to be close to that of Isa 65:20, discussed above, perhaps only for subversion's sake the syntax is negated. In Isaiah there will not be one who has *failed* to live out one's life, but in Jubi-

---

111. See §3.4.4.1 below. Charles noted the unusual feature of gradual restoration (*The Book of Jubilees*, 149).

lees there will not be one who *has* lived out one's life. In Isaiah there will be *no* infant (implicitly infant mortality), but in Jubilees *all* will be infants.

> 23:29 They will complete and live their entire lifetimes peacefully and joyfully. There will be neither a satan nor any evil one who will destroy. For their entire lifetimes will be times of blessing and healing.

The immediate context does not strictly require that "satans and evil ones" be nonhuman entities, but the generic framework warrants comparison with the key eschatological agents of the apocalypses. By alluding to such agents now, Jubilees points out the lack of mention in the just told eschatological scenario. Even when they do appear here, they are mentioned only as being absent. Whereas Jubilees plays with the idea of angels and demons elsewhere in the book, in the eschatological moment on the temporal axis, where such agents typically figure most prominently, Jubilees excludes them entirely. It is not the case that Jubilees simply forgot about the spatial axis when composing this subversive little historical apocalypse, and the argument is not merely from silence. Jubilees subverts an expectation of cosmic agents consummating a catastrophic conflict by describing a past eschatology devoid of angelic or demonic influence.

> 23:30 Then the Lord will heal his servants. They will rise and see great peace. He will expel his enemies. The righteous will see (this), offer praise, and be very happy forever and ever. They will see all their punishments and curses on their enemies. 23:31 Their bones will rest in the earth and their spirits will be very happy. They will know that the Lord is one who executes judgment but shows kindness to hundreds and thousands and to all who love him.

If not for the rest of the book, one might imagine that God's servants refer only to a specific group within Israel, comparable to those who receive a new name in Isa 65:15. Even if it is implied that some were righteous and some were not, the overall emphasis in the book is on the unity of Israel, and the context here is not concerned with the vindication of a particular group or validation of a new priesthood.[112] If "they will rise" connotes resurrection or exaltation of the dead, then the connotation is

---

112. For the lack of sectarianism in Jubilees, see §2.2.1.4 below. For the lack of a new or reformed priesthood, see §3.4.4.4.

quickly subverted. The nation rises in peace and prosperity. The resolution is along the lines of "rest in peace" or a "good death." Dualism of body and soul should not be projected here.

Relatively speaking, vindictiveness against foreign invaders is also fairly mild. The main punishment is being sent home—the restoration of separation between Israel and the nations. Curses are mentioned but not elaborated, requiring the reader to recall from earlier in the chapter that the curses are the curses of life as we know it. It seems that the nations, in their own lands, continue to experience mortality at the age of seventy or eighty, shovel snow, and get stomach aches, while Israel alone comes to its intended blessings. Whereas a historical apocalypse typically imagines a radical reversal, with graphic vindication and vengeance, Jubilees imagines a gradual fulfillment of the original plan of creation. Notice also that God does the expelling—it is never the case that a sword is given to the righteous to kill anyone. Jubilees imagines an ideal restoration in its own terms, but the contrast with other imagined ideals is stark. Jubilees expresses very different eschatological ideals, and the contrast is sharpened by literary evocation of the apocalypses.

> 23:32 Now you, Moses, write down these words because this is how it is written and entered in the testimony of the heavenly tablets for the history of eternity.

Last but not least, Jubilees reminds the reader of the narrative framework of revelation that ties all the apocalyptic literary elements into true use of the literary genre "apocalypse." The definition of the genre is fully present, while the ideas separate this chapter and the rest of the book from the typical apocalypses.

1.3.4. Conclusion

This cursory tour leaves many questions unanswered but should give a general sense of the level at which subversion occurs. Jubilees does not single out a particular text or a particular group. The subversion is not limited to a few passages or a few issues. Jubilees uses all the core literary elements and discusses the implicit issues but says about those issues the opposite of what apocalypses typically say. After considering the details of the subversion through close comparison of individual issues in chapters 2–4, chapter 5 will venture to explain why an author would use the genre in such a way. It is normal for texts to express different ideas, and not every articulation of different ideas constitutes subversion. Yet the literary genre forces a comparison. It raises reader expectations and introduces a dialogue with previous knowledge of apocalypses. Jubilees does not merely disagree with the apocalypses; it subverts them through the use of their literary morphology.

Even within a literary genre, it is normal for any one text to introduce innovation and adapt borrowed literary elements and ideas in new ways to fit new circumstances and to express the author's own ideas. At a certain level, there is remarkable diversity among the apocalypses that existed by the time of Jubilees. Not every apocalypse that introduces new ideas can be called subversive. Jubilees, however, goes beyond innovation. First, on a purely literary level one can observe that Jubilees *radically* changes *every* idea inherent in the literary genre. Second, one can look to cultural and historical context to gauge which issues would have been significant sources of confrontation, beyond what we could imagine as friendly or incidental differences in emphasis. To be sure, the rift in ideas between Jubilees and other apocalypses is not comparable to the rift over issues of Hellenistic assimilation, the gymnasium, foreign objects and persons in the temple, and foregoing circumcision entirely. Wars may not have been fought over the explanation of suffering, and groups may not have defined their orthodoxy around eschatological judgment. Nevertheless, it is clear that the subversions in Jubilees are more than minor innovations. With all their diversity in details, the early apocalypses agree at a certain layer of abstraction, a cluster of ideas about the issues inherent in the literary genre. Only Jubilees expresses nonapocalyptic ideas in apocalyptic literary morphology. The author's intent can never be fully recovered. It will become clear, however, that an intent to harmonize or reconcile would have been unrealistic. Jubilees adopts only superficial elements, and says subversive things about them.

2

The Spatial Axis

The use of the genre "apocalypse," by definition, entails use of literary contents from the spatial axis, particularly cosmic beings such as angels and demons. The use of these literary features implies some treatment of the significance of cosmic beings for humanity. Thus far, Jubilees is like contemporary apocalypses. Despite variation in the details, contemporary apocalypses typically attribute great significance to cosmic forces for the origin of evil, the progression of human history, and the resolution of evil. Jubilees breaks this convention. Jubilees uses the genre to deal with the significance of cosmic forces but inverts the view typical of the apocalypses. Jubilees blames humanity for the origin of evil and the flood, postulates that Israel is exempt from angelic rule and demonic affliction, and simply writes angels and demons out of the plan for the resolution of evil. This is not to say that angelic beings play no role in Jubilees except to be unimportant. The apocalyptic view of human agency is only one of many concerns in the book of Jubilees, and, like many nonapocalypses, Jubilees does use angels to solve exegetical problems. The core issue is the view of nonhuman sources of evil and suffering. Jubilees uses the genre but inverts the claim typically expressed through the genre.

The view of angels and demons constitutes the core of this chapter, but along the same lines as the agency of nonhuman forces we will consider the classification and agency of groups within humanity. Even if the genre does not necessarily entail a classification of humanity, it is the case that contemporary apocalypses eschew Jewish unity, particularly in the present by singling out an elect group within Israel for vindication and in the future by including all nations. Jubilees does not deny that some are more righteous than others or that the return to righteousness begins with a few and progresses slowly. Yet in chapter 23 and throughout the book, Jubilees treats all Israel without internal division (other than the traditional distinction of the sons of Levi). Furthermore, while significant differences exist between Daniel and the Animal Apocalypse on the view of violence, Jubilees differs even where these agree by rejecting any form of human participation in eschatological violence. Although the issues of human classification and violence are less central to the spatial axis than the agency of angels and demons, it is important to consider the departure of Jubilees from the typical apocalypses on these issues. The subversion of the apocalypses in Jubilees is not limited to theological abstractions but entails tangible social implications. One should not overstate the explicitness of the argument or overemphasize this among the many concerns of the book of Jubilees. However, it does seem to follow from this pattern that Jubilees rejects in principle the dissolution of Jewish unity and particularly sectarian violence in the present and in eschatological hopes.

In this chapter in particular we must keep in mind that there is no apocalyptic system of doctrines, only a cluster of compatible ideas. In both superficial imagery and substantial implications, the emphasis in Daniel differs from the Enochic works, which themselves speak in multiple voices. If one is comparing only Daniel and Enochic apocalypses, one finds significant differences in the way that humans and nonhuman forces are imagined to function in the cosmic drama. The present concern is neither to develop nor to deny these differences but to attempt to show that, in the broader frame of contemporary Jewish thought, Daniel and Enochic works stand together in ways that Jubilees stands apart. Jubilees is similar to these works in the use of the genre "apocalypse," the basic tenets common to Judaism at the time, and even some further notions. Indeed, there is no single "nonapocalyptic" set of ideas or social group. Yet, as we consider the coherence and the diversity of Jewish thought in antiquity, it is important not to miss the exceptional use of the genre "apocalypse" in Jubilees.

This chapter will not exhaust the issues related to the spatial axis. The "heavenly tablets," to be discussed in the chapter on revelation, also pertain to the spatial axis. Also related to the temporal axis, the earthly restoration contrasts with distant places of judgment. Similarly, the emphasis on the holiness of Zion and Jerusalem stands out (Jub. 1:28–29; 4:26; 8:19; 18:13). The "angelic liturgy" is yet another way in which Jubilees develops the spatial axis and again contrasts with other angelic liturgies.[1] A

---

1. The angels serve as precedent or analogy for the special rank of Israel and its priesthood in Sabbath observance (Jub. 2:17–21, 28), circumcision (15:27), and the liturgy (30:18; 31:14).

number of other issues could be developed if one were inclined to argue from trajectory and later developments. For example, in light of Josephus's description of the Essenes as naming angels (*B.J.* 2.142), it stands out that Jubilees does not name the revealing angel or any other angel,[2] apart from the disputed case of Mastema.[3] Rather, we will focus on the issue of angels and demons in five parts: evil before the flood, evil after the flood, angelic mediation, a leader of evil, and cosmic agents in the eschatological crisis and restoration. We will then consider the classification of humanity and the views of violence.

2.1. Angels and Demons

The apocalypses typically explain the human situation in terms of independent cosmic agents. Bad angels and demons explain the presence of evil and suffering, and even good angels can be temporarily impeded or otherwise inefficient. Jubilees uses angels to fill certain exegetical needs and addresses their significance in human affairs. Unlike the apocalypses, however, Jubilees denies that the angels are in any way independent, capricious or incompetent forces interfering in the relationship between God and Israel. Even when Jubilees deals with ideas that are associated with evil in other apocalypses, Jubilees always holds to a simple principle, ወገብሩ ፡ ጎይላቲሁ ፡ ለእግዚአብሔር ፡ ኩሎ ፡ ዘመጠነ ፡ አዘዞሙ ፡ እግዚአብሔር, "The Lord's forces did everything that the Lord ordered them" (Jub. 49:4). There are no cosmic forces outside God's control.

This section focuses on the significance of angels and demons with respect to the presence of evil. The five subsections will span three time periods, over which angels and demons decrease in significance, approaching zero. The three chronological categories important for this issue in Jubilees are: before the flood, after the division of the nations, and the eschatological sequence.

---

2. One might even consider the possibility that Jubilees not only abstains from the naming of angels but subtly jabs at the naming of angels in 1 En. 6:7 (and 69:2 [Parables]) by identifying Danel not as an angel but a human patriarch. In Jub. 4:20, Danel is Enoch's father-in-law. The safest assumption is that this is a coincidence stemming from two independent attempts to imagine appropriate names. It would create a dissonance, however, if the audience made a connection. Would a fan of the Enochic literature rather imagine that Enoch married a female giant or that the Book of the Watchers errs in naming a patriarch as an angel?

3. See §2.1.4 below.

2.1.1. BEFORE THE FLOOD: THE ORIGIN OF EVIL

Jubilees draws from the Book of the Watchers in interpreting Genesis and manipulates the details to convey its own view of the origin of evil. Consequently, the Book of the Watchers will be particularly important in this section, but we are ultimately concerned with the apocalyptic view of the origin of evil in general. The apocalyptic literary genre and typical ideas are not tied to a particular narrative on the origin of sin, and a variety of emphases can be found even within the Enochic literature. Without referring to the descent of the watchers, Daniel just as strongly uses the genre "apocalypse" to convey a nonhuman origin of evil. The apocalypses, through a variety of narratives, understand the origin of evil in terms other than the divine or human will. Jubilees differs not only in the narrative details of the Book of the Watchers, but in the general view of evil otherwise shared by the early apocalypses.

2.1.1.1. The Enochic Apocalypses

In the Book of the Watchers (1 En. 1–36) evil begins as a rebellion in heaven that is subsequently imposed onto earthly affairs. At most, the angels differ from other forms of preexistent forces of chaos at enmity with God in that they presumably had good standing in heaven previously.[4] One might even read 1 En. 15:7, "therefore I did not make women among you," to indicate that God had created the watchers. Even so, the watchers are introduced in the story as willful rebels with no particular emphasis on a good origin or nature. More important, the rebellion occurred in heaven, not on earth. The sin is not an error but a willful revolt. Shemihazah knows he that "shall be guilty of a great sin" and pursues it anyway (1 En. 6:3). Asael, likewise, never had a benevolent mission but learned a "stolen mystery" that is responsible for all the evils on the earth (1 En. 16:3; 10:8).

The Book of the Watchers mentions Adam and Eve without developing them as an etiology of evil (1 En. 32:6).[5] Readers influenced by Paul and

---

4. According to 1 En. 9:7, God had previously given authority to Shemihazah.
5. Remarkably, Jubilees seems to fundamentally agree on not reading Eden as the origin of sin. The Book of the Watchers seems to suggest that evil originated through the events of Gen 6, not Gen 3. Jubilees seems to suggest that evil does not exist, but rather "there is no injustice" (Jub. 5:13). Adam sinned, and Adam was punished with death for that sin. Adam may be the first example of sin and punishment, but there

Augustine may have trouble understanding Gen 3 as other than an explanation of "original sin," but that seems not to have been the case before our era.[6] The moderating factor of human responsibility in the Book of the Watchers comes rather in the extent to which angelic sin and punishment is typological for human (particularly priestly) sin and punishment.[7] Evil comes from without, but we should avoid the exaggeration that the Book of the Watchers and other early apocalypses leave no room for human responsibility for participation in evil.

Scholars differ as to the extent to which the understanding of the origin of evil in the Book of the Watchers is implicit in other Enochic apocalypses. Although Paolo Sacchi understood this as the foundational idea of Enochic and apocalyptic literature,[8] it does seem that the position in the Book of the Watchers was moderated in other apocalypses.[9] In 1 En. 80:6, found in the Astronomical Book, the stars go astray first: "Many heads of the stars will stray from the command and will change their ways

---

does not seem to be a lasting contagion of sin caused by Adam (see especially the new and righteous creation after the flood, Jub. 5:12). Jubilees repeats the basic story of sin in Eden in Jub. 3:17–31 with remarkably little addition or variation. Whereas Gen 3 might seem to suggest that labor is a lasting consequence of Adam's sin, Jubilees emphasizes that labor was the original plan for humanity, and Adam labored for seven years before the sin. Hence, the two verses introducing the sin describe the labor of Adam and Eve, with noticeable repetition of words for "work" (Jub. 3:15–16). The other apparent lasting consequence of the sin was wearing clothes, but (in objection to the Hellenistic gymnasium) Jubilees approves of wearing clothes, as written on the heavenly tablets (Jub. 3:31). Jubilees does correlate sin and longevity, and Adam's "early" death at 930 is the result of sin, but Jubilees does not say that anyone past or future was meant to be immortal or that later people die young because of Adam or Eve. Rather, the ideal life span approaches one thousand years (Jub. 23:27). Adam died slightly short of that because of a minor sin, not because he permanently infested the earth with evil.

6. Gary A. Anderson, *The Genesis of Perfection: Adam and Eve in Jewish and Christian Imagination* (Louisville: Westminster John Knox, 2001), 209–10.

7. See especially George W. E. Nickelsburg, "Enoch, Levi, and Peter: Recipients of Revelation in Upper Galilee," *JBL* 100 (1981): 575–600; David Winston Suter, "Fallen Angel, Fallen Priest: The Problem of Family Purity in 1 Enoch 6–16," *HUCA* 50 (1979): 115–35.

8. Sacchi, *Jewish Apocalyptic and Its History*, 107.

9. Annette Yoshiko Reed, *Fallen Angels and the History of Judaism and Christianity: The Reception of Enochic Literature* (New York: Cambridge University Press, 2005), 73–74.

and actions and will not appear at the times prescribed for them."[10] The Animal Apocalypse alludes to the tradition of the fall of the watchers in 86:1 but develops the apocalyptic view of evil less in terms of primordial origins and more in terms of the subsequent amplification of evil. Human responsibility appears in the background, as in 89:54, but the climax in the author's present is explained by cosmic agents.

If we were to expand our chronological scope to the Epistle of Enoch (other than the Apocalypse of Weeks)[11] we would find a significant development from the view of agency typical of the early apocalypses, although not as significant as might first appear.[12] The main difference is that cosmic good and evil are translated into human society, but an ontological division between the righteous and the wicked remains. This view of evil is as much a contiguous development of the early apocalyptic view as it is a reform. It is still the case that suffering is imposed on the righteous from without, apart from the will of God or any just punishment. It is still the case that divine sovereignty is impeded in the present, and vindication and justice exist beyond this life. In particular, 98:4 has drawn attention as a qualification or reform of the Book of the Watchers.[13] Although the verse is textually difficult, the sense is clear enough that human sin is not excused by supernatural imposition. The Book of the Watchers did not say humans have no responsibility for their actions, and the Epistle does not diverge from a view of evil as imposed from without. Even if the trajectory

---

10. James C. VanderKam and George W. E. Nickelsburg, *1 Enoch: A New Translation, Based on the Hermeneia Commentary* (Minneapolis: Fortress, 2004).

11. For a discussion of the date of the main body of the Epistle, see Loren T. Stuckenbruck, *1 Enoch 91–108* (CEJL; Berlin: de Gruyter, 2007), 211–15. Stuckenbruck believes Jubilees reflects awareness of the entire Epistle, indicating a date prior to the Maccabean revolt. The argument is based on the distinctiveness of the term "testimony" in the Epistle. Although Jubilees does indicate Enoch wrote a testimony, it should be noted that "testimony" is a very frequent term in Jubilees (twenty-four times in VanderKam's translation). Consequently, using the term in connection with Enoch may not bear the weight of demonstrating a specific reference to the body of the Epistle. George W. E. Nickelsburg also dates the Epistle early but dates Jubilees even earlier, arguing that Jubilees does not reflect awareness of the Epistle (*1 Enoch: A Commentary on the Book of 1 Enoch* [Hermeneia; Minneapolis: Fortress, 2001], 427).

12. Consider alternatively Paolo Sacchi's account of the relationship between the Epistle of Enoch and the Book of the Watchers. Sacchi views the Epistle as direct and "conscious opposition" (*Jewish Apocalyptic and Its History*, 146).

13. See Stuckenbruck, *1 Enoch 91–108*, 343–47.

culminating in the Epistle of Enoch existed at the time of Jubilees, it still fits as a reform within the cluster of apocalyptic ideas.

2.1.1.2. The Danielic Apocalypses

Daniel provides the clearest example of a view of the origin of evil that is independent of the Book of the Watchers and yet aligns on the more abstract level of ideas. Daniel does not narrate an explanation of the origin of evil per se but uses imagery that reflects a view of evil arising and acting, independent of human sin and divine will. The beasts in Dan 7 come neither from heaven nor humanity but arise from the sea, evoking the ancient images of the rivals of God, Yam and Leviathan. Although the second beast is told קוּמִי אֲכֻלִי בְּשַׂר שַׂגִּיא, "arise, devour much flesh" (7:5), this does not suggest that the beasts arise at the command of God to chastise sin. The beasts are not fallen angels, but certainly not human. Daniel's prayer in Dan 9 assumes Israel's responsibility for its own suffering, but the revealed explanation differs in asserting an external source of evil and a resolution independent of human repentance or other action. The prince of the kingdom of Persia in Dan 10:13 acts in independent opposition to God and Israel. The "little horn" is more complex in that a human figure is partly signified, but the apocalyptic view focuses on the cosmic forces of evil behind the human façade. The actions attributed to the horn in 8:10–25 and 11:36 are not merely human. Jewish thinkers could agree that God's victory and sovereignty are *ultimately* assured and that humans are ultimately responsible for their role in sin. The apocalypses are distinctive in the view that evil exists outside the will of God, is not for the chastisement of human sin, and can temporarily impede divine justice.

2.1.1.3. Jubilees

Jubilees bears a resemblance to the Book of the Watchers in the interpretation of Gen 6 but modifies details and undermines the broader implications of the apocalyptic view of the origin of evil.[14] Jubilees emphasizes that the watchers were created by God. In 2:2, Jubilees interprets the first day of creation to include creation of all the spirits who serve before God.

---

14. Some of these ideas appeared already in Todd R. Hanneken, "Angels and Demons in the Book of Jubilees and Contemporary Apocalypses," *Henoch* 28.2 (2006): 11–25.

Jubilees introduces the watchers as creatures of God, while the Book of the Watchers introduces them as willful rebels, if not necessarily preexistent forces of cosmic opposition. Jubilees emphasizes that the watchers were sent by God with a good mission (4:15; 5:6) and essentially err by getting into bad marriages. Although intermarriage was not a light matter to the author of Jubilees, and inappropriate priestly marriages have been found to resonate behind the Book of the Watchers,[15] we should recognize the difference between earthly lust and a cosmic rebellion imposed onto human affairs.[16]

One can also see the contrasting emphasis on culpability in the function of Enoch's testimony in the Book of the Watchers and Jubilees. In the former, Enoch's main function is to testify against the watchers (12:4–13:3; 16:2–4). Nothing is said of human sin or the "wives" of the watchers.[17] Jubilees does mention once that Enoch had testified to the watchers (4:22), but emphasizes that Enoch's primary role is to testify to humankind.

> Now he [Enoch] is there [Eden, not heaven] writing down the judgment and condemnation of the world and all the wickedness of *mankind*. (Jub. 4:23, emphasis added; likewise 4:19)

The case of the exogamous watchers is useful as a paradigm for human exogamy, but it is a closed case with, as we shall see, no lasting effects on Israel.[18] The sin of the watchers is deemphasized but not eliminated; it is recycled as an example of sin, not an etiology of sin.[19]

---

15. See above, n. 7.

16. Recently Segal has argued convincingly that the separation of the descent of the watchers from the sin of the watchers meets a chronological need to place the descent in the days of Jared but the sin at 120 years before the flood (Segal, *The Book of Jubilees*, 132). Be that as it may, the change fits a larger pattern of the view of evil in Jubilees. The detail can reflect a view of evil and assist a chronological concern at the same time.

17. For textual difficulties in 1 En. 19:2, and the implications of the fate of the women for their culpability, see Kelley Coblentz Bautch, "What Becomes of the Angels' 'Wives'? A Text-Critical Study of 1 Enoch 19:2," *JBL* 125 (2006): 766–80. See also the T. Reu. 5:6, which blames the women for seducing the watchers.

18. A similar conclusion was arrived at independently by Segal: "The Watchers story has been transformed into a paradigm of reward and punishment, and the presentation of God as a just, righteous judge" (*The Book of Jubilees*, 140). See further §3.3.3.2 in the present work.

19. VanderKam, "The Angel Story in the Book of Jubilees," 170. For a different

The good mission of the watchers in Jubilees brings us to the issue of angelic instruction, a point on which Jubilees inverts a basic theme in the Book of the Watchers and paints a picture of the cosmos that differs from the contemporary apocalypses. Jubilees introduces angelic instruction as licit and righteous, in contrast to the illicit instruction of a stolen mystery.

> The angels of the Lord who were called Watchers descended to earth to teach mankind and to do what is just and upright upon the earth. (Jub. 4:15)

Jubilees does not abandon the motif of illicit instruction, however, but transfers it to after the division of the nations. As we shall see in the next subsection, Jubilees' twist on the apocalyptic view of evil is to limit its domain to the Gentiles. Thus, Jubilees never mentions illicit teaching of the watchers as a source of sin or suffering until Noah's great-grandson Kainan finds an inscription teaching bad astronomy (Jub. 8:3). Jubilees transfers the idea of illicit teaching from a cosmic rebellion that corrupts the earth from without to an explanation of foreign astronomy. The adaptation of the illicit teaching motif in Jubilees is striking not only in how the details diverge from the Book of the Watchers but especially in light of the fact that Jubilees otherwise presents angels as mindless transmitters of licit teaching.[20]

---

but compatible analysis, see Loren T. Stuckenbruck, "The Origins of Evil in Jewish Apocalyptic Tradition: The Interpretation of Gen 6:1–4 in the Second and Third Centuries B.C.E.," in *The Fall of the Angels* (ed. Christoph Auffarth and Loren T. Stuckenbruck; Themes in Biblical Narrative 6; Leiden: Brill, 2004), 111–15. Likewise idem, "The Book of Jubilees and the Origin of Evil," in Boccaccini and Ibba, *Enoch and the Mosaic Torah*, 294–308.

20. The twist on the motif of angelic instruction in the Book of the Watchers is symptomatic of a general fundamental difference between the book of Jubilees and the apocalypses. As we shall continue to see, the apocalypses often portray even good angels as relatively fallible independent entities, both in instruction and otherwise. With the possible but explicable exception of Kainan's inscription, angels in Jubilees always obey orders. This is also true of Mastema, as we shall see below. A few passages pertain to teaching in particular. Jub. 6:35 emphasizes that the revealing angel adds nothing independently: "For I know and from now on will inform you—not from my own mind because this is the way the book is written in front of me, and the divisions of times are ordained on the heavenly tablets." Again, 12:22 emphasizes that the revealing angel is merely a conduit: "the word of the Lord was sent to him through me." It may at first appear that Jubilees participates in a pattern of understanding

The apocalypses typically paint human sin and suffering in the shadow of cosmic evil. Even before the flood, Jubilees paints a different picture of the origin and nature of evil. The dramatic contrast, however, comes after the division of the nations. Jubilees does not deny the existence of evil or super-human agency, but it does claim that demons and their afflictions are assigned exclusively to Gentiles. The apocalyptic view of evil is accurate for Gentiles, but for Israel under the covenant it could not be more wrong.

2.1.2. After the Flood: The Persistence of Demons

Jubilees departs from the typical apocalyptic ideas most subtly in the period before the flood. Jubilees departs most radically in denying angels and demons any role in the eschatological climax and restoration, such as it is in Jubilees. In the period between the flood and the eschaton Jubilees makes use of three features of the apocalypses in atypical ways. In this subsection we consider the role of demons in the apocalypses and Jubilees' innovations in asserting immunity for Israel and incorporating demons under the will of God. The next two subsections consider the related issues of angelic mediation and the leader of evil. It continues to be the case that "the Lord's forces do all that the Lord commanded them," and evil has no sovereignty, even temporarily, outside the divine will. Jubilees twists the

---

theophanies as angelic visitations in order to maintain divine transcendence, but the situation is not quite so simple. In some cases Jubilees adds the presence of angels where it is not explicit in Genesis (Jub. 16:1 introduces angels, perhaps to add consistency to Gen 18:1-2, "The Lord appeared ... he saw three men."). In other cases where Genesis indicates that an angel spoke, Jubilees adds that the angel spoke the words of God (Gen 22:11 || Jub. 18:9, 14). Often enough, a theophany in Genesis appears in Jubilees with no addition or removal of angels (Jub. 14:1; 15:3; 24:9; 24:22; 44:5 || Gen 15:1; 17:1; 26:2; 26:24; 46:24). At Jub. 32:20 an angel follows up on a vision of God to fill in detail and answer any questions (based on the theophany in Gen 35:9 but presumably influenced by the wrestler in Gen 32). On two occasions something like a revelation is described without reference to angels ("spirit of righteousness," 25:15; "spirit of prophecy," 31:12). In the Babel account the angels are present as in Genesis, but any hint of an independent voice or action is excised. Angels tutor Abram in Hebrew (Jub. 12:25-27) and supervise Noah's division of the earth (in Jub. 8:10, 20 the angel frames and authorizes the allotment to Shem by placing "the word of the Lord in [Noah's] mouth."). For more analysis of angelic instruction in Jubilees, see Annette Yoshiko Reed, "Enochic and Mosaic Traditions in Jubilees: The Evidence of Angelology and Demonology," in Boccaccini and Ibba, *Enoch and the Mosaic Torah*, 353-68.

apocalyptic view of evil forces by saying that it is only true for the other nations and those of Israel who join them.

2.1.2.1. The Early Apocalypses

Demons per se do not appear in all the apocalypses, nor are they limited to the apocalypses (e.g., Tobit). They are, however, a convenient way of expressing the apocalyptic idea that humanity is afflicted by supernatural evil that cannot be explained as just chastisement from God in proportion to sinfulness. Again, the details of the treatment in Jubilees most resemble the Book of the Watchers, but the implications extend to the level of ideas shared by the Book of the Watchers, Daniel, the Animal Apocalypse, and so forth. In the typical apocalypses, whether by way of demons, beasts, or ineffective angels, Israel experiences unjust suffering as a result of external evil. All Jewish sources at the time could agree that God's superiority and ultimate victory were assured and that human action could have some significance. Jubilees is distinctive among the apocalypses, however, in denying that God's just sovereignty is suspended or seriously challenged. Demons and affliction are the divine plan for the Gentiles, but Israel is immune simply by staying away from the Gentiles. In order to match the claim of Jubilees, Daniel would have to say that the beasts afflict all nations except Israel or that God sent the little horn to mislead the Gentiles from converting to Judaism.

2.1.2.2. Jubilees

Jubilees follows the Book of the Watchers on the basic idea of the existence and origin of demons.[21] In the Book of the Watchers the demons continue to afflict the righteous unchecked until the final judgment (1 En. 15:8–16:1). Jubilees, on the other hand, is unique among the apocalypses in asserting a 90 percent reduction in the number of demons (Jub. 10:9).[22]

---

21. Michel Testuz (*Les idées religieuses*, 83) has pointed out that Jubilees does not make it perfectly clear that the demons are the spirits of the giants, rather than the half-brothers of the giants, but it does seem likely enough that Jubilees assumes the explanation of the Book of the Watchers that the children of the watchers are giants while they live and persist as demons after their bodies are slaughtered.

22. On a related matter, apocalypses sometimes suggest that corruption and sin perseveres not only in demons but within humanity as some kind of genetic defect. These texts look forward to the establishment of a "new and righteous nature" for

In numbers alone Jubilees deemphasizes demons. We shall return below to the role of Mastema in this account, but we can say here that the 10 percent who remain do so at the will of God. Furthermore, Jubilees shifts the role of demons from capricious affliction of the innocent to a form of divine justice, እስመ ፡ ዐቢይ ፡ እከዮሙ· ፡ ለውሉድ ፡ ሰብእ, "because great is the evil of humanity" (Jub. 10:8). More strikingly, the affliction of the nations is not punishment in the Deuteronomistic sense of prompting repentance but part of the divine plan to lead astray all nations except Israel (Jub. 15:31). Jubilees develops an idea that is already found in the ancient versions of Pss 96:5 and 106:35 that other gods and whatever power may be perceived in other religions are simply demons (Jub. 1:11; 11:4).[23]

Jubilees establishes with two details that observance of the covenant grants Israel immunity from the demons. First, Noah receives revelation and writes books that provide immunity from demons. This notion seems to have inspired the later idea of a medical book, likely in the pattern of competitive historiography, ultimately influencing the Book of Asaph the Physician.[24] Although it may be the case, as a number of scholars believe, that the author of Jubilees had in mind an actual collection of writings attributed to Noah,[25] the mention in Jubilees can be explained within the

---

humanity (perhaps drawing from Ezek 36:26, etc.). In Jub. 5:12, it has already happened. Segal also notes that the day of judgment and new creation in the Book of the Watchers is eschatological, whereas in Jub. 5:10–12 it refers to the flood (*The Book of Jubilees*, 137, 139).

23. VanderKam, "The Demons in the *Book of Jubilees*," 354.

24. See Martha Himmelfarb, "Some Echoes of *Jubilees* in Medieval Hebrew Literature," in *Tracing the Threads: Studies in the Vitality of Jewish Pseudepigrapha* (ed. John C. Reeves; Atlanta: Scholars Press, 1994), 115–41; Elinor Lieber, "Asaf's 'Book of Medicines': A Hebrew Encyclopedia of Greek and Jewish Medicine, Possibly Compiled in Byzantium on an Indian Model," *Dumbarton Oaks Papers* 38 (1984): 233–49; Adolph Jellinek, "ספר נח," in בית המדרש (Yerushalayim: Sifre Vahrmann, 1967), 155–60.

25. The idea of a "Book of Noah" appears a number of times in antiquity. Although scholars disagree as to whether the burden of proof is to prove or disprove the existence of an actual book behind these references, it can at least be agreed that no one coherent composition is likely to account for all the contents attributed to such a book. The ancients may not have shared our concern for the lines between imagining Noah as a scribal figure, actually composing works from Noah's point of view, and compiling and standardizing a collection that can be called *The* Book of Noah. It is far from certain that a single standard Book of Noah existed, but it is clear that Noah was imagined as a scribe, and composition from Noah's point of view is hardly unlikely.

literary motif of ancestral books. Jubilees ultimately aims to assert that the Levites came into sole possession of all the legitimate writings of the ancestors (Jub. 45:16). Furthermore, as will be discussed in the chapter on revelation, the heavenly tablets existed from creation and were gradually revealed, but they contain nothing that is not revealed to Moses at Sinai. Thus, the Books of Noah anticipate typologically the Torah of Moses.[26] The important point is that the study of revealed books grants immunity from demons (Jub. 10:13). Jubilees emphasizes that these books were transmitted only to Shem and ultimately only to Levi. In the context of the continuation, it is impossible that any nation besides Israel (and further, any authority besides the Levites) has books of revealed knowledge that grant immunity from demons. The "medicine" foreshadows study and observance of the law, which appears again as the means to guarantee quality and length of life (Jub. 23:26).

Second, although demons have the potential function of punishing sin, Israel alone has the means of forgiveness of sin. As long as Israel obeys the covenant and separates from the nations, they are immune in the first place, but even if they do sin they have the unique opportunity to be forgiven through the Day of Atonement (Jub. 5:17–18). In addition to the removal of accumulated guilt on the Day of Atonement, proper observance of Passover functions preemptively to keep away any plagues for the coming year (Jub. 49:15). Thus, for Jubilees the apocalyptic view of affliction by evil forces, and demons in particular, is not false, but it is only true of other nations.[27] Demons do exist as an explanation for whatever power may be perceived in foreign religion, and they do serve to warn those of Israel who may be tempted to stray from endogamy, separation, and piety under the traditional authorities in Jerusalem. They also function to explain affliction in biblical Israel that might otherwise be attributed to God. This aspect will be addressed below in connection with Mastema. Even when governed by Mastema, the demons afflict only sinners and only with divine permission. The fact that demons are apportioned to

---

For bibliography and a sound discussion leading to a slightly different conclusion, see Michael E. Stone, "The Book(s) Attributed to Noah," *DSD* 13 (2006): 4–23; and Stone, Amihay, and Hillel, *Noah and His Book(s)*.

26. Jubilees maintains that Moses renews and completes the covenant that had existed previously (Jub. 6:18–19; 14:20). See also page 288 below.

27. One might wonder if this implies an accusation that the apocalyptic perspective is nonnative or overly influenced by foreign ideas.

some but not all of Noah's children explains why Jubilees does not address the origin of the demons from the slain giants in the narrative sequence before the flood, but only after the flood and the apportionment of lots to Noah's descendents (Jub. 10:1).[28] Israel's immunity from cosmic evil, or cosmic fallibility of any kind, even temporarily, is guaranteed not only by the books of the covenant and the festivals but by the next point, the uninterrupted and unmediated governance of Israel by God.

2.1.3. Angelic Mediation

We have ample evidence that around and before the time of Jubilees a diversity of thought existed in Judaism on the issue of angelic governance. It may not be the case that *only* apocalypses understand God's sovereignty as temporarily mediated by imperfect angels, but it is the case that several apocalypses emphasize this view and that Jubilees is the only apocalypse that emphatically rejects it. Again, none of the perspectives denies that God will *ultimately* be victorious or that good and powerful angels exist. The apocalyptic claim is that unjust suffering exists in Israel temporarily while angelic sovereigns over Israel are either wicked themselves or matched by their wicked opponents.

2.1.3.1. Evidence outside the Apocalypses

Before coming to the apocalypses, we should note some external traces of this issue in antiquity. We will not resolve indirectly related questions such as the date, priority, or mechanism of exegetical variation. The best known case of the issue of angelic mediation appearing in variant texts is at Deut 32:8. Here the Masoretic Text, in agreement with the Samaritan Pentateuch, gives,

בְּהַנְחֵל עֶלְיוֹן גּוֹיִם בְּהַפְרִידוֹ בְּנֵי אָדָם יַצֵּב גְּבֻלֹת עַמִּים לְמִסְפַּר בְּנֵי יִשְׂרָאֵל:

> When the Most High designated the heritage of the nations, in creating the divisions of humankind, he set up the boundaries of peoples in proportion to the number of Israelites. (Deut 32:8, MT)

---

28. Hanneken, "Angels and Demons," 18.

The Septuagint, however, suggests a *Vorlage* of בני אלהים, which is supported by 4QDeut^j (בני אלוהים, column 12 line 14):²⁹

> ὅτε διεμέριζεν ὁ ὕψιστος ἔθνη, ὡς διέσπειρεν υἱοὺς Αδαμ ἔστησεν ὅρια ἐθνῶν κατὰ ἀριθμὸν ἀγγέλων θεοῦ

> When the Most High distributed the nations, when he separated humankind, he set up the boundaries of peoples in proportion to the number of angels of God. (Deut 32:8, LXX)

Targum Pseudo-Jonathan reflects knowledge of both readings,

> When the Most High gave the world as an inheritance to the peoples who came from the sons of Noah, when he divided the writings and languages among mankind in the generation of the division, at that time he casts lots on seventy angels, the leaders of the nations [שובעין מלאכיא ורברבי עממין], with whom it was revealed to see the city; and at that time he established the borders of the nations according to the sum of the number of the seventy souls of Israel [שובעין נפשתא דישראל] who went down to Egypt. (Deut 32:8, Targum Pseudo-Jonathan)³⁰

The significance of these variants has already been established.³¹ In Deut 32:8 the issue is not explicitly whether Israel is apportioned to a minor divinity but whether nations in general are so proportioned. Deuteronomy 29:25 (both MT and LXX) supports the idea that other nations are apportioned to other divine beings but that Israel is apportioned (directly) to God.

וַיֵּלְכוּ וַיַּעַבְדוּ אֱלֹהִים אֲחֵרִים וַיִּשְׁתַּחֲווּ לָהֶם אֱלֹהִים אֲשֶׁר לֹא־יְדָעוּם וְלֹא חָלַק לָהֶם:

καὶ πορευθέντες ἐλάτρευσαν θεοῖς ἑτέροις καὶ προσεκύνησαν αὐτοῖς οἷς οὐκ ἠπίσταντο οὐδὲ διένειμεν αὐτοῖς

---

29. Eugene Ulrich and Frank Moore Cross, *Qumran Cave 4.IX, Deuteronomy, Joshua, Judges, Kings* (DJD 14; Oxford: Clarendon, 1995), 90.

30. Translation Ernest G. Clarke, *Targum Pseudo-Jonathan: Deuteronomy* (ArBib 5B; Collegeville, Minn.: Liturgical Press, 1998), 90.

31. See especially VanderKam, "The Demons in the *Book of Jubilees*," 352–54. See also, Russell, *Method and Message*, 248.

They went and served other gods and worshiped them, gods whom they did not know and whom he did not allot to them. (Deut 29:25, MT and LXX; see also 4:19)

Our principal concern is not which is original or whether the variant is more the cause or more the consequence of the disputed issue, but that a diversity of views existed.

The interpretation of Third Isaiah often stands behind differences between Jubilees and contemporary apocalypses. Thus it is entirely fitting to consider also a similar case in the text of Isa 63:9, although we are claiming a connection only as analogy, not cause. Here the difference is found in the Qere and Ketiv of the Masoretic Text. The Masoretic Qere and verse division disagree with the Ketiv and the LXX.[32]

... ἐκ πάσης θλίψεως. οὐ πρέσβυς οὐδὲ ἄγγελος, (לא ציר ומלאך)[33] ἀλλ' αὐτὸς κύριος ἔσωσεν αὐτοὺς

... from all their distress. Neither a delegate nor an angel, but the Lord himself saved them. (Isa 63:9, LXX)

בְּכָל־צָרָתָם ׀ לֹא [margin: לוֹ] צָר וּמַלְאַךְ פָּנָיו הוֹשִׁיעָם

In all their distress was his distress. And the angel of his presence saved them. (Isa 63:9, Masoretic Qere)[34]

The issue seems to go back to Exodus, which includes different images of who led Israel: an angel (מַלְאַךְ הָאֱלֹהִים הַהֹלֵךְ לִפְנֵי מַחֲנֵה יִשְׂרָאֵל) in 14:19,[35] or God directly (פָּנַי יֵלֵכוּ) in 33:14–15. The issue in the variants of Isa 63:9 is whether salvation can be attributed to an angel of the presence. Whereas the LXX reflects a negative valuation of an angelic mediator of divine salvation ("Neither a delegate nor an angel, but the Lord himself"),

---

32. 1QIsa[a] presents expected and minor variations.

33. Isac Leo Seeligmann, *The Septuagint Version of Isaiah: A Discussion of Its Problems* (Leiden: Brill, 1948), 62.

34. Hanson (*The Dawn of Apocalyptic*, 80–84) translates the consonantal text, "... in all their distress. Not a messenger, nor an angel, but his own Presence saved them."

35. Likewise Num 20:16. Jub. 48:13 assigns a role to the angel of the presence while maintaining, "The Lord brought them out." See Segal, *The Book of Jubilees*, 217 n. 41.

the Masoretes either accept or prefer the idea of a faithful angelic agent of a transcendent God ("the angel of his presence").

One more external witness reflects the same concern in a more certain historical and social context. The Hebrew base of Sirach can be easily dated to the first quarter of the second century B.C.E., and even if one suspected liberties in translation on behalf of the grandson, one can still be sure of a chronological proximity to Jubilees. We should not overestimate the alignment between Jubilees and Sirach, but it does help that the relationship between Sirach and the apocalypses has been studied thoroughly.[36] By all accounts the ideas in Sirach differ from those typical of the apocalypses. The difference holds for the issue at hand, as Sirach makes clear in 17:17:

> To every nation he appointed a ruler, but Israel is the portion of the Lord.[37]

Although the parallel with Deut 32:8 is unmistakable, the context does not suggest that the author is simply following a version of Deuteronomy. Rather, the context confirms that Sirach is concerned with the issue at hand in its own right. God's governance over Israel, awareness of sin, and justice in punishment is never delayed, mediated, or obfuscated by angelic bureaucracy.[38]

---

36. Argall's characterization as rivalry seems most precise, but others have described the situation as indirect polemic (Wright) or direct polemic (Boccaccini and Olyan). See Randal A. Argall, *1 Enoch and Sirach: A Comparative Literary and Conceptual Analysis of the Themes of Revelation, Creation and Judgment* (SBLEJL 8; Atlanta: Scholars Press, 1995), 250; Benjamin G. Wright, "'Fear the Lord and Honor the Priest': Ben Sira as Defender of the Jerusalem Priesthood," in *The Book of Ben Sira in Modern Research: Proceedings of the First International Ben Sira Conference, 28-31 July 1996, Soesterberg, Netherlands* (ed. Pancratius C. Beentjes; Berlin: de Gruyter, 1997), 220; Gabriele Boccaccini, *Middle Judaism: Jewish Thought, 300 B.C.E. to 200 C.E* (Minneapolis: Fortress, 1991), 80; Saul M. Olyan, "Ben Sira's Relationship to the Priesthood," *HTR* 80 (1987): 279-80.

37. The Hebrew manuscripts do not preserve this verse. See Pancratius C. Beentjes, *The Book of Ben Sira in Hebrew: A Text Edition of All Extant Hebrew Manuscripts and a Synopsis of All Parallel Hebrew Ben Sira Texts* (VTSup 68; Leiden: Brill, 1997).

38. This sample hardly exhausts the relevant sources. One could continue by considering the role of angels as executioners (Exod 12:23; Gen 18) or intercessors (Zech 1:12; Job 33:23). The idea of wicked angels as patrons of wicked kings and kingdoms appears in Isa 24:21, and 1 En. 100:5 (Epistle) refers to the angelic guardian of the

2.1.3.2. The Early Apocalypses

We find the same issue, but a different perspective, in several early apocalypses. The Animal Apocalypse provides the most detailed account, but the Book of the Watchers and Daniel convey the same basic claim. Here the issue is not the wickedness of the wicked angels, although we do find more of these in the Animal Apocalypse, but the inefficiency of the relatively good angels. The implication seems to be that God would never tolerate the present state of injustice, so some kink in the system must explain the present while maintaining the ultimate justice and supremacy of God. The Animal Apocalypse develops an idea like the one in Deut 32:8 to the conclusion that rule over Israel has been outsourced to seventy angels, which are homologous with seventy nations (1 En. 89:59). These angels degrade from mean to evil. The idea that God would outsource sovereignty over Israel is at odds with the perspective already seen in Sirach and soon to be seen in Jubilees. This by itself, however, is only part of the problem. According to the Animal Apocalypse, Israel does have its own guardian apart from the blind and wicked angels. Israel's angel is good, but nevertheless limited as an intermediary and presently powerless, except to take detailed notes for the sake of justice in the future (1 En. 89:71).

Likewise in the Book of the Watchers, one does find wicked angels, as already discussed with respect to the origin of evil, but the further issue is that even the good angels are basically bureaucrats, receiving complaints and compiling reports with considerable delay (1 En. 9:1–4). The issue is not whether Michael is good or bad but whether any angel, rather than God directly, is in charge of the chosen people (1 En. 20:15). Again in Daniel, the first part of the issue is the fact that the holy ones are left at the mercy of a beast for a certain period (Dan 7:25). The second part is that even the good angels are at the limit of their means to keep evil in check. Again, God's ultimate victory is certain, but the myriad myriads of God's power are reserved for the future (Dan 7:10). As of 10:21 the forces of good number two, וְאֵין אֶחָד מִתְחַזֵּק עִמִּי עַל־אֵלֶּה כִּי אִם־מִיכָאֵל שַׂרְכֶם, "there is no one who supports me against them except Michael, your prince" (see also 12:1). Regardless of variations in the narrative details, the apocalypses

---

righteous. Michael serves as a mediator in T. Dan 6:2 (cf. 1 Tim 2:5), and angels fill a priestly function in T. Levi 3:5.

typically convey the idea that God's sovereignty is temporarily impeded both by the wickedness of some cosmic forces and the inefficiency or inefficacy of the good cosmic forces.

2.1.3.3. Jubilees

Jubilees conveys a different view. We should avoid two exaggerations. First, it is not the case that Jubilees is obsessed with this issue; it is a long book, and several comments to this effect do not mean it is a primary concern. Also, it is not necessarily the case that Jubilees is engaging in direct polemic; the relevant comments are spread out in the book, and there is no particular section where Jubilees sustains an assault on the apocalypses on this issue. Far from these two exaggerations, we can still say confidently that Jubilees conveys ideas that conflict significantly from the ideas typically conveyed by the genre "apocalypse." Furthermore, it is precisely in using the typical features of apocalypses that it expresses these conflicting views, either inserting a "not" or saying that it is true of other nations but not Israel.

The clearest example appears in Jub. 15:31-32. Here Jubilees follows apocalypses in addressing the issue of angelic princes over nations but denies their view of the relevance of these spirits for Israel. They never rule over Israel, God's sovereignty is direct and absolute, and the misleading that the angels do against other nations they do at the command of God.

> He sanctified them and gathered (them) from all mankind. For there are many nations and many peoples and all belong to him. He made spirits rule over all in order to lead them astray from following him. But over Israel he made no angel or spirit rule because he alone is their ruler. He will guard them and require them for himself from his angels, his spirits, and everyone, and all his powers so that he may guard them and bless them and so that they may be his and he theirs from now and forever. (Jub. 15:31-32)

As we shall continue to see, Mastema and the demons are indistinct from other angels in the divine commission to lead astray the Gentiles (Jub. 10:3, 8; 12:20; 19:28). The lack of outsourcing of sovereignty over Israel is reinforced in Jub. 16:17-18 and 19:28-29 (see also 21:20).[39]

---

39. The same basic perspective that God never abandons or outsources sovereignty over Israel appears in other passages, such as Jub. 1:5-6, 18, which diverges

> But one of Isaac's sons would become a holy progeny and would not be numbered among the nations, for he would become the share of the Most High. All his descendants had fallen into that (share) which God owns so that they would become a people whom the Lord possesses out of all the nations… (Jub. 16:17–18)
>
> May the Lord God become your father and you his first-born son and people for all time… (Jub. 19:29)

In light of this pattern, there can be no doubt that "Jacob's guardian" in Jub. 35:17 is none other than God directly:

> Jacob's guardian is greater and more powerful, glorious, and praiseworthy that Esau's guardian. (Jub. 35:17; 4QpapJub^h 2 II:11–12)

This is not to say that angels have no role in God's governance of the cosmos. In Jub. 4:6 angels do report sin, but in context they are a foil for God's omniscience, not an explanation for how evil prospers under an inefficient cosmic judicial system. According to Jubilees there is no inefficiency or delay in God's just governance. The Gentiles are misled at the command of God, but Israel is protected by keeping the covenant and simply by keeping their distance from the nations. Without explicitly referring to Deut 32:8, Isa 63:9, or Sir 17:17, Jubilees clearly takes the position that angelic princes are assigned to other nations. They mislead, but not out of incompetence or infidelity; they only mislead the Gentiles, and they only do so at God's command. God deals with Israel directly, and whatever suffering they endure comes directly from God.

Thus far we have seen several ways in which Jubilees, unlike contemporary apocalypses, denies the relevance of evil or fallible cosmic forces for Israel. Now we come to the idea of a leader of evil forces against God and how the figure of Mastema in Jubilees diverges at the level of ideas.

2.1.4. The Leader of Evil

The history of religions approach to the figure of Satan has left a few impediments to understanding Mastema in the book of Jubilees. First, there has been a tendency to approach the Satan myth as a single tradition articu-

---

from the parallel source in Deut 31:17 to make clear that God never abandons Israel, even as temporary punishment.

lated with many synonymous names and titles. It is worth paying attention to the significance of the choice of the term "Mastema" in Jubilees. Second, there has been a tendency to view this single tradition as a linear development from "primitive" to "advanced" ideas about Satan. Although it is certainly true that our discussion would look different if we compared Mastema to the Satan of the Middle Ages, Jubilees cannot be explained as a different developmental stage of the same idea. Third, there has been a tendency to read early texts in light of later interpretations—indeed, it is difficult not to. Although the Book of the Watchers certainly influenced later accounts such as 2 En. 29–31, it is not the case in the Book of the Watchers that Shemihazah and Asael continue to rule over armies of evil. Similarly, the distinction between Satan and the antichrist nascent in the Apocalypse of John and soon expanded by interpreters cannot determine our categories when reading Daniel. Indeed, one cannot really say that the apocalypses at the time of Jubilees reflect a defined "Satan" figure, at least not without arguing from trajectory or apocalypses of ambiguous date. It is at least clear that contemporary apocalypses maintain a view of evil as a cosmic force apart from and in opposition to God. The figure of Mastema in Jubilees is one way in which Jubilees contradicts this view. In a broader chronological scope, the figure of Mastema in Jubilees is comparable to other traditions about a prince of demons, but when one compares what is said about each figure, one finds that Mastema in Jubilees contrasts significantly with the superficially similar leaders of evil.

2.1.4.1. Terms, Names, and Titles

Before describing what can be found in contemporary apocalypses, we should say a few words about the terms used in Jubilees and their relationship to the terms in received scripture. It has been questioned whether Mastema is even a name in Jubilees.[40] There is no doubt that Jubilees is referring to an individual figure with this term, but to the extent to which we can distinguish between a name, a title, and a description of a role, it seems unlikely that Mastema is a name. This is a subtle distinction but worth noting. Josephus and the Essenes as such come later, but it is at least curious that Josephus tells us that the Essenes hold the names of the angels

---

40. James C. VanderKam, *Textual and Historical Studies in the Book of Jubilees* (Missoula, Mont.: Scholars Press, 1977), 266.

among their prized secret wisdom (*B.J.* 2.142). The early apocalypses fit this trajectory,[41] whereas Jubilees, with the questionable exception of Mastema, names no angels.

Jubilees is not, in using the term "Mastema," drawing directly on an earlier tradition that is known to us. The Qumran Jubilees fragments do not preserve the term משטמה, but the "Pseudo" Jubilees fragments and the Book of Asaph[42] do, making it likely that the term was used in the original composition of Jubilees. The fact that the translators transliterated this term is fortunate for us but does not affect the discussion of whether it was originally a name or title. Prior to Jubilees, the term "Mastema" itself is known to us only from Hos 9. There is no clear connection between Hos 9 and Jubilees. There is no evidence that the term in Hosea refers to a personal figure. The LXX, BDB, and several modern translations render respectively, μανία, animosity, harassment, hostility, and hatred. If one looks more broadly for the root שטם, one finds little help. It seems most likely that the choice of the term Mastema in Jubilees is governed by two factors. First, the word exists as a term for hostility, which does point the reader in the right direction. Second, the word resembles, but is not, השטן, which conjures the reader's knowledge of S/satan(s) without actually identifying Mastema as such.[43] The idea of this particular figure is conjured, but the divergence is posted in the term itself. As we shall see, Jubilees has an agenda for the term "satans" apart from what is said about Mastema.

Before turning to the terms "Mastema," "satans," "Beliar," and "Molech" in Jubilees, it will also be helpful to mention the attested usage of the term משטמה in and after Jubilees. Even though Jubilees was an influential document at Qumran and the term משטמה is attested in sectarian and probably nonsectarian works, it is never used unambiguously as a proper noun, and it is often used unambiguously as a common noun.[44] To be sure, it could be part of a title or way of referring to a particular figure, and any

---

41. Dan 8:16; 9:21; 10:13, 21; 12:1; 1 En. 6:7; 9:1; 20:1–8; etc.

42. See n. 48 below.

43. See below on Jub. 10:11, which has been taken as identifying Mastema as Satan (Charles, *Jubilees*, 81).

44. If one accepts that plural or possessive forms (משטמתו) are not proper nouns (regardless of allusiveness) then one eliminates 1QS 3:23; 4QCatena A 9:5; 4QBer^a; and 4Q390. In other cases it is perfectly clear that Mastema/hostility is an attribute of Belial, not a separate figure (1QMilḥamah 13:4, 11). In cases influenced by Jubilees, it remains as ambiguous as it is in Jubilees whether it is a name per se. As with Jubilees, it is used in construct with שר or מלאך in CD 16:5 and Pseudo-Jubilees. It might be

use of the term would be suggestive at some level, but neither before nor after Jubilees was the term accepted as primarily a proper noun. At the risk of belaboring a minor point and making too much of the distinction between a proper noun and a title or role, the same is true of Jubilees. The term almost always appears in construct with "prince." The term could easily be translated as "Harsh Prince," if one were more concerned with translating original meaning than conveying allusions and connections with the history of interpretation.[45] None of this is to deny that this prince is a particular figure in Jubilees or that this figure can be compared to the particular figures elsewhere referred to as Satan, the satan, or satans.

Although the two references to "Beliar" in Jubilees were once counted as evidence of a different source from that which used the term "Mastema,"[46] it not likely that these nouns refer to Mastema or any individual figure at all. Just as בליעל is often used in received scripture, Jubilees uses the equivalent noun in two construct phrases in the senses, rendered by JPS (1985), "scoundrels" and "base thoughts" (Jub. 1:20; 15:33; Deut 13:14; 15:9). In Jub. 1:20 the phrase መንፈሰ ፡ ቤልሐር (unjust spirit, literally: spirit of Belial) is parallel to መንፈሰ ፡ ጽድቅ (just spirit, literally: spirit of righteousness). We should overcome associations from later developments, particularly in the War Scroll and Testaments of the Twelve Patriarchs, which put Belial in direct contrast with God as an independent rival figure. Jubilees also uses the term "Moloch" in the common sense, but no one has suggested that this refers to an active agent in the cosmic drama (Jub. 30:10).[47]

The word "satan" appears five times in the Ethiopic book of Jubilees. Four of those are in nearly identical phrases: አልቦ ፡ (መኑሂ ፡) ሰይጣን ፡

---

somewhat surprising if a morphologically feminine form were used as a name for an angel (the last consonant of שמיחזה is not a gender marker).

45. Compare the decisions of Géza Vermès (*The Complete Dead Sea Scrolls in English* [New York: Allen Lane/Penguin, 1997], 137) and Florentino García-Martínez (Florentino García Martínez and Eibert Tigchelaar, *The Dead Sea Scrolls Study Edition* [Leiden Brill, 1999], 565; Florentino García Martínez, *The Dead Sea Scrolls Translated: the Qumran Texts in English* (2nd ed.; Leiden: Brill; Grand Rapids: Eerdmans, 1996], 39) in translating "Angel of Persecution" and "angel Mastema," respectively, in the context of the Jubilees citation in CD 16:5.

46. Testuz, *Les idées religieuses*, 41. For the present purposes the variant forms *Beliar* and *Belial* are not distinguished.

47. Segal offers an excellent review of the meanings of "Belial" in *The Book of Jubilees*, 251–56. Segal concludes differently, however, that Belial is synonymous with Mastema in Jubilees (182 n. 5, 253 nn. 24, 28).

ወአልቦ፡ (መኑ፡) እኩይ፡ "there will be no satan or any evil one" (Jub. 23:29; 40:9; 46:2; 50:5). Two of these refer to an imagined future, but the other two refer to the peace and prosperity in Egypt under Joseph's governance. Notably, in all four of these instances the term is indefinite, parallel with "any evil one," and negated (they are mentioned as *not* existing). It is expected for Ethiopic to use a singular noun with the negative ("not any satan," rather than, "not any satans"). In none of these cases is a supernatural sense required. The designation "satans" seems to be a general term for adversaries, likely including human as well as demonic troublemakers. Jubilees 10:11 refers to a figure "the satan" or "Satan," but this is easily corrected to "Mastema" on the basis of the Book of Asaph the Physician.[48] This work, though late, is clearly related to the book of Jubilees (arguably from a common source, a dependent work, or Jubilees itself).[49] While a broader comparison would show even more strongly the close relationship, the relevant portion, aligned with the Ethiopic, is as follows:

אך אחד מעשרה הניח להתהלך בארץ לפני שר המשטמה

But he left a tenth to go about on the earth before the prince of Mastema.[50]

ወኀሠራቶሙ፡ አትረፍነ፡ ከመ፡ ይኩኑ፡ ቅድመ፡ ሰይጣን፡ ዲበ፡ ምድር፡ ፡፡

... while we left a tenth of them to exercise power on the earth before the satan. (Jub. 10:11)

While the Greek and Ethiopic transmitters of Jubilees could easily, based on later associations, have confused "Satan" for "Mastema," it is less likely that a medieval Jewish physician would have substituted "Mastema" for "Satan." Even without recourse to the Hebrew Book of Asaph the Physician, an emendation would be easily justified. The context clearly refers

---

48. This work appears in Jellinek and is partially included by Charles in an appendix. See Jellinek, "ספר נח," 155–60; Charles, *Jubilees*, 179.

49. Himmelfarb ("Some Echoes of *Jubilees*," 130) doubts that the author knew the entire book of Jubilees, but she perhaps underestimates other parallels. For example, she asserts, "None of the ills of *Jubilees* is unambiguously a physical ailment," but one could easily link illness and mortality to wickedness on the basis of Jub. 23.

50. The redactor did not render משטמה השר, as might have been expected if it was understood as a proper noun (cf. at the beginning, Mount Lubar, לובר ההר).

to Mastema (thus, if 10:11 did read "Satan," there would be no doubt that Jubilees identifies the two names as one figure). The fact that Jubilees uses "satans" differently in four other places makes clear that a transmitter, and not the author, made the identification. Thus we can say confidently that the original composition of Jubilees only used "satans" to refer to adversaries in the most general sense.[51]

2.1.4.2. Satan in Nonapocalypse Received Scriptures

Much has been written on the origins and development of the "Satan" tradition, of which only a narrow slice is relevant here.[52] Before reviewing contemporary apocalypses, we will consider the use of the term in received scripture. Even in a few references one finds a diversity of views. For a supernatural figure identified with the term one must examine Num 22, Job 1–2, Zech 3, 1 Chr 21:1, and perhaps Ps 109:6.[53] In the last case, the indefinite noun could be taken as a human, but in the context of the verb פקד and with Deut 32:8, it could also be interpreted in line with the position in Jubilees that angels were appointed over nations to mislead them (Jub. 15:31; see also 12:20). Without suggesting a linear historical development, one might observe a spectrum of insidiousness in the other four sources. In Num 22 the indefinite noun refers to a role that is filled by an angel, but the opposition is to Balaam and certainly not to God or any positive figure. In Job 1–2 the noun with the definite article refers to an individual figure among the בני האלהים, "sons of God." Here a greater degree of insidiousness appears in that the figure acts against a righteous person and wields destructive power. It is still very much the case, however, that the figure is entirely subject to God for permission before doing anything more than making accusations.

---

51. Segal, however, reads Jub. 10:11 with the Ethiopic and identifies Mastema with Satan (*The Book of Jubilees*, 176 n. 19).

52. Jeffrey Burton Russell, *The Devil: Perceptions of Evil from Antiquity to Primitive Christianity* (Ithaca, N.Y.: Cornell University Press, 1977); Neil Forsyth, *The Old Enemy: Satan and the Combat Myth* (Princeton: Princeton University Press, 1987); Elaine Pagels, *The Origin of Satan* (New York: Random House, 1995); T. J. Wray and Gregory Mobley, *The Birth of Satan: Tracing the Devil's Biblical Roots* (New York: Palgrave Macmillan, 2005); Henry Ansgar Kelly, *Satan: A Biography* (Cambridge: Cambridge University Press, 2006).

53. The verbal root appears in several psalms in reference to human opponents. The indefinite noun refers to some human opponents in Samuel and Kings.

Again with the definite article, such a figure acts in Zech 3 against a righteous person. This time the accusation is more insidious in as much as it appears to be a groundless accusation. Even here the accuser is just doing the job of accusing and hardly wields any power against God. For our purposes, 1 Chr 21:1 presents the most interesting case. Here שטן appears without the definite article as a particular cosmic figure and quite likely should be taken as a proper noun.[54] The figure in this verse is quite insidious indeed, arising against Israel and inciting David to do something against the will of God that will bring death and destruction. The interesting issue from the perspective of the study of Jubilees is that 2 Sam 24:1 relates the same story, except God is the one who incites David.[55] Jubilees also displays the tendency to assign to a distinct figure the unbecoming deeds previously attributed directly to God. Received scripture conveys a variety of ideas about a heavenly accuser, the most insidious of which is more insidious than Mastema in Jubilees.[56]

2.1.4.3. The Early Apocalypses

When we turn to the apocalypses known to have existed by the time of Jubilees we find neither the terminology nor the idea in the narrow sense of an eternal cosmic figure dedicated to opposition to God or righteous humans. Consequently, at least in the earlier period, it is a fallacy to identify "Satan" as an apocalyptic motif. The discussion still belongs in the present work, however, not because the figure of Satan is typically apocalyptic, but because the idea is related to what has already been considered about the nature of evil. The beasts in Daniel, the fallen watchers, and the national princes in Daniel and the Animal Apocalypse differ from the idea of Satan not only in terminology but in permanence.[57] No one figure rules over evil throughout all time. There is, however, a pattern of supernatural

---

54. JPS, NRSV, and RSV translate as a proper noun, whereas the NAB translates "a satan."

55. First Chr 21 interprets "the anger of the Lord" in 1 Sam 24 as an independent figure. See Segal, *The Book of Jubilees*, 209 n. 19.

56. In 1 Chronicles the figure arises and acts independently and succeeds in causing great destruction. Although the story indirectly leads to the temple in Jerusalem, there is no explicit mention either that God had willed the whole sequence or that the "Satan" was put to shame.

57. See the next chapter, on the temporal axis. Apocalypses typically view evil not so much as a persistent state or gradual progression but as an infestation that surges

opposition. The narrative detail of a specific eternal ruler of evil is not particularly tied to the apocalypses, but the idea of independent cosmic evil is. It is true that Jubilees manipulates certain details in other notions of "satan," but the main interest for this study is how Jubilees uses the figure of Mastema to undermine the idea of cosmic opposition to God.

2.1.4.4. Mastema in Jubilees

In Jubilees, Mastema is no enemy of God. Mastema does the dirty work of leading other nations from God and carrying out violent missions when commanded by God. Mastema fills certain exegetical needs and explains whatever dark power might be perceived in foreign religion but emphatically lacks power over Israel under the law and plays no role whatsoever in the eschatological crisis where one might expect a showdown between the forces of good and evil. Mastema never claims victory or rule over Israel, only shame. Arguably, Mastema never sins and is never judged.[58] We will consider the functions of Mastema in two categories. First, we will consider the role of Mastema in carrying out God's plan for the nations. Second, we will consider the use of Mastema to interpret the biblical history of Israel.

As we have already seen, God commands angels and demons to rule over *other* nations, not only because of their wickedness, but also to lead them astray because God intends to be God for only one nation (Jub. 15:31). Mastema appears in three passages as administrator of the demons assigned by God to other nations. As we have already seen, Jubilees allows for some diminished role for demons to explain whatever power may be perceived in foreign religion. On the narrative level, Mastema fills the function of advocacy for the demons. Most important, Mastema does not

---

twice in world history: once before the flood and again before the final judgment. Thus, at this stage, a permanent figure of evil would not fit well.

58. Jub. 10:8 may refer to a future time when Mastema is to be judged, but if so it is peculiar that the only mention of this possibility comes from the mouth of Mastema. In the context of the verse, "before me ... the authority of my will," it seems more likely that ቅድመ ፡ ኩነኔየ should be read in the sense of "before my authority," rather than "during the time prior to when I am to be punished." Manuscript 58 supports reading "before me," which, even if an error, is an error from the context. Manuscripts 35 (prior to correction) and 38 read "before the judgment." Segal (*The Book of Jubilees*, 177) suggests reading "before my punishment" as chronological sequence: first the demons do the job of destroying and misleading, and then Mastema does the job of punishing.

act against the will of God. Mastema simply points out that the demons serve a valuable function for afflicting sinners. Mastema persuades God but does not exercise any power against God.

Mastema's next appearance develops the identification of idolatry and demon-worship. Abram's experience as a youth illustrates the difference between being misled into idolatry and following reason to God. The idolaters are placed under Mastema's control (Jub. 11:5), which takes the form of diminished harvest (11:11). Abram demonstrates his ability to outwit Mastema first with agricultural invention, then by uncovering the deception of idolatry and divination. The logical conclusion to the contrast is that Abraham's religion has the power to defeat whatever power may exist behind foreign religion. Although Mastema is not mentioned by name (or office, as it were), in chapter 15 the connection is easily made when God commissions other powers to rule over other nations but to stay away from Israel. In Jub. 19:28 the function of Mastema is to remove other nations from following God, with the intent that no children of Israel would follow the other nations in their wrong direction. Most important, the function of Mastema and the demons is the function given to them at the command of God. Jubilees does not deny that any of Israel have ever abandoned their protection from demons by associating with the other nations, subjecting themselves to their punishment. Two emphases, however, remain distinctive: the defeat of the demons is easily accomplished, for Israel, with repentance; and the demons do not afflict the righteous—they may try, but they succeed only in shaming themselves. They are vehicles for just punishment, not an explanation for unjust suffering.

Mastema also has a second function that does pertain directly to Israel. Mastema becomes the agent of actions that Genesis and Exodus had attributed to God but that Jubilees (among other ancient interpretations) viewed to be unfitting of a supremely benevolent God. In each case Jubilees continues to emphasize that Mastema operates within the limits of the command of God. Mastema never claims any victory over Israel. Mastema does the dirty work of God but never acts against God. In the first instance, Jubilees uses Mastema to solve two theological problems stemming from Gen 22. First, Jubilees reconciles Gen 22:12 with the principle of divine omniscience by reading "now I know" as "now I have made known."[59] Borrowing a page

---

59. James L. Kugel, *Traditions of the Bible: A Guide to the Bible as It Was at the Start of the Common Era* (Cambridge: Harvard University Press, 1998), 302.

from Job, Jubilees uses Mastema to explain to whom Abraham's righteousness needed to be made known. The fact that God did know how it would turn out leads to the second point. While the inexplicable and cruel demand in Gen 22 might seem unfitting for a benevolent and loving God, Jubilees gives God a good reason for the trial. The trial becomes an opportunity to put Mastema to shame. Arguably, by the time of the revelation of the law Mastema learns that Israel is off-limits, since Mastema does not appear in the eschatological sequence or any of the "predictions" relative to the time of Moses. (Mastema's final status in the narrative is having been bound—perhaps Mastema remains bound permanently.) On the one hand, Mastema does fill the role attributed to the accuser in Job 1–2 (which itself is one of the less insidious roles attached to the term).[60] On the other hand, Mastema fills the role attributed to God in Gen 22. Jubilees is constrained by received scripture and the theological principles of God's benevolence and omniscience. Jubilees uses the figure of Mastema to the extent of deflecting any appearances of cruelty or witlessness from God, far short of creating an opponent to God's just sovereignty.

In the same way, on several occasions in the life of Moses, Mastema takes on functions that had been attributed to God directly. The theological problems are familiar: Why does God try to kill Moses?[61] Why do the Egyptian magicians have any supernatural power?[62] Even when the slaughter of the Egyptians is justified, how is God's role in bloodshed to be understood?[63] Mastema is a harsh figure to the extent of taking on the

---

60. Mastema is associated with the verb "accuse" in Jub. 48:15. When one reads the book as a whole, one discovers a more general divergence from the idea of a heavenly accuser (satan) as a bad thing. In the view of Jubilees, justice reigns persistently. Thus, the accusing that goes on in Jubilees generally is positive accusation of the wicked (Jub. 4:6, 23–24). When one has perfect trust in the judicial system, the office of accuser is hardly sinister.

61. In Exod 4:24–26, Moses might appear lax with the commandments, while his Egyptian wife becomes his savior. In Jubilees, neither circumcision nor Zipporah are mentioned, but Mastema does start to take on the role of advocate for the Egyptians, and the revealing angel becomes the savior.

62. Jubilees does not oppose the idea that some power can be perceived in other religions but emphasizes that is it only destructive, never constructive (Jub. 48:10). Even at that, the higher angels can deprive such magicians of their feeble power (48:11).

63. Whereas God kills the Egyptian firstborns in Exod 11:4; 12:12–13, 27, 29, in Jub. 49:2 God only gives the command, and Mastema's forces do the dirty work.

harshness otherwise attributed to God, but not evil in a dualistic sense that necessitates an opposition to God.[64] Jubilees 48:3–4 is the borderline case which demonstrates the limit on how hard Jubilees pushes the point that cosmic agents do not successfully interfere in the direct rule of Israel by God. There Mastema does what God does in Exodus 4:24 (trying to kill Moses) and is thwarted by the angel of the presence. One might count this as an exception to the overall pattern of inverting the apocalyptic idea of angelic agency, but the constraining factor is the interpretation of scripture with a particular set of theological presuppositions. The need to explain Exodus 4:24 trumps the inclination to subvert apocalyptic ideas. Even though Mastema appears here as an enemy, Mastema is still not successful or out of control for any length of time.[65]

Although Jubilees *tends* to separate harsh action from God directly, the tendency slips, for example, when the same forces are described as "Mastema's forces" in 49:2 and then "the Lord's forces" in 49:4. At every turn Mastema either acts under direct command of God or is allowed to act for a specific purpose before being quickly restrained. It is in this context that we find the maxim used to introduce this section, ወገብሩ ፡ ኃይላቲሁ ፡ ለእግዚአብሔር ፡ ኵሎ ፡ ዘመጠነ ፡ አዘዞሙ ፡ እግዚአብሔር, "The Lord's

---

Jubilees perhaps finds Mastema suggested in Exod 12:23, הַמַּשְׁחִית "the Destroyer." See further Betsy Halpern-Amaru, "The Festivals of Pesaḥ and Massot in the Book of Jubilees," in Boccaccini and Ibba, *Enoch and the Mosaic Torah*, 309–22.

64. Michael Mach ("Demons," *EDSS* 1:190) discusses the fact that "demons" are not necessarily opposed to God: "it is not self-evident that heavenly beings with negative effects on humans are necessarily opposed to God. They may just fulfill his will, and their deeds will then appear as punishing acts (e.g., … 1QS, iv.12–13…)."

65. Michael Segal (*The Book of Jubilees*, 226–27) perceives a theological seam between Jub. 48 and 49, with the former portraying Mastema as an independent entity and patron of Egypt, and the latter portraying Mastema as strictly subordinate to God. The seam should not be called a contradiction, however. Jub. 2 and 15 show that lower angels can be assigned to rule over nations and still be divine envoys. Both Jub. 48 and 49 convey a view of God in complete control; it is just that Jub. 48 must work harder to interpret the dramatic opposition in the Exodus narrative. Even in Jub. 48, Mastema is hardly a menacing figure. It is true that Mastema is *permitted* to do things in 48:10 and Mastema's forces are *sent* to do things in 49:2, and perhaps that difference in tone may suggest a compositional process in which Jub. 48 is more derivative than 49 (though each is derivative in its own way). The seam is not a sloppy contradiction but has been largely (if not perfectly) smoothed over with other changes. If Jub. 48 differs in tone with Jub. 49 over whether Mastema is permitted or sent to do bad things, it concurs in more important verbs such as "not allowed," "deprived," and "put to shame."

forces did everything that the Lord ordered them" (Jub. 49:4). One might even find humor in the back-and-forth pattern of Mastema's unbinding and binding in Jub. 48:15–18. The dominion of the beasts in Daniel and the shepherds in the Animal Apocalypse, though temporary, is sustained enough to achieve substantial unjust suffering. In contrast, God uses Mastema in short, controlled bursts to the end of destroying the Egyptians and profiting Israel (Jub. 48:18). Mastema never succeeds in causing any suffering in Israel. Conspicuously, Mastema is never associated with any actual harm done by the Egyptians, such as the idea to throw infant boys into the river.[66] To the extent to which Mastema is comparable to an angelic prince of the Egyptians (Jub. 48:3), the advocacy is that of a clumsy stooge.

We can conclude that Jubilees does not at all convey the idea of Satan that *modern* readers seem to persistently expect.[67] The expectations of the original audience may well have been different, however. To the extent to which Jubilees creates reader expectations about a "satan" figure, it does so by using the plural indefinite noun "satans" and a similar (but different) term, "Mastema." The genre "apocalypse," at the time of Jubilees, does not necessarily create an expectation of a particular eternal cosmic enemy of God and the righteous. To the extent to which there may have been a reader expectation that a figure named "Mastema" would be insidious, Jubilees can be said to subvert that expectation.

Even though the particular motif of a single eternal accuser or harsh prince is not typical of the apocalypses, the idea of cosmic agents of unjust oppression is. Jubilees develops the idea of Mastema as a foil for God's hostility toward other nations and specific cases of biblical interpretation. Most important, Jubilees never wavers on the claim that God's sovereignty and benevolence toward Israel is absolute, unmediated, and uninterrupted.

The main difference, besides use of the term, between the idea of Satan as an eternal ruler of all enmity against God and the beasts or corrupt

---

66. Daniel and the Animal Apocalypse, on the other hand, are trying to explain forces that are succeeding quite well in harming the righteous (Dan 7:21, 25; 8:10–12; 11:36; 1 En. 89:65–90:13).

67. Russell, *Method and Message*, 257. It is less surprising that treatments that focus on the Christian idea of Satan, spending no more than a chapter on the pre-Christian background of the idea, flatten Mastema into later developments. For example, three works of this nature make the same mistake in asserting that Mastema, not God, orders Abraham to sacrifice Isaac: Russell, *The Devil*, 204; Pagels, *The Origin of Satan*, 54; Wray and Mobley, *The Birth of Satan*, 103. The same specific error is made in Russell, *The Devil*, 51. None of these sources cite another for this misinformation.

angels that do appear in contemporary apocalypses is that the enemies of God in the apocalypses are temporally limited. Their rise is associated with the climax of history, a final showdown between good and evil. In the next section we will see how Mastema, demons, and satans, such as they do function in Jubilees, are the temporal inverse of the eschatological enemies of God in the apocalypses. Mastema never appears in any of the "predictive" passages, referring to the future relative to Moses. When Jubilees turns to the eschatological conflict and restoration in chapter 23, no angels or demons play any role whatsoever on either side. Rather than becoming more prominent toward the end, in Jubilees such forces lose significance.

2.1.5. Angels and Demons in the Eschatological Crisis and Restoration

This subsection brings us to the clearest case of difference between Jubilees and contemporary apocalypses. For the sake of organization we are considering the spatial axis and the temporal axis in separate chapters, but the apocalypses are most distinctive at the nexus of the two axes. In this subsection we consider the agents of the spatial axis at the eschatological moment on the temporal axis. The differences between Jubilees and contemporary apocalypses are sometimes subtle, as in the accounts of the origin of evil. When we look for the roles of supernatural agents in the eschatological climax, the difference is unmistakable. Especially in the historical apocalypses, but also in the cosmic tours, supernatural agents, good and bad, are most active in the climax of evil, the final conflict, the judgment, and the restoration. In Jubilees the situation is reversed. Angels and demons serve certain functions in the normal progress of history, but in all the versions of eschatological cruxes in Jubilees the only agents are humans and God directly. This is especially clear in Jub. 23, which emphasizes the roles of humans and God and then only mentions satans and evil ones as being absent. As we will see more in the next chapter, the idea of future eschatology takes some twists in Jubilees, so we will also consider the absence of angelic agents in *all* the judgment scenarios in Jubilees. First we will consider the role of supernatural agents (besides God) in eschatological scenarios in contemporary apocalypses.

2.1.5.1. The Early Apocalypses

The ideas of reversal in history and supernatural agency are hardly exclusive to the apocalypses. Even the idea that forces other than God and humans might be responsible for dark moments in history should be read as a broader tendency. It is distinctive that the apocalypses typically emphasize the agency of cosmic forces of evil in eschatological climaxes. What is most distinctive is the need to assign to cosmic figures other than God directly the battle for righteousness, the judgment, and the restoration. It would take us too far afield to venture an explanation of *why* this is the case, but a few examples will demonstrate that it is the case.

As we have already seen, the beasts in Dan 7 convey the idea of supernatural forces of evil rising and climaxing in an eschatological conflict. This view is typical of the apocalypses but has precedent in "cosmic" struggles between *God* and Rahab or Yam, for example.[68] The greater innovation comes in the agency of God in Dan 7. God retains *ultimate* sovereignty but appoints another cosmic figure, the human-like figure of Dan 7:13, to exercise dominion. Other texts may mention hosts who fight with or for God (e.g. 2 Kgs 6:16–17), but only in apocalypses do angelic figures gain such importance.[69] In other parts of the same chapter God assigns dominion to "the Holy Ones of the Most High." Although angelic beings are homologous with their earthly counterparts, the primary and distinctively apocalyptic emphasis here is on the angelic agents (Dan 7:18, 22, 27).[70] In a number of other apocalypses it is conspicuous that God does not destroy, judge, or restore directly but appoints angels to do these things. God does not even appear in Dan 12. In the Book of the Watchers God issues commands, but angels carry out all the actions, good and bad. The Animal Apocalypse makes more room for human agency but still views the human struggle as a façade for the cosmic struggle (1 En. 90:13–14). In the judgment and restoration of 90:20–27 the verbs are plural, indicating the seven archangels as subjects. The same emphasis on angelic agents on

---

68. See, for example, Job 26:7, 12–13; Isa 51:9–10.
69. Even Third Isaiah, often discussed as a forerunner of apocalyptic ideas, emphasizes God's direct and solitary action (Isa 63:5; 66:16). The LXX reading of 63:9 also fits this pattern. The MT Qere would be an exception, but in the context of past salvation, not future eschatology.
70. Collins, *Apocalyptic Imagination*, 104–5.

both sides of the eschatological struggle is true in the Epistle of Enoch, 1 En. 100:4, and other passages.[71]

In many cases passive verbs prevent us from asserting that the active agent is a cosmic being other than God, but in light of the preceding pattern one might imagine as much. The tendency to avoid mention of direct action by God is at least noteworthy. Thus for example, "without human hand" (Dan 8:25; likewise 9:27) contrasts in tone and probably meaning with assertions about the exercise of God's right hand (e.g. Exod 15:6). The Apocalypse of Weeks in particular uses passive verbs that do not explicitly support but certainly fit with this pattern.[72]

We will consider the details of human participation in eschatological violence in the last section of this chapter. In the meantime we can at least say that the apocalypses do not typically emphasize the impact of human agency on the progress of history, but rather the agency of good and bad forces other than God and humans.[73] This is true in general and especially in the eschatological conflict, judgment, and restoration.

2.1.5.2. Jubilees

We have already seen some significant differences between Jubilees and the typical apocalypses on the issues raised by the literary genre. When we turn to the eschatological scenarios in Jubilees, the difference is more

---

71. The Testament of Moses is not discussed in depth because it is not an apocalypse and it is difficult to be sure what parts are contemporary with Jubilees. A broader discussion would include the work, however, because it does deal with many of the ideas inherent to the apocalyptic literary genre and often aligns more with Jubilees than the typical apocalypses. On this issue in particular we find a mixture of both emphases. God both consecrates an angel to take vengeance and then rises from the throne to punish the Gentiles (T. Mos. 10:2–3).

72. Even in passages that do emphasize angelic agency, passive verbs sometimes suggest a more complex view of agency. Thus for example, the human-like figure in Dan 7 receives dominion only after someone or something else destroys the beast, and again in Dan 11:45 the avatar of evil is destroyed (by whom?) before Michael arises and the woes truly begin.

73. Thus, for example, the martyrs of Dan 11:32–35 do not impede the march of evil in verses 36–45. Although a number of explanations have been given for the prayer in Dan 9, all can agree that the emphasis on human sin and repentance is out of place in the work. One certainly gets the impression that Daniel's prayer was not worth a hearing and certainly did not impact the revelation (9:23). See section 4.1.2.2.

pronounced. All other things being equal, Jubilees avoids angelic agency in any function of judgment and salvation. This is not to say, however, that Jubilees always avoids any semblance of angelic function other than teaching. In particular, as we have seen, Jubilees accounts for some of the drama and unbecoming deeds of the Exodus story with recourse to angelic agency.[74] The lesser issue is that Jubilees is constrained by the base text. The greater issue is that Jubilees does not present the Exodus as an eschatological judgment of the Egyptians. Jubilees also follows the Book of the Watchers in specifying that angels bound the fallen watchers. There are limits to the lengths to which Jubilees goes to downplay angelic agency in judgment when constrained by other factors, such as the interest in asserting that sin never goes unpunished. We should not imagine that the author of Jubilees had the issue of angelic agency front and center. It is the case, however, that Jubilees conveys a view that differs from the typical apocalypses on agents other than God and humans, especially in an eschatological context.

Jubilees 23. The primary eschatological scenario in Jubilees is chapter 23. The emphasis on human culpability for the "final woes" is itself distinctive. More distinctive still is the fact that the woes, particularly foreign invasion, are sent directly by God: there are no beasts arising or angelic princes conspiring or becoming blind; God acts directly for the clear purpose of punishing human sin.

> There will be a great punishment from the Lord for the actions of that generation. (Jub. 23:22)

Those who study the law (23:26) are not merely guaranteeing their own resurrection (Dan 11) or allying themselves with a cosmic super-power (1 En. 90:12–16) but actually initiating the restoration themselves. God takes over for all functions other than Torah study and never commissions any other being to carry out any aspect of the restoration. No angels or humans are given swords to carry out vengeance or any other particular

---

74. Even here it would be a mistake to miss the emphasis on the agency of God and Moses. In 48:13 the revealing angel does take some credit, and Mastema has a role, but God and Moses continue to govern most action. Often enough this is just a matter of following scripture, but Jub. 48:5 has God perform the type of action that one typically expects angels to do in apocalypses: "The Lord took revenge on all their gods and burned them up."

action. God does the healing and expelling of enemies, while the righteous need only witness God's direct and singular action:

> Then the Lord will heal his servants. They will rise and see great peace. He will expel his enemies. The righteous will see (this), offer praise, and be very happy forever and ever. They will see all their punishments and curses on their enemies. (Jub. 23:30)

As if to guarantee that the reader noticed the conspicuous silence, the sequence makes clear that "there will be no satan or evil one" (Jub. 23:29).

Some scholars have read this phrase as proof of the importance of Satan in Jubilees,[75] but here and in three other comments like it the word "no" must be taken into account. Except for one instance where emendation is well-supported, (Jub. 10:11), satans are mentioned only when they are absent.[76] Their presence otherwise may follow logically, but noting the lack of satans does not emphasize that satans are otherwise prominent. We have already considered the extremely qualified role of demons in Jubilees and the likelihood that "satans" is a more general category than demons that includes human trouble-makers. Furthermore, the absence of satans does not exclusively refer to eschatological utopia but in two other instances refers to the time of peace and prosperity in Egypt under Joseph (40:9; 46:2). The next chapter will return to the fact that the eschatological restoration is a restoration of natural good things that are perceived to have already existed in the past. Jubilees 23 both *says* that agents other than God and humans are absent and follows through on this assertion in the account of events.

The rest of the book. Jubilees 23 is the most detailed eschatological account in Jubilees, but the same point holds for similar mentions throughout the book. At the end of the book, Jub. 50:5 makes a brief reference to a future time of purity and security in similar terms,

> The jubilees will pass by until Israel is pure of every sexual evil, impurity, contamination, sin, and error. Then they will live confidently in the entire land. They will no longer have any satan or any evil person. The land will be pure from that time until eternity. (Jub. 50:5)

---

75. See, for example, Wray and Mobley, *The Birth of Satan*, 104.
76. See above, §2.1.4.1: "Terms, Names and Titles."

The context makes clear that it is the responsibility of Israel to observe purity laws, and God in turn will establish prosperity and security. No nonhuman force prevents Israel from being pure, and no being other than God establishes prosperity and security. Another passage establishes a high view of the agency of Israel in the cosmos, although an eschatological chronology is not explicit. Abraham says of the descendants of Jacob,

> May they serve (the purpose of) laying heaven's foundations, making the earth firm, and renewing all the luminaries which are above the firmament. (Jub. 19:25)

Even if it is not necessarily eschatological here, it draws on images that are typically eschatological in the apocalypses. Notably, the roles are reversed. Here Israel contributes to restoring the heavens and the earth. In the apocalypses, angelic agency dominates human affairs.[77]

Jubilees 1 also resembles the historical apocalypses in giving an after-the-fact account of the history of Israel after the time of Moses. This chapter continues the pattern of never mentioning demonic agency against Israel in the covenantal period, except with a negation. The "curses" of Israel are not demonic but covenantal. God and God alone afflicts Israel, and only in proportion to their sin for the purpose of prompting repentance (Jub. 1:10). Jubilees 1:11 mentions the demons as objects to whom the sinners of Israel will sacrifice their children. Even here, where the logic applied to other nations would imply that the demons afflict them in turn, Jubilees denies that any besides God will afflict Israel (see again Jub. 15:31). Likewise, the prayer of Moses mentions the "spirit of Belial" (perhaps better translated, as JPS does Deut 15:9, "base thought"),[78] but again with the negative modifier: "may it *not* rule over them." Arguably, this might not refer to an eschatological sequence per se and thus may not fit well in this subsection. It only strengthens the case if even in quasi-eschatological scenarios (besides Jub. 23 and 50) angelic and demonic forces have no influence over Israel. Of course, the narrative focus of the book predates Sinai,

---

77. The intercessory role of Enoch supports this more than it qualifies it, not only because Enoch is elevated to angelic status, but because the Book of the Watchers emphasizes that the roles *should* be reversed (1 En. 15:2). Enoch's (failed) intercessory mission and his testimony do not negate the overwhelming emphasis on good and bad angels in the origin and judgment of evil.

78. See page 73 above.

but it remains striking that Jubilees says much about angels and demons, but nothing but denial when it comes to Israel under the covenant and in the future restoration.

The next chapter will suggest that Jubilees does not follow the Book of the Watchers in the expectation of a deferred, universal day of judgment (1 En. 10:12; 16:1). In anticipation of this, it is worth adding here that the various national days of judgment throughout Jubilees (that is, judgment of other nations) do not involve angelic agents of judgment. For example, the judgment of Lot's descendants in 16:9 takes a singular verb with God as a subject. Similarly, Jubilees removes angelic judgment where it existed in Genesis in the Babel story. Genesis 11:7 might suggest to some (without recourse to the "royal we") that God acted with angelic allies against Babel, הָבָה נֵרְדָה וְנָבְלָה שָׁם שְׂפָתָם, "Come, let us go down there and babble their language." Jubilees 10:23, however, allows no angelic agency. One would hardly say that Jubilees eliminates angels in general. On the contrary, Jubilees develops the issue of their role in God's cosmos. What Jubilees says about them, however, is striking. They teach, reveal, and do other things on direct orders (Jub. 49:4), but they do not do what they typically do in apocalypses, particularly afflict, fight, judge, and restore in an eschatological context.

2.2. HUMANS

2.2.1. GROUPS

The previous section studied several ways in which Jubilees uses the typical apocalyptic literary elements of angels and demons but says atypical things about them. These kinds of agents are the core of the spatial axis that partly defines the genre "apocalypse."[79] The spatial axis can also address the order of humanity from a transcendent perspective. The classification of humanity, particularly for purposes of eschatological salvation, is a frequent, though not definitive, element of the apocalypses. Not all apocalypses deal with issues of election or take positions that can be called sectarian, proto-sectarian, or, in the other direction, universalistic.

---

79. Jubilees does not dwell on their domains. An exhaustive study might consider the angelic liturgy, the heavenly geography, the ranks of angels (and how they mirror the ranks of humans), the noncorruption of heaven in the version of the sinful watchers, the holy places, and the (lack of) nonearthly places of judgment and reward.

The genre may not necessarily raise the issue of human classification to the same extent as the angelic and related agents of the spatial axis. There may be an empirical basis at the time of Jubilees, however, for associating the apocalypses with exclusivist or universalistic tendencies. Contemporary apocalypses often define an elect group within Israel for special (or sole) status in the restoration, while abandoning or condemning other parts of Israel. The category "descendant of Jacob" can be abandoned in the other direction if outsiders are included as equals or above parts of Israel. On this issue as well, Jubilees expresses a very different position. Other than the traditional distinction of Levites and the high priest, the category "Israel" is of absolute significance for Jubilees. No Gentiles are welcome, and no groups within Israel are singled out for special punishment or reward.

Again, a few simplifications and overstatements must be avoided. The issue of universalism is more difficult than the election of a remnant within Israel in as much as it is not always clear whether the other nations are "converting" and joining Israel or if the category "Israel" is being abandoned. Consequently, we will focus our efforts on the idea of an elect group within Israel that is saved while the rest of Israel is condemned. We must also avoid the exaggeration that Jubilees is particularly conciliatory. The unity of Israel does *not* take the form of tolerance of different attitudes toward calendar, exogamy, and other legal issues. Although the Animal Apocalypse is usually one of the clearest points of contrast with Jubilees, they overlap here in imagining Israel unified behind the one true way (their own). Even here, however, contrast can be seen in whether the anticipated unification of Israel is viewed as the vindictive destruction of enemies within Israel or as a snowballing movement of peaceful enlightenment and prosperity. Finally, we should not identify the literary treatment of exclusivity of election with the social reality of sectarianism (nor deny the possibility of certain relationships).[80] We do not know how large or isolated the group of the author of Jubilees may have been. We cannot be sure how reasonable it may have been at the time to hope that a certain

---

80. Albert I. Baumgarten takes a very different approach to the same texts, using social science, but comes to similar conclusions. Jubilees is not sectarian. The radical insistence on separation between Jews and Gentiles later *fueled* sectarianism once the Hasmoneans established a dynasty that accommodated Gentiles. Jubilees itself, however, is presectarian. See *The Flourishing of Jewish Sects in the Maccabean Era: An Interpretation* (JSJSup 55; Leiden: Brill, 1997), 86.

calendar would be restored or established. We know that Israel was never, in fact, united behind the study of the law as taught by Jubilees. The point is that Jubilees imagined that it would be.

2.2.1.1. Third Isaiah

A number of passages from received scripture could be brought as background to the second-century ideas about election and group definition. Perhaps the most demonstrably relevant passages come from Third Isaiah. It seems likely that the influence of Isaiah, including these chapters, was widespread. The interpretation, not the status, of Isaiah was disputed. In Third Isaiah we find the category "Israel" challenged in both directions: election of an internal remnant, and inclusion of non-Israel. On a literary level alone (ch. 5 will turn to the question of social realities at the time of composition), the text lends itself to the idea that not all of Israel has a share in the future hope. For example, Isa 65:9 can suggest salvation of an elect group within Israel by reading a partitive use of מִן.

וְהוֹצֵאתִי מִיַּעֲקֹב זֶרַע וּמִיהוּדָה יוֹרֵשׁ הָרָי
וִירֵשׁוּהָ בְחִירַי וַעֲבָדַי יִשְׁכְּנוּ־שָׁמָּה:

I will take out a part of Jacob as a seed; a portion of Judah is about to take possession of my mountains.
My chosen ones will take possession of the land; my servants will settle there. (Isa 65:9)

The idea that God's sovereignty and worship will extend beyond Israel to all humanity is not particularly rare, as for example in Isa 66:18. The more controversial assertion appears in Isa 66:21, which seems to suggest that some foreigners will be accepted as priests and Levites.[81] The dissolution of the category "Israel," both in designating a subgroup and elevating outsiders, is not the exclusive domain of the apocalypses. Nevertheless, a number of apocalypses designate an elect group within Israel (other than the traditional categories of priests and Levites) and include some outside

---

81. Even if it is the Israelites brought back by the foreigners who become priests and Levites, this constitutes a radical reworking of social categories.

Israel. The debate centers on the social mechanism of continuity, not the existence of similar patterns.[82]

2.2.1.2. The Enochic Apocalypses

Before proceeding with the earliest known apocalypses, the Book of the Watchers and the Astronomical Book, it will be helpful to clarify what is implied by dealing with these works as "contemporary" to Jubilees. We need not defend or contest any of the theories of the social setting of the original composition of these works; we are dealing with them as literature, as read at the time of Jubilees. Thus it does not matter what these works *originally* meant with the use of terms such as "chosen," "righteous," "elect," and "plant." It is clear enough from dependent texts, both before and shortly after Jubilees, that they were interpreted to mean a new elect group within Judaism that often potentially includes non-Jews. One finds in the introduction to the Book of the Watchers a polarity (not to suggest dualism per se) between "wicked," "sinners" and the "elect," "chosen," "righteous." The Book of the Watchers plays with a homology of *Urzeit* and *Endzeit*, so the references are often complex. The identification of "the righteous" changes along the temporal axis, but the scenario seems to run along the same lines as the Apocalypse of Weeks. The elect "plant of righteousness and truth" (1 En. 10:16) can refer to Noah, Abraham, or, ultimately, a sect. The plant is pruned, such that the "righteous" refers to a smaller group as time goes on.[83] Then, following a time of vindication, all the remaining people will join the sect and become righteous themselves (1 En. 10:20-21). The most relevant point is that in the Book of the Watchers the key categories of righteous and wicked are not tied to the categories of Jew and Gentile in the past, present, or future.

Any discussion of the Astronomical Book must be qualified by the fact that we are not sure how much of the wording of the Ethiopic version reflects the most ancient version or what versions should be classified as examples of the genre "apocalypse."[84] It is not the case that the main body

---

82. The classic work on the sociological relationship between Third Isaiah and later apocalypticism is Hanson, *The Dawn of Apocalyptic*.

83. For a survey of plant imagery, see Patrick A. Tiller, "The 'Eternal Planting' in the Dead Sea Scrolls," *DSD* 4 (1997): 312-35. Tiller notes that Jubilees is distinctive in maintaining an exclusive identification of the plant and Israel (323-24).

84. Collins, *Apocalyptic Imagination*, 60-61, especially note 49.

of the Astronomical Book focuses on human groups. Nevertheless, we do find language within the same pattern, "the good will inform the good about righteousness, the righteous will rejoice with the righteous, and they will greet each other" (1 En. 81:8). The specificity comes not in the terminology but in the associated actions. "The righteous" are defined as those who study certain texts and use a certain calendar (1 En. 82:4). Similarly, a concrete criterion can be understood in "Those who understand will not sleep and will listen with their ear to learn this wisdom. It will be more pleasing to them than fine food to those who eat" (1 En. 82:3). Thus "righteous" and similar terms are no longer simply adjectives but designations for a definable group. We have to be careful about arguing from silence with respect to any acknowledgment of Israel as a meaningful group, yet one does get the sense that wisdom is not limited to one of the nations descended from Enoch (1 En. 82:2). Indeed, it seems likely that the choice of Enoch as the voice of "pseudepigraphy" reflects an idea of universal law that applies to all humanity. The wise and righteous are neither all of Israel nor only Israel.

The Apocalypse of Weeks uses a fundamental literary pattern of periods of history culminating in election of an individual or group for salvation.[85] The text emphasizes a theme of election that ultimately includes only a group within Israel. The idea of the pattern is not radical. The Pentateuch certainly fits concentric circles of election in Noah (over everyone), Abraham (over everyone), Isaac (over Ishmael), Jacob (over Esau), Levi, Aaron, and Phinehas. Three points are, however, distinctive. First, the history varies in a tendentious way at the end. The election of Enoch (week 1), Noah (week 2), and Abraham (week 3) are the least disputed.[86] The election of the covenant, tabernacle, and temple (weeks 4 and 5) are not particularly tendentious, except in the avoidance of figures such as Aaron, Phinehas, and Zadok. In the sixth week, the relevant point is not so much the heavenly ascent of Elijah but the unchoosing of Israel. The chosen plant is cut down, as it were, to a chosen root. Nothing good is said of the postexilic period either, except that at its end a new group would be

---

85. See especially ibid., 65.

86. Positive inclusion of Enoch in salvation history may have become disputed in some much later texts, but it is not the case that the figure of Enoch defined a sect of Judaism in the second century B.C.E. or that Jews could not agree to say something nice about Enoch as part of the history of righteous figures (e.g., Genesis, Sirach, Jubilees).

chosen. We need not consider every plausible speculation about this group and how it correlates with external evidence.[87] The internal evidence is perfectly clear that this apocalypse hopes for salvation of only a group, not all of Israel. A second distinctive point should be observed in the violent vindictiveness of this group against the rest of Israel (1 En. 91:11–13; end of week 7, week 8). Third, after the wicked of Israel descend to punishment, the other nations ascend to equality in an (apparently new) covenant of righteousness (1 En. 91:14; week 9).

The rest of the Epistle of Enoch fits the same pattern, perhaps less emphatically so than the Apocalypse of Weeks. "Righteous" is more than an adjective; "the righteous" are defined by possession of certain books (1 En. 104:13). Scholars have emphasized different aspects of "testifying against the sons of the earth" (1 En. 105:1). This may indeed mean that the group is not cloistered or detached to such an extent that they have no contact with others.[88] Nevertheless, the role of testifying *against* is hardly a mark of solidarity. The Epistle of Enoch certain fits the pattern presently under discussion, although there are still legitimate reservations on whether it should be counted as a contemporary apocalypse.

With a tinge of military propaganda, the Animal Apocalypse attempts to portray the nation united in suffering under the oppression of foreign rulers and a few bad sheep, as it were. The promised resolution also emphasizes unity and equality. We have the means to read through the propaganda and know that quite a bit of Israel fell outside the view of who has a place in the restoration. The unity envisaged comes only with the deaths of all opposed to the rule of Judah Maccabee. Historically, it is easy to identify the Animal Apocalypse as an exclusive, partisan perspective. Literarily, the images of unity must be balanced with the images of vindication and vengeance.

The Animal Apocalypse portrays not so much a single group as an alliance and not so much orthodoxy as loyalty to the right side of a (civil) war. Although the Animal Apocalypse may emphasize foreign oppression more than civil war, even without recourse to other sources we can find evidence of a divided view of Israel. On the good side one finds an alliance of a pietistic movement that had previously taken to violence without success, together with the military forces of Judah Maccabee. The former

---

87. Stuckenbruck, *1 Enoch 91–108*, 124–28.
88. Collins, *Apocalyptic Imagination*, 71; Stuckenbruck, *1 Enoch 91–108*, 215–16.

are allegorized by young lambs that open their eyes, the latter by rams (1 En. 90:6–10). On the bad side one needs to read past the other nations to find the references to the enemies within Israel. First, a group of Jews is portrayed as blind and deaf, apparently in as much as they reject the reforms of the pietistic movement (90:7). After the revolt begins, some or much of Israel is blamed for not supporting it. The tone is not bitterness, as if enemy collaborators, but exhortation to aid those who are being persecuted unjustly (for starting a revolt). Unfortunately for the casual reader, Tiller and Nickelsburg present in their main texts an emendation that is not required or supported by any manuscript.[89] They emend "wild sheep" to "wild beasts," removing a clear reference to a group of Jews who are viewed as the enemy and allied with the foreign oppressor. We may not know how the numbers were divided between those of Israel who supported Judah Maccabee, those who sought neutrality, and those who sought to put down his revolt. It is at least clear, however, that the Animal Apocalypse identifies a group of Jews as the enemy.

The case becomes unmistakable in the restoration. The judgment culminates in the fiery torment of the "blinded sheep," the Jews who refused to join the pietists and the Maccabean side of the civil war. The enmity is magnified by placing these opponents in the same judgment as the cosmic forces of evil from the beginning of time and the history of oppression in Israel. Although the Animal Apocalypse attempts to portray the enemy as foreign oppressors and a handful of traitors, the eschatological judgment shows the true interest. There may be foreign armies to defeat, but the burning of bones in the fiery abyss is reserved for enemies within Israel, along with the cosmic forces of evil.

After the military victory is decided, as the envisaged restoration unfolds, the other nations actually fare quite well. Again, we should not conflate the variations on universalism. The foreign nations are "included" in the restoration not as equals but as a second class below "the sheep that remained" (1 En. 90:30). The vindication of Israel is an important step in the restoration. As the restoration continues, however, the Animal Apocalypse undoes the election of Israel and the division of the nations.[90]

---

89. Patrick A. Tiller, *A Commentary on the Animal Apocalypse of I Enoch* (Atlanta: Scholars, 1993), 358 n. 8, 363–64; VanderKam and Nickelsburg, *1 Enoch: A New Translation*, 133 n. g; Nickelsburg, *Commentary on 1 Enoch*, 389 n. 16b.

90. The verse might be understood such that "they" refers only to the Gentiles

And I saw until all their species were transformed, and they all became white cattle. (1 En. 90:38, Tiller's translation)

This may not be universalistic inclusiveness in the sense of tolerance of diversity, but it is the case that the Animal Apocalypse, in the more abstract moments, holds an ideal vision that does not separate Israel from the rest of humanity. To be sure, liberation from foreign oppression is the short-term rallying cry, but the true enemies of the Animal Apocalypse, as seen by long-term hopes, are those of Israel who do not support the pietistic movement and the Maccabean fighters. Thus we find that the "big tent" images of a unified Israel and humanity (1 En. 90:36) operate within a view of humanity that is deeply vindictive and thoroughly at odds with the principles and practice of Jewish unity.

2.2.1.3. The Danielic Apocalypses

Multiple categories or groups within Israel appear in the final apocalypse of Daniel. The first and "lowest" category is actually the least relevant to the pattern under consideration. It was not disputed that some Jews could be described as עֹזְבֵי בְּרִית קֹדֶשׁ, "those who abandon the holy covenant," (Dan 11:30; see also 11:32, מַרְשִׁיעֵי בְרִית, "violators of the covenant"). Daniel does not claim that most Jews fit this category or dwell on a particular vindictiveness toward them (12:2 not withstanding). At the other end, the category of הַמַּשְׂכִּלִים, "the enlightened," suggests a group.[91] They seem to be a subcategory of עַם יֹדְעֵי אֱלֹהָיו, "the people that know their God," those specifically in the role of teaching (Dan 11:32–33). Member-

---

mentioned in the previous verse. Thus, the Gentiles become cattle while the Jews remain sheep. However, it would be surprising in the next verse if God rejoices over the Gentiles but not the Jews. Furthermore, the decline of history earlier in the account (and the livestock market) appear to value white cattle over white sheep. If the Animal Apocalypse suggests that Gentiles will ultimately have higher status than Jews, then there is a different but deeper conflict with Jubilees. However, the more likely interpretation is that the diversification and degradation of species will be reversed and the final state will resemble the original plan of creation in that all people will become one nation (species). See also Tiller, *Commentary on the Animal Apocalypse*, 383–88.

91. Daniel 1:4 should be read in the same vein. Daniel and his comrades may not be the historical founders of the group that produced the final apocalypse of Daniel, but they are implicitly identified as analogous forerunners (מַשְׂכִּילִים בְּכָל־חָכְמָה, "those enlightened in every wisdom").

ship among the משכילים, together with martyrdom, establishes a special future status in the restoration, or rather, transformation (Dan 12:1–3). The condemnation of the wicked of Israel and the elevation of the most righteous is only the periphery of the issue, however.

The heart of the issue is the attitude toward the majority of Israel, referred to in Daniel as רבים, "the multitude," or עם, "the nation." On the one hand, Daniel does not treat the nation with contempt—they are teachable and worthy of teaching (Dan 11:33; 12:3). On the other hand, there is no expectation that the teaching will be received by all or will be efficacious in historical time (Dan 11:33–35). The bottom line is the eschatological hope, articulated in Dan 12:1:

בָּעֵת הַהִיא יִמָּלֵט עַמְּךָ כָּל־הַנִּמְצָא כָּתוּב בַּסֵּפֶר

> At that time your people will be delivered, everyone found written in the book.

All of Israel will be tested and given the opportunity to learn wisdom, but only some of them are expected to endure or be restored after death. To be sure, Daniel is not narrowly dualistic, notwithstanding a contrast of wicked and wise in 12:10. There are several degrees of eschatological hopes for parts of Israel, including the extremes of everlasting disgrace and shining like the splendor of the firmament. Intermediate degrees seem to include death without resurrection, endurance without death, and everlasting life (12:2–3). The main point is that Daniel singles out a group within Israel for special eschatological reward and abandons hope that all Israel will be united in the restoration.

It would take an elaborate discussion to account for the view of foreign nations in Dan 10–12 and in the framework of the redacted work. One can at least say that the category עם (nation) retains significance and can refer to all Israel or a qualified subgroup, but not foreign converts (Dan 11:14, 32–33; see also 12:4). Interestingly, Dan 12 makes no mention of other nations. Removal may be implicit, but Dan 12 does not emphasize punishment, conversion, or submission.

In conclusion, Daniel describes multiple categories within Israel, apparently based on orthodoxy, rather than tribal or familial descent (such as Levite, Zadokite, etc.).[92] Daniel 10–12 is not radically vindictive

---

92. Interestingly, different Daniel traditions identify his tribal affiliation differ-

THE SPATIAL AXIS   97

or dualistic but does imagine a restoration in which group or class membership determines eschatological status, with the extremes of everlasting reward, everlasting punishment, and some middle ground. Daniel is not as extreme as the Apocalypse of Weeks, but certainly within a cluster of views that assigns eschatological status to groups within Israel.

2.2.1.4. Jubilees

When we turn to Jubilees, we find that the category "Israel" is of absolute and eternal significance, from creation to restoration. The vision of unity does not take the form of tolerance of diversity, but it is striking relative to its day and relative to the other apocalypses. Jubilees insists on the unity and exclusivity of Israel. No foreigners are included. The traditional distinction of the descendents of Levi is maintained, but no new groups are designated for eschatological reward or punishment.[93]

When Michel Testuz combed Jubilees for an indicator of the group that produced the book, he found the phrase "all the elect ones of Israel" (ለኩሎሙ ፡ ኅሩያን ፡ እስራኤል) in Jub. 1:29, which he took as an early term for the group that become known as the Essenes.[94] By itself, or only in the context of an apocalypse, this ambiguous phrase suggests an elite group within Israel. Indeed, this kind of language is somewhat typical for the apocalypses and typically conveys some degree of elitism. But when we look at what the book of Jubilees says about election and the unity of Israel, we find overwhelming data that Jubilees emphatically views *all* of Israel as elect. This may be explained partly by the primary narrative setting in the period from creation to the arrival at Sinai, and it will be important to pay close attention to chapter 23. After surveying the overwhelming emphasis of the book as a whole, the isolated instance of the phrase "all the elect ones of Israel" in Jub. 1:29 appears in a new light. The phrase may evoke

---

ently. Dan 1:6 claims descent from Judah, while the Old Greek opening of Bel and the Serpent identifies him as a priest.

93. This basic observation was already made by Nickelsburg: "Strikingly different from 1 Enoch, the author [of Jubilees] emphasizes Israel's status as the covenantal people and proscribes interaction with the Gentiles and certainly the preaching of an eschatological *kerygma* that might lead to the salvation of the Gentiles" ("The Nature and Function of Revelation," 106).

94. Testuz, *Les idées religieuses*, 33.

associations with the idea that only a portion of Israel is ultimately elected for salvation, but the idea is not sustained.[95]

Apart from some irrelevant uses of the term (e.g., "select warriors," Jub. 37:6–14), the election of Levi (Jub. 30:18), and 1:29, Jubilees uses the language of election only for all of Israel.[96] We shall return to the election of Levi. First we will survey the language of election, then related phrases such as "righteous plant," and, finally, the frequent use of the word "all" in phrases such as "all of Jacob's descendants." Besides the ambiguous case in 1:29, five chapters discuss or at least refer to the election of Israel as a people (2:20; 15:30; 19:18; 22:9–10; 33:11). Even Abram is not described as chosen, and Ishmael and Esau are emphatically not chosen, since descent from Abraham does not constitute election,

> For the Lord did not draw near to himself either Ishmael, his sons, his brothers, or Esau. He did not choose them (simply) because they were among Abraham's children, for he knew them. But he chose Israel to be his people. He sanctified them and gathered (them) from all mankind. (Jub. 15:30–31)

Although chapter 23 does not use the language of election, one certainly finds in 2:20 that the election will not expire (see also 22:9–10).

> I have chosen the descendants of Jacob among all of those whom I have seen. I have recorded them as my first-born son and have sanctified them for myself throughout the ages of eternity. (Jub. 2:20; 4QJub^a VII:11–12)

The same is true when we turn to related language. The phrase "righteous plant" refers to *all* of Israel in Jub. 1:16; 16:26; 21:24; and 36:6. Jubilees 21:24 is particularly interesting because the language resonates with the

---

95. One should also consider the possibility that the text is corrupt, but no manuscripts attest a nonconstruct form that would support a reading such as "all of the chosen [people], Israel."

96. Since neither a concordance nor an electronic copy of Ethiopic Jubilees is available, this assertion is based on searching an electronic copy of VanderKam's translation for forms including (s)elect, choice, choose, or chose(n). The uses counted as irrelevant are the selection of choice warriors for battle in 37:6–14, the choice offering in 16:23, the watchers marrying whomever they choose in 5:1 and 7:21, Abram choosing God in 12:19, and the place God has chosen for the temple in 32:10.

typical language of the apocalypses, but the context establishes a meaning that is contrary to the meaning in the apocalypses.

> [God] will raise from you [Isaac] a righteous plant [Jacob] in all the earth throughout all the history of the earth. (Jub. 21:24; 4QJub^f 1:7–8)

If such a sentence were uncovered as a fragment, one might not guess that the righteous plant is the entire people of Israel, but in the context of an address to Isaac and the clear tendency throughout Jubilees, the language takes on an unexpected meaning. Finally, Jubilees often uses words like "all" in phrases such as "all of them will be called children of the living God" (Jub. 1:25), "all Jacob's children" (1:28), and "may all your [Jacob's] descendants become blessed and holy descendants" (25:18). Jubilees uses strong language for the unity of Israel, but before making a strong conclusion we should consider one moderating point and one exception.

Jubilees emphasizes that the category "Israel" has singular and eternal significance in the classification of humanity. The emphasis on "all" suggests that the entire nation will eternally enjoy that status. Jubilees does not single out a group within Israel for eschatological reward or condemnation. This position is moderated by the fact that some individuals may sin and be punished with death. For example, in 30:22 individual Israelites who violate the covenant are subject to being erased from the book of the living and recorded as enemies. Yet it is precisely because they remain under the covenant that they are punished under the covenant. As we shall see when we read Jub. 23 for the temporal axis, Jubilees does not view the covenantal curses as an unexercised threat. The covenantal relationship between God and all of Israel is not reconsidered. The potential for individual Israelites to sin and be cut off moderates but does not negate the overwhelming emphasis on the election of all Israel.[97]

---

97. Michael Segal (*The Book of Jubilees*, 241–43) has demonstrated that the limits to which we can speak of Jubilees as nonsectarian is established by Jub. 15:26: "Anyone who is born, the flesh of whose private parts has not been circumcised by the eighth day does not belong to the people of the pact." Here we learn that a descendant of Jacob can cease to be a member of God's people by violating the covenant of circumcision. This constitutes at least one ingredient of sectarianism, namely, the ability to argue that someone who claims to be a Jew and is ethnically a Jew is not really a Jew. This would not be so controversial if it spoke only of the assimilationists who "covered over" their circumcision (1 Macc 1:15). Jubilees may also imply that Jews who *do* practice circumcision, but according to a different legal ruling, can also be excluded

Also, the elevation of Levi might be considered an exception to the rejection of division within Israel, but the major differences are that this group designation is traditional and in received scripture, and the role of the group is not eschatological.[98] The scope of the present work does not justify a lengthy discussion as to whether Jubilees participates in polemic between priestly groups. Although it is true that Jubilees does not make clear reference to Zadok and says less than one might expect of Aaron and Phinehas,[99] the simplest explanation is that the status of the Aaronides over the Levites was not hotly contested, and Jubilees focuses on the narrative setting before the establishment of the cult.[100] Furthermore, the

---

from God's people. Jubilees emphasizes circumcision on the eighth day, whereas the Mishnah accommodates a delay in case of illness or Sabbath (m. Šabb. 19:5). There are chronological difficulties in implying that Jubilees excommunicated adherents to the Mishnah. It is also hard to imagine, in practical terms, that the author would not have accepted as a Jew someone who followed the right teachings in all ways except having parents who procrastinated. The biggest problem with making such judgments from this passage is that the overall emphasis is elsewhere. The passage very clearly condemns those who forego circumcision entirely. It also explains how Ishmael, though circumcised, is excluded from God's people. It may also exclude Idumeans or others who practice circumcision differently. It may also exclude adult converts to Judaism (who are excluded elsewhere if not here). Only behind all these emphases might one also claim that the passage denies the Judaism of devout Jews who follow a different legal ruling. It seems better to say that Jubilees is proto-sectarian. It has rigid social categories that lead to sectarianism, but the original composition emphasizes the unity of Israel without anticipating that its own rulings would contribute to sectarianism. For the contributions of Baumgarten and Himmelfarb on Jubilees and sectarianism, see ch. 5 n. 44.

98. See §3.4.4.4.

99. Phinehas is not mentioned by name, but the expansion of the zeal of Levi for purity and endogamy is clearly modeled on Phinehas. See Num 25 and Jub. 30.

100. Scholars since Wellhausen have traced the tumultuous history of priestly groups from the rise of professional priests to the late and disputed familial distinctions of Levites, Aaronide priests, and high priests. Although disputes about priestly status frequently occurred, some scholars have overestimated the extent to which the pre-exilic disputes extended into the second century B.C.E. As early as the Chronicler, and certainly by the mid-second century B.C.E. in Jerusalem's priestly circles, the ascending status of all Israel, Levites, and priests (if not the high priesthood) had ceased to be hotly disputed. Thus, the fact that Jubilees elevates Levi is primarily a function of the ancestral time period in which the book is set. Although Aaron might have appeared more at the end of the book, the decision not to develop further the establishment of the priestly cult is not a snub on Aaron or propaganda for a pan-Levitical priesthood. Even more so, the lack of a "prediction" of the distinction of Phinehas or Zadok

acknowledgement of the traditional role of the sons of Levi but the lack of additional privilege supports the present point that Jubilees emphasizes the unity of Israel.[101]

The narrative setting may partly explain some of the emphasis on the unity of Israel, but again the true views come out in the eschatological hopes. Thus we turn to Jub. 23. The first key to understanding groups in chapter 23 is that "children" (בנים) is not necessarily a technical term for a particular and defined group of Jews in the second century B.C.E. If this is part of a pattern of allusion or similarity to the Animal Apocalypse, or a particular group behind the Animal Apocalypse and Damascus Document, one must look past the term and consider whether similar things are said about the בנים in each case. Even within chapter 23, scholars have mistakenly identified the two uses of the term as references to the same group, despite the different actions and evaluations associated with them.[102] Jubilees 23 first uses the term in verse 16 for the youths who revolt against their elders. There are no good reasons to assume that Jubilees has anything nice to say about these militants, although there are bad reasons, and good reasons to think the opposite. The bad reasons are based on association with other apocalypses and accounts of the Maccabean revolt (especially 1 Maccabees) that praise the militants.[103] The good reasons to think

---

can be explained by the overwhelming tendency to stay in the narrative setting, with only general predictive passages. See Julius Wellhausen, *Prolegomena to the History of Israel* (Edinburgh: Black, 1885; repr., Atlanta: Scholars Press, 1994), 121–51; Saul M. Olyan, "Zadok's Origins and the Tribal Politics of David," *JBL* 101 (1982): 177–93; idem, "Ben Sira's Relationship to the Priesthood," 261–86; Joseph Blenkinsopp, "The Judaean Priesthood during the Neo-Babylonian and Achaemenid Periods: A Hypothetical Reconstruction," *CBQ* 60 (1998): 25–43; Aelred Cody, *A History of Old Testament Priesthood* (Rome: Pontifical Biblical Institute, 1969), 146–92; Frank Moore Cross, *Canaanite Myth and Hebrew Epic: Essays in the History of the Religion of Israel* (Cambridge: Harvard University Press, 1973), 195–215; Gary N. Knoppers, "Hierodules, Priests, or Janitors? The Levites in Chronicles and the History of the Israelite Priesthood," *JBL* 118 (1999): 49–72; Walther Zimmerli, *Ezekiel: A Commentary on the Book of the Prophet Ezekiel* (Hermeneia; Philadelphia: Fortress, 1979), 456–59.

101. The special status of Levi may keep us from talking about *equality* of all Israel in Jubilees, but we can still talk about *unity*. In the second century B.C.E., the voices for abolishing any hierarchical distinctions were the voices against unity, and the voices for the traditional categories were the voices for unity.

102. Werman, "ספר היובלים ועדת קומרן," 49–50; Testuz, *Les idées religieuses*, 166.

103. See §5.3 for discussion of the evidence that Jubilees was written shortly after the Maccabean revolt, most likely between 159 and 152 B.C.E. Even if Jubilees had been

the opposite are based on the chapter itself.[104] Jubilees 23:16–21 refers to a Jewish civil war, punished by God in 23:22–25. Even if one accusation or another applies to one side and not the other, neither side is right. Nothing good is said about either side, and nothing good comes of the fighting. The repeated use of "all" and the inclusive plural pronouns ("they") include all participants in the civil war. When God intervenes, God punishes both sides. Contrary to the Animal Apocalypse, the "Day of the Lord" is no vindication for militants. The בנים who appear in Jub. 23:26 are the exact opposite in action and in consequence.[105] Rather than fighting, they study the laws. Rather than bringing on the wrath of God, they bring on the blessings of God. Even if we entertain the possibility that they are the same people reformed, the transformation of group identity is so radical as to prohibit a simple identification.[106] The relationship between the functions of the children in 23:26 and the children in 23:16 is a relationship of strong contrast.[107] If anything is to be made of the repeated terminology, it is an accentuated contrast.

---

composed earlier than the Maccabean revolt and did refer to a smaller or imaginary civil conflict, the present point about rejection of sectarian violence would remain.

104. John J. Collins suggested that the reference to the children who take up arms in Jub. 23:16 "is ambivalent at best, and may be read as disapproving" ("Pseudepigraphy and Group Formation in Second Temple Judaism," in *Pseudepigraphic Perspectives: The Apocrypha and Pseudepigrapha in Light of the Dead Sea Scrolls* [ed. Esther G. Chazon, Avital Pinnick, and Michael E. Stone; STDJ 31; Leiden: Brill, 1999], 53).

105. Collins (ibid.) also notes that 23:26 need not refer to a specific group within Israel nor be identified with the militant group in 23:16. This should be taken as a correction to a conflation in an earlier work: "the 'children' who begin to study the laws and rise up and drive out their adversaries can be plausibly identified with the Hasidim or a wing of that party" (*Apocalyptic Imagination*, 83). To be precise, God drives out the enemies, after God drove them in as a result of the "children" rising up. The children who study in 23:26 do not drive out enemies.

106. One might argue that verse 26 describes a reform of the same basic party, but even if that is the case, it is more a reconstitution than a reform. Presumably the pietistic militants considered themselves faithful to the law. If Jubilees were referring to the same group, it would be denying any legitimacy, not only to their militancy, but to their former adherence to scripture by saying, "They will *begin* to study the laws, seek out the commands and return to the right way."

107. If one wished to speak exhaustively about "children" in the sequence, one would also consider 23:18, which explicitly blames the children of men (ው·ሕ·ጹ ፡ ሰብእ, presumably בני אדם) for the plague, and 23:25, which describes the curse of the children (ደቂቅ). These points illustrate further that "children" is not a technical term for a particular group.

Remarkably, Jubilees does not single out any groups within Israel for special punishment or reward. In as much as there is a tension between collective guilt and punishment versus individual guilt and punishment, Jub. 23 favors the side of collective guilt and punishment. Although one might get the sense that the Jews who die fighting each other deserve what they get (23:20), vindictiveness is lacking in the war account, and especially the punishment and restoration accounts. The initial phase of punishment comes as a famine, with the emphasis that all, not only the militants on both sides, suffer (23:18). The "great punishment from the Lord" applies to everyone (23:22). Even more explicitly, the armies God sends to punish Israel will "show partiality to no one." What is truly remarkable, however, is the lack of judgment or vindictiveness in the eschatological restoration. The "enemies" who are expelled in 23:30 are best understood as the foreign armies who had been sent in as punishment. The eschatological hope for foreigners is not vindictive punishment, submission, or incorporation but simply "go home."[108] The restoration restores the national boundaries laid out with care in Jub. 9. While Israel enjoys its covenantal blessings, the other nations continue to experience the "curses" of normal life specified earlier in the chapter. Jubilees does not dwell on vengeance against foreigners, much less a group within Israel.

Likewise, on the other side, those who began the trend of studying the laws are not mentioned again for special reward. The reversal of the pattern in life span applies to everyone (23:27), as did the decrease. There is a mild discussion of things being made right for righteous individuals, but two observations are essential. First, neither God's "servants" nor "the righteous" are a group; they do not refer back to any group or actions previously discussed. They are a class of individuals described by an attribute. The idea that God rewards righteous individuals is hardly sectarian polemic. Second, even if one takes 23:30 as a form of resurrection, which is not necessary,[109] the resurrected are only awakened long enough to see that everything turned out alright. Then they return to resting in

---

108. This is true of the eschatological framework in Jub. 23. In other contexts one does find the idea of other nations serving Israel (Jub. 22:11; 38:14).

109. It is not explicit that that those who rise had been dead. The verb "to rise" could refer to any improvement in situation. The preceding verb, "to heal," may suggest reversal of death but could be any suffering. The general emphasis of the context is not the replacement of death with eternal life but the replacement of violent and unnatural death with peaceful death in very old age.

peace (23:31). We should not insist on binary positions on the afterlife in second century B.C.E. Jewish thought. Sirach attests the idea of a good or bad death, but not an afterlife per se.[110] Jubilees does not say much more than that those who suffered a bad death unjustly will be set right so they can rest in peace. Certainly no one is becoming a luminary or enjoying eternal, unimaginable bliss. Finally, the "kindness" in 23:31 is not limited to an elite organization but shown to "hundreds and thousands and to all who love God." The eschatological punishments and rewards, such as they may be, are not the vindication of a separatist group but the restoration of an idealized past. The category "Israel" continues to be the only meaningful category for the classification of humanity, and its separation, intended from creation, finally becomes realized in the expulsion of foreigners and restoration of boundaries. *Contra* Testuz, Collins has noted that Jubilees lacks a group designation such as "chosen righteous."[111] The evidence permits a further conclusion that Jubilees not only lacks but rejects a group designation within Israel, other than the traditional priestly categories.

This subsection has shown some significant differences between Jubilees and contemporary apocalypses. Even if the issue of human classification is not necessarily implied by the use of the genre "apocalypse," and even if the apocalypses do not form a coherent cluster of views on the status of other nations in the future restoration, some major contrasts are evident. Contemporary apocalypses consistently qualify or reject the significance of the category "Israel." Often enough, the category dissolves, and foreign nations are incorporated in some way. Jubilees rejects this possibility. The apocalypses are more consistent on the elevation of a new group within Israel, particularly in eschatological contexts. The eschatological hope for the author of Jubilees is not that the author or author's group would rule over Israel or be singled out for salvation but that they would provide the model by which the entire nation would be restored and united. Even though there is not consistency in the apocalypses on the issue of human classification, they do cluster together in a basic perspective. Jubilees addresses the issues but does not share the perspective.[112]

---

110. Sir 1:12–13 (10–11); 11:26–28; 30:4–6; 41:1–13.
111. Collins, *Apocalyptic Imagination*, 74.
112. A more thorough study would also consider the Testament of Moses, although it is not an apocalypse and not uniformly contemporary. There may be interesting affinities with Jubilees in the idea that membership among the Jewish people

2.2.2. Violence

In the previous section we saw samples of how views of group definition can extend to violence and how Jub. 23 opposes the Jewish civil war. When we focus on the issue of violence in this section we find a number of moderating factors on both sides. Yet it remains the case that the apocalypses, with all their diversity, stand together on some form of an endorsement of violence. Jubilees, in contrast, frequently reflects a principled aversion to violence, especially violence between Jews. Three major moderating factors and two methodological caveats should be considered from the outset.

First, we can say empirically that violence is typically addressed in contemporary apocalypses, but it is not part of the definition of the literary genre. Many sources that do not use the genre "apocalypse" also develop divine violence, human violence, or divine violence through human agency.[113] Nevertheless, it is not a coincidence that the apocalypses bring a twist to the relationship between human and cosmic violence. One might argue this from social psychology if one develops the idea that "apocalypse" is the genre of choice for the marginalized and alienated. One could also argue that the spatial axis imposes a cosmic significance to human action, even when all obvious factors suggest insignificance and the chain of cause and effect cannot be seen from a human perspective. Thus, the genre amplifies the significance of individual human action beyond the scope of mundane reality. Typically, the apocalypses amplify human violence and facilitation of violence to cosmic proportions. Jubilees, in contrast, amplifies the significance of nonmilitant religious observance.[114]

Second, we should be clear that the apocalypses offer vastly different interpretations of *how* the call to violence plays out. The Animal Apoca-

---

and observance of the law are decisive and that righteousness and disobedience are personal attributes, not group ones.

113. See, for example, 2 Kgs 6:16–17. Again, Third Isaiah is especially interesting because, though not an apocalypse, several ideas relate to apocalypses that come later (Hanson, *The Dawn of Apocalyptic*). Isa 63:3 and 66:16 provide influential, graphic descriptions of God's feet, fire, and sword spilling much blood. Other passages, such as Isa 57:12–13, more clearly direct those violent hopes against other Jews.

114. Although one can rightly speak of "determinism" in some apocalypses, it should not be overstated as to diminish the function of legitimizing a call to action. That which is determined highlights by elimination that which remains to be determined.

lypse expresses a relatively practical hope of human armies inspiring an angel and God to join the battle. The hope Daniel articulates is less practical (or more realistic, depending on how one looks at it) in that the decision to stand up to evil will not be efficacious in the short term. Daniel emphasizes the efficaciousness of nonhuman intervention. One should not, however, miss the endorsement of violence in Daniel or the eschatological hope of those who die in battle. Even Daniel, and certainly other apocalypses, include violence in their earthly call to action and supernatural hopes.

Third, we should not portray Jubilees as a predecessor to Gandhi in principled opposition to all forms of violence. Jubilees assesses positively the biblical wars of the patriarchs, even where the Pentateuch left ambiguity. Also, in the judgments of individual nations, which differ from the eschatological scenario of Jub. 23, Jubilees extends the idea of violent destruction of Sodom and Gomorrah to the destruction of other nations (past or future). However, one should not be quick to assume that Jubilees presents the wars of the patriarchs as models to be replicated or God as judging nations through the armies of Israel.

Finally, two lesser issues should be noted. First, the critical reader needs to look past the double standard of "violence is always righteous when I do it and always wicked when others do it." We are not comparing the views of the violence of other nations (although it is interesting that Jubilees portrays foreign armies as divine punishment). Nor should we focus only on interpretation of particular historical events. As much as is possible, we should investigate the views of violence in principle. Second, it is certainly true that Jubilees writes from a different historical perspective on the Jewish civil war. We need not deny that historical retrospect partly explains the more critical view of Jubilees and the more optimistic view of the Animal Apocalypse, nor need we compare Jubilees to less critical retrospectives (1–2 Maccabees). The point here is *that* Jubilees differs in its evaluation of violence, not *why* Jubilees differs.

We will begin the discussion with the contemporary readings of earlier apocalypses, then consider the contemporary apocalypses. We will consider Daniel carefully, noting how it differs from Enochic apocalypses but emphasizing the remaining positive value of violence. Finally, we will consider how violence can continue to be justified in Jubilees but becomes qualified within a framework that is critical of violence.

2.2.2.1. The Enochic Apocalypses

The earliest apocalypses differ in that they were apparently written at a time when the perceived conflicts were relatively bloodless, or at least less immediate. We do not find specific evaluation of the Jewish civil war, but we do find a positive assessment of violence. The most obvious assessment of violence in these works set before the flood comes out in the explanation of the flood. Any account of a universal flood, including the Genesis account, is necessarily violent, but the Genesis account is notoriously vague on causality. The early Enochic works "justify" the flood as vengeance against sinners. Thus, although the Astronomical Book does not dwell on the matter, we read, "the apostate will drown with the apostate" (81:8). The interest in the flood came to be the idea that the past obliteration of sinners was a model for a forthcoming obliteration. Thus, the violent judgment is typologically past but eschatologically future. It is true that Enoch and Noah do not appear as warriors,[115] but the early Enoch apocalypses do lend themselves to a homologous interpretation of angelic and human violence. If the past angelic vengeance did not *require* human participation in the imminent fulfillment of the type (*imitatio angelorum*), it certainly did not prohibit it, as evident in apocalypses that build on the early traditions with specific calls to human violence.

The apocalypses closer to the time of Jubilees dispel any doubt as to whether God commissions humans to take vengeance on humans, just as God commissions angels to take vengeance on angels. The heroes of the Animal Apocalypse can be identified as a historical army, and in 90:19 that army will be given a big sword to go out and kill "all the wild beasts" (including other Jews, the wild sheep of 90:16).[116] Similarly, in the Apocalypse of Weeks a sword is given to the righteous to execute judgment on the wicked and pillage (91:12–13). If the rest of the Epistle is later, it is all the more striking that its graphic images of violence may have developed outside the

---

115. Enoch reprimands regarding vengeance that will come but does not execute judgment himself (1 En. 13:8). A positive assessment of vengeance is clear even when the role of humans in the typology is unclear.

116. This applies to the Animal Apocalypse as we have it, not the version that may have existed prior to a pro-Maccabean revision. The latest study to isolate references to the Maccabean crisis from the rest of the work is Daniel Assefa, *L'Apocalypse des animaux (1 Hen 85–90): Une propagande militaire? Approches narrative, historico-critique, perspectives théologiques* (JSJSup 120; Leiden: Brill, 2007).

context of reaction to wartime events. For example, the Epistle of Enoch 98:12 reads,

> Now be it known to you that you will be delivered into the hands of the righteous, and they will cut off your necks, and they will kill you and not spare you. (1 En. 98:12, Nickelsburg's translation)

Human agency has come a long way. One might find a sadistic tinge in the punishment in 95:3 and 96:1, "as you desire." We have at least two contemporary apocalypses and a roughly contemporary apocalypse that establish the extreme of historical and anticipated human violence against other humans, including Jews.

2.2.2.2. The Danielic Apocalypses

If one were comparing only Daniel and the Enochic apocalypses, one would rightly find significant differences to emphasize. When one adds Jubilees to the consideration, however, one finds at the level of ideas about violence that Daniel and the Enochic apocalypses stand together in ways that Jubilees stands apart. The crux of the prescribed human action is Dan 11:32–35, but first some other tendencies in the compilation should be considered. A form of the phrase "not by human hand" appears in Dan 2:34, 45 and 8:25 (cf. 11:45). Similarly, Dan 7:11 implies no human action in the slaying of the beast (even the human-like figure appears only after the beast is slain). In the final apocalypse the human action prescribed in 11:32–35 does not bring about immediate victory in earthly terms. Consistently in Daniel, the cosmic feats are left to cosmic forces. Daniel has no illusions that the Maccabean soldiers, even with their angelophanies, will bring about the desired victory.

In terms of practical expectations, Daniel departs from the pro-Maccabean texts. At the more abstract level of ideas, however, we do not find a categorical rejection of empire, violence, or armed human action.[117] In

---

117. There is a rejection of a bad kind of empire and violence, but in Daniel the opposite of a wicked kingdom is not the absence of domination, but domination by holy ones, replete with violent vindication. Many scholars would describe Daniel as nonviolent, pacifist, or quietist. See, most recently, Portier-Young, *Apocalypse against Empire*, 223–79. The following addresses the difficult question of whether the enlightened ones encouraged violence among the commoners "who know their God." There

Dan 2 the means to restoring the kingdom of Israel is supernatural, but it is still a violent kingdom that will shatter all other kingdoms (2:44). Similarly, Dan 7 looks to transfer, not abolish, dominion and empire. Indestructible is not the same as peaceful. Even with the emphasis on supernatural agency and angelic representation of the nation of Israel, Dan 7 does not anticipate a day when humans cease to lord over others. The *means* shift to supernatural intervention, but the anticipated end is basically victory in terms of earthly empire, not a utopian vision of peace and universal direct governance by God.

Before coming to the crux of normative human response in Dan 11:32–35, we should mention Dan 11:14.

וּבָעִתִּים הָהֵם רַבִּים יַעַמְדוּ עַל־מֶלֶךְ הַנֶּגֶב וּבְנֵי ׀ פָּרִיצֵי עַמְּךָ יִנַּשְּׂאוּ לְהַעֲמִיד חָזוֹן וְנִכְשָׁלוּ׃

> In those times many will rise against the king of the south, and the violent ones of your people will raise themselves to fulfill the vision, but they will stumble. (Dan 11:14, Collins's translation)

Whether the anti-Ptolemaic group was pro-Seleucid or pro-independence, we find a negative evaluation both in the language used to describe them (בני פריצי עמך) and in their efficaciousness (נכשלו). Although visions were given military significance at other times (e.g., 1 En. 90:14; 2 Macc 3:25; 11:8), we cannot specifically identify this group.[118] This is a negative assessment of a militant uprising, but it is not the last word on human resistance.

Between the review of past history and the anticipation of future events, Dan 11 offers only a few verses of explicit guidance on what humans should do in the present. We should distinguish "the people who know their God" (עַם יֹדְעֵי אֱלֹהָיו) from "the enlightened among the people" (מַשְׂכִּילֵי עָם).[119] They are obviously on the same side, but they have different descriptions, functions, and fates. The latter are a subcat-

---

is a good case that they did not reject violent resistance, even if they did contextualize it in a larger view of God's plan. Giving meaning to defeat in battle is not the same as rejecting battle. Disagreement about this difficult point, however, should not distract from the clearer and more fundamental point that Daniel is replete with literary violence throughout the imagined hopes for future vindication.

118. See Collins, *Daniel: A Commentary*, 380.
119. For a different view, see Collins, *Apocalyptic Imagination*, 111.

egory of the former. All the knowledgeable resist, but only one role in the resistance is teaching (we shall return to whether fighting is also a legitimate role in the resistance). First, the term המשכילים is stronger than היודעים, suggesting a more elite subgroup. Second, the actions are different. We should not imagine that only wisdom teachers knew their God and "stood up." It makes more sense if a broader class stood up to resist in a variety of ways, and only a subclass was devoted to teaching. Third, the fate of the general class and subclass are treated differently, both here and in 12:2–3. It is true that the verb "fall" is used for both, but 11:35 is redundant if we flatten any distinction of subclass. The other verbs are distinct. In 12:2–3 the רבים are simply resurrected, but the משכילים are elevated to become luminaries.

To summarize, the general category of those on the correct side is called "the people who know their God" and "the multitude." They stand firm and take action (יַחֲזִקוּ וְעָשׂוּ) and receive proper instruction. They suffer sword, flame, captivity, and plunder and receive little help from some insincere ones. Afterward they will rise to everlasting life. The more specific subcategory among those on the right side refers to those who are devoted to teaching wisdom (theologians for the cause, if you will). They are mostly called משכילים and described as מַצְדִּיקֵי הָרַבִּים in 12:3. They will teach the multitude, and like the multitude some of them fall, but for them it serves a different function: to refine, purify, and whiten them. Afterward they become like stars forever.

Now we consider the likelihood that fighting was part of the prescribed resistance.[120] The verbs חזק and עשה may not specify military action, but they do not preclude it, and the fate of this resistance movement suggests that they had been doing more than praying in their attics. Daniel 6:10 and 2 Maccabees may portray the least confrontational forms of piety as magnets for wicked persecutors, but other sources and historical probability suggest that martyrdom came first to the soldiers. Thus, while the martyrs of 1 Macc 2 were killed while they refused to fight on the Sabbath, it is most likely that they were being chased in the desert because of their eagerness

---

120. Gordon Zerbe refutes the claims that the enlightened ones rejected military action outright but still holds that they may have followed a path of passive resistance themselves. See his " 'Pacifism' and 'Passive Resistance' in Apocalyptic Writings: A Critical Evaluation," in *The Pseudepigrapha and Early Biblical Interpretation* (ed. James H. Charlesworth and Craig A. Evans; Studies in Scripture in Early Judaism and Christianity 2; Sheffield: JSOT Press, 1993), 66–75.

to fight on the other six days.[121] Only if a group is organized for a purpose can it be defeated, helped, or joined (11:34). Military struggle is the most likely of the possibilities. Although there is not as much clarity as we might like on the action taken by the masses, the more important point is the basic claim that violence is salvific. Violence is not efficacious in military terms, but it is not a vain or sinful effort either (as it is in Jubilees). Enduring violence is salvific, and it at least seems likely that violent resistance was advocated, even if the only expectation was to prove fidelity and draw martyrdom.[122]

We should not assume that the group that produced Dan 10–12 is described in 1–2 Maccabees or any other text. Daniel does not take a high view of Judah Maccabee, and certainly not of Antiochus Epiphanes, but this does not reduce the possibilities to quietism. The apocalypse was not composed with a sword in the hand, but the balance of evidence suggests that the group of wisdom teachers with which the author identified taught and supported armed resistance. Although they did not expect military resistance to be efficacious in a practical and immediate sense prior to divine intervention at the appointed time, and they reserved the highest reward for themselves, they did promise the fallen fighters everlasting life (Dan 12:2). Even in a cosmic crisis, the decision of the individual still matters, not because one can determine history but because one can determine one's own eternal life. Despite the many differences from the Animal Apocalypse, at the level of ideas Daniel shares a favorable view of cosmic violence and promotes human participation therein.

2.2.2.3. Jubilees

In subtle ways Jubilees reflects a critical view of violence. Jubilees is not written for the purpose of critiquing violence in principle, and other factors, such as justification of the patriarchs, easily trump the skepticism toward the efficacy of violence. Yet one finds various comments throughout Jubilees that suggest a perspective opposed to violence. Again, one

---

121. Similarly, Victor Tcherikover, *Hellenistic Civilization and the Jews* (Philadelphia: Jewish Publication Society of America, 1959), 198.

122. H. H. Rowley (*The Relevance of Apocalyptic*, 21, 108) also makes a distinction between supporting the Maccabees and expecting them to succeed by military might. He claims that Daniel supports the Maccabees while emphasizing that victory will come from God.

finds the perspective reflected most truly in the eschatological hopes. Jubilees 23 includes violence in the sin and punishment phase, but the repentance and restoration phases are marked by the absence of violent resistance, conquest, or vindication by any agents. First we will look at some of the positive portrayals of violence that must moderate any conclusions, and then we will look at the critical passages and evaluate the relationship between the competing interests. The data can be understood as reflecting a deep skepticism toward the efficacy of violence, within which isolated instances of violence may be necessary as a last resort.

Jubilees is not a statement of the author's personal philosophy. The author is constrained by received scripture, theological and exegetical principles, and historical context. The distinctive set of ideas comes out in how the author navigates these constraints. To be sure, normative violence appears in Genesis, and even ambiguous violence at the hands of patriarchs becomes normative in Jubilees. Thus, not only do we see Abraham fighting against Chedorlaomer (Jub. 13:25), but we find Jacob's reservations in the Pentateuch about the slaughter of Shechem resolved as emphatically justified in heaven (30:23). There is no downplaying the fact that the interests in Jubilees in justifying biblical heroes, elevating Levi in particular, and condemning exogamy take precedence over any skepticism about the efficaciousness of armed aggression. In this context we read the most favorable portrayal of violence in Jubilees:

> It [the slaughter of Shechem] was a just act for them [Levi and Simeon] and was recorded as a just act for them. Levi's descendants were chosen for the priesthood and as levites to serve before the Lord as we (do) for all time. Levi and his sons will be blessed forever because he was eager to carry out justice, punishment, and revenge on all who rise against Israel. (Jub. 30:17–18)

Jubilees identifies the issue and the outcome with Num 25, where Phinehas acts violently against exogamy[123] and receives a blessing for it. Even for a Jewish author not aligned with priestly interests, the justification of Phinehas was not in question. Jubilees' endorsement of Phinehas is hardly, however, an endorsement of any historical figure who invoked Phinehas

---

123. Jub. 30:7–16 emphasizes that the problem that Levi addressed was exogamy, not the rape of twelve-year-old girls.

to justify killing other Jews (1 Macc 2:26, 54).[124] The author neither denied nor avoided the positive evaluation of biblical violence. Jubilees is not a radical and principled rejection of all violence, yet we will see how Jubilees works the nonnegotiable instances of just violence into a basic framework that is critical of violent approaches.

The other set of moderating data is the judgment of nations. The next chapter will show that Jubilees does not follow other apocalypses in the view that all the nations and the cosmos are to be judged at once. Every nation faces judgment, but judgment happens in historical, not eschatological, time. It is important to distinguish eschatological violence from historical violence when studying the core attitude, but historical violence is violence nonetheless. In some cases it is questionable whether Jubilees is venting violent hatred against a nation or explaining how it happened that a biblical enemy of Israel has ceased to exist by the second century B.C.E. (e.g., the Amorites in Jub. 29:11). Jubilees 24 involves complicated issues of the texts and interpretation of Genesis, other received writings on the Philistines, and contemporary attitudes and events, but the bottom line is clear. The Philistines were to be eradicated. Whether past (Babel, Sodom and Gomorrah, Amorites), contemporary (apparently the Philistines), or future, Jubilees is not reluctant to imagine that whole nations would be eradicated for their ancestral and collective sins. This is not a vision of universal peace and tolerance,[125] but it is not military propaganda either. Jubilees does not challenge traditional national enmity, but the agents for the judgment of nations are God and other nations.[126]

---

124. The violence of Levi and Phinehas is normative but not prescriptive. Any individual Jew who carries out revenge could not expect to be blessed with an eternal priesthood, at least as far as Jubilees is concerned. This is not to suggest that Jubilees directly engages arguments for the Hasmonean priesthood, only that it gives no indications of supporting that kind of argument. Modern readers should be careful not to mistake, based on later developments, an interpretation of Genesis and Numbers for political propaganda.

125. Even making peace takes the form of imposing tribute in 34:9 and 38:12.

126. Only in Jub. 24:29 would one have to consider seriously the possibility that Jubilees endorses a Jewish army eradicating a population. This likely reflects a historical reality that some Jewish forces made war on some traditionally Philistine cities, and Jubilees is certainly not sorry about that (see Charles, *Jubilees*, 154–55). Yet it remains striking that this brief allusion appears in the context of a lengthy emphasis on a much larger program for the judgment of the Philistines. The passage emphasizes the ancestral curse recorded on the heavenly tablets, the majority action of the Greeks

The justification of biblical wars and the expectation that the enemies of Israel did or would share the fate of Sodom and Gomorrah moderate the extent to which we can speak of a nonviolent perspective in Jubilees. Relative to its day and relative to other apocalypses, however, a number of contrasts on the level of ideas are striking. Jubilees accepts the occasional necessity of war and violent justice but leans in the direction of skepticism toward the efficacy of violence. First, but least, we will consider two negative comments on the etiology of warfare. Second, we will consider the prohibition of fighting on the Sabbath, which amounts to a prohibition of joining an army in the first place. Third, we will consider the frequent discussions that reflect a concern with and opposition to fraternal strife. Finally, we shall return to Jub. 23, which condemns the Jewish civil war and imagines a restoration without violent retribution by anyone against anyone.

The first point can bear little weight in light of the frequent tendency to condemn the warfare of others while celebrating one's own. Nevertheless, it is worth mentioning that in two places Jubilees identifies the origin and nature of warfare as demonic. In Jub. 11:2–5 demons inspire idolaters to shed blood, and in 5:9 the first civil war occurs between the giants. Obviously the defensive actions of the patriarchs are not demonic. Even if demons drive idolaters to initiate wars, the patriarchs are justified in fighting back. Even for its day it is not a strong position to say that wicked ones start wars and righteous people defend themselves. It does, however, fit a tendency to view war as no more than a necessary evil.

Second, and more significantly, the legal ruling in Jubilees prohibiting fighting on the Sabbath amounts to a prohibition of joining an army in the first place, at least when the enemy does not share the principle. Very early in the revolt, religious militants realized that fighting on six days and resting on the Sabbath was not a viable option. After the events described in 1 Macc 2, it became clear that soldiers had to be prepared either to fight on the Sabbath or face martyrdom. Jubilees does not develop the idea of martyrdom (or related ideas of vicarious suffering or innocent blood forcing God to act), resurrection, or an afterlife other than resting in peace. We may therefore conclude that Jubilees was promoting a third option: do not be a soldier. Common sense and 1 Macc 2 establish that a soldier

---

and Antiochus in particular (to explain the singular nouns in Jub. 24:28), and the more supernatural eternal curse described in the poetic section.

who refuses to fight on the Sabbath will die, and Jub. 50:13 establishes that a soldier who does fight on the Sabbath will die. The ruling amounts to a prohibition against being a militant.[127]

The third point is striking not so much in content as in the number of occasions on which it is emphasized. Jubilees, writing in the wake of a civil war, repeatedly condemns fraternal strife and praises fraternal harmony, both within Israel and with Ishmael and Esau. Besides the more general cases (Cain and Abel, the self-destructive war of the giants), in Jub. 20:2 Abraham proposes alliance and unity not only between the descendants of Isaac and Ishmael but also all the sons of Keturah. In 42:25 Joseph tests for "peaceful thoughts" between his brothers, and in 46:1–2 Israelite unity is equated with prosperity and lack of satans or evil ones. The relationship between Jacob and Esau is naturally much more complicated, but Jubilees continually emphasizes the ideal of fraternal harmony.[128] The ideal of brotherly love between Jacob and Esau is emphasized in 35:20; 36:4, 11, and so forth. The subsequent chapters develop, as literature does, the tensions and drama in such a tenuous relationship across a number of conflicting characters. The resolution reveals the perspective of the author of Jubilees. Despite his ups and downs, Esau himself comes off relatively well. The blame for the history of tension shifts to his sons, which creates an opening for the later descendants to return to their original roots of reconciling with Israel. Jacob finally recognizes the necessity of self-defense, even against his brother, but regrets the situation and commands mercy:

> They sent to their father (to ask) whether they should make peace with them or kill them. Jacob sent word to his sons to make peace. (Jub. 38:11–12)

---

127. One might also consider the ruling against bloodshed in Jub. 6:8. One might argue that here Jubilees is simply following Gen 9:6, but just because Genesis said it does not mean the author of Jubilees did not believe it. One might also argue that shedding blood refers to murder but not war, but shedding blood on the earth does refer to war in Jub. 23:20.

128. Doron Mendels attempted to explain these chapters in terms of the political situation at the time of composition. His basic observation that Jubilees promotes the idea of alliance is correct. However, he underestimates the extent to which Jubilees is concerned with the issues in Genesis rather than particular current events. See *The Land of Israel as a Political Concept in Hasmonean Literature: Recourse to History in Second Century B.C. Claims to the Holy Land* (TSAJ 15; Tübingen: Mohr Siebeck, 1987), 57–88.

Peace takes the form of tribute. Perhaps the constraint of contemporary circumstance appears again. On the literary level, Jubilees promotes the ideal of fraternal harmony between the descendants of Jacob and Esau. In light of the tensions and conflicts known to have existed in the second century, the moderate (but not absolute) conciliatory tone of Jubilees is all the more striking.

Finally, we return to Jub. 23 from the perspective of attitudes toward violence. As will be discussed further in chapter 5, Jub. 23 condones none of the factions fighting in the civil war. Closely related is the fact that Jubilees views the "shedding of much blood" not as a glorious thing but as an inherently wicked thing that arouses punishment from God. Fighting, regardless of intentions, is neither righteous nor efficacious:

> They will stand up with swords and warfare in order to bring them back to the way; but they will not be brought back until[129] much blood is shed on the earth by each group. (Jub. 23:20)

The closest Jub. 23 comes to a positive view of violence (but still not very positive) is the foreign nations who invade Israel, since they are at least doing the will of God (23:22). The point is not that those who are fighting are sinful; the point is that fighting is sinful. Nothing good comes from any of the fighting. The only human agents of salvation are those who repent and study the laws. This virtue does not lead them to military victory. Even God, who takes on the entire remaining agency in the restoration, does not judge or punish anyone. Presumably the surviving warriors will repent and join those who have already repented and begun to study the laws properly. The closest thing to retribution is that God expels the enemies, but without violence. God had sent the nations in as punishment; now God is simply sending them home after the repentance. Separation from the nations is absolutely essential to the eschatological hope of Jubilees, but vengeance is not. Other passages discuss the judgment of individual nations, and some of them may have eschatological twists, but the core description of the eschatological restoration is completely nonviolent. The same is true of the other eschatological notes: Jub. 1:22–25; 50:5; and 19:25.

---

129. In context it is clear that "until" (እስከ) does not mean that they will eventually succeed in bringing anyone back to the right way even after much blood is shed.

Jubilees is not radically nonviolent when faced with other constraints. The eschatological hopes reveal the priorities of the author when least constrained. We need not argue that the author made a deliberate attempt to promote a systematic theology of just war; we simply observe that, when left to imagine an ideal future, vengeance did not make the author's list of priorities. The author promotes peace within Israel and as much as possible with the descendants of Esau and Ishmael. In principle, self-defense can be necessary, but violent activism is neither salvific nor permissible if it conflicts with the Sabbath. Judgment is a function of God, not Israel, and even then it is not always as violent as one would expect from an apocalypse. Apocalypses say different things about violence, but they typically portray violent vindication favorably, especially in the eschatological hopes. It is precisely in chapter 23 that Jubilees especially uses the genre "apocalypse," especially critiques violence as the means for humans to bring about blessing, and especially describes a nonviolent vision of the future.

An apocalypse, by definition, offers a broad view of the cosmos, a perspective that can be seen only with recourse to special revelation. Apocalypses always include cosmic agents, such as angels and demons, or their domains. The broad perspective often includes a broad view of humanity with an implicit interpretation of its divisions. Sometimes the orders of humanity and the orders of cosmic forces blur together.

Typically in apocalypses, the cosmic and global forces impose on an expectation of the way things should be between an all-good God and a good group of people. Cosmic forces can be of mixed quality, but the significance is seen as major, and the net significance in the present is seen as negative. The agents of the cosmos are in conflict, and the orders of humanity are subject to revision and reversal. Those to whom the nature of the conflict is revealed become involved in the conflict.

In Jubilees, nothing can impose itself between Israel and God. Israel can sin by dividing against itself or intermarrying with other nations, and God can use nations to punish Israel. Yet the covenantal relationship, like the cosmos itself, remains under tight control. Angels and demons exist but have no direct significance for Israel. Other nations exist but have no wisdom that the descendants of Levi do not have and have no power over Israel except as tools of divine punishment. The only significant agents are God and Israel. The role of Israel is to study and obey the covenant. Even before Jacob was born, even before the world was created, the order of the cosmos was established the way it will always be. Jubilees offers its own broad perspective of a cosmos tightly ordered around the eternal covenant between God and Israel. Jubilees uses the literary genre of the apocalypses to subvert the typical apocalyptic ideas.

3
The Temporal Axis

Just as apocalypses describe the agents of the cosmic drama from a broad perspective, apocalypses also describe the content or meaning of history from a broad perspective. Apocalypses situate the reader in a view of history that is not empirically obvious and offer some expectation of the future, either directly or by extrapolation from precedent and pattern. Jubilees also provides a view of history that encompasses its beginning, its structure, its turning point, and its goal. We shall see that Jubilees fits the definition of the literary genre "apocalypse" in revealing a transcendent view of the temporal axis and conveys ideas about eschatology (except in the narrowest sense of absolutely final cosmic catastrophe). When one examines what Jubilees says about the meaning of history and eschatology in particular, one finds that Jubilees consistently adapts and frequently inverts the ideas typically conveyed by contemporary apocalypses.

Early apocalypses typically view history in exponential deterioration and expect a radical reversal with radical reward and punishment. Jubilees 23, which most directly follows the format of the historical apocalypse, evokes images of radical eschatology but in a framework of gradual decline and restoration. Jubilees applies a pattern of sin, punishment, repentance, and restoration to the broadest possible view of history. Although the situation should not be reduced to apocalyptic versus Deuteronomistic theology, the pattern of apocalyptic eschatology might be better described as sin (of others), suffering (of selves), punishment (of others), and glorification (of selves). Both Jubilees and contemporary apocalypses deal with issues of sin and punishment of Israel and the nations but place punishment differently in the scheme of history. In Jub. 23 Israel is punished by God according to the covenantal curses, leading to repentance and permanent restoration. Other chapters discuss the judgment of other nations, but those passages should not be simply inserted into the eschatological sequence of chapter 23 as if misplaced folios. As we shall see, the judgment of other nations is not particularly eschatological. Jubilees is an apocalypse because it deals with the larger pattern of sin and restoration in history, but not every instance of sin and punishment is eschatological.

The central issue of the temporal axis is the turning point of history. In Jubilees, the turning point is already in the past and the restoration has begun. Jubilees also differs from other apocalypses in the view of history as ordered and good from the beginning, such that it needs to be restored and fulfilled but not replaced with a new creation (or covenant, nation, geography, temple, or calendar). The four sections of this chapter will consider the decline of history, the final woes, the judgment, and the restoration. On each of these issues Jubilees is comparable in that we can easily identify passages for comparison. When we carry out the comparison, however, we find that the positions on these issues contrast significantly with the positions of other apocalypses.

3.1. The Decline of History

Apocalypses vary in the range and specific content of the transcendent view of history, but apocalypses at the time of Jubilees typically portray the present moment as a radical breakdown of the course of history. The present is neither normal nor sustainable but a recent crisis of justice that demands immediate divine intervention. A broad perspective reveals that current wickedness is either unprecedented or has precedent just before the flood. Either way, a moment of catastrophic judgment and salvation is imminent. Jubilees adopts not only the broad scope of history but also the idea of a pattern of decline. What Jubilees says about the decline of history, however, differs significantly from what apocalypses typically say. In Jubilees the decline is not exponential but gradual, with most of the change in the distant past. Jubilees normalizes the course of history and takes the urgency out of the view of the present.

3.1.1. The Enochic Apocalypses

The Book of the Watchers is a cosmic-tour apocalypse, not a historical apocalypse. This limits the extent to which one can specifically stratify the decline of history from the final woes or the restoration from the judgment. Even a cosmic-tour apocalypse considers implicitly the temporal axis. The next section on the final woes will better handle the relationship between suffering and eschatological intervention. The more salient point for this section follows from the *Urzeit* typology. The Book of the Watchers does not survey all of history, but the implication is that only twice in the history of the cosmos has the situation degraded so badly that God's forces must intervene to "reboot," as it were. Without commenting on the period in between, the Book of the Watchers indicates to the reader that the need for judgment exists in the present in a way unprecedented since the days of Noah. As if it were not clear enough in the main text, the introduction makes explicit that the revelation of Enoch's heavenly tour is not for the generation of the flood but for a distant generation (1 En. 1:2). The same implication applies to 1 En. 80, found within the Astronomical Book.

What we have found implicit in the Book of the Watchers becomes explicit in the historical apocalypses of the Apocalypse of Weeks and the Animal Apocalypse. The Apocalypse of Weeks says nothing bad about the first, third, fourth, or fifth weeks. A prototype of the final intervention is found in the second week: "in it will be the first end" (1 En. 93:4). In brief but certain terms, deceit and violence "spring up," as opposed to a culmination of sin beginning with Adam and Cain in the first week. The sixth and seventh weeks represent the fuller and later downward spiral. The decline begins in the sixth week with blindness and straying from wisdom but deteriorates considerably in the seventh week with pervasive perversity.[1] The general message, for our present purposes, is that the status quo is not normal. Most weeks have been righteous enough, but the present state of the world is utterly corrupt. Only once before has there been even a partial precedent for the present state of wickedness, and that ended with universal judgment and limited salvation. Those identified as the "perverse generation" are not the kinds of sinners the world has always endured, or even the culmination of a gradual process, but a unique and radical rise of evil. "Gradual" may be a relative term, since two "weeks" of history is still a long time, but the decline is not gradual over the whole span of history, and there is an exponential decline from blind to perverse.

The Animal Apocalypse describes the exponential decline of the postexilic period at greater length. To be sure, the postexilic period is not the only instance of injustice, but it is unique in the rate and extent of decline. Both the good and the bad of biblical history fit into the summary. The description of the period of the judges fits fairly well with the preexilic period in general: "sometimes their eyes were opened, and sometimes they

---

1. Stuckenbruck, *1 Enoch 91–108*, 58–59.

were blinded, until another sheep arose and led them and brought them all back, and their eyes were opened" (1 En. 89:41). The balance of justice is stable and relatively good. Only with the exile does the situation change drastically. The decline starts slowly before exponentially deteriorating. At first the Babylonians receive the relatively mild accusation, "they began to kill and destroy many more than they had been commanded" (1 En. 89:65). In the Persian period the problem grows to include not only the shepherds and beasts but the sheep as well: "the eyes of the sheep were blind, and they did not see, and their shepherds likewise" (1 En. 89:74). In the Hellenistic period, particularly in the second century, both the shepherds and sheep reach a profound low point. The last twelve shepherds destroy more than their predecessors (1 En. 90:17), so much more as to cause Enoch to lament this period in particular (90:3). One shepherd joins directly in attacking the righteous (90:13). Even stronger language describes the sheep at this low point of history: "they were extremely deaf, and their eyes were extremely and excessively blinded" (90:7).

The Animal Apocalypse differs from the other apocalypses in a number of particulars and, being longer, incorporates other instances of sin and punishment in the sweep of history. At the level of ideas, the view of history is the same. The apocalyptic scope of history puts the present moment in a superlative perspective. The message is that never has history seen more heinous injustice. History has shown, however, the inevitability of divine intervention to punish sinners and reward the righteous. The logical conclusion is that a proportionately radical reversal of history will occur any moment now.

Furthermore, we should consider the "narrative bridge" of 1 En. 91, not because it is necessarily contemporary with Jubilees, but because it is in fact an excellent bridge between the Animal Apocalypse and the Apocalypse of Weeks. That is, it describes succinctly the underlying set of ideas that holds together these two rather different apocalypses, and by extension the *Urzeit* typology of the Book of the Watchers, as they eventually came to be viewed as a coherent collection.

> For I know that the state of violence will grow strong on the earth,
> and a great scourge will be consummated on the earth.
>
> Indeed, all iniquity will be consummated,
> but it will be cut off from its roots,
> and its whole structure will vanish. [the flood]

> And again [in the post-exilic period], iniquity will be consummated on the earth,
> and all the deeds of iniquity and violence and sin will prevail again.
>
> And when sin and iniquity and blasphemy and violence increase in every deed,
> and perversity and sin and uncleanness increase… (1 En. 91:5–7, Nickelsburg's translation)

We have yet to consider Daniel and Jubilees in this section, but continuing with the rest of the passage will preview nicely the following sections: the final woes, the judgment and the restoration.

> … a great scourge will come from heaven upon all these,
> and the holy Lord will come forth in wrath and with a scourge,
> to execute judgment upon the earth.
>
> And in those days, violence will be cut off from its roots,
> as well as the roots of iniquity, together with deceit,
> and they will be destroyed from under heaven.
>
> And all the idols of the nations will be given up,
> and the tower(s) will be burned with fire.
>
> They will be removed from all the earth,
> and they will be thrown into the fiery judgment,
> and they will be destroyed in fierce, everlasting judgment.
>
> And the righteous will arise from his sleep,
> and wisdom will arise and be given to them. (1 En. 91:7–10, Nickelsburg's translation)

Thus we have an outline of a view of history that runs through a series of apocalypses as they came to be read together. In order to speak of an apocalyptic view of history we must also consider the apocalypses and collection of Daniel.

3.1.2. The Danielic Apocalypses and the Book of Daniel

The Danielic apocalypses, like the Enochic apocalypses, vary in framework and details but revolve around a consistent view of the exponential decline of history in the postexilic period. Perhaps the most basic difference is that the scope of history considered in the Danielic apocalypses begins with the Babylonian exile and consequently excludes diluvian protology. The view of history is nevertheless sufficiently broad to be transcendent on the temporal axis. The decline of history pervades all the apocalypses in Daniel, even Dan 8, which by itself does not follow through on the temporal axis to judgment and restoration. Furthermore, the collection of the twelve-chapter book of Daniel casts an apocalyptic light on Dan 2, a court tale that would not be considered an apocalypse by itself.[2]

The basic structure of the vision of Dan 2 relates the decline of history.[3] One could also call the decline "exponential" in that clay is significantly less valuable than the first three materials, all the more so in the unstable compound with iron (Dan 2:43). In the apocalypses the decline of history is less a matter of decreasing glory and more a matter of increasing wickedness, but the core notion of decline is the same. In Dan 7 the fourth beast is considerably worse than the first three, דְּחִילָה וְאֵימְתָנִי וְתַקִּיפָא יַתִּירָא... וְהִיא מְשַׁנְּיָה מִן־כָּל־חֵיוָתָא דִּי קָדָמַיהּ, "fearsome and terrible and exceedingly strong. ... It was different from all the other beasts that were before it" (Dan 7:7, Collins's translation). The exponential decline continues as even for this beast the tenth horn is worst of all (Dan 7:20). Likewise in Dan 8, Media and Persia are dangerous, but Alexander more so and Antiochus Epiphanes most of all. Daniel 9 offers yet another variation on the same theme. The entire postexilic period is designated for suffering, and within that period the situation degrades exponentially. Contrary to Daniel's presumption, the exilic period is the least of the problem. The return lingers seven "weeks" without construction. When construction does come, it does not resolve the problem. Distressful times only magnify in the final "weeks" as cataclysm and desolations envelop all (Dan 9:26). In Dan 10–11 the decline of history is spread over a number of details, but the nadir of history is clear in Antiochus Epiphanes, both generally and in particular statements such as, וְעָשָׂה אֲשֶׁר לֹא־עָשׂוּ אֲבֹתָיו וַאֲבוֹת אֲבֹתָיו, "he will do what his ancestors had not done" (Dan 11:24).

---

2. On the relationship of Dan 2 to the apocalypses proper, see Collins, *Apocalyptic Imagination*, 90–91.

3. Even if a historical-critical case can be made for an original reading of the four materials as four kings, rather than four kingdoms, the "kingdom" version was established by the time of Jubilees. See Collins, *Daniel: A Commentary*, 169.

The decline of history is used in different ways, and one should not imagine that we have explained the central theme of Daniel by identifying a pervasive perspective of the temporal axis. It is the case, however, that all the Danielic apocalypses attest the view of exponential decline on the temporal axis, and the twelve-chapter collection connects this theme with the court tale in chapter 2. From the Danielic and Enochic apocalypses we can be sure what the transcendent view of the temporal axis typically conveyed at the time of Jubilees: the "present" of the audience is a unique crisis, close to the bottom of a catastrophic deterioration of history. Implicitly or explicitly, a broad view of history shows that the present state of injustice is not normal or tolerable from a divine perspective.

3.1.3. Jubilees

Jubilees manipulates the transcendent view of history in decline in a subtle but profound way. At first Jubilees appears to be "apocalyptic" not only in literary genre but in part of the layer of ideas. Indeed, Jubilees uses more of what is generic about the apocalypses than purely literary elements in that it adopts not only the transcendent view of history but also the idea of decline. The key is to ask what Jubilees says about the decline of history. Again we find that Jubilees uses enough of what is generic about the apocalypses to evoke a reader expectation but inverts the core idea. The difference might be stated as briefly as radical versus gradual, but such a summary would not do justice to the significance of the implications. Apocalypses typically invoke the broad view of history to claim that the present period and present moment are radical departures from what is normal in the scope of history and tolerable in a view from heaven. The present moment becomes imperative precisely because the nadir of history, or the climax of evil, is recent and radical. Jubilees takes the edge off the apocalyptic view of history.

The barometer of the decline of history in Jub. 23 is life span. The point of departure for the Jubilees "apocalypse" is the problem of the correlation between longevity and righteousness. As will be discussed in chapter 4, Jubilees weaves together several sources even on this departure from the "rewritten" narrative of Genesis–Exodus. The point here is that Jubilees weaves together these sources specifically to establish the *gradual* nature of the decline of history. Jubilees connects the former nineteen jubilees, Abraham's four jubilees, Moses' two and a half jubilees, two jubilees from Isa 65:20, and one and a half jubilees from Ps 90:10. Whereas the decline of history in apocalypses is typically dramatic and recent, the decline of life span in Jubilees is gradual and mostly long past. The descent stretches over the entire span of history from creation to the present.[4] The first generations saw most of the decline, whereas the decline is empirically undetectable in recent generations.[5] The "apocalyptic" scope of history is as broad as possible, but the present period is an organic continuation of the process of history, not a sudden deterioration demanding radical intervention. The shape of the curve is the opposite of the exponential decline typical of apocalypses. The present generation stands not in the freefall of a catastrophic plummet but at a relatively flat point along a decline spread across history. In this way, Jubilees diffuses the urgency that is so essential to the apocalyptic view of history.

The effect of this is consistent with what we found in the previous chapter. There we found that the turn of history does not depend on agents besides Israel. Here it seems that the recent events of sin and chastisement were not determined by a pattern of history outside of human control. Contrary to what one might expect from an apocalypse, there is no indica-

---

4. James M. Scott (*On Earth as in Heaven: The Restoration of Sacred Time and Sacred Space in the Book of Jubilees* [JSJSup 91; Leiden: Brill, 2005], 106–7) obfuscated this point in order to make the data fit his hypothesis of three periods of history in Jub. 23. In fact, the gradual decline continues after Moses both in Jubilees and in received scripture. In no source does the death of Moses mark a sudden transition in life span. Joshua, for example, lives to 110 years. In Jubilees, the transition from Moses' 2.5 jubilees life span to the "normal" 1.5 jubilees life span is mediated by a 2.0 jubilees life span (Jub. 23:11). Scott is correct that Jub. 23:25 should not be taken literally to mean that restoration will not happen until after a generation in which no one lives longer than a few weeks (118–19), but even a literary image cannot be ignored. Rather, it serves to establish the point that the gradual decrease in longevity continues from Adam to the great repentance. Moses is not a turning point in longevity, just another point on the gradual decline.

Furthermore, Paul notwithstanding (Rom 8:2), it does not make sense to present the giving of the law as marking a new era of even more premature death. Scott is at pains to suggest that the diminished life span after the giving of the law results from the golden calf or covenantal disobedience. The calf is not mentioned in Jubilees, and the punishment of mortality applies to all humanity and thus could not result from Israel's disobedience of its covenant (107 n. 72, 116). See also the critique of Scott in Berner, *Jahre, Jahrwochen und Jubiläen*, 307–9.

5. The following section on the final woes will deal with the issue of infant mortality in Jub. 23:25.

tion of a determined time or auspicious dates for the events in Jub. 23.[6] The responsibility is purely human. God had predicted that Israel would sin and require chastisement before repenting, but it could have been another generation.[7] The events were foreseen by God, but the exact timing was not predetermined.

3.2. THE FINAL WOES

This section focuses on what is said about the turning point of history, which can typically be described well as "final woes."[8] It is not the case that

---

6. "Indeed, none of the [eschatological] passages in *Jubilees* offers anything resembling a timetable in any unit of measurements" (Himmelfarb, "Torah, Testimony, and Heavenly Tablets," 24). Christoph Berner makes a similar observation and argues that Jub. 23:14–31 must have been added by a redactor who was not concerned with heptadic chronology (*Jahre, Jahrwochen und Jubiläen*, 239–48).

7. The emphasis on human action remains the case even if one accepts David Lambert's argument that Jubilees does not call for repentance in the sense of turning away from sin but rather recognition of sinfulness and reliance on God's foreordained grace. See his "Did Israel Believe That Redemption Awaited Its Repentance? The Case of *Jubilees* 1," *CBQ* 68 (2006): 631–50. It is far from clear, however, that Jubilees recognizes this distinction, which becomes most clear in later sources. Even in Lambert's central passage, Jub. 1:23, the Israelites return to God *before* God circumcises their minds. Lambert's arguments for discounting repentance in the rest of the book are not convincing (Jub. 1:15; 5:17; 23:26). The case is even clearer if one considers purity. Israel is expected to reject and avoid impurity, not recognize their impurity and wait for God to purify them (20:3, 6; 21:3; 30:22; 41:26; 50:5). God may have some role, but even the Day of Atonement is described as Israelites purifying themselves (34:19).

8. To be clear, other scholars have used "final woes" and related terminology to refer more generally to bad things in an eschatological context. I am using the term more narrowly to identify a stage that mediates or bridges the decline of history (or the rise of sinfulness) and the judgment. For a discussion from the perspective of New Testament scholarship on various terms, see Brant Pitre, *Jesus, the Tribulation, and the End of the Exile: Restoration Eschatology and the Origin of the Atonement* (WUNT 2/204; Tübingen: Mohr Siebeck, 2005), 29. Pitre sometimes distinguishes "the Great Tribulation" in a sense narrower than "the tribulation" (61), but he defines them together as "the common Jewish expectation of a final time of suffering and trial that will take place at the end of the age" (29), which often includes the exilic and postexilic periods (70). See also Mark Dubis, *Messianic Woes in First Peter: Suffering and Eschatology in 1 Peter 4:12–19* (Studies in Biblical Literature 33; New York: Lang, 2002); and Dale C. Allison, *The End of the Ages Has Come: An Early Interpretation of the Passion and Resurrection of Jesus* (Philadelphia: Fortress, 1985).

apocalypses always distinguish a stage of final woes apart from the decline of history and the judgment. Sometimes the final woes are most striking not in how they are distinct from the decline of history and the judgment but how they bridge the two. Apocalypses do focus on an eschatological turning point, and that turning point is typically catastrophic (i.e., woeful). The woes are final at least in as much as they mark the last of the woes, but they also typically bring about significant permanent destruction, though not necessarily a complete end of the world. The apocalypses often place the beginning of the final woes in the reader's present, with the consummation of the woes in the future. Variation can be found in many details, most notably in whether a period of final woes can be separated in the narrative between the decline and the judgment. It is significant, however, that the apocalypses develop a stage that mediates or bridges the nadir of history and the restoration. The duration of time between the onset of the nadir of history and the final resolution can be long or short, but some intervening stage appears. Although restoration, vindication, and reward for the righteous are inevitable, the apocalypses often convey some sense that things are going to get worse before they get better.

In some cases final woes can be clearly distinguished from the decline of history and the judgment. The final woes can differ from the previous decline of history if evil escalates from a natural to a supernatural plane or from earthly to cosmic. Sometimes the pattern of evil culminates such that it overwhelms the persecutors as well as the persecuted. The final woes can blend with the judgment but can often be distinguished if the righteous must suffer or endure the final woes prior to their reward (perhaps as a period of testing) or if a formal and permanent judgment comes at a distinct later stage. The final woes are typically future or not yet fully realized.[9] There is no single coherent "final woes" motif standard to all the apocalypses. There is, however, a cluster of views of the temporal axis that imagines a catastrophic nadir of history to be followed by supernatural destruction before finally leading to restoration.

---

9. Of course, one must be careful not to equate supernatural with unrealized. Certainly angelophanies were perceived to have occurred, and natural disasters could have been interpreted as supernatural cosmic upheaval.

3.2.1. The Enochic Apocalypses

The Book of the Watchers does not explicitly distinguish an intermediate period, but one does get a clear sense that the righteous remnant is rewarded only after enduring a harsh period of violent judgment. First, a preliminary observation should be made about the "trigger" for divine intervention. The climax of evil, not repentance, triggers the divine intervention. There is no cycle of sin, punishment, repentance, and restoration; rather, the righteous and the wicked are ontologically distinct all along. Similarly, the punishment has no pedagogical function to prompt repentance. Punishment is retribution, not chastisement.

Even if the desolation of the earth by the teaching of Asael (1 En. 10:8) is classified as typological of the decline of history/rise of evil, the woes that fall between the intervention of God and the vindication of the righteous can be studied as final woes. Although the first divine command at the intervention is to instruct Noah on his self-preservation, the Book of the Watchers lends itself to the idea that things get worse before they get better when God's angels intervene. The most obvious example would be the flood itself. Even though it is primarily a judgment of the wicked, even for the righteous it is a difficulty to endure prior to the realization of the restoration. The war of the giants can also be considered in this category, in as much as violence increases before vindication comes.[10] Depending on whether one imagines Noah just barely escaping all this violence or comfortably secured all along (1 En. 10:3), the image of intermediate escalation of violence may not be so central to understanding the Book of the Watchers by itself. When grouped with other apocalypses, however, it fits a pattern that violence and destruction is expected to increase following divine intervention but prior to the vindication of the righteous.[11]

---

10. Interestingly, the war of the giants becomes something of a middle-judgment. Although it is divine judgment in as much as God initiates the war, it is not sudden and overt divine judgment. Rather, the Book of the Watchers suggests a more natural principle that the wicked will succumb to their own violence prior to overt divine judgment. This point, by itself, can also be found in Jubilees, but the meaning changes in the recontextualization. In the Book of the Watchers the giants are prototypes for latter-day tyrants, while in Jubilees they are simply examples of sinners punished. Jub. 5 is historical, not eschatological. See also 1 En. 88:2.

11. See also, in the introduction, 1 En. 1:7–8. Massive destruction often precedes the vindication of the righteous in the apocalypses.

First Enoch 80, found within the Astronomical Book, brings very different details but fits a pattern of a consummation of evil of cosmic proportions prior to the separation of the righteous and wicked for reward and punishment. Chapter 80 covers three degrees of cosmic degeneration. At the most mundane level, mis-harvest could be a direct consequence of improper calculation of seasons. Drought would not be a natural consequence of calendrical error, but it is a natural event in itself that could easily be interpreted as the result of sin. The chapter introduces final woes in a more narrow sense by predicting the impact of sin on a third level: the sky will stand still and the moon will change course and become brighter (1 En. 80:2, 4). Two observations follow. First, the particularly unnatural predictions are necessarily for the future, as such events could not have been claimed to have already occurred. Second, the deterioration of nature necessarily applies to all humans, with no escape for the righteous. This becomes explicit: "Evil will multiply against them, and punishment will come upon them to destroy all" (1 En. 80:8). Presumably the wise will benefit from a proper understanding of this cosmic catastrophe, but they are affected nonetheless. The date and development of the chapter pose problems,[12] but in general terms the chapter supports the general pattern. By the time of Jubilees, the expectation of final cosmic catastrophe in the near future came to be associated with the genre "apocalypse."

The Apocalypse of Weeks provides only a brief glimpse of a period of hardship apart from the decline of history and the judgment. The rise of the perverse generation in the seventh week is the culmination of the decline of history. Even though it is violent and implies a struggle of sorts, the slaughter of the wicked in the eighth week gives no indication of hardship for the righteous, so it would be better characterized as a stage of judgment than a final woe. Although the Apocalypse of Weeks does not emphasize the woes at the end of the seventh week, a reader can easily get the sense that the conflict between the perverse generation and the chosen will get worse before it gets better. In the seventh week the chosen receive wisdom, which certainly provides the benefit of understanding and hope for imminent vindication, but they do not receive the sword and victory until the eighth week (which is certainly future relative to the reader's present). Different texts provide different details of the conflict at the end

---

12. George W. E. Nickelsburg and James C. VanderKam, *1 Enoch 2: A Commentary on the Book of 1 Enoch, Chapters 37–82* (Hermeneia; Minneapolis: Fortress, 2011), 359–65.

THE TEMPORAL AXIS   131

of the seventh week, but in any case it is clear that the chosen must endure a period of conflict equipped with nothing but wisdom and knowledge before they will receive military victory in the eighth week.[13] The eighth week may be near but will not come until the forces of evil finish unraveling in the "present" conflict.

The Animal Apocalypse expands the historical detail of a conflict comparable to that implied, especially in the Ethiopic, at the end of the seventh week of the Apocalypse of Weeks. Before addressing the final woes, we should note a possible expansion of the proto-woes of the Book of the Watchers. In addition to the war of the giants and the flood, the Animal Apocalypse may add a meteor-like image of stones cast from heaven, if one can have any confidence in the text after reading the copious attempts at explanation and reconstruction (1 En. 88:3).[14] Even if the Animal Apocalypse does not expand the images of cosmic catastrophe of the Book of the Watchers, it at least "seconds" and builds on its account of the former judgment.

The perspective on the Maccabean revolt in the Animal Apocalypse is somewhat constrained by reality and its function as a sort of military propaganda.[15] Nevertheless, we can still identify the set of beliefs that

---

13. 4Q212 (Enoch^g) fragment 1, column 4 line 14 is read by Nickelsburg, ולהון עקרין אשי חמסא ועבד שקרא בה למעבד[דין], "and they will uproot the foundations of violence, and the structure of deceit in it, to execute [judgment]." The Ethiopic text is longer. Although one must be particularly suspect of the Ethiopic in light of the displacement of 91:11–17, the Ethiopic text does make at least as much sense. Here one finds a time of mutual destruction of bullies and blasphemers, ወእምኔሁ ፡ ይትነዘሙ ፡ አሥራወ ፡ ዐመፃ ፡ ወኃጥአን ፡ ይጥሀጕሉ ፡ በሰይፍ ፡ እምነ ፡ ጽሩፋን ፡ ይትነዘሙ ፡ በኵሉ ፡ መካን ፡ ወእለ ፡ ይሐልዩዎ ፡ ለግፍዕ ፡ ወእለ ፡ ይገብርዎ ፡ ለጽርፈት ፡ ይጥሀጕሉ ፡ በመጥ በሕት, "And then the roots of iniquity will be cut off, and sinners will perish by the sword; some of the blasphemers they will be cut off in every place; and those who plan violence and those who commit blasphemy will perish by the sword" (Nickelsburg, *1 Enoch: A Commentary*, 436; Stuckenbruck, *1 Enoch 91–108*, 128–30).

14. See especially Tiller, *Commentary on the Animal Apocalypse*, 254–55; also Nickelsburg, *1 Enoch: A Commentary*, 374–75. For lack of clear reason why the Animal Apocalypse would go beyond the Book of the Watchers where it otherwise follows so closely, it seems the image is dependent on the image of the watchers bound and cast into pits of sharp rocks and covered over (1 En. 10:5).

15. See, however, Assefa, *Une propagande militaire*. Assefa rejects the view that the Animal Apocalypse supports or is even compatible with the Maccabean revolt. He views the work as predating the revolt, except 90:13–15 (and 90:31 and 38b even later). He argues that neither the original nor the interpolation is militaristic. Rather, foreign

shapes the perspective. The reality is that neither the pietists (חסידים) nor Judah Maccabee enjoyed immediate decisive victory. The distinctive interpretation of the reality is that it is precisely in losing that the rebels guarantee their victory. By struggling for what is right but not themselves succeeding, the Maccabees provoke their angel and God to intercede on their behalf. Depending on how one interprets the doublet of 1 En. 90:13–18,[16] the author may imagine that the woes are past and the pattern of military victory has begun, or that the righteous but losing resistance must continue before decisive divine intervention establishes victory. Either way, it is not the victory of Judah Maccabee that brings about divine salvation, but the unjust suffering. If anything, the revolt brings a heightening of woes in 90:11. In verses 12 and 13 Judah Maccabee is not victorious but only struggles, endures, and cries out. When the angel does intervene, it does not mark the end but the turning point of the conflict. The struggle carries on, but the "woe" of the battles shifts from Judah Maccabee to his opponents.

We may or may not have an idea that the situation will get worse before it gets better. Although foreign angels do participate in the attack on

---

oppression should be accepted as punishment from God and met with repentance. He also sees the ultimate inclusion of all nations and the rejection of the temple as incompatible with the Maccabean revolt.

Assefa successfully illustrates different perspectives and retrospectives within the general position of opposition to Antiochus Epiphanes. In particular, the views of the temple and Gentiles certainly do differ in the Animal Apocalypse and 1 Maccabees. However, this conflict does not leave the Animal Apocalypse incompatible with military resistance in general or Judah Maccabee in particular (see also 1 Macc 2:27–43 for evidence of different theological views among those who supported military opposition). There may also be a surprising but small extent to which the sins of Israel bring on the suffering. Whatever divine commission the seventy shepherds once had, they went well beyond it. However complex the compositional history of the work may be, the work consistently praises resistance to foreign oppression.

16. Scholars differ on whether the doublet in 1 En. 90 should be read as a literary feature produced by a single author or as evidence of stages of composition. Personally, I prefer to read the doublet as a coherent literary device. According to my read, the point of the passage is to extrapolate from precedent to authorize bold claims for imminent victory. The doublet can be represented schematically as A B C A' B' C'. In a past battle (A) an angel helped us (B), resulting in a great victory (C). Now, in the next even bigger battle (A'), an even greater theophany will occur (B'), resulting in a final victory (C'). Tiller (*Commentary on the Animal Apocalypse*, 71) considers a "stylistic device" option but concludes otherwise.

Judah Maccabee (90:13) and God does strike the earth with a staff of wrath (90:18), we do not quite have an image of the righteous enduring a cosmic catastrophe. We do, however, have a theology of final woes. The outrageous suffering that the righteous endure in their struggle is not merely a feature of the decline of history before restoration takes place. Rather, endurance of the woes brings about divine vindication and restoration. The Animal Apocalypse supports Judah Maccabee by giving meaning to suffering, not by denying the fact that he was unable to protect the people from slaughter or claim substantial immediate victory.

Even if the Epistle of Enoch is not clearly contemporary with Jubilees, it is worth considering because it clarifies some distinctions that seem to be operative in other apocalypses. One should not impose on the various images in the Epistle of Enoch a rational sequence of events. One can, however, identify a spectrum of aspects of judgment ranging from relatively mundane consequences of wickedness, to a "collapse of iniquity," to havoc of nature, to a "definitive theophany"[17] and final judgment. Along this spectrum the status of the righteous ranges from victims, to caught in the fray, to protected from punishment all around, to enjoying vindication and vengeance.[18] Although there is no consistent chronology, one might find something of a sequence of aspects (rather than a mere list of synonyms) listed in 1 En. 94:9: "you have been prepared for the day of bloodshed, and the day of darkness, and the day of great judgment." To some extent the third aspect or "day" can be conceptually separated from the previous two. While the third belongs clearly to the following sections on judgment and restoration, the first two are better treated as "final woes," even if the righteous are protected from the worst of them. The definitive theophany and the vindication of the righteous are inevitable but not immediate. Each of these three days or aspects is imminent but unfulfilled,

---

17. This phrase is used by Nickelsburg, *1 Enoch: A Commentary*, 425.

18. Even if some of the suffering of the righteous described in the Epistle, 1 En. 103:9–15, belongs to the decline of history, the woes extend at least through the nadir of history. The righteous will not have to hide on the great day of judgment (1 En. 104:5), but they appear very much in need of protection as chaos and violence overtakes the earth (96:2; 100:5). The righteous are either protected like Noah or resurrected (103:4), but either way the righteous must endure until the reversal is complete. See also 1 En. 94:11–95:1.

unlike the persecution of the righteous as part of the decline of history (see especially 1 En. 103:9–15).[19]

The first aspect, the day of bloodshed, seems to include a "collapse of iniquity" such that the wicked destroy not only the righteous but themselves as well. Two passages describe such a phase of chaos and war prior to the theophany. The longer of these extends from 1 En. 99:16 to 100:6. God initiates the destruction, and the angels assist (99:16, 100:4), although their involvement is known only to the wise. This aspect is comparable to the war of the giants in the Book of the Watchers. "Iniquity collapses" (1 En. 100:6) not merely under its own weight, but with some help. The war is natural in means (sword) but exceptional in cause (divine), object (against one's own beloved), and result (blood flowing to a horse's breast). The final collapse of iniquity seems to be further described from a perspective related to women in the infant-abandoning chaos and bloodshed of 1 En. 99:4–6.

The second aspect, the day of darkness, resonates with the judgment through the forces of nature described in 1 En. 100:11–13.[20] The cosmic nature of the final woes was already found in 1 En. 80 (in the Astronomical Book) and implicit in the Book of the Watchers in that, like the flood waters already used, the cosmos contains places and storehouses of elements that can be used for judgment. In the Epistle of Enoch the elements take an active role in judgment, not only in being withheld (dew and rain) or inundating (cold, snow, and frost) but in testifying. Before God has the last word, chaos and punishment extend to the natural order. The Epistle does not develop how the righteous get through this, but it is at least clear that, unlike the wicked, they endure (1 En. 100:13). As the final judgment of the "definitive theophany" dawns, the earth is in confusion, the luminaries shake, and a "flood of fire" comes down (1 En. 102:1–3).

The bottom line in the Epistle of Enoch is that justice is absent in the present and chaos will increase before order is restored. The fundamental instruction for the righteous is, "endure." As mentioned above, the "narrative bridge" situates the final woes in a succinct summary of the basic eschatological expectation of several Enochic apocalypses (91:7; page 122 above). The notion of final woes varies in the Enochic apocalypses but revolves around the idea that a catastrophe like the flood is about to happen

---

19. Nickelsburg, *1 Enoch: A Commentary*, 425.
20. See also 1 En. 101:2.

again. The basic common view of the final woes is that the righteous must endure as wickedness consummates to overtake the wicked themselves, and chaos and destruction extend throughout the cosmos before justice will be restored. Without making reference to the flood, the apocalypses in Daniel reflect a similar underlying notion.

3.2.2. The Danielic Apocalypses

The descriptions of Antiochus Epiphanes in Dan 8 and 9 extend the idea of the decline of history to an extreme that could be classified as final woes. Antiochus Epiphanes is more than just the culmination of the decline of history in that his evil wreaks havoc on everyone, not only the righteous and holy in Israel. Daniel 9:26 might suggest that even the death of Antiochus Epiphanes would not be the end of the war and desolations: וְקִצּוֹ בַשֶּׁטֶף וְעַד קֵץ מִלְחָמָה נֶחֱרֶצֶת שֹׁמֵמוֹת, "his end will be torrential, yet desolations will be until the end of the determined war." Daniel 12 pushes further, however, to imagine an even worse period for the righteous to endure, after the death of Antiochus Epiphanes and *after* the beginning of the divine intervention.

> At that time Michael, the great prince who stands over your people, will stand up, and it will be a time of distress such that has not been from when nations came to be until that time. At that time your people will be delivered—all those found written in the book. (Dan 12:1)

Strikingly, the rise of Michael does not bring deliverance immediately, but only after even more woes. Indeed, one might well think that the woes, and particularly death, are useful or even necessary for salvation. In 11:35 death serves the function of refining, purifying, and whitening (also 12:10). Even if the undead qualify for reward in 12:3, the dead are singled out for everlasting life in 12:2. It is not the case that death is strictly required. Yet, by the time we read Dan 12:12, אַשְׁרֵי הַמְחַכֶּה וְיַגִּיעַ לְיָמִים אֶלֶף שְׁלֹשׁ מֵאוֹת שְׁלֹשִׁים וַחֲמִשָּׁה, "happy is the one who endures and comes to 1,335 days," it is clear that enduring against death is less important than enduring against apostasy. Despite significant differences, the woes in the last apocalypse of Daniel resemble the Animal Apocalypse in the assignment of a salvific function to the final woes. Daniel also joins the other apocalypses in the general view that evil will increase to the extremity of the imagination before the final reversal of woe.

3.2.3. JUBILEES

Jubilees 23 adopts the generic features of the final woes in the other apocalypses but subverts their typical meaning. Jubilees 23 evokes images of natural catastrophe, civil war, and invasion that precede an eschatological restoration. It places these predictions in an ancient setting and uses language features typical of historical apocalypses such as "in those days," "then it will be said," and so forth.[21] Arguably, Jub. 23 develops more formal aspects of the final woes than any single previous apocalypse. Inarguably, Jub. 23 evokes a reader expectation of ideas about final woes comparable to other apocalypses. The message about those final woes is dissonant with such an expectation. In Jub. 23 the final woes are not that final and not that woeful. Jubilees 23 undermines the typical meaning of the final woes through two basic means. First, the "woes" are punishments directly ordained by God and justly imposed on sinners according to the terms of the covenant in order to prompt repentance. As will be discussed further in chapter 4 on the view of revelation, Jubilees draws its "prediction" of the final woes not from new revelation but by reading the covenant curses as predictions. Second, the "woes" have already been fulfilled by the reader's present. Even compared to the covenant curses, but especially compared to the apocalypses, the woes of Jub. 23 are toned down. Rather than stretching the imagination with extreme catastrophe, Jub. 23 reduces the curses to events that have already happened in the course of history. As we shall see, the fulfillment of the covenant curses, which can be taken as prerequisites for the restoration, allows Jubilees to argue that the restoration period has already begun. Both of these points require further elaboration.

3.2.3.1. The "Final Woes" Are Just Chastisement from God as Prescribed by the Covenant

Jubilees 23 follows a familiar pattern of human sin and divine punishment following the terms and punishments of the covenant, particularly in Lev 26 and Deut 28. The sin is human sin within Israel, not a cosmic or even international evil force. The sin that "that evil generation" commits, including injustice and impurity, all comes down to covenantal infidelity.

---

21. It also gives the "final woes" in a rather long list in Jub. 23:13, which may resonate with a tendency among the apocalypses. See Stone, "Lists of Revealed Things," 414–52.

because of their abandoning the covenant that the Lord made between them and himself so that they should observe and perform all his commands, ordinances, and all his laws without deviating to the left or right. (Jub. 23:16)

The reduction of life span to one and a half jubilees can be attributed to the general wickedness of all humankind, but all the other woes appear in this covenantal framework of Jewish sin and just divine punishment.[22] In other apocalypses Jewish covenantal infidelity might appear as at most a subordinate factor (e.g., 1 En. 89:60). In other apocalypses the wicked afflict the chosen and God destroys the wicked—and the chosen may have to endure while God destroys the wicked. The other apocalypses do not, however, explain the final woes as God chastising God's people.

The pattern of inversion applies to divine punishment as well. In Enochic apocalypses the war of the giants is a form of divine punishment, but the civil war in Jub. 23 is part of the sin against God. God does not "send a sword" or in any way commission the civil war in Jub. 23:16–21. Some may claim to kill on God's behalf, "but neither truly nor rightly" (Jub. 23:21). God's negative evaluation of the Jewish civil war is made clear by God's punishment of it, first in famine (23:18) and then in foreign invasion (23:22–24). Although Jub. 23 does not say that God sent the famine, it is implicit not only in that God controls nature but also from the pattern in received scripture that God punishes sin with famine and diminishment of natural bounty. The implicit becomes explicit in the second phase of divine punishment: "there will be a great punishment from the Lord for the actions of that generation" (Jub. 23:22). In chapter 2 we saw how Jub. 23 centers on the agency of Israel and God, eliminating cosmic evil and reducing the nations to pawns. Here we examine the same material from a perspective of the placement of suffering in an eschatological framework. The turning point of history comes about not as a divine intervention to reverse the climax of evil. The turning point comes about as a result of repentance. The preceding woes are explicable as sin and just punishment.

---

22. Cana Werman also notices a distinction between two different types of guilt in Jub. 23: a general guilt that applies to the nations, and a covenantal guilt that applies to Israel ("ספר היובלים ועדת קומרן," 43). This important observation is not best explained, however, by postulating that one author thought the Gentiles were sinful while another thought Israel had been sinful. For further discussion of the problem, see Hanneken, "The Book of Jubilees among the Apocalypses," 129 n. 43, 436–39.

In several apocalypses enduring unjust suffering has the positive result of calling God to action. In Jubilees the suffering is just and has the positive result of calling Israel to repentance. Furthermore, the woes of famine and invasion are not a crisis of justice to be rectified but the enforcement of covenantal justice.

The connection to the covenantal curses is apparent not only in the explicit framework of "they will abandon the covenant ... God will punish" but also in the details of the punishment. Jubilees is not a line-for-line retelling of Deut 28 or Lev 26, but almost every detail in Jub. 23 has a parallel in these chapters. An examination of these parallels establishes the present point that Jub. 23 recontextualizes the final woes as covenantal chastisement. The parallels also bring us to the next point, that the final woes are toned down to fit the claim that the covenantal prediction has already been fulfilled and the restoration begun.

3.2.3.2. The "Final Woes" Have Already Been Fulfilled

For convenience, one can organize the woes in Jub. 23 under the categories of sickness, famine, and invasion. The first category is anticipated in Jub. 23:12 but detailed in 23:13:

> blow upon blow, wound upon wound, distress upon distress, bad news upon bad news, disease upon disease, and every (kind of) bad punishment like this, one with the other: disease and stomach pains. (Jub. 23:13)

The continuation of the list will be considered in the second category. For the sake of brevity, we will focus on Deut 28, although the same points can generally be made from Lev 26. Deuteronomy 28:21–22, 27–28, 35, 59–61 list comparable illness.

> The LORD will make the pestilence cling to you until it has consumed you off the land that you are entering to possess. The LORD will afflict you with consumption, fever, inflammation, with fiery heat and drought, and with blight and mildew; they shall pursue you until you perish. (Deut 28:21–22, NRSV)

> The LORD will afflict you with the boils of Egypt, with ulcers, scurvy, and itch, of which you cannot be healed. The LORD will afflict you with madness, blindness, and confusion of mind. (Deut 28:27–28, NRSV)

The LORD will strike you on the knees and on the legs with grievous boils of which you cannot be healed, from the sole of your foot to the crown of your head. (Deut 28:35, NRSV)

Then the LORD will overwhelm both you and your offspring with severe and lasting afflictions and grievous and lasting maladies. He will bring back upon you all the diseases of Egypt, of which you were in dread, and they shall cling to you. Every other malady and affliction, even though not recorded in the book of this law, the LORD will inflict on you until you are destroyed. (Deut 28:59–61, NRSV)

The apocalypses do not include ordinary sickness among the final woes; indeed, "ordinary" is a key difference between the woes in Jubilees and those in the apocalypses. Knowing how closely Jubilees depends on received scripture, it is not surprising that Jubilees draws from the contents of the covenant curses to provide the final woes of the genre "apocalypse." It is striking, however, that Jubilees recasts the covenant curses in such a way that they could easily be said to have been fulfilled already. An interpreter might imagine that the threats of Deut 28 are not conditional threats but predictions to be fulfilled before an end to all suffering can come about. While one might wonder if the extremes of Deut 28 had yet been fulfilled, the disease curses *as retold in Jubilees* have already been fulfilled.

The second category follows the same pattern of framing the covenant curses in such a way that they have already been fulfilled. Jubilees 23 lists woes related to famine and forces of nature first in the continuation of 23:13, then in 23:18 following the Jewish civil war.

… ወአስሐትያ ፡ ወበረድ ፡ ወሐመዳ ፡ ወነበርጸው ፡ ወሰከሕካሕ ፡ ወሰያዛዝ ፡ ወዐባር …

… snow, hail, frost, fever [or: heat], cold [Ethiopic ambiguous, Latin has *frigora*, Leslau offers "chaff"[23]], numbness, famine… (Jub. 23:13)

ናሁ ፡ ምድር ፡ ትትሐጕል ፡ በእንተ ፡ ኵሉ ፡ ምግባሮሙ ፡ ወአልቦ ፡ ዘርአ ፡ ወይን ፡ ወአልቦ ፡ ቅብእ ፡ እስመ ፡ ኵሉ ፡ ካሕድ ፡ ምግባሪሆሙ ፡ ወኵሎሙ ፡

---

23. One might wonder if אבק "dust, soot" in Deut 28:24 could lie behind the rare Ethiopic word ነበርጸው for which Wolf Leslau gives "chaff" (*Comparative Dictionary of Ge'ez [Classical Ethiopic]: Ge'ez-English, English-Ge'ez, with an Index of the Semitic Roots* [Wiesbaden: Harrassowitz, 1987]).

ይትሐጕሉ ፡ ኅቡረ ፡ አራዊት ፡ ወእንስሳ ፡ ወአዕዋፍ ፡፡ ወኵሉ ፡ ዓሣተ ፡ ባሕር ፡
እምቅድመ ፡ ውሉድ ፡ ሰብእ

> The earth will indeed be destroyed [or: diminished] because of all that they do. There will be no produce [or: seed] from the vine and no oil because what they do (constitutes) complete disobedience [literally: every disobedience is their practice]. All will be destroyed [or: diminished] together—animals, cattle, birds, and all fish of the sea—because of mankind. (Jub. 23:18)

For this category we should examine the parallels not only with Deut 28 but also with other texts in order to examine how borrowed language changes meaning in the new context. Deuteronomy 28 describes famine and afflictions of nature in 22–24 and 38–40.

> The LORD will afflict you with consumption, fever, inflammation, with fiery heat and drought, and with blight and mildew; they shall pursue you until you perish. The sky over your head shall be bronze, and the earth under you iron. The LORD will change the rain of your land into powder [אָבָק], and only dust shall come down upon you from the sky until you are destroyed. (Deut 28:22–24, NRSV)

> You shall carry much seed into the field but shall gather little in, for the locust shall consume it. You shall plant vineyards and dress them, but you shall neither drink the wine nor gather the grapes, for the worm shall eat them. You shall have olive trees throughout all your territory, but you shall not anoint yourself with the oil, for your olives shall drop off. (Deut 28:38–40, NRSV)

Again, the sky of copper and earth of iron is a harsher image than that given in Jubilees, and everything in Jubilees could be easily considered fulfilled. The correspondence is even closer in the next part, abbreviated in Jubilees. This is especially true in light of VanderKam's demonstration that by a simple loss of a conjunction the present Ethiopic text could have come from an original "seed, wine and oil."[24] The situation gets more interesting with the destruction of land, water, and sky animals in Jubilees.

---

24. VanderKam, *The Book of Jubilees*, 2:144. This phrase also occurs in Deut 28:51, although in the context of foreign invasion rather than diminishment of natural bounty: דָּגָן תִּירוֹשׁ וְיִצְהָר, "grain, wine, and oil."

Although Deut 28 lists slaughter and theft of livestock by foreigners in the next category (invasion), the image in Jubilees is not theft and not limited to domesticated or even land animals. One should not think that Jubilees is simply extending the famine to fishing and hunting. On the contrary, Jubilees tends to shorten and tone down Deut 28 and Lev 26. Indeed, we must look elsewhere for the source of such an image. The flood is a natural place to look for an idea of destruction of all life on earth, but the immediate problem is that the flood described in Genesis (like any flood) would not have killed fish. If anything, it would take an amplified sequel to the flood to destroy fish. An amplified sequel to the flood is implicit or explicit in the Enochic apocalypses, but one does not find the detail of the destruction of fish. In as much as the image fits the category of cosmic destruction it certainly evokes the parallel tendency in the apocalypses. Yet, the specific image leads us away from the apocalypses and the idea of "final woes." What is said about this diminishment of nature as a result of human sin differs from what is sometimes said about cosmic destruction in the apocalypses. Although Zeph 1:3 is also comparable, the closest parallel to Jub. 23:18 is Hos 4:3. Even if one does not accept that the author or the audience would have made such a connection, the passage is at least illustrative of how such language could be used in a nonapocalyptic, nonfinal framework.

עַל־כֵּן ׀ תֶּאֱבַל הָאָרֶץ
וְאֻמְלַל כָּל־יוֹשֵׁב בָּהּ
בְּחַיַּת הַשָּׂדֶה וּבְעוֹף הַשָּׁמָיִם
וְגַם־דְּגֵי הַיָּם יֵאָסֵפוּ׃

    Thus the land dries up.
    Everything that dwells on it languishes.
    Everything among the beasts of the field and the birds of the sky,
    Even the fish of the sea are withheld (Hos 4:3)

This passage might have been understood as a condemnation of a fertility cult, such that diminishment of fertility was a fitting punishment for idolatry intended to increase fertility. At any rate, the point is that the passage describes diminished fertility, not a cataclysmic end of all life. One should be careful not to overtranslate the verbs אבל, אמל, and אסף. The idea is of drying up, languishing, and being withheld, not destruction. It is also clearly a punishment from God for the covenantal infidelity of Israel.

Both points are also true of Jubilees. The continuation of Jub. 23 makes clear that 23:18 does not describe the catastrophic destruction of all life but rather a diminishment of bounty comparable to the diminishment of life span. The Ethiopic verbs in this verse (from the root ሀጕለ, "to lose") need not indicate catastrophic destruction. VanderKam's rendering "destroyed" is possible, but so is "deprived" or "diminished." It stands to reason that such a polyvalence operated in the Hebrew original. Also, the lack of fertility is clearly punishment of covenantal infidelity, not an extermination of universal wickedness and contamination. After all, the world proceeds unimpeded in the next verse. On the one hand, the language helps evoke comparison with the second flood or other forms of universal catastrophe in the apocalypses. On the other hand, in context and in light of the connection with received scripture (Hosea), the diminishment of fertility as a result of covenantal disobedience takes on a very different meaning. In this light, it makes sense that the diminishment of fertility does not appear in Deut 28: it is not woeful enough.

The climactic third category of punishment is foreign invasion. In this case the woes are indeed woeful, but still no more so than the covenant curses, and they do not go beyond events already fulfilled in the 160s B.C.E. More important, the foreign invasion is not the climax of injustice and evil against God, but just punishment from God according to the terms of the covenant. This category, too, is previewed in the list in Jub. 23:13 but expanded at length in 23:22–23.

> ... death, sword, captivity, and every (sort of) blow and difficulty. (Jub. 23:13)

> There will be a great punishment from the Lord for the actions of that generation. He will deliver them to the sword, judgment, captivity, plundering, and devouring. He will arouse against them the sinful nations who will have no mercy or kindness for them and who will show partiality to no one, whether old or young, or anyone at all, because they are evil and strong so that they are more evil than all mankind. They will cause chaos in Israel and sin against Jacob. Much blood will be shed on the earth, and there will be no one who gathers up (corpses) or who buries (them). (Jub. 23:22–32)

Twenty-nine verses in Deut 28 describe invasion and exile of some kind. The point is not that foreign invasion links Jub. 23 to the covenant curses more than the apocalypses, although two details are worth noting. The main point is that the explanation of foreign invasion in Jubilees is the same as in Deuteronomy, contrary to the apocalypses. Furthermore, the curses of Deut 28 are toned down to exclude woes not already fulfilled in the 160s B.C.E.

Two details connect Jub. 23 to Deut 28. Chapter 5 will discuss how the slaughter in 1 Macc 7:17 became related to Ps 79 for the image that none were left to bury. Although Jubilees uses language from Ps 79, the idea was also "predicted" in Deuteronomy:

> Your corpses shall be food for every bird of the air and animal of the earth, and there shall be no one to frighten them away. (Deut 28:26)

Additionally, the specific mention that ruthless foreign invaders would show partiality neither to the aged nor the young comes straight from Deuteronomy:

> ... a grim-faced nation showing no respect to the old or favor to the young. (Deut 28:50)

Despite the similarities in general idea and specific details, there is also a striking difference in that Jub. 23 excises any curses that cannot be counted as already fulfilled, such that the restoration could have already begun. The more striking general absence is the idea of exile. The Assyrian and/or Babylonian exile is mentioned in Jub. 1, but no such mention is made in the "recent" historical apocalypse. Since the historical persecutions of the 160s B.C.E. did not include exile and the author did not anticipate exile happening again prior to restoration, this curse was simply omitted.[25] Furthermore, as bad as the worst of the woes in Jub. 23 may be (although some of them are strikingly quotidian, such as stomach aches and death at the age of seventy or eighty), the woes in Jubilees are still toned down relative to the covenant curses. For example, Deut 28:53–57 describes the most outstanding citizens reduced to eating their children and afterbirth and greedily refusing to share with the rest of the family. Among the threats

---

25. Betsy Halpern-Amaru (*Rewriting the Bible: Land and Covenant in Post-biblical Jewish Literature* [Valley Forge, Pa.: Trinity Press International, 1994], 53) discusses other shifts in the way Jubilees reads Deuteronomy that result from their different historical contexts. At the time of Jubilees, exile was no longer a threat, so the biblical land theology was adapted.

read as predictions, this one apparently was not fulfilled in recent memory. The other apocalypses, which typically imagine the situation getting worse before it gets better, might simply have kept this prediction (if they were to base their final woes on the covenant curses). As we shall see, for Jubilees, things have already started to get better, and the beginning of the gradual restoration is already realized.

Finally we come to the main issue that sets the explanation of foreign invasion in Jub. 23 apart from the apocalypses. Jubilees 23:22–23 emphasizes three times that the punishment is from the Lord, that the Lord delivers Israel to punishment, and that the Lord arouses against them the sinners of the nations. Deuteronomy 28 also inserts frequent reminders that the curses are actively imposed by God as just punishment such as: וְעָבַדְתָּ אֶת־אֹיְבֶיךָ אֲשֶׁר יְשַׁלְּחֶנּוּ יְהוָה בָּךְ, "You will serve your enemies, whom the Lord will send against you" (Deut 28:48), and יִשָּׂא יְהוָה עָלֶיךָ גּוֹי, "The Lord will raise a nation against you" (28:49). The typical apocalypses, however, do not really entertain the idea that persecution of the chosen by outsiders occurs at the will of God.[26] Foreign armies represent external forces of evil acting unjustly. At most God waits to restore justice while the wicked pile up enough sin to warrant their absolute destruction. In the typical apocalypses, the climax of evil is anything but a just act of God in a covenantal framework intended to prompt repentance.

3.2.3.3. The White Children

Thus far Jubilees has frequently evoked formal elements of the genre "apocalypse" but consistently adapted them to convey a very different view of the temporal axis. Any such manipulation of reader expectations can be called subversive in a general sense, but not necessarily intended

---

26. The Animal Apocalypse attributes such action by God to the destruction of the northern kingdom, which only enhances the contrast with the very different description of the "present" destruction (1 En. 89:55). The Animal Apocalypse also includes some possibility that part of the beginning of the decline of history started according to God's command, but the situation quickly degrades beyond any punishment conceivably willed by God (1 En. 89:65).

As discussed in chapter 2, Dan 9:11 represents a view external to the apocalypse. See Collins, *Apocalyptic Imagination*, 108–9; idem, *Daniel: A Commentary*, 360; Andreas Bedenbender, *Der Gott der Welt tritt auf den Sinai: Entstehung, Entwicklung und Funktionsweise der frühjüdischen Apokalyptik* (ANTZ 8; Berlin: Institut Kirche und Judentum, 2000), 238–40.

to ridicule. In some examples, one might think the discord is simply the by-product of reframing a Deuteronomistic view of suffering in the framework of the apocalypses. (Although even at that one would have to evaluate the significance of such a decision.) The borrowing and adapting of literary features to tell a different point of view could be explained in a number of ways. As we come to Jub. 23:24–25 we find some of the stronger evidence in favor of humor or intent to ridicule.[27]

Chapter 5 will consider the overlap in historical context of Jubilees with other apocalypses. For now we are more concerned with the overlap in literary features of Jub. 23:24:

> At that time they will cry out and call and pray to be rescued from the power of the sinful nations, but there will be no one who rescues (them). (Jub. 23:24)

First, one might compare this passage to the Animal Apocalypse. In both apocalypses we find "crying out" at an eschatological climax. In the Animal Apocalypse, the lambs and the rams cry out first to the sheep but ultimately for divine assistance, such that the angel and God intervene to support the rams in battle (1 En. 89:6, 10, 11, 13). Although the initial cry of the lambs to the deaf sheep is ineffective, the subsequent cries are successful first in rousing an army and second in enlisting the angel and God directly to provide military support. The image of crying out suggests that the Maccabees raise a just complaint that is heeded by the nonwild sheep and by God. Jubilees 23:24 could be understood to reject the possibility that the prayer of the Maccabees was or would be heeded by God. As will be discussed in chapter 5, Jubilees counts the Maccabees among the self-righteous sinful Jews who kill other Jews. Since the punishment comes from God as a result of Jews killing other Jews, praying to God with a sword in hand will not cause God to rescue anyone.

Jubilees 23:24 possibly echoes another apocalypse: "When they fall they will receive little help, and many will join them insincerely" (Dan 11:34, Collins's translation). Here we find a more skeptical assessment of

---

27. Literary critics distinguish Horatian and Juvenalian satire on the basis of whether it is poking fun in a friendly way or is a bitter attack. An openness to comparable possibilities should be brought to the consideration of Jub. 23:24–25. See Chris Baldick, *The Oxford Dictionary of Literary Terms* (3rd ed.; Oxford: Oxford University Press, 2008).

human forces creating an efficacious alliance. Skeptical as the *maskilim* may be of the masses, however, we have already seen Jubilees' skepticism that *any* militants are on the right track. Militants are not a little help, but *no* help. Indeed, they are the problem addressed in Jub. 23:16–21. Interestingly enough, the next verse in Daniel brings us to the next verse in Jub. 23.

Much has been said in attempts to explain the white children in Jub. 23:25.[28]

> The children's heads will turn white with gray hair. A child who is three weeks of age will look old like one whose years are 100, and their condition will be destroyed through distress and pain. (Jub. 23:25)

The old-man infant of Isa 65:20 is relevant to the pattern of longevity already discussed as part of the decline of history but does not account for the image of white-headed children.[29] We already have copious reason to be critical of any assumptions that an image in Jubilees means what it means in other apocalypses. The path to understanding this verse is to ask three questions: (1) What is typically said of white children in apocalypses? (2) What is typically said of white children in received scripture? (3) What is said of white children in Jubilees?

The apocalypses and related traditions consistently present the images of whiteness and/or children positively. Regardless of one's best guess as to the existence of a Book of Noah, or the date of 1 En. 106:2 and the Genesis Apocryphon, one can be confident that a positive image of a snow-white birth of Noah existed by the time of Jubilees. Even if such a traditional image was not expressed exclusively in the genre "apocalypse," it is easy to link the image to the apocalypses. The components "white" and "child" also appear somewhat distinctively in the apocalypses. Thus in Dan 11:35 the wise are "whitened" by the final woes and death. In the Animal Apocalypse white represents goodness and holiness, and the rams become white in the restoration (1 En. 90:32). Although הבנים, "the children," was not a technical term for a particular group, there certainly are examples that

---

28. A very different attempt at explanation was offered by André Caquot, "Les enfants aux cheveux blancs: Réflexions sur un motif," in *Mélanges d'histoire des religions offerts à Henri-Charles Puech* (Paris: Presses Universitaires de France, 1974), 161–72.

29. See further below, §4.1.3.2, "Third Isaiah in Jubilees 23."

allude to a group or class in such a way.³⁰ The white children in Jubilees may not be a direct reference to any one apocalypse in particular, but that is not the issue. The issue is that, based on what one typically finds in apocalypses by the time of Jubilees, one would expect white children to be a good thing, probably associated with the circles responsible for composition.³¹

There may be a tendency for the modern reader to assume that the positive valuation of "white children" is universal rather than particular to the apocalypses. In fact, whiteness is not typically equated with holiness in nonapocalypses, even if there are some examples (Ps 51:9). In Leviticus a child with a white head is something that should be brought to the priest to be declared unclean and cast out of the camp (Lev 13:3). Miriam turning white is practically viewed as a "final woe" by Moses and Aaron in Num 12:12 (see also Exod 4:6). Thus a white child is not necessarily a good thing in received scripture.

Finally we come to the big question: What is said about these white children in Jubilees? Simply put, they *are* the final woe. They are the bottom of the decline of history (measured according to life span) and the last item mentioned before the restoration. The curses of old age and sickness climax in a hyperbolic, one might say ridiculous, image of an infant that looks like an old man. To be sure, Jubilees maintains subtlety, but once one entertains the possibility of subversive treatment of apocalyptic generic elements, and once one asks the right questions, the Jubilees apocalypse sounds considerably less apocalyptic.

The main point is that Jubilees adopts the temporal scope and the eschatological nexus of the genre "apocalypse" and uses the genre to convey an alternative view of history and the present moment, that the worst is over and the restoration has already begun. This main point does not rule out, however, the possibility that the primary audience could have perceived a serendipitous disparaging reference to the self-identification imagery of groups associated with the apocalypses. In light of the general pattern that Jubilees evokes but inverts reader expectations of the genre "apocalypse," we might also understand Jub. 23:25 as a subversive evocation of apocalyptic imagery. Jubilees uses an image that evokes the tendency of apocalypses

---

30. See Kister, "לתולדות כת האיסיים," 8–9.

31. One might also consider a later text, the Parables of Enoch. A white head is certainly a good thing in reference to the "head of days" (God; cf. the Ancient of Days in Dan 7:9, 13), whose "head was like white wool" (1 En. 46:1).

to generate hyperbolic images and the positive valuation on "whiteness" and "children." Significantly, however, Jubilees inverts the valuation of the image and, by extension, any groups that self-identified in similar terms.

As we are about to see, it is no accident that the final woes in Jubilees are all either quotidian (stomach aches, mortality at seventy or eighty years) or realized in the reader's recent history (famine, invasion). Even the hyperbolic image of white children dying young is realized in the rise of sectarianism and civil war. The climax of the final woes (or the fulfillment of the "predictions" of covenantal curses) is a prerequisite for the restoration. We now turn to the significance of a fact that has long been at least partially recognized: the eschatology of Jubilees is realized. The next verse describes the only condition for the turning point, a condition that is realized in the mind of the author of Jubilees in the author's own audience.

> In those days the children will begin to study the laws, to seek out the commands, and to return to the right way. (Jub. 23:26)

From the perspective of the author, the final woes are already fulfilled, the proper "seeking out" of the law has begun, and the gradual restoration is underway. Charles and others recognized this much but imagined a "temporary kingdom" prior to a still-future cosmic judgment in order to reconcile the realized eschatology of Jub. 23 with their own expectation of a unique final judgment in an apocalypse.[32] As we shall see, the end of the woes and the beginning of the gradual restoration in Jubilees is not temporary. Jubilees does not eliminate the idea of judgment but diverges from the typical apocalypses by divorcing judgment from eschatology.[33]

3.3. The Judgment

The previous chapter considered some distinctive issues of the agents and objects of judgment. This chapter turns to the issue of when judgment occurs on the temporal axis. The issue of judgment in some form is common in Judaism. Jubilees evokes the apocalypses in particular not

---

32. Charles, *Jubilees*, lxxxvii, 9–10, 150. Charles's comment on Jub. 23:30 in particular will be of interest in the following section. See also Testuz, *Les idées religieuses*, 168–69; Davenport, *The Eschatology of the Book of Jubilees*, 41; Rowley, *The Relevance of Apocalyptic*, 61; Russell, *Method and Message*, 269, 292.

33. For the realized "new creation" in Jub. 1:29 and 5:12, see §3.4.4.2. below.

only with the generic framework of revelation and a transcendent scope of the spatial and temporal axes but also in generic language, including "great day of judgment." A subject of disagreement was whether judgment was deferred to a future consummation in which the entire cosmos would be judged at once or if judgment occurred incrementally on a rolling basis for individual persons and nations. This issue has already been observed with respect to Sirach and parts of 1 Enoch.[34] The Enochic and Danielic apocalypses defer judgment to a unique (or unique after the flood) future consummation and universal judgment. Jubilees uses generic features to evoke a similar reader expectation but in fact divorces the idea of judgment from the eschatological nexus. Jubilees presents a pattern of rolling judgment spread out along the temporal axis, past and future. When we ask what is said about the "great day of judgment," we find that each nation faces its own great day of judgment (or more than one), but there is no one day of universal judgment. Some nations, such as Sodom and Gomorrah, have already been judged, while others will yet be judged, unrelated to the restoration of Israel. Jubilees 23 teases a suggestion of a "great day of judgment" but goes on to describe an eschatological sequence devoid of judgment scenes.

In the following subsections we will discuss the other apocalypses only briefly for the simple point that they view a single cosmic judgment as integral to the turning point on the temporal axis. When we turn to Jubilees we will address first what is said (and not said) in chapter 23 and then the rest of the book. If one examined only chapter 23, one might think that Jubilees rejects judgment apart from chastisement for sin to prompt repentance. In fact, various nations do suffer a "final" judgment, but the distinctive issue remains that judgment of individual nations is ongoing throughout history. Only with great effort have scholars forced the individual descriptions of judgment into the eschatological scheme of Jub. 23.

3.3.1. The Enochic Apocalypses

Scholars may not agree *why* the idea developed in Judaism that empires will yet be judged by God well after their decline from power.[35] Regardless of

---

34. Argall, *1 Enoch and Sirach*, 247.

35. Perhaps a sense persisted that Babylon, for example, deserved worse punishment than simply being replaced by a new superpower. Perhaps there was a sense that the evil behind Babylon persisted and simply put on new clothes in other empires. On

the explanation, the present concern is simply that the apocalypses at the time of Jubilees typically convey the idea that a cosmic judgment remains in the future apart from political decline or even death. We can sample a few statements to this effect without exhausting the interesting data relevant to a study focused on the intricacies of ideas of judgment.

The Book of the Watchers states particularly explicitly the idea of deferred universal judgment:

> Thus they will make desolate until the day of the consummation of the great judgment, when the great age will be consummated. It will be consummated all at once. (1 En. 16:1, Nickelsburg's translation)

Other passages support the singularity of *the* day of judgment.[36] To be precise, one might speak of two universal judgments: the flood and the final judgment typified by the flood. Even such a typology does not prevent us from speaking of an exceptional cosmic judgment deferred until the (near) future and linked to an eschatological turning point. Although we are focusing on the temporal locus of judgment, it is also relevant that punishment is basically supernatural in the Book of the Watchers and basically natural in Jubilees (and Sirach).[37] An exceptional, deferred, eschatological judgment is not a superficial feature of the Book of the Watchers but one of the most central ideas.

Skipping over some distinct nuances, such as the stages and agents of judgment, the Apocalypse of Weeks and Animal Apocalypse revolve around the same basic premise that judgment is deferred until a final batch

---

a different level, perhaps there was an interpretive problem when curses in authoritative texts appeared not to have been fulfilled in history. Perhaps sometimes history had nothing to do with it, but the idea of deferred stages resolved textual contradictions. The canonical apocalypses in Daniel have been studied more, but the same issue applies to other apocalypses.

36. The "hollow places" described in 22:1–14 are separated according to something of a preliminary judgment but are primarily holding chambers until the deferred day of judgment, "until the day (on) which they will be judged, and until the time of the day of the end of the great judgment that will be exacted from them" (1 En. 22:4).

Even if one questions the date of the superscription itself, it succinctly summarizes the concern for the singular eschatological axis: "the day of tribulation" (1 En. 1:1). It is striking, however, that the enemies are simply "removed" as they are in Jubilees. In the rest of the Book of the Watchers, worse things than removal occur.

37. Argall, *1 Enoch and Sirach*, 230, 242.

process that will judge the sinners of all ages at once. In the Apocalypse of Weeks one finds more an era than a day of judgment. Judgment occurs first in earthly military terms and culminates with the final judgment of all cosmic beings. Even where textual problems plague more detailed considerations, the eschatological focus on judgment pervades all variants.[38] The Animal Apocalypse provides a clear example of a period in which judgment is deferred (1 En. 89:77), followed by a single formal batch judgment of all the cosmic and human (sheep) sinners (90:20-27). Incidents of judgment are not excluded from previous history (e.g. 89:54-58, the northern kingdom), but the scale of the final judgment is unique. The idea of an exceptional deferred judgment pervades the narrative bridge and the Epistle of Enoch as well.[39] The Enochic apocalypses include significant internal variations in the details, yet they cluster around a core idea that judgment is deferred until an exceptional, imminent, universal consummation. This judgment is fundamentally linked on the temporal axis to the eschatological turning point.

3.3.2. The Danielic Apocalypses and the Book of Daniel

The apocalypses of Daniel, plus Dan 2, share variations on the basic idea that reward and punishment does not occur in this life or throughout history but is deferred until a future time. Again, we include the court tale in Dan 2 because the redaction of the book of Daniel reframes the chapter in the context of the apocalypses. One striking feature of Dan 2 is that the image of a single statue is an awkward expression for a succession of kingdoms, especially since the sequence works down, rather than up.[40] The important issue for us is that the first kingdoms, even if they are supplanted in a political sense, are not judged until the end, when all kingdoms are destroyed together. The awkwardness can only be par-

---

38. For example, all readings of 1 En. 91:15 build around the basic idea found in 4QEn^g, דין עלמא וקץ דינא רבא. See Nickelsburg, *1 Enoch: A Commentary*, 437; Stuckenbruck, *1 Enoch 91-108*, 148-49.

39. See 1 En. 91:7-9; 92:4-5; 94:9; 96:8; 98:8; 100:4; 102:1-3. Even if some degree of individual retribution is immediate after death (1 En. 103:8), individual judgment is deferred until death, and earthly judgment is deferred until a future date.

40. The image would seem to require that the foundation existed in some sense even before the head (unless statues are constructed from the top down).

tially explained by the preexistence of such a tradition.⁴¹ No author was constrained to express this idea in this image, and we have independent confirmation of the belief that the consummation of judgment occurs all at once. The Danielic apocalypses confirm the idea that political decline (or even death) does not fill the need for judgment. Daniel 2 offers a particularly striking image of deferred batch judgment, but the basic idea is hardly limited to this chapter.

Daniel 7 offers an interesting variation on the same basic idea. It is at least clear that the rise of a beast does not amount to judgment of the previous beast.⁴² The interesting variation is that, not only do the first three beasts survive until the great judgment scene, but they seem to receive a deferment of punishment:

> As for the rest of the beasts,⁴³ their dominion was taken away, and an extension of life was given to them for a time and a season. (Dan 7:12, Collins's translation)

Rather than attempting to explain this as reflecting historical reality or a practical hope that a new Jewish kingdom would conquer one kingdom at a time, the verse should be understood as a way of emphasizing the wickedness and punishment of the last beast.⁴⁴ Furthermore, the deferred or lessened punishment does not negate the basic principle that the court judged all the beasts in one sitting (Dan 7:10).⁴⁵ The variation does not challenge the basic pattern of decline of history, final woes, judgment, and restoration nor the idea that the judgment is a single universal judgment tied to the eschatological axis.

The remaining apocalypses lack detailed judgment scenes but follow the basic idea that justice is deferred until an appointed time. Unlike Dan

---

41. See Collins, *Daniel: A Commentary*, 166–70, on this issue, particularly for the contributions of Swain and Grayson.

42. Collins (ibid., 298, 304) has suggested that the devouring of much flesh refers to the Median conquest of the Babylonians, but even if this is the case the first beast continues to exist.

43. The Old Greek is more vague on who receives the deferment: τοὺς κύκλῳ αὐτοῦ, "those around him."

44. Collins, *Daniel: A Commentary*, 304.

45. Dan 7:12 seems to suggest that the destruction of these beasts is imminent, while 7:27 may suggest that they are destroyed as kingdoms only in that they become subject to the everlasting kingdom.

7, Dan 8:7 gives the impression that one kingdom is indeed destroyed by the next, but this fits perfectly well with the idea expanded in Dan 10–12 that the rise and fall of earthly power is separate from final justice. If it were possible to separate Dan 8 and 9 as isolated apocalypses, one might speak of an eschatological expectation that emphasizes woes and end of woes without an elaborate judgment or restoration. As it is, Dan 8 and 9 should be understood as presuming a judgment and restoration expanded elsewhere. Daniel 9 ends with a brief promise that the desolator will be destroyed at the appointed time: עַד־כָּלָה וְנֶחֱרָצָה תִּתַּךְ עַל־שֹׁמֵם, "until the determined destruction is poured upon the desolator." Daniel 10–12 spends more time on the decline of history than on the judgment, but one still finds the basic theme that God's justice is not realized in the rise and fall of political forces but is deferred until an appointed time. In the present time, justice for kingdoms and individuals is absent or inverted. Only at a future date will a single great eschatological judgment bring justice to the living and the dead (Dan 12:2). This brief survey is not intended to downplay the variations between the Danielic apocalypses on the issue of judgment but to show the common core of the basic position that justice is deferred until a future consummation in which all will be judged. The variations between the Danielic and Enochic apocalypses are even greater, but the basic apocalyptic idea of a deferred, universal, and eschatological judgment is consistently expressed in these apocalypses.

3.3.3. Jubilees

Judgment is a major issue in Jubilees as well, but Jubilees varies significantly from the apocalypses by divorcing judgment from eschatology. Each nation has its own day of judgment, and individuals receive justice within their lifetimes (or in their deaths). The turning point of history does not lead directly to any judgment of anyone, but only the removal of divine punishment. There is no one day or period in which all are judged. Some nations have already been judged (the most obvious example being Sodom and Gomorrah). Other nations will be judged by God in the future, but not in a way directly tied to the restoration of Israel. Judgment may be deferred in the traditional sense that God's mercy allows time for repentance or the fulfillment of warrant for a certain punishment (cf. Gen 15:16).[46] The grace

---

46. There does not seem to be an "instant karma" position in contemporary texts.

period, however, applies to individual nations and not the cosmos. Judgment occurs as necessary throughout history. There is no time in which divine justice is suspended nor any particular time in which it will be enacted.

We will begin by considering Jub. 23. As was the case with demonic agency, Jub. 23 is not merely silent on the idea of judgment but inverts the idea. Then we will consider what is said about days of judgment in other parts of Jubilees. We must reject the assumption that Jubilees has a systematic scheme of a single judgment that the reader must assemble by scavenging various comments throughout the book.[47] A more objective clarity can be gained by focusing on the temporal dimension, asking *when* judgment takes place in each passage. In some instances it is clear that, despite language evocative of the apocalypses, the judgment has already taken place in the distant past.

3.3.3.1. Jubilees 23

Jubilees 23 does not downplay the idea of judgment. Rather, it incorporates judgment (among other generic features of the apocalypses) but changes the context and sequence so as to change the meaning. Thus, Jub. 23 evokes the reader expectation based on the apocalypses, among other means, by using the phrase "great day of judgment."

> All the generations that will come into being from now until the great day of judgment will grow old quickly—before they complete two jubilees. (Jub. 23:11)

This great day of judgment does indeed refer to the eschatological turning point in life span, but the subversion comes in what is said about this great

---

Ben Sira holds that judgment can be deferred out of divine mercy within a person's lifetime, but justice catches up no later than the moment of death.

47. Testuz (*Les idées religieuses*, 175) and Scott (*On Earth as in Heaven*, 69 n. 119) patch together disparate passages in Jubilees and present it as a single consistent scenario. Both scholars claim that a set of esoteric oral explanations would have accompanied the written text to decode its enigmas. Although it is plausible that a written text would have been accompanied by oral teaching, the present work is content to explicate the written text, and not reconstruct what is at best plausible. I also doubt Scott's assertion that "Jubilees' milieu values secret knowledge" or that Jubilees "like a cryptogram, requires specialized, insider knowledge and decoding."

day of judgment. Based on other apocalypses, one would expect this judgment to refer to the punishment of the nations, followed by the vindication of the chosen. This is not the case in Jubilees.

In a sense the original problem in Jub. 23 is that Abraham and the elect are indistinct from other nations according to the criterion of life span, which is often associated with righteousness. Theoretically (as Jubilees sees it), righteousness and covenantal fidelity should grant not only security in the land but length of life to the degree exemplified by the first generations. Jubilees asserts that this will become the case once Israel seeks out the law in the right way. The other side of this coin is that the other nations will not have security in the land of Israel and will not have the blessings of health and longevity. They are "punished" only in the sense that they leave the land of Israel and continue to suffer the same 1.5 Jubilee mortality, stomach aches, pains, and violence that they had always suffered.

> Then the Lord will heal his servants. They will rise and see great peace. He will expel his enemies. The righteous will see (this), offer praise, and be very happy forever and ever. They will see all their punishments and curses on their enemies. (Jub. 23:30)

The difference is the elevation of Israel, not any new or supernatural punishment of the nations. There is no explicit court or judgment scene. This is not the "great day of judgment." We must look elsewhere for the great day of judgment in Jub. 23.

In Jub. 23, the divine punishment is not against nations and forces of evil but rather is chastisement of Israel for its sins, by means of the nations (Jub. 23:22–23). At the level of ideas, the pattern is not decline of history, final woes, judgment, restoration, but a pattern of sin, punishment, repentance, restoration. It is not just that Jub. 23 follows a Deuteronomistic pattern but that it uses apocalyptic literary elements to describe it. Neither Deuteronomy nor any text prior to Jubilees uses the genre "apocalypse" or the phrase "great day of judgment" to refer to covenantal curses. Some references to the "day of the Lord" may be more proximate than others, but the term never refers to a Deuteronomistic chastisement to promote repentance. Conversely, no apocalypse prior to Jubilees portrays the final woes as just judgment from God to prompt the elect to repentance. Jubilees uses the language of "great day of judgment" in an eschatological framework but inverts the meaning to refer to covenantal chastisement rather than final destruction of evil. In Jub. 23 the great day of judgment is not the reversal of the "final" woes that Israel suffers but the woes themselves. Judgment does not follow but precedes the turning point of history and thus is eschatological only in a very atypical sense.

Unlike the theophany judgment scenes and nonnatural punishments in other apocalypses, the judgments in chapter 23 could certainly have already happened in history. As we saw in the last section, the final woes, which are really the main acts of justice in Jub. 23, are realized. The sending home of invaders is hardly a judgment, but that, too, was realized. As we will consider in more detail in chapter 5, the "eschatological" sequence well through the judgment matches what we can tell of recent history from 1 Maccabees. We can certainly find the "sin" phase of the Jewish civil war, the initial woes of famine, and the second woes of invasion (Bacchides in 1 Macc 9). The repentance phase requires only studying and seeking the laws, which would have been understood as realized in the audience of the book of Jubilees. The nonmilitary expulsion of enemies occurred in the withdrawal of Bacchides in 1 Macc 9. The author may have merely asserted that the Gentiles continue to suffer illness, violence, and mortality (while the righteous are gradually escaping such suffering, as we shall see). Thus, the eschatological judgments in Jub. 23 differ from the typical judgments in apocalypses in that they could have been perceived as already realized.

Although Jub. 23 has no judgment or punishment of the nations other than going home and continuing in the same "curses" of mortality, illness, and violence, this is not to say that individual nations do not face noneschatological judgment elsewhere in Jubilees. The rolling, noneschatological nature of these judgments can be seen in those that have already occurred. The use of apocalyptic language to describe judgment that is already fulfilled, and not typological in the sense of the flood, contributes to the dissonance in reader expectations based on other apocalypses.

Jubilees places judgment in realized natural history, as opposed to supernatural hyperbolic judgment, and views justice and judgment as an ongoing, rolling process, as opposed to one deferred batch judgment. Jubilees is not, however, soft on judgment. Every individual and nation will be judged (although Israel has special opportunities for forgiveness). Judgment can be harsh in Jubilees, but harshness alone is not distinctive of the apocalypses. The place of judgment on the temporal axis is what distinguishes the apocalyptic view of judgment. As we consider judgment in the rest of the book, two themes are consistently clear: judgment is a rolling process, and judgment is realized. We will consider judgment in the rest of Jubilees in three categories: the main judgment discourse with

THE TEMPORAL AXIS 157

respect to the flood in Jub. 5, the role of Enoch, and passages about individual nations.

3.3.3.2. The Judgment Discourse in Jubilees 5

Jubilees uses the phrase "great day of judgment" in one place outside of chapter 23: Jub. 5:10 refers to the flood, not a date future relative to Moses or the readers of the book. The flood is a realized example of judgment that demonstrates the ongoing principles of judgment; it is not a type for a particular future judgment.[48] The passage depends upon and evokes the Book of the Watchers, but it diverges significantly:

ወአበዊሆሙሰ ፡ ይኔጽሩ ፡ ወእምድኅረዝ ፡ ተአስሩ ፡ ውስተ ፡ መዓምቅቲሃ ፡ ለምድር ፡ እስከ ፡ ዕለተ ፡ ደይን ፡ ዐባይ ፡ ለከዊነ ፡ ኩነኔ ፡ ዲበ ፡ ኩሎሙ ፡ እለ ፡ አማስኑ ፡ ፍናዊሆሙ ፡ ወምግባሪሆሙ ፡ ቅድመ ፡ እግዚአብሔር ፡፡ ወደምሰሰ ፡ ኩሎ ፡ እመካኖሙ ፡ ወኢተርፈ ፡ አሐዱ ፡ እምኔሆሙ ፡ ዘኢኮነነ ፡ በኩሉ ፡ እከዮሙ።[49]

> As for their fathers [the watchers who fathered the giants], they were watching [the obliteration of the giants], and afterwards they were bound in the depths of the earth until the great day of judgment so there would be punishment on all those who had corrupted their ways and deeds before the Lord. God obliterated all from their place so that not one of them survived that God did not judge all his wickedness. (Jub. 5:10–11)

One immediately notices that there are no future verbs (the only imperfect is "they were watching").[50] In contrast to the Book of the Watchers, which portrays the flood as a prototype of a single final great day of judgment,

---

48. Segal came to a similar conclusion, "The Watchers story has been transformed into a paradigm of reward and punishment, and the presentation of God as a just, righteous judge" (*The Book of Jubilees*, 140). See also page 58 above.
49. All Ethiopic text comes from vol. 1 of VanderKam, *The Book of Jubilees*.
50. Since I am the first to argue that Jubilees thoroughly departs from the apocalyptic view of judgment, it is not surprising that previous translators have attempted to accommodate the text to the expectation of a future judgment. They have varied in their willingness to emend the text for this purpose. Charles (*Jubilees*, 44–45) simply emended the verbs, suggesting that the Greek translator mistook Hebrew converted perfects for ordinary perfects. It is not the case that this error appears with any frequency in the translation of Jubilees. VanderKam noted the lack of warrant for emendation. The same tendency can be seen, however, in his decision to translate the infini-

the flood itself was a great judgment. The binding of the watchers was not a way of deferring their judgment to a later, final time; it was their punishment as part of the judgment of the flood. The "great day of judgment" consists of the death of the giants, the binding of the watchers, and the drowning of all sinners. Everyone has already been judged. The continuation makes clear that the flood is viewed as an example of God's unwavering justice, not a type for deferred cosmic upheaval: ወአልቦ ፡ ዐመፃ ... በእንተ ፡ ኩሉ ... ይኬንና, "there is no injustice. ... God exercises judgment regarding each individual" (Jub. 5:13, 15). Although the genre and certain images cue the reader to the Book of the Watchers, the ideas of judgment are more aligned with those of Ben Sira.[51] God's mercy can create a short grace period, but it is never the case that God's justice is suspended until an appointed time.

3.3.3.3. The Role of Enoch in Judgment

Jubilees also addresses the role of Enoch as part of the claim that judgment is perfectly realized without delay. Enoch serves as a witness to divine justice in the past and leaves writings to warn future generations, but Enoch does not have an eschatological function or return for any judgment scene after the flood. Enoch's first function, to witness judgment executed through the war of the giants and the flood, is not so subversive except for the fact that the flood is a fully realized example of judgment, not a prototype for an eschatological judgment. The Animal Apocalypse also portrays Enoch as a witness to judgment:

> And they said to me, "Stay here until you see all that happens to those elephants and camels and asses and to the stars and to the cattle and all of them." (1 En. 87:4, Nickelsburg's translation)

---

tive as a future. Hence he translates, "when there will be condemnation on all" where I translate, "so there would be punishment on all" (*The Book of Jubilees*, 2:33).

51. I do not mean to suggest that Ben Sira and Jubilees are genetically related or that there was a faction of Judaism that included both. I do find it helpful that Randall Argall has shown that Sirach and 1 Enoch share a significant common ground and develop certain distinctive ideas. The relationship between Jubilees and the Book of the Watchers in this case strikes me as analogous. See Argall, *1 Enoch and Sirach*.

Enoch also "witnesses" through a vision the final judgment in 90:20–27 and in the Book of the Watchers the places of judgment reserved for the future. Based on analogy from other apocalypses, it is tempting to find Enoch in Jubilees as an immortal scribe recording all sin and returning in the final judgment to testify against the wicked. In fact, Enoch has no ongoing function, even if one does not read Jub. 7:39 to say that Enoch died.[52] Rather, Enoch's lasting legacy is through his writings, which serve to warn subsequent generations of the generic punishments for sin on any given day of judgment.

Enoch's witness of the judgment of the generation before the flood is discussed in Jub. 4:24, and the testimony of his writings is described 10:17 and 4:19. Jubilees 4:24 and 10:17 are so closely parallel that they should be read together, despite the basic difference that one refers to Enoch himself and the other to his writings.

እስመ ፡ ህየ ፡ ተውህበ ፡ ውእቱ ፡
ለትእምርት ፡ ወከመ ፡ ያስምዕ ፡
ላዕለ ፡ ኩሉ ፡ ደቂቀ ፡ ሰብእ ፡
ከመ ፡ ይንግር ፡
ኩሎ ፡ ግብረ ፡ ትውልድ ፡
እስከ ፡ አመ ፡ ዕለተ ፡ ደይን

because he [Enoch] was assigned to that place [Eden]
as a sign and to testify
to all humanity
so that he could tell
every deed of (that) generation
up to (its) day of judgment. (Jub. 4:24)

እስመ ፡ ግብሩ ፡ ለሄኖክ ፡ ፍጥረት ፡ ውእቱ ፡
ለስምዕ ፡
ለትዝምደ ፡ ዓለም ፡
ከመ ፡ ይንግር ፡
ኩነኔ[53] ፡ ኩሎ ፡ ግብረ ፡ ለትውልደ ፡ ትውልድ ፡
በዕለተ ፡ ደይን ።

---

52. In Jub. 4:23 the emphatic particle ናሁ (הנה) need not specify the time of activity with respect to Moses.

53. One of the better manuscripts, manuscript 35, gives "the punishment for...." Even manuscript 25 could be understood in this sense. See VanderKam, *The Book of Jubilees*, 1:63.

> because Enoch's work was something created
> as a testimony
> for the whole time of the (human) race,
> so that it should tell
> to every generation the punishment for every deed[54]
> on the day of judgment.[55] (Jub. 10:17)

In the first instance, Enoch witnesses the deeds and judgment of the generation judged in the flood, but his testimony of these facts for subsequent generations appear only through his writings, not some eschatological return. Thus, in Jub. 10:17 the subject has changed from Enoch to Enoch's writings. Neither the phrase "the day of judgment" nor any other passage in Jubilees requires that there be only one day of judgment. Rather, every generation is judged and punished in its own time. The only alternative would be to assume a future date at which every generation would be resurrected to face judgment, but such an idea is not to be found in Jubilees.[56] As we now turn to individual nations, we shall see that God's justice against individuals and nations is ongoing throughout history, not limited to one or two instances of protological and eschatological judgment.

---

54. The word order has been changed, since English prefers the indirect object to precede the direct object. "Every generation" are the ones told; "the punishment for every deed" is what they are told.

55. I understand "on the day of judgment" as referring to when the punishment will be, not when the testimony will tell the punishment.

56. It is clearly the case that the wicked do not rise for judgment. Jub. 23:31, "the bones [of the righteous] will rest in the earth and their spirits will be very happy," is not much of an afterlife and should be understood more in the sense of "rest in peace." Jub. 23:30, "[God's servants] will rise [ይትነሥኡ] and see great peace," refers to the prosperity of the living, not the resurrection of the dead. Charles finds immortality of the soul but notes the absence of resurrection of the body (*Jubilees*, lxxxix). Volz notes that the only trace of the dead in the restoration is in Jub. 23:31, where they become aware of the restoration without participating in it. See Paul Volz, *Die Eschatologie der jüdischen Gemeinde im neutestamentlichen Zeitalter, nach den Quellen der rabbinischen, apokalyptischen und apokryphen Literatur dargestellt* (Tübingen: Mohr Siebeck, 1934), 29. Rowley finds "no hint of resurrection" (*The Relevance of Apocalyptic*, 61).

3.3.3.4. The Judgment of Individual Nations

Any number of individuals in Jubilees receive their just punishment at or before the moment of death.[57] The more difficult case is the judgment of the nations. Jubilees treats the judgment of each nation separately. Some nations are yet to be judged, some have already been judged, and some continue to exist but have been justly subjugated.

The clearest case of judgment fulfilled in the past, according to Jubilees, is the judgment of Sodom. This judgment is not typological for a single future judgment but an example of God's open policy of judgment. Sodom had its day of judgment in Gen 19:24–25 and Jub. 16:5. More important, the same policy of nondeferred judgment extends to other nations:

> The Lord will execute judgment in the same way in the places where people commit the same sort of impure actions as Sodom—just like the judgment on Sodom. (Jub. 16:6)

Whereas Jubilees mentions the flood only once after Noah, as a chronological reference point (Jub. 23:9), Jubilees mentions Sodom in five different passages, three of which refer to Sodom as an example of judgment beyond the Genesis narrative (Jub. 13; 16; 20:5–6; 22:22; 36:10).[58] Jubilees includes the flood as an example of judgment but prefers the example of Sodom. The emphasis on the judgment of an individual city contrasts sharply with the deferred cosmic judgment in Daniel and especially the flood typology of the Enochic apocalypses. Of course, the idea of using

---

57. Cain, for example, not only avoids capital punishment but receives something of a special protection in Gen 4:15. In Jub. 4:31 Cain was eventually killed "by a just punishment." Jub. 7:33 maintains that the earth will be purified (indicative) by the blood of the one who shed the blood (cf. Gen 9:6; Num 35:33). Apparently judgment for individuals can be deferred within a lifetime, but no later than the moment of death.

58. Jub. 9:15 does not mention a particular nation but may vaguely reference the punishment of Sodom (sword and fire) as applicable to nations that violate the ordained borders. Another resonance would be Isa 66:16: "For by fire will the Lord execute judgment, and by his sword, on all flesh; and those slain by the Lord shall be many" (NRSV). While the Isaiah passage imagines sudden mass judgment of all flesh, no such suggestion is found in Jubilees. It is also relevant that the punishment for stealing territory (sword and fire) is the means by which Judah conquered Jerusalem in Judg 1:8. Jub. 9 in general deals with the accusation that the Jews "stole" the land of Canaan, to which Jubilees responds that they stole it *back* from Canaan.

Sodom as evidence of the real threat of God's punishment is not novel to Jubilees, but it is unprecedented in apocalypses.[59] Sodom is a clear case of judgment that has already happened in a noneschatological framework that could happen again at any time. The judgment of Sodom and analogous days of judgment illustrate how strong language of judgment ("day of turmoil and curse, of anger and wrath," Jub. 36:10) can be used to describe a harsh judgment that is not universal. It is universality and eschatology, not harshness, that distinguishes the apocalyptic view of judgment.

Even though limited to a single place, Sodom is a case of punishment by absolute destruction. Judgment is not always synonymous with complete destruction in Jubilees. For example, Egypt was judged for its sins with the plagues, but it continues to exist (Jub. 14:14). In the cases of the Moabites and the Philistines, the angel "predicts" to Moses that they will be judged, but it is difficult to say if the judgment was perceived as fulfilled prior to the second century B.C.E. There is reason to believe that these ancient peoples (not place names) were considered extinct, in which case Jubilees can be partly understood as explaining the past judgment of these nations. Even if they exist in some sense but lack the power they once had, they could still be considered already judged. Whereas we have every reason to believe that the typical apocalypses had contemporary enemies in mind when they promised imminent judgment, we should not assume that Jubilees is relating contemporary politics in cursing the descendants of Lot and Caphtor. Even if they were not considered judged to extinction by the time of Jubilees, we still should look to theological and interpretive problems to explain the harsh judgment of these nations. First, we shall consider how the curse of the Philistines arises from Genesis, not second-century oppression by that particular people. Then we will consider the problem that may lie at the root of the condemnation of both Lot and Esau.

In Gen 26:28 Isaac seems to make an oath (אָלָה) and a covenant (בְּרִית) with a Philistine king. Although this could be a problem for many interpreters, we have reason to believe that making covenants with surrounding peoples was an especially hot issue in the mid-second century B.C.E.

---

59. In received scripture the example of Sodom is used in Deuteronomy, Isaiah, Jeremiah, Ezekiel, Amos, and Zephaniah. I do not count the Testaments of Napthali and Benjamin or 2 Enoch as contemporary.

In those days certain renegades [υἱοὶ παράνομοι] came out from Israel and misled many, saying, "Let us go and make a covenant with the nations around us." (1 Macc 1:11)

VanderKam has convincingly shown the importance of this issue not just in one or two passages in Jubilees but in the broadest explanation of the "origins and purposes" of Jubilees.[60] This oath and covenant of Isaac is precisely the problem that leads to the account in Jubilees of the effects of the oath and ultimately the curse of the Philistines (Jub. 24:28-30). It is not impossible that Jubilees could have used the term "Philistines" to refer to enemies in the second century B.C.E. The main concern, however, behind the harshness in Jub. 24 has less to do with the Philistines per se and more to do with making covenants with surrounding nations. In other apocalypses we might assume that a curse on a nation is hoped to be fulfilled in the imminent future, but in Jubilees it seems not to matter when it did or will happen. There is nothing eschatological about the judgment of the Philistines predicted in Jub. 24:28-30, and it has nothing to do with Jub. 23.

Although one might question whether Moab was considered judged in the past, the descendents of Esau were certainly understood as alive at the time of the author. On the one hand, one should not deny that the author of Jubilees has a contemporary people in mind in Jub. 38:14: "The Edomites have not extricated themselves from the yoke of servitude which Jacob's sons imposed on them until today."[61] On the other hand, one should not think that Jubilees is primarily concerned with contemporary politics in its treatment of Esau and his descendants.[62] Genesis suffices to explain

---

60. James C. VanderKam, "The Origins and Purposes of the Book of Jubilees," in *Studies in the Book of Jubilees* (ed. Matthias Albani, Jörg Frey, and Armin Lange; TSAJ 65; Tübingen: Mohr Siebeck, 1997), 3-24. Elsewhere VanderKam demonstrates the significance of Exod 23:32, "You shall make no covenant with them," for the selection of the scriptural setting of Jubilees; see his "The Scriptural Setting of the Book of Jubilees," *DSD* 13 (2006): 69. See also Dan 9:27 for the issue of a ברית between Antiochus and the Jewish masses. Josephus also gives his own special condemnation of Jews not resolving their problems internally but running off to foreign leaders to support their selfish plots (e.g., *B.J.* 1.31-32).

61. The ensuing king list would seem to require that the Edomites have long since lost sovereignty, or at least noteworthy kings. Loss of sovereignty can be a form of judgment.

62. For an approach very much centered on contemporary politics, see Mendels, *Land of Israel*, 57-88.

the complex treatment of the relationship between Jacob/Israel and Esau/Edom. Likewise, the status of Lot is a famous ambiguity in Jewish biblical interpretation.[63] Although the particular interpretive problems with Lot and Esau are very different, there may be a broad issue that begins to account for the harsh judgment of both nations in Jubilees.

The basic issue, it seems, goes back to the categorization of humanity discussed in the previous chapter, on the spatial axis. Israel is an absolute category for the division of humanity. There is no partial credit for brothers or cousins of Jacob. For purposes of marriage, purity, covenant, temple, and eschatological restoration, all of non-Israel is completely excluded, regardless of what may have been temporarily acceptable in the time of the patriarchs. Jubilees is bound by the complexities of received scripture but uses judgment to resolve all ambiguities about related peoples. The treatment of Esau is complex, but the bottom line is simple: Esau and all his descendants will be destroyed (Jub. 35:14; 36:10). Likewise, the family tie between Abraham and his nephew does not extend to their descendants (16:9). God's promises, particularly for mercy from total judgment, apply to Israel alone. Israel's historical extended family and allies have been or will be judged like every other nation, but there is nothing eschatological about their judgments.

The harsh judgment in Jubilees of Caphtor, Lot, and even Esau is not the product of contemporary oppression or political tension. Rather, their rejection resolves theological problems in authoritative texts. This alone would be a significant point of contrast with what one typically finds in the apocalypses. It also brings us back to our general point for this section. The idea of judgment is important for Jubilees, but judgment is not anchored on the temporal axis. Each nation is judged individually, but none of these judgments is tied to the reader's present or the restoration in Jub. 23. The turning point in Jub. 23 brings separation between Israel and the nations, but not final judgment of any or all nations. The only punishment in Jub. 23 is the covenantal punishment of Israel leading to repentance, and the worst that happens to the other nations is that they are sent home and left out of the restoration of Israel.[64] There is harsh judgment in Jubilees, but harshness does not distinguish the apocalyptic view of judgment. Judgment is a rolling process for individual nations, rather than a single batch

---

63. Kugel, *Traditions of the Bible*, 329–31.

64. As discussed in the previous chapter on the spatial axis, the apocalypses often make room for other nations in the restoration.

judgment deferred to a future time. Jubilees has the literary components of the genre, including language such as "great day of judgment," a turning point of history, and the theme of judgment. Jubilees sounds like other apocalypses but assembles the pieces in such a way as to undermine the view of judgment on the temporal axis typically found in the apocalypses.

3.4. The Restoration

The restoration in Jubilees is distinctive on two temporal issues. First, the restoration is gradual and has already begun. Second, the restoration restores and fulfills the original plan of creation. The first issue is relatively simple and clear. From a temporal perspective, the restoration typically happens quickly and radically, such that one could not claim that it has already happened in history. In Jubilees, the restoration is gradual and has already begun, casting a very different light on the present moment. The issue is not the degree of the change but the temporal nature of the change and time relative to the present.

The second issue is subtle and complex. The other apocalypses are not uniform in the details of the "new" creation and the implied critique of the former creation, but they do converge around a negative evaluation of the present world order. This issue allows us to step back from the particulars of Jub. 23 and grasp the more fundamental perspective conveyed throughout the book. Jubilees maintains a fundamentally positive, even Panglossian, view of creation, received scripture, the temple, the priesthood, national identity, and social structure in general. The "new creation" in Jubilees is a restoration and making permanent of things that have already existed in biblical history. It is not a rejection of the world or the history of Israel. There is no new covenant, new temple, new social order, or new creation other than the fulfillment and making permanent of the original plan of creation. We will consider the other apocalypses for both issues, then consider Jubilees in two sections, first the gradual and realized restoration in Jub. 23 and then the view of old creation in Jubilees as a whole.[65]

---

65. Some of the ideas pertaining to this point already appeared in print in Todd R. Hanneken, "Creation and New Creation in the Hebrew Bible and Early Jewish Literature," in *God, Grace, and Creation* (ed. Philip Rossi; College Theology Society Annual 55; Maryknoll, N.Y.: Orbis, 2010), 79–93.

3.4.1. Third Isaiah

Once again, it is not the case that the positions in Third Isaiah align uniformly with either the apocalypses or Jubilees, but it is the case that Third Isaiah forms the background to the disputed issues at hand. On the first issue, Third Isaiah clearly conveys the idea of a rapid and radical reversal in the near future, as, for example, in, 63:19–64:1:

> If only you would tear open the heavens and come down,
> The mountains would shudder from your presence
> As fire in kindling boils water.[66]

Radical reversal is not unique to Third Isaiah, but the language of new creation is distinctively clear in Third Isaiah, especially 65:17:

> So look! I am about to create a new heavens and a new earth.
> Former things will not be remembered or even cross the mind.[67]

It is also evident that Jubilees has this passage (65:20) in mind when treating the issue of life span, as discussed above. If read literally, Isa 65:17–25 contributes the image of ecological discontinuity, that is, a rewriting of the basic laws of nature and a complete replacement of earth and sky. The more persistent point in Third Isaiah is the revision of the social order, not only class but priesthood (Isa 61:6; 66:21) and national identity (56:8).[68] On the issue of the status of the old creation, it is not the case that the early apocalypses consistently dwell on the replacement of the old creation with a new creation, such that the treatment in Jubilees should be understood as a direct response to the apocalypses. Rather, Third Isaiah raises the idea of a new creation, and the apocalypses and Jubilees develop the idea in different directions. For Jubilees, the restoration is new in the sense of renewal or restoring the past. In the apocalypses, there is less about the world that is worth saving (even if the starkest imagery of total ecological replacement develops later).

---

66. See also 58:8; 59:19; 61:11; 62:11; 63:4; 66:12.
67. Reprised, with emphasis on everlasting, in Isa 66:22.
68. Consider also the שֵׁם אַחֵר, "different name" in Isa 65:15.

3.4.2. The Enochic Apocalypses

The Enochic apocalypses clearly and consistently imagine a rapid and radical restoration, a restoration that could not have been called realized.[69] The Enochic apocalypses are not uniform in how they imagine the continuity between the old creation and the new creation. The Book of the Watchers resembles Jubilees in imagining a restoration to Eden. Other Enochic apocalypses either suggest or state that the whole world will pass away. The issue is not merely the view of flora and fauna but the valuation of salvation history after Eden. Jubilees and the Book of the Watchers end up back in Eden, in a sense, but Jubilees takes more with it, including the Torah, temple, priesthood, and national boundaries.

The Book of the Watchers speaks of two judgments at once. The former model, in the days of Noah, is realized, but the second, more complete judgment remains for the future. The restoration description in 1 En. 10:16–11:2 indicates that the future fulfillment will be far more glorious than the prototype.[70] As for the second issue, the Book of the Watchers is actually very similar to Jubilees in that it imagines a restoration that is like the beginning of the old creation. This is particularly so in that longevity is restored (but not immortality)[71] and in the use of references to Eden in the description of the restoration. The restoration is radical but could still be considered a restoration of precedent and the original plan of creation, other than the removal of that dangerous tree.[72] The question of what is *not* found in the restoration is a bit trickier. We should be

---

69. Grant Macaskill (*Revealed Wisdom and Inaugurated Eschatology in Ancient Judaism and Early Christianity* [JSJSup 115; Leiden: Brill, 2007], 45) emphasizes an aspect in which the eschatology of 1 Enoch is not entirely future. He calls the eschatology inaugurated in as much as the revelation of wisdom to a remnant group (including opening their eyes) has already occurred. One could add that the decline of history and beginning of the final woes are also typically realized. Nevertheless, the judgment and restoration are thoroughly unrealized. The reversal of history is in the imminent future, but in the future nonetheless.

70. See especially 1:4–7 and 25:3. For a recent discussion of the future judgment in the Book of the Watchers, set in the context of the past judgment, see ibid., 33–34.

71. 1 En. 5:9 ("the number of their days they will complete"); 25:4–6 ("such as your fathers lived also in their days").

72. 1 En. 10:16–11:2; 25:4–6. This description applies to the redacted Book of the Watchers as a whole as it existed by the time of Jubilees. The discussion would be considerably more complicated if one were to distinguish the historical development

skeptical of arguments from silence or later developments. The lack of reference to the Sinai covenant should be primarily understood in terms of the ancient setting and "audience" (i.e., the fact that the testimony of Enoch, unlike the Torah of Moses, applies to all of humanity). Nevertheless, it is the case that the Book of the Watchers does nothing to rule out the possibility, for later interpreters, that the final restoration would be a world without Torah, national boundaries, hierocracy, or perhaps even a temple.

The Astronomical Book develops a less-detailed vision of the restoration, and one should be suspect of the antiquity (relative to Jubilees) of some parts. I briefly note two items that contribute to the idea of the entire earth and sky being replaced with a new earth and sky. First, 1 En. 72:1, "how every year of the world will be forever, until a new creation lasting forever is made," could suggest that the new creation will discontinue the world and history as we know it. Second, the phrase "for the generations of the world" (1 En. 81:2; 82:1) could mean that there will be no more generations in this world after the predictions are fulfilled. To be sure, the relationship between the old and new creation is not emphasized in the Astronomical Book.

Again, the Apocalypse of Weeks is striking in that three "weeks" of history pass between the turning point and the final end of history. Be that as it may, one would not call the restoration in the Apocalypse of Weeks gradual in the sense of imperceptible or potentially realized, as we shall see in Jubilees. Even the initial reversal at the beginning of the eighth week is more radical than could have been understood to have already happened. The present of the reader is the end of the seventh week.[73] One effect of "spreading out" the destruction of the old is that contempt for multiple aspects of creation can be conveyed. One of the first "changes" to be made is that a temple will be built to replace the first temple (the second is not even acknowledged).

The next change is that, as Nickelsburg translates, "righteous law [דין קשוט] will be revealed to all the sons of the whole earth … and all humankind will look to the path of everlasting righteousness" (1 En. 91:14). One problem with concluding from this that the law of Moses

---

of the components of 1–5, 6–11, 12–16, 17–19, and 20–36. See Stuckenbruck, *1 Enoch 91–108*, 6 n. 7.

73. VanderKam, "Studies in the Apocalypse of Weeks," 377–79 (521–23 in the 1984 publication); Nickelsburg, *1 Enoch: A Commentary*, 441.

is viewed as unrighteous is that דין קשוט is probably better rendered as Nickelsburg himself twice renders it in the Apocalypse of Weeks, "righteous judgment."[74] Another problem is that the law of Moses was called "a covenant for all generations" in 1 En. 93:6. This is not to suggest that the Apocalypse of Weeks embraces the law of Moses without reservation. Rather, the point is to place the emphasis where the Apocalypse of Weeks does, on the extension to all humanity. The problem with the law of Moses is *not* that it is not righteous or even that it is not eternal but that it was revealed only to Israel, not all humanity. Whether the righteous judgment revealed to all nations is identical to the Mosaic Torah, similar but adapted to a new audience, or completely different, the major shift in the ninth week is that national boundaries are dissolved. To the extent to which the Apocalypse of Weeks downplays the eternal validity of the Torah of Moses, the author of Jubilees must be seething mad, but the extension of law (or revealed righteous judgment) to the other nations is no more tolerable.

Last, and probably least among the issues at hand, the heaven is thrown out and replaced with a new, improved heaven that is seven times brighter. The need for a new cosmos says nothing good about the original cosmos; even if it was not made corrupt, it has become irreparably corrupt. Although ecological discontinuity may seem more radical to the modern reader, at the time the issues of the legitimacy of the Second Temple and national boundaries were seven times hotter than the luminaries of the firmament.

The same basic set of ideas is expressed in the Animal Apocalypse. On the first issue, it is again clear that the radical restoration is unrealized. Even if angelophanies were perceived in history, the earth opening up to swallow foreign armies, and everything thereafter, was not fulfilled in the second century. As for the second issue, creation may be restored more than replaced, but it is restored to a time without nations, Torah, or, arguably, hierocracy. The temple is emphatically rejected and replaced. History essentially reverses and goes back to the original creation of Adam. The Animal Apocalypse implies what the Book of the Watchers did not: the division of humanity into nations will be reversed, as all will again become

---

74. See the discussion in Nickelsburg, *1 Enoch: A Commentary*, 449. The phrase also appears without requiring a sense of "law" in 4Q197 (Tob[b]), 4Q205 (En[d]), 4Q213a (Levi[b]) (cf. 4Q246). Stuckenbruck translates "the righteous judgment" (*1 Enoch 91–108*, 139–42).

one "species" (1 En. 90:38).[75] Even more explicitly than the Apocalypse of Weeks, the Animal Apocalypse rejects the legitimacy or recoverability of the Second Temple and calls for tearing down the "old house" and building a new one (1 En. 90:28–29). The birth of the new leader may be more ambiguous, but this does not sound like a restoration of the Zadokite priesthood or Davidic monarchy (1 En. 89:12).[76] Of course, other elements, such as the reversal of the diaspora, were not controversial (1 En. 90:33). The Animal Apocalypse does not extend its critique to the heavens or the earth by adding a replacement heaven or earth, nor does it deal with longevity or immortality. One could even say that the end goal of the restoration is simply the return to the original plan. Contrary to Jubilees, the original plan did not include the separation of Israel, the received structures of authority, or explicit importance of the revelation at Sinai.

3.4.3. The Danielic Apocalypses and the Book of Daniel

The apocalypses in Daniel and Dan 2 convey an expectation of a sudden radical reversal that has not yet taken place. There is nothing gradual about the sudden supernatural destruction of the world's empires and the establishment of a Jewish empire far superior to any previous empire (Dan 2:35, 44). Scholars may continue to disagree about certain details in Dan 7, but second-century Judea saw no dominion served by all peoples. The resurrection in Dan 12 likewise stands outside of realized history. Like the Enochic apocalypses, there is nothing subtle or gradual about the restorations conceived in Daniel. The book conveys optimism for the future but a very negative view of the present.

The view of the former order reflected in the new order is more ambiguous and should not be inflated to a major concern. On the one hand, the establishment of a global Jewish empire surpassing all previous empires is not a restoration of even the most glorified past. On the other hand, it is very much earthly. In Dan 12 the highest level of reward is outside the earthly realm (at least figuratively), but this is not exactly a rejection of the value of creation. There may not be emphasis on the restoration as a Torah-centered society, but a rejection or replacement is not suggested

---

75. For the argument that Jews as well as Gentiles become white cattle at the conclusion of the Animal Apocalypse, see ch. 2 n. 90.

76. In order to parallel the last white bull, it would have to go back at least to Isaac.

either.⁷⁷ Once the abomination that desolates the temple is removed, the temple can apparently recover fully. The restoration surpasses the world as we know it but does not particularly replace it. Daniel has a negative view of the present moment but not salvation history as a whole. Daniel is more neutral on this issue and certainly does not contrast with Jubilees as sharply as the Apocalypse of Weeks and the Animal Apocalypse.

3.4.4. Jubilees

Jubilees takes a very different view of the temporal nature of the restoration than the contemporary apocalypses. First, the restoration in Jub. 23 is gradual, which is a difference by itself, but, more importantly, this leads to the conclusion that the restoration has already begun. The genre "apocalypse" still functions to create an imperative view of the present moment, but it is a positive view of the present. Second, Jub. 1 identifies the indwelling of the sanctuary in the restoration with the indwelling of the sanctuary in the days of Aaron. The restoration will make permanent, not replace, the traditional sanctuary and priesthood. Third, in the book as a whole the restoration restores and fulfills the original plan of creation without introducing a "new" creation.

Although we have not found uniformity in the apocalypses on the recoverability of creation and salvation history since Eden, relative to Jubilees, the apocalypses are either silent or overtly negative on the continuity of the Jewish tradition in the restoration. The Apocalypse of Weeks and the Animal Apocalypse do not speak for all the apocalypses, but they do speak loudly on the rejection of exclusive revelation and temple for Israel, as well as the traditional structure of priestly authority. No apocalypse besides Jubilees overtly counters this view. Thus, the negative view is associated with the apocalypses even if it is not a standard component. Although it has been noted that Jubilees takes a positive view of the temple, priesthood, Jewish particularism, and the law and covenant associated with Sinai, we will consider these issues from the perspective of the eschatological restoration. According to Jubilees, nothing new is needed, except to fulfill the old. The restoration stabilizes but does not change or add to the original

---

77. See §4.1.2.2 below on the view of Jeremiah and the Torah of Moses implied in Dan 9.

plan of creation, including the law, people, land, temple, priesthood, and calendar of Israel received from long ago.

3.4.4.1. The Restoration in Jubilees 23 Is Gradual and Has Already Begun

Scholars since Charles have noted that the restoration in Jubilees is gradual,[78] and Russell seems to have grasped some of the significance of the fact that Jubilees stands out among apocalypses for an "evolutionary rather than cataclysmic" restoration.[79] Further significance comes from the context of the present work. This is not one way that Jubilees is different but the climax of a pattern of differences. Not only is the restoration gradual; it has already begun. The repentance phase (itself distinctive among early apocalypses),[80] which has already begun in as much as the book has any audience, leads directly to a gradual restoration. Although the end result is dramatic, there are no ahistorical conditions or predictions to be fulfilled before the blessings begin.

> In those days the children will begin to study the laws, to seek out the commands, and to return to the right way. The days will begin to become numerous and increase, and mankind as well—generation by generation and day by day until their lifetimes approach one thousand years and to more years than the number of days (had been). (Jub. 23:26–27)[81]

---

78. Charles, *Jubilees*, 149; Rowley, *The Relevance of Apocalyptic*, 61.

79. Russell, *Method and Message*, 268 n. 4.

80. Even if one counts the lambs opening their eyes in the Animal Apocalypse as a form of repentance, it does not lead directly to restoration but rather to final woes. In general, and perhaps also in the Animal Apocalypse, the Apocalypse of Weeks is more typical in the view that the chosen are chosen because they are already righteous (if for any reason at all), not because they repented prior to receiving esoteric revelation. Again, I do not count the prayer in Dan 9 as an endorsed explanation of the situation in the last days.

81. James Kugel demonstrates how this obscure phrase relates to Ps 90:14–15, שַׂבְּעֵנוּ בַבֹּקֶר חַסְדֶּךָ וּנְרַנְּנָה וְנִשְׂמְחָה בְּכָל־יָמֵינוּ שַׂמְּחֵנוּ כִּימוֹת עִנִּיתָנוּ שְׁנוֹת רָאִינוּ רָעָה, "Satisfy us in the morning with your kindness that we may shout and be glad all our days. Make us glad like/according to the days of our affliction, the years we saw misfortune." While it would make no sense to ask to be gladdened like the days one was afflicted, Jubilees makes sense of it by asserting that in the restoration Israel would get back the days humanity had lost to punishment for wickedness and be happy all the days they were miserable. See James L. Kugel, "The Jubilees Apocalypse," *DSD* 1 (1994): 333–34. It is difficult to translate in such a way that stays close to the Ethiopic

Since the restoration in life span is gradual, it would have been impossible to falsify the claim. Indeed, since the time of composition was a time of peace following a period of civil war, famine, and occupation (see ch. 5), an increase in life expectancy would have been apparent. The restoration of longevity is not immortality, but returning to the original plan for humanity in Eden. This, by itself, is not so different from the Book of the Watchers, but other differences will become apparent in the next subsection. Compared to other apocalypses, it is striking that the restoration does not go beyond what had once been the case in the ideal past. Even the climax of restoration in Jub. 23 does not go beyond what is imagined to have already been the case in the "old" creation. The old creation may need to be restored to its former glory, but it does not need to be replaced. We see this in Jub. 23 with respect to longevity, but more points like this will come out when we consider the rest of the book.

It would be an overreaction to lump Jubilees with later examples of realized eschatology, but we should not miss the significance of the difference between Jubilees and contemporary apocalypses. We should consider how the view of the present moment in Jubilees differs from what a reader would expect. Jubilees still amplifies the significance of the present moment, but it shifts from a moment of crisis to a moment of opportunity. The hope and promises are no longer mediated by threats and pessimism. The plan of restoration does not require new revelation but a return to traditional social and textual authorities. The promises are not complicated by external agents or arbitrarily appointed dates; rather, the continuing restoration of history depends only on the decision of the people of Israel. The audience is called to Torah study, not warfare or martyrdom. Jubilees asserts that the worst is over. The difference between Jubilees and contemporary apocalypses on the temporal relationship between the present and the restoration (i.e., whether the restoration has begun) should be more than a footnote in the study of Jewish thought and literature in antiquity.

---

while making clear the allusion and the meaning. The basic idea, drawing from Jub. 4:30 ("[Adam] lacked seventy years from one thousand years because one thousand years are one day in the testimony of heaven"), is that if humanity now lives seventy years and is given back the number of years of Adam, they will reach the one thousand years that was originally intended.

3.4.4.2. Jubilees 1:26–29 Identifies the Indwelling of the Sanctuary in the Restoration with the Indwelling of the Sanctuary of Aaron

The description of the new creation and indwelling of the sanctuary in Jub. 1:26–29 is complex and allusive. Surprisingly, Jubilees presents these features, typically envisioned for the eschatological future, as complete in the days of Moses, in the distant past for the original audience. The first key to understanding Jub. 1:29 is to observe that it is the last of three formulations of the scope of the book. The double-meanings of Jub. 1:29 could have been confusing to the ancient audience, as they have been to modern scholars, but Jub. 1:26–28 should help the reader. In the first formulation, God commands Moses to write down the book of Jubilees. In the second, God commands the angel of the presence to dictate to Moses the book of Jubilees. Finally, Jub. 1:29 describes the scope of the tablets that the angel dictated to Moses. While the third may add an eschatological twist on the first two formulations, it does not contradict them. In all three cases the scope of the book is from Gen 1 up to but excluding Exod 25–Lev 9, that is, through Exod 24. In other words, the book covers from the creation up to (not through) the building and indwelling of the sanctuary of God in the midst of Israel. Besides the consistency of the three iterations, the actual book supports this observation;[82] Jubilees narrates the time from

---

82. VanderKam deals with the problem that the actual scope of Jubilees does not support the reading that Jub. 1:26, 29 refer exclusively to an "end." However, even with chapter 23, Jubilees does not include the contents of all of history. Many passages in Jubilees claim to give the laws and chronological structure that will apply to all of history but not the specific events. Jub. 1, like Deuteronomy, predicts a pattern of sin, punishment, repentance, and restoration but is hardly a predetermined chronology. Deuteronomy and Jub. 1 support the idea that Moses received some sense of what would happen to Israel in the future but not specific chronology of events. See James C. VanderKam, "Studies on the Prologue and Jubilees 1," in *For a Later Generation: The Transformation of Tradition in Israel, Early Judaism, and Early Christianity* (ed. Randal A. Argall, Beverly Bow, and Rodney Alan Werline; Harrisburg, Pa.: Trinity Press International, 2000), 272–73.

Berner (*Jahre, Jahrwochen und Jubiläen*, 239–48) considers the tension to be a contradiction that could not have been produced by a single author. He claims the original work presented the time of creation through Moses in a heptadic chronology. A later redactor added Jub. 1:5–28 and 23:14–31 to extend the scope past the days of Moses, but that redactor neglected the heptadic chronology of the original author. It seems more likely that the passages that speak of "for all time" mean that the laws related in Jubilees are for all time, not that Jubilees relates the events of all time.

creation through Exod 24.[83] The addition of an eschatological, permanent dimension adds to but does not negate the basic sense. The dwelling of God among Israel will happen again and will happen permanently, but it has already happened and will basically be the fulfillment, not replacement, of the plan in the heavenly tablets (a.k.a. the Priestly source) for the priesthood and sanctuary of Aaron.

The first of three iterations clearly states the scope, up to the indwelling of the sanctuary.

> Now write down the entire account that I am making known to you on this mountain from beginning to end, how it is to be in every division of time—as it is in the law and the testimony—into its weeks for jubilees forever, until the time when I descend and dwell with them forever and ever." (Jub. 1:26, my translation)[84]

As it happens, the indwelling that began in Lev 9 was interrupted by sin, but it was intended then for all eternity and will happen again successfully. Jubilees 1:26 cannot be understood to mean that the book of Jubilees will chronicle all the events of all time, but only the divisions of time that are to be for all time and the events from creation until the *original* sanctuary. If ቀዳሚ ፡ ወደኃሪ, "what is first and what is last," resonates with the typical apocalypses, the resonance in language accentuates discord in the ideas sustained; Jubilees does not develop an end of time per se, even in chapter 23.[85] Chronicles shows that "first and last" can simply mean

---

83. VanderKam, "Scriptural Setting," 61–72.

84. Cf. Exod 25:8, "They are to make a sanctuary for me that I may dwell among them"; also Exod 29:45; Num 5:3; 35:34.

85. In the Latin text of Jub. 45:14, Jacob informs his children what would happen to them in their last days in the land of Egypt, which is to say, the exodus. The Ethiopic duplicates "what would happen to them" so that Jacob tells them *both* what would happen to them in Egypt *and* what would happen to them in the last days (although Ethiopic manuscripts 21, 35 and 63 omit the conjunction). Scribal error could go in either direction (duplicating or dropping), but two factors are decisive in favor of the Latin. First, Jubilees does not use the language or the idea of "last days" or "end of time" in chapter 23. Indeed, history changes course when Israel repents, but history never ends. Second, the passage in Jubilees is based on Gen 49, but it *removes* all the predictive content. At best, Jubilees would be acknowledging an eschatological prediction, not retelling or expanding it. It is much more likely, however, that Jubilees used the phrase בְּאַחֲרִית הַיָּמִים from Gen 49:1 in the basic sense of "in days to come," i.e., the time to come in Egypt. The eschatological use of the phrase explains why later

"complete contents (of a book)," without the later connotation of an end of the cosmos.[86]

The second iteration states even more clearly and succinctly the scope of Jubilees as it is carried out in the rest of the book:

> Then he said to an angel of the presence, "Dictate [4Q216 IV, להכתיב] to Moses from the beginning of creation until the time when my sanctuary [መቅደሥ] is built among them forever and ever." (Jub. 1:27, my translation)

Again, it is true that the sanctuary built among Israel in Exod 25–Lev 9 did not persist uninterrupted for eternity, but it was planned for eternity, and the same basic plan will become stable for eternity. The formulation is ambiguous enough to tease an expectation that Jubilees will describe events after the days of Moses and Aaron, but those expectations are soon subverted. The next verse goes on to connect the theophany in Lev 9 with the theophany in 2 Chr 7:3 on Mount Zion. The long-term plan for the dwelling of God in the holy place indeed refers to Zion and Jerusalem, but that addition does not negate the connection to the immediate fulfillment in the time following the revelation of the book of Jubilees to Moses. The building of the sanctuary has two temporal meanings: the simple sense of the time of Exod 25, and the permanent sense future relative to the audience. There is only one object, however. Jubilees identifies the eternal sanctuary as the sanctuary of Aaron.

Jubilees 1:29 pushes further the polyvalence, but we should not emend away the basic meaning that the scope of Jubilees is from the creation in Gen 1 up to the indwelling of God in Exod 25–Lev 9. The future relative to the second-century audience is a restoration of the immediate future relative to Moses. It is important to recognize the multiple connotations of "making new." In one sense the creation in Gen 1 was making new. In another sense the priestly cult of Aaron has cosmic significance for atonement and renewal. In yet another sense the eschatological future relative

---

transmitters would give it an "end of time" meaning that was not operative in the original composition. Another possible sense would be "in the last days of the era," which would mean the same thing, since the first era of 2,450 years ends with the exodus and journey in the desert.

86. Deutero-Isaiah notwithstanding (41:4; 44:6; 48:12), the phrase could simply refer to completeness in treating the subject matter, as it does frequently in Chronicles (1 Chr 29:29; 2 Chr 9:29; 12:15; 16:11; 20:34; 25:26; 26:22; 28:26; 35:27).

to the audience will be a renewal. All three senses are active in Jub. 1:29. The basic "from … until" structure can be aligned with the previous two iterations and the actual contents of the rest of the book. There are two "from" clauses, which iterates that the heavenly tablets existed from the beginning of creation. Both refer to the creation as described in Gen 1. First comes the claim that the law, testimony, and calendar of the heavenly tablets existed from creation:

> from the time the law and the testimony were created—for the weeks of their jubilees, year by year in their full number, and their jubilees. (Jub. 1:29)

Although Genesis does not make clear that the law was created at or before the creation of the world, Jubilees is not alone in this perspective.[87]

The second "from" clause is, in a sense, a more conventional way of referring to the creation of the heavens and earth as it is known in Gen 1. In another sense, the text as we have it seems to go beyond the creation in Gen 1. Although previous scholars have felt compelled to emend, another way to make sense of the text is to understand "creating new" at multiple levels. Thus, the *terminus a quo* of Jubilees is still the original creation:

> እምዕለተ ፡ ፍጥረት ፡ ሐዳስ ፡ አም ፡ ይትሐደስ ፡ ሰማያት ፡ ወምድር ፡ ወኩሉ ፡ ፍጥረቶሙ...
>
> from the time of new creation, when the heavens become new, along with the earth, and all their creatures… (Jub. 1:29)

Without context, this verse could be understood as an eschatological prediction, as if Jubilees were to narrate starting with a time future relative to Moses and the second-century audience.[88] The immediate context and the

---

87. With the help of Prov 8:22, Wisdom and vicariously Torah were considered the prerequisites of creation (Kugel, *Traditions of the Bible*, 54).

88. Thus it is on the basis of context, rather than grammar, that I seek a more ambiguous or neutral translation than that of VanderKam, "from … the time of the new creation when the heavens, the earth, and all their creatures will be renewed [subjunctive]." The bigger difference is that VanderKam inserts an emendation, "[the time of the creation until]." Although not supported by manuscripts, the emendation is a reasonable attempt to make simple sense of the passage. I suggest that the passage has a complex but meaningful sense without emendation.

actual contents of the book discord with such an understanding and thus demands an alternative understanding of ambiguous terms and nonperfective conjugation.[89] The claim is not that this is a *simple* way of referring to the creation in Gen 1. Jubilees is intentionally playing against an understanding of "new creation" that suggests that the first creation was flawed. The heavens and earth were already made new in the original creation. Any other new creation will be a restoration, not a rejection of the original new creation in Gen 1.[90]

A further assertion about the original creation has perplexed scholars. VanderKam is justified in departing from the base manuscript (25) to include ለሰማይ, "with respect to heaven, heavenly" (manuscript 35). The meaning, however, does not make sense with VanderKam's emendation, as he has the verse reading "the creatures of the earth will be renewed … like the creatures of the earth." Rather, Jubilees is saying here what it says elsewhere, that there is a correlation between heavenly beings and earthly beings.[91] The lower angels maintain the forces of nature and govern the other nations, the angels of holiness mirror the people of Israel (without mediating sovereignty), and the angels of the presence mirror the Levites:[92]

… በከመ ፡ ኃይላቲሆሙ ፡ ለሰማይ ፡ ወበከመ ፡ ኩሉ ፡ ፍጥረት ፡ ምድር…

… in accordance with the heavenly powers, to each an earthly creature…
(Jub. 1:29)[93]

This correspondence refers to an aspect of the original creation in Jub. 2:2.

---

89. Thomas O. Lambdin (*Introduction to Classical Ethiopic (Ge'ez)* [HSS 24; Missoula, Mont.: Scholars Press, 1978], 437) suggests using the English past tense to translate an Ethiopic subjunctive subordinate to a past frame of reference. In the present circumstance, the joy is in the multivalence, since to "become new" is not clearly marked as past or future.

90. The same term ፍጥረት ፡ ሐዳስ, "new creation," appears in the sense of restoration, not replacement, of the past creation in Jub. 5:12, where it is translated by VanderKam as "new … nature." There the context is the "day of judgment" that was the flood, ወገብረ ፡ ለኩሉ ፡ ግብሩ ፡ ፍጥረት ፡ ሐዳስ ፡ ወጻድቅተ, literally, "And God made for all God's works a new and righteous creation." Again, the "day of judgment" and "new creation" here are past relative to Moses.

91. See the discussion of Deut 32:8; 4:19; 29:25 in §2.1.3, "Angelic Mediation."

92. See Jub. 30:18 and n. 112 below.

93. Cf. VanderKam, "like the powers of the sky and like all the creatures of the earth."

Finally, we come to the easy part, the "until" clause. Although the sanctuary was restored several times in Jewish history, its "creation" refers primarily to the time of Moses and Aaron.[94] Thus, in the simple sense, the temporal extent of the book is up to the creation of the sanctuary:

... እስከ ፡ አመ ፡ ይትፈጠር ፡ መቅደስ ፡ እግዚአብሔር

... until the time when the sanctuary of the Lord will be created. (Jub. 1:29)

This basic "until" clause matches perfectly with the previous two iterations and the actual scope of the book. None of this is to deny that Jubilees is playing on multiple temporal levels. Moses' reception of the heavenly tablets in Exod 24 is followed by the creation and indwelling of God in the sanctuary, and the obvious analogy is that the study of the heavenly tablets in the time of the audience will lead directly to the renewal of the sanctuary and indwelling of God.[95] The plan for restoration is a return to the plan of creation laid out from the beginning of creation through the time the heavenly tablets were fully revealed to Israel at Sinai. This first era, the jubilee of jubilees, provides the plan for eternity. The future will stabilize and fulfill, not supersede, the original plan. Ambiguous or multivalent language of new creation resonates with the apocalypses enough to evoke reader expectations of the ideas conveyed, but those expectations are subverted by the meaning sustained in context.

Jubilees 1:29 goes on to include the subsequent plan for the sanctuary. Here we see as strongly as ever the very high opinion that Jubilees has for the priestly cult. Purity is a prerequisite for the sanctuary, but once the

---

94. Exodus and Leviticus do not use the root ברא to refer to the construction of the sanctuary, but for Jubilees the original and final constructions of the sanctuary are identified as part of the fulfillment of creation. The Temple Scroll also speaks of the sanctuary as something created by God (29:8–10). Eyal Regev ("Jubilees, Qumran, and the Essenes," in Boccaccini and Ibba, *Enoch and the Mosaic Torah*, 426–40) argues that this passage in the Temple Scroll is dependent on Jubilees. Isa 4:5 would also be relevant to a consideration of "creation" in relationship to the sanctuary.

95. Although it is not explicit, the pattern of Moses' study of the heavenly tablets leading to the making new of Aaron's sanctuary could correlate with the study and renewal in the time of the audience (Jub. 23:26–31). The healing discussed in the following paragraph also applies to Jub. 23:30.

sanctuary is in operation it has power to benefit not only Israel, but the luminaries:

በኢየሩሳሌም ፡ በደብረ ፡ ጽዮን ፡ ኩሉ.⁹⁶ ፡ ብርሃናት ፡ ይትሐደሱ ፡ ለፈውስ ፡ ወለሰላም ፡ ወለበረከት ፡ ለኩሎሙ ፡ ኅሩያነ ፡ እስራኤል ፡ ወከመ ፡ ይኩን ፡ ከማሁ ፡ እምይእቲ ፡ ዕለት ፡ ወእስከ ፡ ኩሉ ፡ መዋዕለ ፡ ምድር ፡፡

> In Jerusalem, on Mount Zion, all the luminaries will be renewed for healing, health, and blessing of all the chosen, Israel,⁹⁷ so that it will remain so from then on, for all the days of the earth. (Jub. 1:29)

Remarkably, this reverses the direction of influence that one typically finds in apocalypses. Jubilees 19:25 also conveys the idea that Israel renews the luminaries and makes firm the earth.

> May they serve (the purpose of) laying heaven's foundations, making the earth firm, and renewing all the luminaries that are above the firmament. (Jub. 19:2)

The priestly cult never realized its full potential in the past, but, once it is rolling properly, the same basic plan will create a self-sustaining cycle. Mount Zion benefits the luminaries, which benefit Israel, which maintains the cult.⁹⁸ After a few false starts, the same basic cult will get running and continue for all time.

---

96. I read with manuscripts 39, 42 and 48 against VanderKam's base text (25) in omitting a conjunction before "all." I am also disregarding the punctuation, which is not included in the critical apparatus. It would not be impossible to read this clause with the preceding sentence, but I do find it helpful to distinguish the creation of the sanctuary from its later development. One must also be suspect of short, unnecessary phrases that could be explained as anti-Samaritan polemic which could have been inserted during the early transmission of Jubilees. VanderKam translates, "… in Jerusalem on Mt. Zion. All the luminaries will be renewed for (the purpose of) healing, health, and blessing for all the elect ones of Israel and so that it may remain this way from that time throughout all the days of the earth."

97. See 2.2.1.4 for how the phrase "elect ones of Israel" cannot refer to a sect. If it is original, it could mean that all Israel is elect, or it could refer to the Levites.

98. Fletcher-Louis ("Jewish Apocalyptic and Apocalypticism," 1605) includes Jub. 19:25 as an example of the relationship between temple and cosmos, or "temple cosmology."

3.4.4.3. The Law Revealed at Sinai Will Not Be Surpassed

Besides the restoration of the original life span and the sanctuary of Aaron, which we already considered, the rest of the book includes four more major ways the restoration fulfills the original plan of creation but does not introduce a fundamentally new replacement. These four aspects, discussed in this and the following three subsections, are: (1) the law of Israel, revealed from the heavenly tablets to Moses at Sinai, will be fulfilled, not surpassed; (2) the people of Israel (the priests to a higher degree, but not all humanity) will be holy (pure, set apart); (3) the land of Israel (Zion to a higher degree but not the whole world) will be holy (pure, set apart); (4) the calendar of Israel will synchronize with the heavenly calendar. The persistent pattern is that everything that is needed for the restoration was established at some point in the history of the world from creation through the sanctuary in the wilderness. There is nothing new except the making permanent of what once existed. Furthermore, the particulars of Jewish history (the division of nations, the exclusive covenant, the priesthood) are not part of the decline of history to be reversed but were the original plan of creation written on the heavenly tablets. It is true that a pedagogical period of Deuteronomistic sin and punishment took place before Israel became ready to sustain its purity.[99] Yet, as Israel turns to study the heavenly tablets, according to Jubilees, the final implementation of the plan of creation is becoming manifest.

Scholars may differ on how the Enochic apocalypses view the eschatological status of the law revealed to Moses. It is not impossible to read some of these works as viewing the Sinai covenant and revelation as insufficient or temporary (something of a stopgap measure). The obvious limitation of a law for Israel at the time of Moses is that it would not suffice to explain the judgment of other nations at any time. Scholars will continue to debate the extent to which the negative evaluation of the Torah of Moses goes beyond addressing this problem.[100]

What is clear is that in Jubilees there is only one set of heavenly tablets, revealed throughout the jubilee of jubilees and completely to Moses,

---

99. The years of study mentioned in Jub. 50:4 ended up surpassing forty by a large margin.

100. This issue is not entirely separable from the interpretation of בְּרִית חֲדָשָׁה in Jer 31:31, most notably in the Damascus Document (CD 6.19; 8.21; 20.12). See also Pesher Habakkuk 2.3; 1QS^b 3.26; 5.5, 21.

and there is only one basic covenant, renewed on occasion throughout history and made permanent (and exclusive) with Israel at Sinai. There is only one true way, and that is the way revealed to Moses. The eternality of the heavenly tablets and their complete revelation to Moses is evident throughout Jubilees and also emphasized in eschatological contexts. Jubilees 23:26 emphasizes that the restoration comes by studying the laws. The eternal unity of revelation is borne out in that the description of the restoration echoes not only the Pentateuch (Deut 7:9, etc.), but also Isaiah (65), and Psalms (90).[101] Jubilees 23 concludes with a reminder that this, like everything written by Moses, is "written and entered in the testimony of the heavenly tablets for the generations of eternity."

Throughout the rest of the book, Jubilees emphasizes that the laws received by Moses will never expire. One might doubt whether the copious language of "forever" and "eternal" used to describe the laws revealed to Moses necessarily applies to the eschatological restoration.[102] Often enough, even stronger language dispels any such doubt. For example, the phrase "this law has no temporal limit" appears six times to describe the laws of blood (Jub. 6:14), tithe (13:26),[103] second tithe (32:10), the Festivals of Tabernacles (16:30) and Passover (49:8), and the prohibition of exogamy (30:10). One should understand this assertion to indicate that the law as a whole has no temporal limit, not only these six. Similarly strong language is used of circumcision:

> This law is for every generation forever. There is no circumcising of days.[104] There is no omitting any of the eight days, for it is an eternal ordinance, ordained and written on the heavenly tablets. (Jub. 15:25, slightly adapted from VanderKam's translation)

---

101. I am not trying to make any suggestions of a canonical nature, only that the authoritative status of Isaiah and Psalms was not clearly distinguished from the law of Moses.

102. Jubilees prologue; 2:33; 3:14; 6:14; 13:25; 32:10; 33:16; 49:17.

103. This verse also suggests that the priesthood will be eternal.

104. The point is clear enough from "eternal ordinance," but the point is even stronger if one reads with Segal, "there is no completion [מולות or מולאת] of days" rather than "there is no circumcising [מולת] of days" (*The Book of Jubilees*, 235). Segal's argument is compelling, but the word should probably be understood as a pun suggesting both meanings rather than one or the other.

In one case, at least partly to deal with unpunished behavior of a patriarch, Jubilees develops the notion that the laws are eternal but are only applicable once they are revealed (and are then applicable ever after).

> For the statute, the punishment, and the law had not been completely revealed to all but (only) in your time as a law of its particular time and as an eternal law for the generations of eternity. There is no time when this law will be at an end. (Jub. 33:16–17)

Besides supporting the present point that the laws revealed at Sinai do not expire in the restoration, this passage demonstrates that the heavenly tablets were not *completely* revealed before Sinai, even though many laws were revealed and followed (or enforced) previously.[105] No previous revelation is as complete as that given to Moses.

3.4.4.4. The Separation of the Israelites Was Planned from the Beginning

The previous chapter considered the categorization of humanity from the perspective of the spatial axis; here we consider the election of Israel on the temporal axis, as both original to the plan of creation and maintained in the restoration. The idea of election was not disputed. The dispute concerned whether humanity would return in the restoration to a unified state with a single religion. The apocalypses and Third Isaiah do not necessarily convey *equality* of all peoples but some degree of inclusion of all nations in a single place of worship. Especially when one views the eschatological restoration as a return to the original plan of creation, it would seem to follow that all the children of Adam would walk with God in paradise.[106] Jubilees cuts off this notion at the source. The election of Israel was not God cutting God's losses and focusing on a remnant as the rest of humanity sinned. Rather, the election of Israel was planned from the beginning of creation and became manifest already in the first week of creation. The

---

105. See also Jub. 36:20, "[Jacob] worshiped the Lord wholeheartedly and in line with the visible commands according to the division of the times of his generation."

106. One should not think that there were only two sets of ideas about universalism: total rejection or total acceptance. One should not conflate the inclusiveness that takes the form of Jews abandoning circumcision, for example, and the inclusiveness that takes the form of asserting that all nations will essentially become Jewish. Jubilees rejects both forms. See James C. VanderKam, "Genesis 1 in Jubilees 2," *DSD* 1 (1994): 319–21; idem, "Origins and Purposes of Jubilees," 20–22.

restoration, it follows, will fulfill the plan of complete separation of Israel. Furthermore, the degrees of holiness within Israel are typified in the creation of the ranks of angels.

The creation account in Jub. 2 climaxes not only with the creation of the Sabbath but the designation of the people to observe the Sabbath.[107]

> [He said to us: "I will now separate for myself] a people among my nations. And [they will keep sabbath. I will sanctify them as my people, and I will bless them. They will be my people and I will be their God.] And he[108] chose the descendants of Jacob among [all of those whom I have seen. I have recorded them as my firstborn son and have sanctified them for myself] for all the age(s) of eternity. The [seventh] day [I will tell them so that they may keep sabbath on it from everything"] (Jub. 2:19–20, 4QJub^a VII:9–12, VanderKam and Milik 1994)

In fact, the Sabbath and Israel are practically identified.

> [There were twenty-two heads of humanity] from Adam until him; and twenty-two k[inds of work were made until the seventh day. The one is blessed and holy and the other is blessed] and holy. Both (literally: this one with this one) were made together for holiness [and for blessing. It was given to this one to be for all times the blessed and holy ones.] This is the testimony and the fir[st] law […] (Jub. 2:23–24, 4QJub^a VII:14–17, VanderKam and Milik 1994)

The Ethiopic continues, "as it was sanctified and blessed on the seventh day" (Jub. 2:24). The election of Israel is not an accident of the deterioration of history, but a central part of the original plan of creation. Furthermore, Israel has exclusive rights to Sabbath holiness (2:31).[109] There never

---

107. This issue has already been elucidated, with extra attention to textual issues, by VanderKam, "Genesis 1 in Jubilees 2," 315–21.

108. The Ethiopic text uses first-person forms throughout.

109. VanderKam translates the previous verse about the angels keeping Sabbath, "before it was made known to *all* humanity." I suggest that the italicized word (ኵሉ) would be better translated as "any of." The exclusivity of Israel's sanctification in the Sabbath is clear in Jub. 2:20, 31. Jubilees may partly be reacting to an interpretive problem between the two versions of the Decalogue as to whether the reason for Sabbath observance theoretically applies to all creation or only Israel.

Lutz Doering discusses related issues and similarly observes the emphasis on exclusive observance of the Sabbath by Israel in "The Concept of the Sabbath in the

was a time when the Sabbath was not observed or was intended to be observed by all nations. Consequently, the eschatological restoration and the fulfillment of the plan of creation is not the universalizing of Sabbath observance but the sanctification of Israel alone in Sabbath observance.

The images of eschatological restoration in the rest of the book follow through on the original plan for the eternal separation of Israel (Jub. 2:33). Numerous passages use language of "eternal" or "forever" to describe the election of the descendents of Jacob (e.g., 15:9, 19; 16:26; 22:23; 25:11; 25:20). The central passage on the exclusivity of the relationship between God and Israel (15:30–32) emphasizes the eternality of the distinction. Jubilees 23 describes the restoration with the driving out of the foreign "enemies"; Jub. 1:22–25 also casts the exclusive relationship between God and Israel in eschatological terms.

The issue is most clear when Jubilees focuses not just on the chosenness of Israel continuing in the restoration but on the separation of Israel being fulfilled in the restoration. Thus, should one suggest that the other nations could become pure and join an inclusive vision of Israel in the restoration, Jubilees makes clear that integration and purity are fundamentally incompatible. Indeed, impurity and exogamy are identified (Jub. 30:8). The mixing of types (Israel and the nations) is fundamentally defiling.[110] Jubilees 30:14–15 elevates exogamy to an eschatological issue, identifying exogamy as the root cause of the "final woes" in Jub. 23.

> Israel will not become clean from this impurity while it has one of the foreign women or if anyone has given one of his daughters to any foreign man. For it is blow upon blow and curse upon curse. Every punishment, blow, and curse will come. If one does this or shuts his eyes to those who do impure things and who defile the Lord's sanctuary and to those who

---

Book of Jubilees," in *Studies in the Book of Jubilees* (ed. Matthias Albani, Jörg Frey, and Armin Lange; TSAJ 65; Tübingen: Mohr Siebeck, 1997), 189–90.

110. This observation about Jubilees has already been made by Jonathan Klawans, *Impurity and Sin in Ancient Judaism* (Oxford: Oxford University Press, 2000), 48. See also Christine Elizabeth Hayes, *Gentile Impurities and Jewish Identities: Intermarriage and Conversion from the Bible to the Talmud* (Oxford: Oxford University Press, 2002), 73–81; Betsy Halpern-Amaru, *The Empowerment of Women in the Book of Jubilees* (JSJSup 60; Leiden: Brill, 1999), 154–59; Himmelfarb, *A Kingdom of Priests*, 70–80; Cana Werman, "*Jubilees* 30: Building a Paradigm for the Ban on Intermarriage," *HTR* 90 (1997): 1–22.

profane his holy name, then the entire nation will be condemned together because of all this impurity and this contamination. (Jub. 30:14–15)

Jubilees is "double-dipping" for explanations of the recent suffering. In Jub. 23 the direct cause was the Jewish civil war, but here the indirect cause is exogamy. Jubilees 50:5 resumes the eschatological significance of exogamy by singling out purity among the laws to which Israel returns, bringing about the restoration. The restoration will not transcend the separation of Israel from the nations; it will make the separation absolute.

Although Jubilees emphasizes the holiness barrier between Israel and the nations, it does not challenge the traditional hierarchy in Israel. The issue at hand is not whether one can distill sentiments about priestly groups from the book of Jubilees[111] but Jubilees' eschatological endorsement of the traditional hierarchy in general. Jubilees 2 establishes both the hierarchy of angels and the analogy between angels and humanity. The angels created on the first day follow three degrees of holiness: the angels of the presence have their counterpart in the descendants of Levi; the angels of holiness have their counterpart in the people of Israel; the angels of natural elements have their counterparts in the nations of the world. The first correspondence is made clear in Jub. 30:18:

Levi's descendants were chosen for the priesthood and as levites to serve before the Lord as we (do) for all time.

The "we" is spoken by the angel of the presence who dictates to Moses (Jub. 1:27). The same point is clear in Jub. 31:14. Again, language of "forever" is used of Levi's elevation in Jub. 32:1. The second correspondence, between the angels of holiness and the people of Israel, is clear in two passages. The angels of holiness do not serve in the heavenly sanctuary, but they do share with the angels of the presence Sabbath observance (Jub. 2:18) and circumcision (15:27).[112] The correspondence between the third tier of

---

111. In an earlier century one might identify the elevation of Levi as a pan-Levite polemic against priestly supremacy. By the time of Chronicles, however, one could say nice things about the Levites without challenging the structure that distinguished the priests above the Levites. See ch. 2 n. 100 above.

112. Jub. 31:14 may call for a moderation of this point. There the Levites are blessed "to serve in his temple like the angels of the presence and like the holy ones." There is at least a difference in language between holy ones (31:14, ቅዱሳን) and angels of holiness (2:18, መላእክት ፡ ቅዱሳት) or angels of sanctification (15:27, መላእክት ፡

angels and the rest of the nations is evident both in the fact that they do not share Sabbath observance and circumcision and in Jub. 15:31, where God appoints these angels of the spirits to other nations.[113]

The point is that on the first day of creation God created a hierarchy of heavenly beings that correlates directly to a hierarchy of earthly beings. Hierocracy is not part of the decline of history but the original plan of creation and a reflection of the heavenly ideal. The eschatological restoration and fulfillment of the original plan of creation will not overthrow the hierocratic structures of authority within Israel but fulfill them. Although the focus of this chapter is to describe the situation with respect to the temporal axis, it has long been observed that Jubilees takes a favorable view of the Jerusalem priesthood (other than recent events).[114] Jubilees 23 in particular does not discuss the eschatological priesthood, yet it is clear from the ranks of angels, the language of "forever," and the discussion below of God dwelling in the temple that the Levitical priesthood is fundamental to the plan for the fulfillment of creation.

3.4.4.5. The Borders of the Land of Israel Will Be Restored, Not Dissolved

On the one hand, one might expect an apocalypse to imagine an eschatological restoration in which Babel and the division of the nations is undone, either in that all humanity becomes united in religion or Israel conquers the world far beyond its traditional borders. On the other hand, the theology of land in the Pentateuch is specific to one land, and the Deuteronomistic vision of conquest pertains to a particular territory. Although

---

ቅዱሳ). It is not necessarily the case that there was a clearly articulated and understood distinction between angels of holiness and holy ones (such as the latter being a more general category). The point is that the different language in 31:14 reflects a different concern. Jub. 31:14 is not concerned with ranks of angels and their distinct roles, as Jub. 2 is. This may mean that the author was not obsessed with absolute precision in specifying the ranks of angels in all possible contexts, but it is not a contradiction that requires different authors. At any rate, there is an analogy between the ranks of angels and the ranks of humanity in several passages.

113. Himmelfarb discusses the correlation between angels and Israel in Jubilees and in a broader context; see *A Kingdom of Priests*, 53–84; idem, "The Book of Jubilees and Early Jewish Mysticism," in Boccaccini and Ibba, *Enoch and the Mosaic Torah*, 384–94.

114. Charles, *Jubilees*, lxxiii. For more on the favorable view of Levi, see above, §2.2.1.4, and Hanneken, "The Book of Jubilees among the Apocalypses," 499–505.

the Ethiopic word ምድር can mean "earth" in the sense of the whole earth, in some instances the word should be read as "the land" in the sense of the territory of Israel.[115] The eschatological restoration in Jubilees secures the borders and purifies the land of Israel; it does not expand into an empire or open the borders for an international place of worship. This can be seen first from the "original" plan of the division under Noah and the promises to Abraham. Some of the eschatological passages are more textually complicated, but they are best understood as fulfilling, not going beyond, the particular promises for the land of Israel.

The division of the land in the days of Noah is eternal, and the promise of land to Abraham applies only to the land of Israel. Jubilees 8 goes to great effort to authorize the right of the descendants of Shem to the land of Israel and to highlight the magnitude of the offense of its theft by Canaan. Again we find language of "eternity" and "forever" used to describe the allotment of territory (Jub. 8:12; 17, 21). Jubilees also makes clear that "lots" were not random or human arbitrariness but were made certain from prophecy and overseen by an angel of the presence (8:10, 18, 20; 9:15). Of course, the main point is that Israel did not steal, but recovered, the "land of Canaan." Jubilees makes no effort to qualify the converse, however. For a descendant of Shem to expand into the territory of another would no less bring a curse. The division of territory under Noah and the curse against territorial expansion is valid for all times and peoples, including Israel in the future.

Jubilees also follows Genesis closely in describing the land promised to Abraham and his descendents as the land of Israel, not the whole planet. In no case does Jubilees go out of its way to remove qualifiers such as "the land that you see," "where you reside," "this land," as one would expect if the author of Jubilees anticipated that the descendants of Abraham would eventually own the whole planet.[116] Following the protological notions of territory, it would be very surprising indeed if Jubilees proposed an eschatological territory of Israel expanded to conquer all lands everywhere.[117]

---

115. Halpern-Amaru, *Rewriting the Bible*, 28, 140–41 n. 19. She shows a greater tendency to read Jubilees as referring to the whole earth rather than the land, especially in the context of rereading "exile from the land" as "destruction from the earth" (44–46).

116. Jub. 13:20; 14:7; 15:10; 22:27; 25:17.

117. See, however, Betsy Halpern-Amaru, who does read a shift toward territorial expansionism. She refers to a change of wording from Gen 28:14 (spread out) to Jub.

Two passages in Jubilees suggest that the eschatological restoration restores security of the land of Israel, while another passage, by itself, could be understood as either the land of Israel or the whole earth. A broader reading of Jubilees suggests understanding the ambiguous reading as particular to the land of Israel, not an instance of dissolution or expansion of borders. The first reference comes at the end of the book:

> The jubilees will pass by until Israel is pure of every sexual evil, impurity, contamination, sin, and error. Then they will live confidently in the entire land. They will no longer have any satan or any evil person. The land will be pure from that time until eternity. (Jub. 50:5)

We have already mentioned this passage for the absence of nonhuman agents on the spatial axis. The point now is that the purity and security of the land in the restoration is best understood as referring to the entire land of Israel, not the entire planet. There is no suggestion of purity bringing conquest, only the fulfillment of the land promises in the Pentateuch. Another brief but clear reference is Jub. 23:30, where God expels the sinners of the nations. The fact that they are expelled, and not eradicated or reformed, requires that other territories remain home to sinners.

Two difficult passages should also be considered. The first, Jub. 32:18–19, is a matter of text criticism. While the Ethiopic makes Israel sounds like a global empire, the Latin text does not. They key phrase in the Ethiopic was translated by VanderKam as "they will rule wherever mankind [anyone] has set foot." The Latin reads, "they will rule wherever they set foot against anyone." The passage echoes Deut 11:24, "Every spot on which your foot treads shall be yours," but there the context makes clear that "the land" is a bordered territory, not the whole surface of the earth (see also Josh 1:3). If the author of Jubilees wished to change this idea to imply global conquest, it would have required more emphasis.[118] The Latin makes more sense in light of Deuteronomy and is more consistent with the view of "the land" in the rest of the book of Jubilees.[119] The "prediction" to Jacob

---

27:23 (increase) as evidence of a deliberate shift in emphasis toward territorial expansion. She also argues from the Ethiopic text of Jub. 32:18–19, but see below for the superiority of the Latin text. Halpern-Amaru, *Rewriting the Bible*, 39–40.

118. The words preserved in 4QpapJub[h] do not suffice to resolve the ambiguity, but the fragment does rule out a longer text that might have emphasized this innovation.

119. For further discussion, including the sense of "under heaven" in Jub. 32:19, see Hanneken, "The Book of Jubilees among the Apocalypses," 442–46.

that kings descended from him will be sovereign in the land does not go beyond what was already fulfilled (relative to the audience) through David and Solomon, even if it remains to be restored permanently in the future.

The second difficult passage is Jub. 4:26, where we have no variant texts to support an emendation.[120] The Ethiopic text claims not only that Zion will be sanctified but also that the land will be sanctified from Zion. Here the problem is not the determination of the "the land" as the bordered territory of Israel or the whole earth but the fact that *sanctification* of the land goes beyond precedent. It is tempting to emend, such that the people are sanctified or the land is purified. Even without emending, it would be possible to understand "the inhabitants of" as implicit, such that the inhabitants of the land are sanctified from Zion. The same sense may be implicit in Jub. 6:2, where Noah atones for all the sins of (the inhabitants of) the land. Although eschatological sanctification of the land would go beyond the restoration of historical precedent, it could still have been understood as the fulfillment of the original plan of creation written on the heavenly tablets. Thus, Jub. 50:2–5 predicts that Israel will become pure, as required for the fulfillment of Lev 25:10.[121] At that point, the fiftieth year will be sanctified, and release (דרור) will be proclaimed in the land. That would bring us within one interpretive move from sanctifying the land itself. New textual evidence would be necessary to achieve certainty on Jub. 4:26, but the basic point remains clear: Jubilees imagines a restoration of the traditional borders of the land of Israel, not an expansion or an opening of the borders to foreigners. Even the "new" in the eschatology of Jubilees is a fulfillment and making permanent of the old.

3.4.4.6. The Eschatological Calendar Will Restore, Not Replace, the Calendar Observed in the Past and in Heaven

It is not the case that apocalypses are typically as concerned with calendrical replacement as Jubilees is with calendrical restoration. Even the Astronomical Book (as we have it) suggests only in passing that a new law for heavenly bodies and time-keeping will be applicable in the new creation (1 En. 72:1). Yet it is important to consider this point because, for Jubilees, calendar fits the larger package: the calendar and festivals that are par-

---

120. For further discussion, see ibid., 447–49.
121. See below page 192.

ticular to Judaism are not, in fact, particular to Judaism but mirrored in the heavenly tablets and heavenly liturgy. The general issue is whether the eschatological future will replace Jewish particularism with some form of universalism, that is, whether Jewish history would end and be replaced with a new universal history. For Jubilees, Jewish particularism, including calendar and festivals, is planned from creation and will be made absolute in the restoration. The basic point is clear in many places in Jubilees.

One should be careful to qualify the calendrical concern of Jubilees. Jubilees is very much concerned with celebrating the festivals at the proper time. Jubilees is also concerned with counting periods of seven years and forty-nine years. The major payoff is in the point that the release of Israel from Egypt and return to its land happens in the fiftieth period of forty-nine years (a jubilee of jubilees comparable to the jubilee year in Lev 25).[122] It is not the case, however, that Jubilees serves as a calendrical handbook. Days of the week are among the issues not addressed in Jubilees, unlike 4Q252.[123] Although Jubilees counts forty-nine-year periods from creation through the entry into the land, it does not apparently extend this count to a second jubilee of jubilees or use larger structures.[124] Thus, although we

---

122. VanderKam, "Studies in the Chronology of the Book of Jubilees," 542.

123. Ben-Dov, "Tradition and Innovation in the Calendar of Jubilees," 276–93.

124. As tempting as it may be for modern scholars to imagine that Jubilees would have had a chronological scheme for history after Moses, attempts to uncover such a scheme in Jubilees, as thorough as they have been, have essentially proved the hypothesis false. It is one thing when one makes great assumptions that succeed in making sense of otherwise nonsensical data. When great assumptions provide no more clarity than what is assumed, the hypothesis should be rejected.

On a small scale, Michel Testuz (*Les idées religieuses*, 165–77) tried to piece together various passages in Jubilees into an eschatological scheme and a future periodization of history. He concluded, however, that no such periodization was evident in Jubilees, and if it existed, it existed only as separate secret information in the inner-circles of the sect. As discussed in chapter 2, I disagree with Testuz's conclusion that Jubilees was written by a sect.

James Scott studied the hypothesis on a much larger scale. The thoroughness and skill of his efforts make it clear, to me at least, that if such a structure were to be found, he would have found it. It is not the case that Jubilees synchronizes events with 294-year or 490-year cycles, beyond coincidence and the sources used (*On Earth as in Heaven*, 237–49). It is not the case that the periods can be made to fit without overlap (52). It is not the case that the proposed system is manifested in Jubilees itself (149) or makes sense of previously nonsensical passages. It is not the case that Scott can find any evidence in Jubilees for dates of major events such as the restoration of the temple

will not overstate the *type* of calendrical concern in Jubilees, it would be difficult to overstate the *degree* of its concern for the dating of festivals. All the usual modes of emphasis are found: the festivals were practiced by the patriarchs (6:24; 7:3; 14:20; 15:1; 16:20; 18:18; 22:1; etc.), they are ordained on the heavenly tablets (6:35; 16:28; 32:28; 49:8), they are observed by angels (6:18)—all at particular times. From the prologue until the last verse of the last chapter, the heavenly tablets are described as calendrical law for "the divisions of the times." One repeatedly finds strong language for the permanence of the festival schedule, including "throughout all the years of eternity" (prologue, 6:24), "all the history of the earth" (16:28), and "no temporal limit because it is ordained forever" (16:30; 49:8). Reform or re-creation of the festival calendar is not even an eschatological possibility. Israel will synchronize its calendar with heaven, not the earthly standards of other nations.

Another type of calendrical concern in Jubilees is the jubilee *year*. It is clear that Jubilees counts a jubilee of jubilees that fulfills, on the national scale, the release and return of Lev 25.[125] Jubilees 50:2-5 also addresses the fiftieth year, in addition to the fiftieth jubilee. The jubilee year is a clear case of a plan outlined on the heavenly tablets but not yet successfully fulfilled in history. The observance and counting of the fiftieth-year release and return is conditional upon possession of the land and purity.[126] The first condition, possession of the land, draws from Lev 25:1 ("when you enter the land…") and explains why there were no jubilee years in the first 2,450 years of creation. Thus, "the year of the jubilee we did not tell you about until the time when you enter into the land of which you will take possession" (Jub. 50:2). The second condition is purity: "the jubilees [i.e., the fiftieth years] will pass by [i.e., they will not be observed or counted]

(148-49). These modest results build on huge assumptions. Although I do like the idea that symmetry and extrapolation are a priori likely, Scott pushes the extent to which one can reconstruct an *Endzeit* from an *Urzeit* (156) and the extent to which "rigorous symmetry" is a principle of Jubilees (148). I simply reject the assumptions that Jubilees is an esoteric work of an esoteric milieu (69 n. 119) or that Jubilees has the same ideas as those found in Daniel and the Apocalypse of Weeks (74, 102, 128, 156) or later documents found at Qumran (23-24). Scott also builds mountains on VanderKam's emendation of Jub. 1:29 without as much as acknowledging that it is an emendation (73). See also the critique of Scott in Berner, *Jahre, Jahrwochen und Jubiläen*, 307-9.

125. VanderKam, "Studies in the Chronology of the Book of Jubilees," 543.

126. The conditional nature of the jubilee year is also supported by Num 36:4: וְאִם־יִהְיֶה הַיֹּבֵל לִבְנֵי יִשְׂרָאֵל, "should the jubilee year occur for the Israelites…".

until Israel is pure" (Jub. 50:5; cf. Lev 25:18). Jubilees 50:3 explains that the jubilee year is different from the sabbatical year in that it is conditional. The sabbatical year is counted no matter what because the land "keeps" the sabbatical year. The jubilee year, however, is the responsibility of Israel: "The land will keep its sabbaths in their dwelling on it, but they [Israel] are to know God's year for the jubilee" (Jub. 50:3).[127] The "eschatological" counting of a fiftieth year is new in the sense that it had not been counted in the past, before Israel became pure. Nevertheless, it still fits the overarching pattern that the eschatological restoration in Jubilees restores, but does not reform or replace, the original plan of creation found in the heavenly tablets revealed to Moses at Sinai.

3.5. Conclusion

Jubilees uses the genre "apocalypse" to convey its own view of the temporal axis. Jubilees expresses a transcendent view of the content and meaning of history. Jubilees gives an overarching pattern that includes creation, the present moment of the reader, and the final stabilization of history. Furthermore, Jubilees is comparable to the typical apocalypses in the four major categories of the temporal axis. Jubilees has something to say about the decline of history, the final woes, the judgment, and the restoration.

What Jubilees says is significantly different from the typical apocalypses. There is a decline of history that will reverse, but the decline is not recent or exponential. Received scripture indicates that a life span of seventy to eighty years is not the original or final plan but a punishment for sin. The decline of history, measured in life span, is less immediate to the reader's present. The change mostly took place long ago and is so gradual that neither the decline nor restoration can be perceived in a single lifetime. Thus, when Jubilees does address recent events, the events are deprived of the context of a climax of history.

The suffering of "recent" history in Jub. 23 evokes the final woes of the apocalypses but differs from them. As we already saw in the previous chapter, the woes are imposed by God as chastisement for the sin of Israel according to the terms of the covenant. Neither cosmic nor international

---

127. For further elaboration, see Hanneken, "The Book of Jubilees among the Apocalypses," 456–59.

forces are responsible. Furthermore, the woes are past. Jubilees says the worst is over, whereas apocalypses often say the worst is yet to come.

The change of history does not depend on enduring until God decides to intervene but on the repentance of Israel. When Israel repents, God will gradually fulfill the covenantal blessings of life and security in the land. The Gentile invaders will be sent home and excluded from the restoration of Israel, but a vengeful judgment is lacking in Jub. 23. Judgment is an important theme elsewhere in Jubilees, but it is not eschatological. God's mercy produces only minor delays in punishment, which can occur for any individual or nation at any time. The beginning of the restoration is also realized in the reader's present. Furthermore, the restoration is, in fact, a restoration, not a replacement with a new creation. God's creation is stretched out over 2,450 years, not seven days, to include the creation of Israel and the earthly counterpart of the heavenly sanctuary. God's original plan for creation is good and does not need to be replaced. The particularism of Jewish history was intended all along; it is not a symptom of the decline of righteousness to a remnant. The exclusive covenant does not need to be replaced, the covenantal relationship does not need to extend to the rest of humanity, and the borders of the land of Israel will neither be opened nor extended beyond the original plan. The priesthood and the sanctuary will be restored, not reformed. The calendar that functioned all along in heaven and among the patriarchs will be restored.

For Jubilees, history—Jewish history in particular—is basically good. History has its ups and downs, but even the recent disaster of the Jewish civil war has meaning according to the idea that suffering comes from God to prompt repentance. Scripture reveals the blessings God has planned for Israel and the relatively simple plan for bringing it about: study of the laws in general and purity in particular. The broad view of history has its larger "down," followed by a permanent "up," but the idea is basically Deuteronomistic, stretched over the whole of history.

4
The View of Revelation

The genre "apocalypse" typically authorizes new revelation. Jubilees, however, uses the genre to authorize revelation that is already authoritative. Both of these statements require significant qualification, but a difference holds between new and derivative. The Jewish apocalypses typically resonate with authoritative literature or use it as a springboard, but neither the contents nor the authority derive primarily from the interpretation of received literature. Jubilees exercises great creativity but fundamentally derives its authority from authoritative materials. Any interpretation needs to be authorized in some way, and perhaps to some degree the importance of received scripture needed to be reauthorized. The use of the genre "apocalypse" to authorize an interpretation closely derived from received scripture, however, goes beyond overkill and beyond atypical. The genre "apocalypse" creates reader expectations that something new is going to be revealed, but Jubilees presents something derivative. The contrast between authorizing new revelation and overauthorizing derivative interpretation, with the appropriate qualifications, occupies the first section of this chapter.

The second section will turn to what is said about revelation. Typically in the apocalypses, revelation is mysterious or coded, and only with recourse to special wisdom or additional revelation can the true meaning and, consequently, the true path to righteousness and divine favor be understood. In Jubilees, however, revelation is foolproof. Jubilees does not convey meaning in codes, it does not interpret Genesis as if a code or allegory, and it downplays codes and enigmas in Genesis itself. Wisdom is not an important category in the view of revelation; it is neither a prerequisite for righteousness nor a consequence of the study of revelation. One must study the law, but the meanings are not secret, mysterious, or particularly hidden. Covenantal fidelity, with its requirements and rewards, is publicly revealed to all Israel, regardless of intelligence.

One might describe the basic observation of the first section as the collision of "apocalypse" and "rewritten Bible" in Jubilees.[1] One might describe the basic observation of the second section as the separation of "apocalypse" from "wisdom" in Jubilees. In light of larger patterns in Jubilees, however, it becomes clear that these are not minor variations on the genre "apocalypse" but rather use of the literary genre to subvert the view of revelation typically conveyed. An apocalypse is fundamentally an uncovering and implicitly an uncovering of something new and mysterious. Jubilees evokes those expectations through literary morphology but subverts them by "uncovering" narratives and laws that are fundamentally familiar.

4.1. The Use and View of Received Authority

The issue of this section is particularly subtle. Although the ultimate claim is that Jubilees differs from contemporary apocalypses in that it is primarily authorized by its dependence on the received scriptures of Israel, there are gray areas on both sides of the distinction. Contemporary apocalypses do gain authority in their resonances with received authority. They sound like something God, a wisdom hero, or a prophet would say, even though one could not derive the content of what is said from any prior source. On the other side, Jubilees, like any interpretive work, needed to authorize itself. If we approach Jubilees from the perspective of methods of authorizing interpretations, we find a difference of degree, since all interpretations use some such methods.[2] If we approach Jubilees from the perspective of reader expectations based on the genre "apocalypse," however, we find a stark division between new and derived revelation.[3] Jubilees falls fundamentally on the "derived" side of the spectrum, and contemporary apocalypses fundamentally on the "new" side.

---

1. For a recent review of the benefits and dangers in the term "rewritten Bible," see Moshe J. Bernstein, "'Rewritten Bible': A Generic Category Which Has Outlived Its Usefulness?" *Textus* 22 (2005): 169–96. Bernstein concludes that, properly used, the category has not outlived its usefulness.

2. Hindy Najman, "Interpretation as Primordial Writing: Jubilees and Its Authority Conferring Strategies," *JSJ* 30 (1999): 379.

3. This distinction was suggested by George W. E. Nickelsburg, "Wisdom and Apocalypticism in Early Judaism," 27–28.

In the broad strokes the case is clear.[4] Often enough, there is no mistaking the difference between mysteries revealed and public traditions rewritten. In some specific instances—Jubilees at its most creative and the Animal Apocalypse at its most derivative—finer analysis is required. Even here, where the points on the spectrum are closest, a distinction can be made. The difference is not apparent if we check only whether derivative and novel points are present, whether familiar authority and recontextualization take place, and whether the simple sense is challenged. The difference comes down to the purpose or end to which received traditions are used. The Animal Apocalypse uses scripture, and inherently interprets scripture, but does not review history to the end of interpreting scripture. The review of history builds to the present moment (1 En. 90:6), at which point scriptural interpretation falls away and institutions such as the priesthood and temple are discussed only as being radically reformed. Daniel 9 is another interesting case, but the base text is not so much interpreted as overlaid with a new revelation that supersedes the original revelation.[5]

The fact that Jubilees has clear concerns based on contemporary context does not negate the basic point that Jubilees is primarily engaged in interpreting scripture. The contrast is not that one is influenced by contemporary concerns and the other is not.[6] The question is not whether Jubilees is "pure" exegesis but whether scripture ceases to be the concern. Sometimes Jubilees solves problems within a passage, sometimes it reconciles two passages, and sometimes it reconciles scripture with theological presuppositions, but scripture is always on the table. In Jub. 23, for

---

4. See the broad survey in James C. VanderKam, "Biblical Interpretation in *1 Enoch* and *Jubilees*," in Charlesworth and Evans, *The Pseudepigrapha and Early Biblical Interpretation*, 96–125; repr. as pages 276–304 in VanderKam, *From Revelation to Canon: Studies in the Hebrew Bible and Second Temple Literature* (Leiden: Brill, 2000). Although much can be said of resonance of the Hebrew Bible in 1 Enoch, this resonance is much looser than the close dependence throughout Jubilees.

5. It is widely observed that apocalypses resonate with received traditions but are not primarily interpretations. See Michael E. Stone, "Apocalyptic Literature," in *Jewish Writings of the Second Temple Period: Apocrypha, Pseudepigrapha, Qumran, Sectarian Writings, Philo, Josephus* (ed. Michael E. Stone; Assen: Van Gorcum; Philadelphia: Fortress, 1984), 390–91, 429; Collins, *Apocalyptic Imagination*, 40.

6. Jubilees, no less than the apocalypses, speaks to contemporary concerns. One might draw a distinction between updating scripture to address contemporary concerns and extrapolating from ancient authorities to address contemporary concerns, but the contemporary concerns remain constant.

example, Jubilees departs from rewriting Genesis–Exodus, but it is still reacting to an interpretation of Third Isaiah with an interpretation of Deut 28 and other texts as an explanation of current events. We cannot be sure how much of the Levi material in Jubilees is received, but it is clear that the Genesis account of Levi the patriarch is filled out on the basis of other material about the priests and Levites. In some cases Jubilees is not interpreting Genesis so much as the other texts that give awkward accounts of the origins of priestly and Levitical privilege.[7]

Novelty is a spectrum, not a binary characteristic, and it is not always easy to measure. We should not underestimate either the extent to which apocalypses can be derivative or the extent to which Jubilees can be creative. Even at the points where Jubilees and the apocalypses most resemble each other, a line can be drawn. Novelty and derivation can take many forms, but at the threshold the reader expectation of novelty from an apocalypse is satisfied when the authority of the revelatory framework addresses problems beyond mortal capability. The interpretation of scripture by weaving together received texts and traditions, however, was already familiar in the human domain.

This novelty functions primarily in the world of the author and audience, although the contrast can be drawn somewhat in the narrative world as well. Jubilees and the apocalypses share a narrative framework that claims authority from a heavenly source through an ancient scribe for subsequent generations (or one subsequent generation). In both cases the truths are claimed to be ancient or timeless. From the perspective of the audience, however, the typical apocalypse reveals information that could not have been guessed by human means and at most resonates with familiar authorities. The typical apocalypse thereby reinforces the expectation

---

7. The Levi material in Jubilees is complicated because we cannot be sure what traditions were received by Jubilees, but even if we were to assume that most of the expansions were "new" in Jubilees, it would still be creativity toward the end of biblical interpretation. It is not necessarily wrong to read Jubilees' interest in the Levites and the temple as indicative of social location, but the field of play is still scripture. Jubilees infuses the Genesis accounts of Levi the patriarch with other scriptural accounts of Levites and priests. Jubilees shifts the etiology of the priesthood from Moses (who had a certain conflict of interests) and the fallout of the golden calf to merit and heavenly design long before. Historical-critical scholars have interpreted the problems of the origins of the priests and Levites as a long history of struggle between priestly groups (see ch. 2 n. 100). Jubilees has a different solution but is interpreting the same sources, along with other traditions only partially known to us.

that an apocalypse uncovers previously hidden things. The typical apocalypse is a new revelation for the audience, even if the narrative plays with the chronology by claiming antiquity for the new revelation. This is all the more true in light of the discussion of the second section of this chapter. Often the narrative presents the revelation as decipherable only to a certain generation, sometimes not even the original ancient recipient of the revelation. In those cases the revelation is "new" for the actual audience, even in the narrative world. For Jubilees, the nonnovelty applies especially to the actual audience, but even in the narrative the heavenly tablets are presented as mostly revealed earlier and the covenant already made and renewed earlier.[8]

Jubilees raises, but does not meet, the expectation of previously inaccessible contents. Jubilees claims to be, or at least leads the reader to expect it to be, something other than what it turns out to be. The typical apocalypse claims to reveal something new, and it does reveal something new. It claims to be an independent revelation, and it is an independent revelation. Jubilees, however, frames itself as if new but is in fact derived. Jubilees claims to be an independent revelation but could just as easily have been "rewritten scripture" without the genre "apocalypse."

Before exploring the novelty, and limits of novelty, of the Enochic apocalypses, the Danielic apocalypses, and then Jubilees, we should clarify the difference between using a received authority and embracing its ideas. We must understand "received" broadly, without illusions of canon, dogma, or denomination.[9] Reception was not all or none. There was no list

---

8. For an insightful articulation of how Deuteronomy uses the claim to repeat what has already been said as a way to advance a new understanding of what has been said, see Bernard M. Levinson, *Legal Revision and Religious Renewal in Ancient Israel* (Cambridge: Cambridge University Press, 2008).

9. A critical understanding of reception and authority of scriptures and scriptural traditions in the second century B.C.E. is an ongoing project. See James C. VanderKam, "Authoritative Literature in the Dead Sea Scrolls," *DSD* 5 (1998): 382–402; idem, "Questions of Canon Viewed through the Dead Sea Scrolls," in *The Canon Debate* (ed. Lee Martin McDonald and James A. Sanders; Peabody, Mass.: Hendrickson, 2002), 91–109; Eugene Ulrich, "The Notion and Definition of Canon," in McDonald and Sanders, *The Canon Debate*, 21–35; idem, "From Literature to Scripture: Reflections on the Growth of a Text's Authoritativeness," *DSD* 10 (2003): 3–25; Shemaryahu Talmon, "The Crystallization of the 'Canon of Hebrew Scriptures' in the Light of Biblical Scrolls from Qumran," in *The Bible as Book* (ed. Edward D. Herbert and Emanuel Tov; London: British Library, 2002), 5–20; John Barton, "The Significance of a Fixed

that established one work as fixed and supremely authoritative and another work as unusable. We cannot assume that Jubilees only acknowledges texts with which it agrees. Jubilees could not deny the fact that Third Isaiah and the Book of the Watchers, for example, were part of the tradition, but Jubilees could reshape the received tradition according to its own ideas.[10] Although we will find that Jubilees embraces the ideas of Deuteronomy more consistently than those of Third Isaiah or the Book of the Watchers, that has no bearing on defining which traditions were received and bore some familiar authority. For practical reasons, we will focus on Jewish traditions known to us in writing, but this is not to deny that received traditions could also be oral or non-Jewish in origin.[11]

Canon of the Hebrew Bible," in *Hebrew Bible/Old Testament: The History of Its Interpretation* (ed. Magne Sæbø; Göttingen: Vandenhoeck and Ruprecht, 1996), 67–83. The social implications of a claim to higher revelation are largely bracketed in the present work but are addressed in John J. Collins, "Ethos and Identity in Jewish Apocalyptic Literature," in *Ethos und Identität: Einheit und Vielfalt des Judentums in hellenistisch-römischer Zeit* (ed. Matthias Konradt and Ulrike Steinert; Studien zu Judentum und Christentum; Paderborn: Schöningh, 2002), 51–65.

10. Recently Loren T. Stuckenbruck described the reshaping of traditions in the Epistle of Enoch, particularly Deuteronomy and the Book of the Watchers. In both cases the Epistle reshapes or proposes a clarified understanding of the traditions without dismissing them. See Stuckenbruck's "The *Epistle of Enoch*: Genre and Authorial Presentation," *DSD* 17 (2010): 410–14. Also, Levinson demonstrated, in *Legal Revision and Religious Renewal*, not only that and why Deuteronomy reshapes legal tradition, but *how* Deuteronomy does so.

11. The perception of "foreign" influence is too thorny an issue to be profitably discussed in the present work, but it does seem promising—if one could move from modern to ancient perceptions of "foreignness" in literature and wisdom—that the apocalyptic view suggests that revealed wisdom can be found among all nations, whereas Jubilees holds that the only legitimate revelation is preserved by the Levites in Jerusalem (Jub. 45:16: "He gave all his books and the books of his fathers to his son Levi so that he could preserve then and renew them for his sons until today").

For influences on the apocalypses from the broader cultural context, see Collins, *Apocalyptic Imagination*, 36–37; Jonathan Z. Smith, "Wisdom and Apocalyptic," in *Religious Syncretism in Antiquity: Essays in Conversation with Geo Widengren* (ed. Birger Albert Pearson; Series on Formative Contemporary Thinkers 1; Missoula, Mont.: Scholars Press, 1975), 131–56; James C. VanderKam, *Enoch and the Growth of an Apocalyptic Tradition* (Washington, D.C.: Catholic Biblical Association of America, 1984), 189; Stone, "Lists of Revealed Things," 438; Hans D. Betz, "On the Problem of the Religio-Historical Understanding of Apocalyptic," *JTC* 6 (1969): 138; Helge S. Kvanvig, *Roots of Apocalyptic: The Mesopotamian Background of the Enoch Figure*

4.1.1. The Enochic Apocalypses

We should avoid the exaggeration that the Enochic apocalypses are discontinuous with or in opposition to Jewish traditions, including the Mosaic Pentateuch.[12] In the Enochic apocalypses the genre functions to authorize revelation that echoes with the familiar but is not derivative of previous revelation. The Enochic apocalypses assume and build on previous Enochic apocalypses, as well as other received traditions, but they do not rewrite or sustain a continuous exposition of received authorities. Simply put, the basic method often labeled "rewritten Bible" and described by Alexander as centripetal interpretation does not apply to the Enochic apocalypses.[13]

---

and of the Son of Man (WMANT 61; Neukirchen-Vluyn: Neukirchener, 1988); David Winston Suter, "Why Galilee? Galilean Regionalism in the Interpretation of 1 'Enoch' 6–16," *Henoch* 25 (2003): 172; Klaus Koch, "History as a Battlefield of Two Antagonistic Powers in the Apocalypse of Weeks and in the Rule of the Community," in *Enoch and Qumran Origins: New Light on a Forgotten Connection* (ed. Gabriele Boccaccini; Grand Rapids: Eerdmans, 2005), 185–99.

12. The view of Moses and the Torah in 1 Enoch is still debated. Among works emphasizing a positive connection are E. P. Sanders, *Paul and Palestinian Judaism: A Comparison of Patterns of Religion* (Philadelphia: Fortress, 1977); Lars Hartman, *Asking for a Meaning: A Study of 1 Enoch 1–5* (ConBNT 12; Lund: Gleerup, 1979). An oppositional relationship, especially prior to the Maccabean revolt, is developed in Sacchi, *Jewish Apocalyptic and Its History*; Boccaccini, *Beyond the Essene Hypothesis*; Bedenbender, *Der Gott der Welt*; idem, "The Place of the Torah in the Early Enoch Literature," in *The Early Enoch Literature* (ed. Gabriele Boccaccini and John J. Collins; JSJSup 121; Leiden: Brill, 2007), 65–79. Nickelsburg tends to fall on the side of negative views but is more sensitive to the extent to which the Torah influences 1 Enoch (see n. 19). The idea of an Enochic Pentateuch goes back to G. H. Dix, "The Enochic Pentateuch," *JTS* 27 (1925–1926): 29–42. The notion was advanced by Jozef T. Milik and Matthew Black in *The Books of Enoch: Aramaic Fragments of Qumrân Cave 4* (Oxford: Clarendon, 1976). It was first refuted by Jonas C. Greenfield and Michael E. Stone, "The Enochic Pentateuch and the Date of the Similitudes," *HTR* 70 (1977): 51–65.

13. Centrifugal expansions "take as their starting-point a single episode of the Bible, or a very short passage, and expand it almost beyond recognition. ... Rewritten Bible texts are centripetal: they come back to the Bible again and again" (Philip S. Alexander, "Retelling the Old Testament," in *It Is Written: Scripture Citing Scripture: Essays in Honour of Barnabas Lindars, SSF* [ed. Donald A. Carson and H. G. M. Williamson; Cambridge: Cambridge University Press, 1988], 117).

4.1.1.1. The Use of Enochic Traditions

Without dwelling on the complexities of the earliest origins of Enochic traditions, there can be no doubt that by the time of Jubilees a set of traditions about Enoch as a recipient of revelation was received and could be used to help authorize further revelation. One can rightly question whether editorial hands might be responsible for certain framework passages that situate individual revelations in the life of Enoch. Nevertheless, the Enochic apocalypses near the time of Jubilees inextricably depend on the figure of Enoch and allude to the content of previous apocalypses, even if strict consistency is not required. The idea of Enochic revelation is received, and Enochic apocalypses can draw on the authority of the figure of Enoch, but the point here is that the content of each apocalypse brings a new revelation. One can certainly speak of redactors reconciling and summarizing, but the corpus builds by accretion of new revelation much more than interpretation of former revelation.

The growth by accretion can be seen already in the combination of the Shemihazah and Asael strands in the Book of the Watchers.[14] Closer to the time of Jubilees, one can see how the narrative framework of the life of Enoch was put to use by the Apocalypse of Weeks.[15] Whether one counts the beginning as 93:1 or 93:3, the Apocalypse of Weeks draws on the experience and revelation of Enoch in particular, in addition to the appropriated language of "Enoch took up his discourse and said…" (1 En. 93:1, 3).[16] The basic content of the revelation, particularly as it approaches the time of the audience, resonates with but is not derived from former revelation.

The Animal Apocalypse demonstrates the limits of derived authority but still fits the basic pattern of the genre authorizing nonderived revelation. First Enoch 86:1–89:1 builds on the Book of the Watchers, among other sources, in the form of summary, not exposition.[17] The Animal

---

14. Only in a loose sense could 1 En. 20–36 be called an interpretive expansion of 1 En. 17–19. See Michael A. Knibb, "The Book of Enoch in the Light of the Qumran Wisdom Literature," in *Wisdom and Apocalypticism in the Dead Sea Scrolls and in the Biblical Tradition* (ed. Florentino García Martínez; BETL 168; Leuven: Peeters, 2003), 210.

15. Stuckenbruck, *1 Enoch 91–108*, 8–14.

16. Ibid., 69–70.

17. See further Nickelsburg, *1 Enoch: A Commentary*, 359–60.

Apocalypse goes on to develop ideas implicit in the Book of the Watchers about the nature of evil and the *Urzeit-Endzeit* typology of judgment. The Animal Apocalypse also shares an idea of division of history comparable to the Apocalypse of Weeks, uses the figure of Enoch, and adopts apocalyptic ideas in general.[18] As much as these resonances and continuities may authorize the Animal Apocalypse, the basic ideas are not derivative. The behavior of the seventy shepherds is consistent with the behavior of angels in the Book of the Watchers, but the explanation of postexilic history as the commissioning of seventy angels to rule Israel is new (see next for the use of Ezek 34). It is not surprising that the historical details of the "present" are not derived from former traditions, but it is striking that the imagined restoration has only thematic similarities with other visions of future restoration. Whereas the Animal Apocalypse uses *early* history as an opportunity to connect with familiar traditions, the details of the restoration do not even attempt consistency with previous apocalypses. This is not to say the genre "apocalypse" is fundamentally opposed to reconciling received revelations of the future, only that a reader at the time of Jubilees would expect an apocalypse to use derived elements as a springboard for thoroughly new revelation.

4.1.1.2. The Use of Non-Enochic Jewish Traditions

The use and the limits of use of received scriptures in the Enochic apocalypses have already been thoroughly analyzed by Nickelsburg and others. We need only review some basic points here, since the present argument does not depend on the more controversial points about the understanding of Mosaic authority. We will give more attention to the Animal Apocalypse, which again demonstrates the greatest extent of derivation from received authority of any contemporary apocalypse, yet still differs substantially from the rewriting found in Jubilees.

---

18. Nickelsburg (ibid., 360) places greater emphasis on the dependence of the Animal Vision on the Apocalypse of Weeks, suggesting that the former may be a "massive elaboration" of the latter. The common intellectual foundation is clear enough, but evidence of literary dependence is lacking, and it would be difficult to argue that the Animal Apocalypse claims or acknowledges such dependence.

Before coming to specific examples, we might consider some general assessments.[19] The extent to which the Enochic apocalypses resonate with and presume received scripture is not lost on Nickelsburg,

> Thus *1 Enoch* represents a remarkable *tour de force* in the religion of Israel. The authors speak in the language and forms of accepted authoritative Scripture (Torah and Prophets) with all its resonances. However, the explicit authority of the text lies not in these real sources, but in its claim to direct revelation received long before Moses or the prophets lived and spoke.[20]

In the same article Nickelsburg goes on to emphasize the novelty of the claims of revelation.

> The Enochic authors, however, claim *fresh* revelation. They do not quote the Hebrew Scriptures and interpret or rewrite those Scriptures in their own terms. Instead they cut themselves loose from the received texts and create new ones.[21]

Although there are many points where the relationship between a received tradition and its use in an Enochic apocalypse can be disputed, we need to step back to see the basic point that concerns us here. For example, if one turns to pages 338–339 in Nickelsburg's aforementioned seminal article on the subject, the language is consistently on the level of, "scriptural nuances ... parallels ... biblical vocabulary ... reminiscent of ... language imitating

---

19. Ibid., 57–61; Nickelsburg, "Scripture in 1 Enoch and 1 Enoch as Scripture," in *Texts and Contexts: Biblical Texts in Their Textual and Situational Contexts: Essays in Honor of Lars Hartman* (ed. Tord Fornberg and David Hellholm; Oslo: Scandanavian University Press, 1995), 333–354; idem, "The Nature and Function of Revelation," 91–107; idem, "Enochic Wisdom: An Alternative to the Mosaic Torah?" in *Hesed Ve-Emet: Studies in Honor of Ernest S. Frerichs* (ed. Jodi Magness and Seymour Gitin; BJS 320; Atlanta: Scholars Press, 1998), 123–32; idem, "Enochic Wisdom and Its Relationship to the Mosaic Torah," in Boccaccini and Collins, *The Early Enoch Literature*, 81–94. Hartman, *Asking for a Meaning*; idem, "An Early Example of Jewish Exegesis: *1 En.* 10:16—11:2," *Neot* 17 (1983): 16–27.

20. Nickelsburg, "Scripture in 1 Enoch and 1 Enoch as Scripture," 346.

21. Ibid., 348–49. I would emphasize a point that Nickelsburg also mentions, that the revelatory setting well before the time of Moses partially accounts for the lack of explicit citation of Mosaic discourse. The issue here is not the lack of direct citation, but the lack of substantial continuity between the "sources" and the resonances (342).

... shaped by biblical accounts."[22] We need not deny the accuracy or the significance of these allusions; we need only observe that the relationship between Jubilees and its sources is radically more direct.

Although a number of classic examples of allusions dominate the discussion of the relationship between Enochic and Mosaic discourse, most of these allusions, whatever the tone or nature of their use, are not the sustained derivative discussions that Alexander calls centripetal.[23] Thus, the dependence on the oracle form, as in Num 22, and the blessing in Deut 33 (1 En. 1) do not really demonstrate the limit of derivation from received authorities in apocalypses contemporary to Jubilees. The use of Gen 5–6 as a springboard is obvious, and Ezek 1–2 (1 En. 14) and Isa 65–66[24] cannot go unmentioned. The most important case for establishing the limit of the extent to which we can say that apocalypses at the time of Jubilees present nonderivative revelation is the Animal Apocalypse, particularly with respect to Ezek 34.

Among the many sources that can be identified behind the Animal Apocalypse, none exerts an influence that is as sustained in theme and imagery as Ezek 34. Biblical history from Genesis through Kings is glossed; the dependence on Ezek 34 (presumably with some help from Zechariah) is more than a gloss. The themes and imagery may be traditional, but Ezek 34 offers a substantial concentration of parallels.[25] The works share the imagery of owner/lord, shepherd (adapted), good sheep, bad sheep, and beasts and the themes of abuse of authority, dispersion, ingathering, divine judgment, and restoration, including a new individual figure.

The resonances of Ezek 34 in the Animal Apocalypse certainly convey a degree of authority, simply in the fact of sounding familiar. However, two factors moderate the extent to which we can say the Animal Apocalypse

---

22. Ibid., 338–39.

23. For the rich mixture of biblical language and imagery, but not close, sustained exegesis, see Hartman, *Asking for a Meaning*. Michael A. Knibb ("The Use of Scripture in *1 Enoch* 17–19," in *Jerusalem, Alexandria, Rome: Studies in Ancient Cultural Interaction in Honour of A. Hilhorst* [ed. Florentino García Martínez and Gerard P. Luttikhuizen; JSJSup 82; Leiden: Brill, 2003], 165–78) discusses parallels in 1 En. 17–19 and the difficulty with identifying shared language as biblical allusion or interpretation.

24. See Nickelsburg, "Scripture in 1 Enoch and 1 Enoch as Scripture," 336.

25. Tiller (*Commentary on the Animal Apocalypse*, 59) places more emphasis on the extent to which the imagery and themes are traditional, whereas Nickelsburg (*1 Enoch: A Commentary*, 391) places more emphasis on the concentration of parallels with Ezek 34 and Zech 11.

derives authority from Ezekiel: first, and more superficially, the Animal Apocalypse makes no such claim; second, the Animal Apocalypse makes no effort to solve problems within Ezekiel, nor does it justify or explain the transitions from "text" to "interpretation." The first point, that the Animal Apocalypse does not claim authority from Ezekiel, goes beyond the fact that the figure of Ezekiel is not referred to by name or allusion. The passage that treats Ezekiel's time not only fails to allude to this particular prophet; it seems to suggest that the "normal" pattern of prophets calling the sheep back to the right way has already been displaced by the commissioning of seventy shepherds (1 En. 89:59–72). The Animal Apocalypse says nothing to suggest a textual relationship, to identify the revelatory settings, or to account for the similarities as a common source.[26] It is one thing for modern scholars to recognize the direct or indirect influence of Ezek 34, but there is no literary acknowledgement of such a dependence. Resonances may be inherently authorizing, but this resonance is not an explicit or primary source of authority for the Animal Apocalypse.

The second point is more substantial. The Animal Apocalypse may be influenced by Ezek 34 and interpret it in a general sense, but it does not solve problems within Ezek 34, nor does it solve the problems that would follow from close comparison of the two "revelations." It does not so much explicate the subtleties of the base text as overlay it with a new layer of revelation. Thus, the Animal Apocalypse does not take up all the images of Ezek 34, such as the polluted water (34:18–19). It does not justify or explain the innovation that the shepherds are neither Jewish nor human. There is no attempt to derive or reconcile the claim that the shepherds are divinely appointed and will not be judged until an appointed time. The Animal Apocalypse does not claim to interpret Ezek 34, nor does it actually do so in the narrow sense of explicating a text.

Individual aspects of the Animal Apocalypse are derivative, but the purpose and conclusion of the work as a whole wanders in a new direction, far from the interpretation of received authority. The genre "apocalypse" authorizes the claim that a fiery abyss will open up and burn the bones of the current temple leadership (90:26–27), not the claim that David ruled Israel after the death of Saul (89:48).

---

26. Contrast this with Jubilees, which claims a relationship with the "first law" (Jub. 6:22), identifies the revelatory setting as Sinai and Exod 24 in particular, and uses the heavenly tablets to assert and explain the unity of all valid revelation.

The Animal Apocalypse represents the limit, not the average, of what we can imagine an informed reader would expect from an apocalypse with respect to derivation of authority and contents of revelation. The Danielic apocalypses (especially Dan 9) bring us to a further set of considerations but ultimately do not surpass the Animal Apocalypse on the spectrum from new to derived authority.

4.1.2. The Danielic Apocalypses

The use of received authorities in the Danielic apocalypses, as in the previous subsection on the Enochic apocalypses, can be separated into the use of Danielic traditions and the use of other received traditions. The dominant (but not only) point for this subsection will be the use of Jeremiah in Dan 9, which is unique among the early apocalypses in explicitly citing a source.[27] In order to understand the use of Jeremiah, we must first consider the use in the apocalypses of traditions found in the court tales. The apocalypses develop the idea found in the court tales of multiple stages of revelation. Daniel 9 presents Jeremiah as a stage of revelation that is legitimate but incomplete. Daniel acknowledges the authority of Jeremiah but does not derive its own authority from Jeremiah. The apocalypse is an independent instance of revelation that relates to but does not derive from a former instance of revelation.

4.1.2.1. The Use of Danielic Traditions

The Danielic apocalypses build on received traditions about Daniel and so appropriate, to an extent, the authority of the Daniel traditions. We should not underestimate the continuities in the Danielic traditions or the extent to which the apocalypses would have sounded familiar and authoritative. These factors moderate, but do not negate, the point that the predominant authorization is the assertion of revelation in the manner of the genre "apocalypse." We will take as a point of departure that the court tales in Dan 3–6 predate and influence the formation of the Danielic apocalypses. Daniel 2 should be treated separately. Since it reflects so many features of the Danielic apocalypses (other than genre), we cannot be as confident where it falls amid the formation of apocalypses around traditions framed

---

27. Collins, *Daniel: A Commentary*, 359.

as court tales.²⁸ We are here concerned only with identifying the continuities, not explaining the mechanisms of continuity.²⁹ Similarly, we are not concerned with explaining the origins of Danielic traditions, only the point at which apocalypses begin to make use of a received tradition about a wisdom hero whose adventures included revealed interpretation. The later Danielic apocalypses (and redactions) also build on the authority of the earlier apocalypses. These continuities should be understood as part of the authorizing strategies of the apocalypses. In general, the continuities contribute a sense of familiarity and consistency. On a deeper level, one of the continuities, the idea of multiple stages of revelation, authorizes the underlying claim that revelation is ongoing and subject to amendment. The Danielic apocalypses not only exhibit but defend the principle of new revelation. Thus it is all the more discordant when a reader finds, in Jubilees, fundamentally derivative revelation in the framework of an apocalypse.

Even if one brackets Dan 2, Dan 4 in particular illustrates a significant number of continuities from the received Danielic traditions into the apocalypses. Here one finds an enhanced agency of angels (Dan 4:10, 14, 32), as well as numerically auspicious chronology (4:22, 26).³⁰ One can find in Dan 5:26–28 the idea of a declining sequence of kingdoms, which becomes developed in Dan 2 and 7, along with imminent doom (if not eschatology proper).³¹ There are similarities in framework between Dan 4 and 2, and Dan 7 has even been called a "midrash" on Dan 2, but Collins distinguishes influence from derivation: "It is a new vision, and the earlier chapter is only one of many influences on it."³² Collins also notes "echoes of terminology" that provide continuity between Dan 7 and the court tales.³³

---

28. An exhaustive study would also be concerned with the Danielic traditions found outside the twelve-chapter redaction.

29. For example, are the apocalypses a linear development of a coherent tradition that also produced the court tales, or should we think of a looser connection? There do seem to be enough continuities that we can at least understand why the writers of the apocalypses would be drawn to develop their works in Danielic terms.

30. It is worth distinguishing prediction and numerical auspiciousness from predestination.

31. The decreasing monetary value of kings behind Dan 5:25 is elaborated by Collins, *Daniel: A Commentary*, 251.

32. Ibid., 323, 173.

33. Ibid., 311. For more continuities and discontinuities between Dan 1–6 and Dan 7, see 294. Ideas such as punishment by burning also reappear (Dan 3:11; 7:11).

Daniel 5:18–21 is exceptional in that it recapitulates a former court tale, but a more general narrative continuity appears in several places in the work as we have it.[34] These facts should caution us against any simplistic generalizations to the effect that apocalypses present purely new revelation without building on received traditions and gaining some authority from the continuity. Yet, on the spectrum from new to derived revelation and authority, Daniel never approaches the extent to which Jubilees derives the content and authority of revelation from received authorities.

Of all the ways in which the Danielic apocalypses build on Danielic traditions, none is more significant for this chapter than the idea of multiple stages of revelation. Indeed, the second section of this chapter will return to the same basic issue from the perspective of the elitism of coded revelation. The idea of multiple stages of revelation can be found in the Danielic court tales and developed further in the apocalypses. It will aid clarity to mention briefly the external but particularly direct formulation found in Pesher Habakkuk:

> God told Habakkuk to write down the things that are going to come upon the last generation, but the fulfillment of the period God did not make known to him. (1Q Pesher Habakkuk 7.1–2)

As we shall soon see, Dan 9 approaches Jeremiah similarly. Nickelsburg has described this idea as "secondary revelation" or "revealed interpretation."[35] It is preferable to speak of multiple stages of revelation, partially in anticipation of outlining three stages without implying secondary or tertiary value in the second and third stages. "Interpretation" is too loaded a term to describe the relationship between the stages, in as much as it may suggest a human activity of derivation.[36]

---

34. For example, Dan 8:27 assumes the work of the king that Daniel was doing in the court tales. Dan 8:1 refers explicitly to a former vision and picks up (however loosely) the imagery of animals and horns. Dan 9:21 refers to the *angelus interpres* of a prior vision. Dan 10:12 evokes Dan 9 for an angel sent as soon as requested (however adapted). Even though the chronological sequence "resets" with the apocalypses, within each part a chronological sequence is presented.

35. Nickelsburg, "The Nature and Function of Revelation," 112.

36. Armin Lange has studied the phenomenon of revealed interpretation in the broader context of the eastern Mediterranean in antiquity. Lange emphasizes continuity in the development of practices of reinterpretation. See his "Interpretation als Offenbarung: Zum Verhältnis von Schriftauslegung und Offenbarung in apokalyp-

The idea of stages of revelation is already found, in some form, in the court tales. Daniel 2, 4, and 5 all include an initial stage of revelation that is divine in origin, legitimate, and meaningful even if the first stage is not sufficient to access that meaning.[37] Daniel 4 and 5 do not perfectly fit the emerging pattern at the second stage in that the interpretation is not (or at least not emphatically) a revelation in its own right. Daniel may appear to interpret the initial revelation from his own wisdom, yet even here the ancient thinker could easily understand Daniel's wisdom as revealed in a general sense. The divine nature of Daniel's wisdom appears in Dan 4:5, 15; 5:11, 14. The interpretation in Dan 5:26–28 rings more of the miraculous than earthly wisdom.

Daniel 2 emphasizes that the second stage is a divine revelation in its own right. Nebuchadnezzar receives a revelation that turns out to be legitimate, but other than motivating him to find a reliable interpretation, the first stage is not sufficient for conveying meaning. The second stage, the interpretation, is itself revealed in Dan 2:19. The independence of this revelation hardly establishes a dichotomy between revealed information and revealed wisdom. Daniel's prayer makes clear that God not only answers questions but gives sages the wisdom to understand hidden things (2:21). Daniel 2 both illustrates a second stage of revelation that is fully independent of human reasoning and claims that the divine wisdom Daniel used in chapters 4 and 5 is itself a form of revelation. Although we might be quick to observe the difference between a revealed interpretation that comes in a night vision following a direct request to God and an interpretation that comes from a wise person "on the spot," Dan 2 seems to be asserting that they are both revelation. Thus, clearly one—and from an ancient perspective three—of the court tales exhibit two stages of revelation. The initial stage is legitimate but not complete by itself.

---

tischer und nichtapokalyptischer Literatur," in García Martínez, *Wisdom and Apocalypticism*, 17–33. Be that as it may, the end result is a distinctive development, as revealed interpretation claims independent revelation as authority over connection to the original text. See further Michael Segal, "Between Bible and Rewritten Bible," in *Biblical Interpretation at Qumran* (ed. Matthias Henze; Studies in the Dead Sea Scrolls and Related Literature; Grand Rapids: Eerdmans, 2005), 10–28.

37. One issue that is not discussed in this chapter is the view of the availability of revelation and revealed wisdom to other nations. Whereas Jubilees claims that even the antediluvian revelations of the heavenly tablets are transmitted to and preserved by Israel alone, Daniel claims that Gentiles have access to preliminary revelation and are able to appreciate its explication.

We should also consider a third stage. If Nebuchadnezzar receives a first-stage "revelation" and Daniel a second-stage "revealed interpretation," it still remains the case that Daniel does not always exactly understand even the interpretation. It remains for the audience to fulfill the third stage of understanding the historical meaning of the revelation. For example, Daniel may have understood that the mixing of clay and iron indicates a failed marriage (2:43), but it remains for the third stage to identify specifically the individuals in question.[38] More explicitly, Daniel does not understand in 12:8 what the enlightened will understand later in 12:10. The unsealing of the vision is part of the third stage (12:4). It might be a stretch for moderns to think of the third stage as a revelation, rather than a realization, but we should not be too quick to dismiss the extent to which insight could be considered revealed wisdom. The point is neither that all stages are equal nor that one is necessarily better than the other but that revelation is spread out over stages and that some degree of revelation is active at each stage.

The idea of multiple stages of revelation underlies all the Danielic apocalypses to varying extents. The major shift is that Daniel's role becomes less active as the second-stage revelation is taken over by an angelic figure. Even when the first and second stages are aspects of the same vision, there remains a striking division of vision and interpretation. The first and second stages are least clearly distinct in Dan 10–12,[39] but in 12:8–10 the division between the second and third stage is explicit. Daniel 9 is the most interesting case, however, and brings us to the next point on the use of non-Danielic received authorities. The first stage of revelation is not Danielic at all, but the revelation received in the book of Jeremiah. While one should not push too far the comparison between Nebuchadnezzar's dream and Jeremiah's prophecy, in both cases the second stage of revelation does not explicate the first in mundane terms but constitutes an independent revelation. The first stage is legitimate but not complete by itself.

To conclude this point, the continuities in the Danielic tradition are such that the Danielic apocalypses are not entirely new. They do derive contents and authority from received sources to a nonnegligible degree, yet these continuities are never so substantial that any Danielic apocalypse

---

38. Collins, *Daniel: A Commentary*, 170.

39. Perhaps this apocalypse presumes the former visions as stage one and presents itself as an elaborate stage two. Thus in Dan 10:1 the דָּבָר נִגְלָה would be stage one and stage two would be בִּינָה לוֹ בַּמַּרְאֶה.

can be called derivative or a rewriting of a former apocalypse or court tale. Furthermore, one of the continuities from the court tales to the apocalypses, the principle of multiple stages of revelation, is practically a manifesto for ongoing revelation and the possibility that received revelation can continue to be amended in unexpected ways.

4.1.2.2. The Use of Non-Danielic Jewish Traditions

The Danielic apocalypses in general contain resonances with received traditions not unlike those characteristic of the Enochic apocalypses.[40] Daniel 9 is an especially interesting case for the use of received authorities in the early apocalypses. Not only is there a citation of Jeremiah, but the explanation of suffering associated with Deuteronomy is cited "as written in the law of Moses." Again, to a certain extent, Daniel derives authority from sounding familiar and continuous with the received traditions of Jeremiah and Deuteronomy, yet the apocalypse of Dan 9 does not derive its own authority directly from these sources. We should avoid the suggestion that Daniel 9 rejects the legitimacy of the revelations to Jeremiah and Moses. Daniel 9 does seem to say, however, that these revelations are not adequate by themselves for properly understanding the situation at the time of the audience. Jeremiah's prophecy needs to be amended with an additional revelation in order to be understood properly. Daniel 9 does not interpret Jeremiah in a derivative sense but rather claims a second stage of revelation. Similarly, Dan 9 does not polemicize against the revelation to

---

40. For example, the elevation of the little horn in Dan 8:10 resonates with the hubris of the day star in Isa 14:12–15. The *angelus interpres* already appeared in Zech 1–6. The throne and related visions of Dan 7 and 10–12 resonate with Ezekiel and perhaps the Book of the Watchers chapter 14. Dan 7 is a classic example of elusive allusions to ancient mythic imagery. For further discussion, see Michael A. Fishbane, *Biblical Interpretation in Ancient Israel* (Oxford: Oxford University Press, 1985), 482–95. It is important not to deny the basic level at which the Danielic apocalypses are continuous with received traditions. This continuity does not negate the contrast between the basically derivative authority of Jubilees and the basically novel authority of the Danielic apocalypses. Collins says of Dan 7 what we may call typical of the early apocalypses: "Whoever composed Daniel 7 was a creative author, not merely a copyist of ancient sources. It should be no surprise that his contribution is a new entity, discontinuous in some respects with all its sources" (*Daniel: A Commentary*, 281–82). The author of Jubilees is also creative but much more continuous with the received authorities.

Moses, but it does suggest that the Deuteronomic explanation of suffering, however adequate it may have been in the past, is not the proper way of understanding the situation at the time of the audience. We will consider the view of the revelation of Jeremiah first, then the portrayal of the Deuteronomic explanation of suffering, before concluding with some general comments about the assertions of authority in the Danielic apocalypses.

According to Dan 9, the word of the Lord is true, but the word of Jeremiah is incomplete. Daniel 9:2 begins with the assumption that the word of the Lord that came to Jeremiah is true:

אֲנִי דָּנִיֵּאל בִּינֹתִי בַּסְּפָרִים מִסְפַּר הַשָּׁנִים אֲשֶׁר הָיָה דְבַר־יְהוָה אֶל־יִרְמִיָה הַנָּבִיא לְמַלֹּאות לְחָרְבוֹת יְרוּשָׁלַָם שִׁבְעִים שָׁנָה

> I, Daniel, observed in the books the number of years that, according to the word of the Lord that came to Jeremiah the prophet, were to fulfill the desolation of Jerusalem: seventy years. (Dan 9:2, Collins's translation)

Jeremiah as we have it mentions the seventy years in three verses, 25:11, 12 and 29:10. The first mentions the ruin (חרבה):

וְהָיְתָה כָּל־הָאָרֶץ הַזֹּאת לְחָרְבָּה לְשַׁמָּה וְעָבְדוּ הַגּוֹיִם הָאֵלֶּה אֶת־מֶלֶךְ בָּבֶל שִׁבְעִים שָׁנָה׃

> This whole land will become a terrible desolation. These nations will serve the king of Babylon for seventy years. (Jer 25:11)

The main innovation in Dan 9 is the "interpretation," which is really an additional revelation, that seventy years are actually seventy weeks of years (Dan 9:24). While this is the major explicit amendment, Dan 9 also exhibits some selective reading of Jeremiah in the understanding of חרבות ירושלם, "the desolation of Jerusalem." Jeremiah 29:10 is apparently ignored or disregarded as a different prophecy of seventy years, since the return to the land is not the fulfillment of the prophecy:

כִּי־כֹה אָמַר יְהוָה כִּי לְפִי מְלֹאת לְבָבֶל שִׁבְעִים שָׁנָה אֶפְקֹד אֶתְכֶם וַהֲקִמֹתִי עֲלֵיכֶם אֶת־דְּבָרִי הַטּוֹב לְהָשִׁיב אֶתְכֶם אֶל־הַמָּקוֹם הַזֶּה׃

> Thus says the LORD: After Babylon's seventy years are completed, I will visit you to fulfill my promise to bring you back to this place. (Jer 29:10)

In Dan 9 the return to the land, the anointed ruler, and the rebuilding are only milestones on the way to true restoration (9:24–26). The conflict implied in Jer 25:12, that the prophecy is fulfilled with the fall of Babylon, would probably have been considered resolved by the perspective in Dan 7:12 that the loss of dominion does not constitute an adequate judgment of Babylon. Whatever may have been thought of Jer 29:10 and considered implicit with regard to Jer 25:12, there remains an important fact that only three words of Jer 25:11 play any role in Dan 9 (שבעים שנה, חרבה, "desolation," "seventy years"), and one of them is trumped by a second revelation.[41] The acceptance of authority is tempered not only by the removal from context, ignoring problems suggested by the context of Jeremiah, but also by the fact that Dan 9 goes against other received "solutions" to the seventy years. Daniel implicitly rejects the adequacy of 2 Chr 36:20–22;[42] Ezra 1:1; and Zech 1:12. The extent to which Dan 9 assumes the veracity of Jer 25:11 should not be mistaken for the canon-conscious interpretation that develops in some circles considerably later.

Daniel 9 transforms seventy years to seventy weeks of years not on the basis of a hook in the text, the context, or other received authority but by claiming equal status as direct revelation. One could point to differences in the concept of revelation claimed in Jeremiah and the concept of revelation claimed in Dan 9 (such as angelic mediation), but the revelations to Jeremiah and Daniel share the same basic source. Daniel does not denigrate the authenticity of Jeremiah's revelatory experience but does suggest that Jeremiah did not receive (or did not record) a complete understanding. Jeremiah's revelation is trumped by a second stage of revelation that is not derivative of former revelation but derives from the same heavenly source as the initial stage. The revised understanding is presented as an explicit revelation, not the product of Daniel's wisdom (but we should

---

41. See Collins, *Daniel: A Commentary*, 359, on the removal of the phrase from context and use "like a symbol in a dream."

42. Fishbane (*Biblical Interpretation in Ancient Israel*, 482) makes a case for understanding Dan 9 as an interpretation of 2 Chr 36:20–22 in light of Leviticus 26. It is important to recognize that even the "new" revelations do not come out of nowhere but out of rich traditions of interpretation. It remains the case that Dan 9 rejects the simple sense of Jer 25 and 2 Chr 36. Relatively speaking, Dan 9 authorizes its substantial innovation as a new revelation more than an as interpretation of 2 Chr 36. Again, there is much gray area on the spectrum of novelty, but Dan 9 is less a borderline case than the Animal Apocalypse, and even there a line can be drawn between the apocalypses and Jubilees (see above, page 205).

not set up fences between explicit narrative revelation and supplementary revelation that comes by way of revealed wisdom). Daniel 9 is rare among the early apocalypses for explicitly citing former revelation, but it is still a new revelation that does not primarily derive its contents and authority from Jeremiah.

Although no particular passage is cited, the explanation of suffering assumed in the prayer of Daniel also comes from received authority, particularly the book of Deuteronomy, כַּאֲשֶׁר כָּתוּב בְּתוֹרַת מֹשֶׁה, "as is written in the Torah of Moses" (Dan 9:11, 13).[43] Although there are different ways of explaining the Deuteronomistic prayer in Dan 9, most scholars agree that it is discordant in the context of the Danielic apocalypses.[44] Most likely, the author incorporated the prayer with full awareness of the tension between the explanation of suffering associated with Deuteronomy and the explanation revealed by the angel in the rest of the chapter.[45] The result is not a denial of the authenticity of Deuteronomy as revelation but an assertion that a different understanding based on new revelation is necessary to understand the present circumstance.[46]

The primary discord is theological, but there are also narrative cues that a different explanation is being offered. First, no one listens to Daniel or lets him finish. The angel departs not as a result of what Daniel says but at the beginning (9:23) and interrupts Daniel while he is still speaking (9:21). Not only does the angel not acknowledge the "confession" of Daniel; the angel proceeds to give a very different explanation.[47] Daniel had assumed that the suffering at hand is a result of the sin of Israel and comes as punishment from God to prompt repentance. The prayer also implies that restoration will come about as a result of repentance and supplication for divine mercy. After interrupting Daniel to break the news that his prayer was not worth listening to, the angel informs him that the time

---

43. See Collins, *Daniel: A Commentary*, 350.

44. Ibid., 359–60.

45. This position is defended by ibid., 348. Likewise Collins, *Apocalyptic Imagination*, 108–9. See also Bedenbender, *Der Gott der Welt* 238–40.

46. As discussed in the chapter on the temporal axis, the apocalypses typically convey a view of the present moment as a radical departure (for the worse) from the normal progress of history. Deuteronomy could be perfectly adequate as an explanation of "normal" suffering, but not the present eschatological crisis.

47. As noted by Collins, "the theology of history in Daniel 9 is very different from the Deuteronomic theology of the prayer. The deliverance promised by the angel is in no sense a response to Daniel's prayer" (*Daniel: A Commentary*, 360).

of restoration is determined and does not depend on repentance. Daniel 9:24 is somewhat difficult, but it does seem that the iniquity involved is not merely that of Israel. The suffering of Israel cannot be completely explained as punishment for its own sins; rather, Israel must wait while sinners build up sufficient merit for complete destruction (לְכַלֵּא הַפֶּשַׁע, "to make the transgression complete").[48] This idea is not new (Gen 15:16), but it does complicate the Deuteronomistic explanation. The sin of Israel and the righteousness of God are not the only parts of the suffering equation; evil is permitted to flourish so that the deferred punishment and reward can be greater (צֶדֶק עֹלָמִים, "everlasting righteousness"). None of this denies that the explanation of suffering and the proposed response written in the law of Moses were legitimate revelation.[49] It does make clear, however, that the present circumstance is not the "normal" circumstance to which Deuteronomy applies. The eschatological sequence is a special time that demands a new revelation in order to be fully understood.

In conclusion, only in an indirect sense do the Danielic apocalypses derive authority from the received authority of Jeremiah and Deuteronomy. There is a familiarity in the continuity, but what is said about the received authorities is that they are not sufficient authorities for the present. Daniel 9 does not solve interpretive problems in Jeremiah and Deuteronomy. Daniel 9 does not claim to explicate what Jeremiah or Deuteronomy mean internally, but to amend them with additional revelation. The major authority of the Danielic apocalypses is the claim to direct revelation provided by the genre "apocalypse." The figure of Daniel contributes authority (perhaps because he was already associated with second-stage revelation), as do the descriptions of Daniel's response (especially 10:8–9) and the progress of history (*vaticinia ex eventu*). In several places the apocalypses simply assert their own veracity (8:26; 10:21; 11:2; 12:7; see also 2:45). The Jewish apocalypses at the time of Jubilees certainly have enough continuity with received authorities that we

---

48. "The traditional Deuteronomic theology, then, which envisages the sin of all Israel, is not adequately nuanced for the situation envisaged in Daniel. Undoubtedly the sins for which atonement must be made include the transgression of Jews who forsake the covenant, but the emphasis is not on the punishment of Israel. Rather the idea is that evil must run its course until the appointed time" (ibid., 354).

49. Collins makes a point about Dan 9 that is important to the general argument of the present work. In Jubilees, as in Daniel, presenting theological understanding in explicit tension with an alternative understanding does not alone constitute polemic: "There is an implicit rejection of the Deuteronomic theology of history in Daniel 9, although the author does not polemicize against it" (ibid., 360).

can easily identify them as Jewish, but when we look closely we find that the genre typically authorizes fundamentally new revelation.

4.1.3. Jubilees

In the previous two subsections we explored the ways in which the typical apocalypses derive contents and authority from received traditions while finding that, on a spectrum from new to derived, they are fundamentally new. In this subsection we will acknowledge the significant ways in which Jubilees is creative and, like any interpretation, needs to authorize itself. From a broad perspective, however, Jubilees is fundamentally derivative from received authorities. This is true not only in how closely it rewrites Genesis and Exodus but in the way it brings in other received authorities even when it departs from the base. Jubilees packs scripture with more scripture. The typical apocalypses are not devoid of scriptural interpretation, but neither do they go about solving problems in a received text in a sustained or systematic way. The interpretation is typically implicit, while the claim to independent revelation is explicit. It is not merely surprising to proceed from an apocalypse framework to a rewriting of publicly received revelations; it is discordant. A reader expects an apocalypse to present revelation that could not be gathered from reason and public knowledge. Jubilees is certainly creative, but it derives its content and authority from received scriptures to a degree unlike any prior apocalypse. Even in the specific cases where the points on the spectrum approach, a line can be drawn between revelation that could only be authorized as independent revelation and interpretation that could stand as learned but mortal interpretation. Jubilees manipulates the line in that it claims to be independent revelation, leading the reader to expect contents that could not stand on human authority, but in fact delivers the type of content familiar to anyone steeped in the tradition of interpretation.

The main qualification to this subsection is the extent to which Jubilees must authorize itself as interpretation. First we shall consider the lesser degree to which Jubilees reauthorizes its base text, Genesis–Exodus. It has been suggested that Genesis needed to be authorized as revelation because, unlike much of the Pentateuch, it does not claim divine authorship.[50] Although this is an interesting potential problem that might be

---

50. Rowland, *The Open Heaven*, 52.

solved by framing the patriarchal stories explicitly as revelation, it is not clear that the author of Jubilees had this problem in mind or that the genre "apocalypse" would have been the most efficient way of addressing it. It seems more likely that by the 150s B.C.E. Genesis was considered an integral part of the law of Moses with the same basis of authority.[51] Jubilees may gesture toward explaining the authority of the received writings, but the primary flow of authority is from the received writings to Jubilees.[52]

A related, and more significant, point is the assertion of the timelessness, not just of Genesis, but of the entire law of Moses. First Maccabees 1:11 suggests a roughly contemporary movement in Judaism that understood the laws separating Israel from the nations as a "late" development that could be disregarded in favor of a former unity. To this, Jubilees seems to respond that all the laws (and the separation of Israel in particular, Jub. 2:19) existed from the beginning of creation.[53] By this explanation Jubilees is not so much authorizing Genesis or Mosaic law per se but authorizing the interpretation that Mosaic law is not temporally limited: there was not a time before it existed, nor will there be a time when it is no longer in effect. Thus we come to the next point, the need for Jubilees to authorize itself as interpretation.

We can be reasonably confident that the audience of Jubilees already accepted the authority of the "first law" written for Moses (Jub. 6:22), which we can identify as some form of the Pentateuch.[54] The greater need

---

51. Hindy Najman (*Seconding Sinai: The Development of Mosaic Discourse in Second Temple Judaism* [JSJSup 77; Leiden: Brill, 2003], 66) emphasizes the extent to which Jubilees gains from the preexistent authority of the Torah but also notes that the authority of the Torah is bolstered: "the laws endorsed by Jubilees are shown to have the authority of Mosaic Torah, while the authority of Mosaic Torah is at the same time shown to be rooted in a heavenly tradition ascribed to God and known to select individuals since the beginnings of history."

52. "Thus they claimed, for their interpretations of authoritative texts, the already established authority of the texts themselves" (ibid., 45).

53. VanderKam, "Origins and Purposes of Jubilees," 18–22. This point was recently elaborated by Segal, leading to an important observation: "The perspectives ... can be reduced to one fundamental notion: God established the entire world order from the beginning of time" (*The Book of Jubilees*, 323).

54. See especially Alexander, "Retelling the Old Testament," 100; VanderKam, "Studies on the Prologue and Jubilees 1," 268–73. We should not think of the Pentateuch so narrowly as to exclude variant readings or teachings that might not have been considered separable from the text in antiquity.

was for Jubilees to authorize itself as the dictation Moses received shortly after receiving the written tablets. Najman has contributed greatly to understanding the authority-conferring strategies in Jubilees.[55] She lists separately three strategies that might be grouped together as the genre "apocalypse" (heavenly tablets, angelic intermediary, reliable recipient), then describes well the authority conferred by recasting biblical traditions, matching the words and solving the problems of the Torah.[56] This section is particularly concerned with the overkill noticed by Najman: "it is remarkable that Jubilees should employ four different strategies when it might be supposed that one would have sufficed."[57] Indeed, this would have been even more striking to the ancient audience, such that it would have been discordant to begin with an apocalypse and continue to hear a rewritten form of publicly received scripture. We should underestimate neither the degree to which any interpretation needs authorization nor the degree to which Jubilees is a creative and novel interpretation. It is significant, however, that no contemporary text brings together "apocalypse" and "rewritten scripture" to such a degree. The rarity of the literary combination points to a tension at the level of ideas. The use of the genre "apocalypse" in Jubilees cannot be explained simply as overenthusiastic authorization of rewritten scripture. The genre brings not only authority, but a set of reader expectations that, when not met, creates discord.

Much work has already been done, though no doubt much remains to be done, to demonstrate the use of received scripture in Jubilees.[58] Jubilees is creative but always works with received materials. Many themes and passages could be brought to illustrate both the creativity and derivativeness of Jubilees, but for the present purposes two points will suffice. First we will consider the use of a feature associated with the apocalypses, the heavenly tablets. Then we will look more closely at chapter 23, a salient

---

55. Najman, "Interpretation as Primordial Writing," 379–410; idem, *Seconding Sinai*.

56. Najman, "Interpretation as Primordial Writing," 380.

57. Ibid., 389, 401.

58. See J. T. A. G. M. van Ruiten, *Primaeval History Interpreted: The Rewriting of Genesis 1–11 in the Book of Jubilees* (JSJSup 66; Leiden: Brill, 2000); John C. Endres, *Biblical Interpretation in the Book of Jubilees* (CBQMS 18; Washington, D.C.: Catholic Biblical Association of America, 1987); Kugel, *Traditions of the Bible*; George J. Brooke, "Exegetical Strategies in Jubilees 1–2: New Light from 4QJubilees^a," in Albani, Frey, and Lange, *Studies in the Book of Jubilees*, 39–57; VanderKam, "Biblical Interpretation in *1 Enoch* and *Jubilees*," 96–125.

example of a passage in which Jubilees departs from the base text of Genesis–Exodus but continues to work with received authority.

4.1.3.1. The Heavenly Tablets

Fortunately, we need not duplicate the extensive work that has been done on the heavenly tablets in Jubilees and in general.[59] A simple but powerful point, for the present purposes, builds directly on the work of García Martínez, who studied all the examples of recourse to heavenly tablets in Jubilees and organized them into five categories, one of which is "new halakot."[60] What is most remarkable here is that *the "new halakot" are not very new.* The tablets reveal the familiar, not the fantastic. To be fair, some of the other categories include some fairly innovative emphases.[61] There

---

59. Florentino García Martínez, "The Heavenly Tablets in the Book of Jubilees," in Albani, Frey, and Lange, *Studies in the Book of Jubilees*, 243–60; Himmelfarb, "Torah, Testimony, and Heavenly Tablets," 25–29; Cana Werman, "The תורה and the תעודה Engraved on The Tablets," *DSD* 9 (2002): 75–103; Leora Ravid, "של המינוח המיוחד לוחות השמים בספר היובלים," *Tarbiz* 68 (1999): 463–471; Leslie Baynes, "'My Life Is Written Before You': The Function of the Motif 'Heavenly Book' in Judeo-Christian Apocalypses, 200 B.C.E.–200 C.E," (Ph.D. dissertation, University of Notre Dame, 2004); Najman, "Interpretation as Primordial Writing," 389–400; VanderKam, *Enoch and the Growth*, 151; Shalom M. Paul, "Heavenly Tablets and the Book of Life," in *The Gaster Festschrift* (ed. David Marcus; New York: ANE Society, 1974), 345–53; Segal; *The Book of Jubilees*, 313–16.

Recently James Kugel ("Interpolations in *Jubilees*," 216–19, 267, 271) has argued that concern with the heavenly tablets indicates the work of an interpolator. If such an interpolator existed, the present work applies to both the author and the interpolator and illustrates further the extent to which they were like-minded, if not literally the same mind.

60. García Martínez, "The Heavenly Tablets in the Book of Jubilees," 255–58.

61. It would take a monograph by itself to consider completely where the 364-day calendar would fall on the spectrum from new to derived. Without resolving every related issue, it is at least plausible that the author and the author's audience could have viewed this calendar as a received authority. Possible but debatable sources of this authority could have been: (1) memory of the way things used to be, with the assumption that they had always been that way; (2) an interpretation of the Astronomical Book of Enoch; and (3) an interpretation of passages that seem to suggest that certain festivals always fall on the same day of the week, combined perhaps with an assumption that the Day of Atonement cannot conflict with the Sabbath, or simply a theological view of a balanced and symmetric universe. Furthermore, Himmelfarb ("Torah, Testimony, and Heavenly Tablets," 26) observes that in most of the passages

is also a certain need to authorize a decision of which of the received traditions should be emphasized. Still, a brief consideration of the six most novel uses of the heavenly tablets will demonstrate that Jubilees derives its authority from received traditions even when it uses a formal feature that cues a contrary reader expectation.

The first "new" legislation is the prohibition of public nudity in Jub. 3:31. While it may be true that the received codes did not exactly anticipate the Hellenistic gymnasium, two considerations limit the novelty of the prohibition. First, Jubilees ties the prohibition to Gen 3:21, where God causes Adam and Eve to wear clothes (וַיַּלְבִּשֵׁם). The conclusion that God wants all humans to wear clothes is closely derivative. The second consideration is more complex but inevitable. Written traditions are significant, but not the only form of received tradition.[62] Using logic related to the logic associated with "natural law," a Jewish writer could easily conclude that there is a cosmic reason for the way things have always been done by every (Semitic) society. The prohibition of nakedness is one of the laws taught by Noah in Jub. 7:20, suggesting that this prohibition was revealed to and incumbent upon all nations, even if Noah's books were only passed on to Shem.[63]

García Martínez classifies as "calendar and feasts," the innovation was the claim that the patriarchs observed the festival calendar, not the festival calendar itself. Put differently, Jubilees must authorize the claim that the traditional way of doing things has the same authority as the law and covenant set down in the Pentateuch. In this case, the traditional festival calendar is as fixed a part of Israel's covenant as the other issues fought over under Seleucid rule. Jubilees does *not* authorize the 364-day calendar as an innovation. For more on the authority of nonwritten tradition, see Kister, "לתולדות כת האיסיים," 1–18. For more on the identification of festival calendar with other non-negotiable covenant requirements, see Segal, *The Book of Jubilees*, 301–3.

62. A later articulation of this issue can be found in Josephus, *A.J.* 13.297, where the Pharisees, unlike the Sadducees, are said to accept regulations handed down but not written. See also Kister, "לתולדות כת האיסיים," 1–18.

63. The relationship between the laws of Noah in Jubilees and the rabbinic Noahide laws was studied by Finkelstein and Albeck. The relationship may not be direct, but Jubilees does have a concept that some laws are revealed to and incumbent upon all humanity, while others are revealed only to Israel. See Chanoch Albeck, *Das Buch der Jubiläen und die Halacha* (Bericht der Hochschule für die Wissenschaft des Judentums 47; Berlin: Berlin-Schöneberg, 1930), 34–59; Louis Finkelstein, "The Book of Jubilees and the Rabbinic Halaka," *HTR* 16 (1923): 59–61; idem, "Some Examples of the Maccabean Halaka," *JBL* 49 (1930): 21–25; idem, "Pre-Maccabean Documents in the Passover Haggadah (Concluded)," *HTR* 36 (1943): 19 n. 128.

The second "new" law attributed to the heavenly tablets states that a murderer is to be punished by the means with which he murdered (Jub. 4:32). The idea here is closely related to the *lex talionis* (Lev 24:19–20). It is possible that Jubilees is implicitly disputing a tendency to "soften" the *lex talionis* with monetary substitution, as found later in rabbinic law.[64] The explicit concern, however, is not whether Cain *should have been* punished but whether he *was* punished. Genesis does not report the death of Cain, but Jubilees asserts that Lev 24 was applied to Cain supernaturally. The law is derivative of Lev 24, and the narrative is derivative of the theological principle that God enforces justice.

The third law listed as "new" by García Martínez is the requirement of circumcision on the eighth day. Again, later evidence indicates differences of opinion about whether the day could be delayed.[65] The heavenly tablets authorize the interpretation that circumcision on the eighth day means on *exactly* the eighth day, but the interpretation is based directly on Genesis and Leviticus. Genesis 17:14 mentions the eighth day in the LXX and Samaritan recensions, as do Gen 17:12 and Lev 12:3 in all recensions.[66]

The fourth example is more interesting. According to Jub. 28:6 the custom cited by Laban of giving the elder daughter before the younger daughter is in fact a law on the heavenly tablets. Of course, we cannot completely ignore the possibility that the author's own conscience suggested that this *should* be a law, but the logic is simply the converse of a basic principle in Jubilees. If the patriarchs practiced the laws, then the practices of the patriarchs must be law. The word of Laban is probably less the authority than the assent of Jacob. The prohibition of marrying two sisters in Lev 18:18 seems to be in the background, although Jubilees does not explain how the law cited by Laban trumps Lev 18:18. The issue

---

64. García Martínez, "The Heavenly Tablets in the Book of Jubilees," 255.

65. See ch. 2 note 97 for further discussion of the halakic disputes that presumably underlie the emphases in Jubilees. In emphasizing *exactly* the eighth day, Jubilees seems to be addressing several or all of the following: (1) interpreting the circumcision of Ishmael as *not* marking inclusion among God's people; (2) opposing those who consider circumcision negotiable in the interest of participating in Hellenistic culture; (3) excluding adult converts; and (4) rejecting the interpretation later found in the Mishnah that allows circumcision to be delayed due to Sabbath or illness. If there is a halakic debate here, Jubilees is "interpreting" the law to mean what it says, against a possible looser interpretation that it means other than what it says. The interpretation in Jubilees is more closely derivative.

66. García Martínez, "The Heavenly Tablets in the Book of Jubilees," 256.

warrants further study, but for the present purposes it is clear that the law is derivative even though it interprets a custom as a law.

The fifth example, Jub. 30:9, demands capital punishment for exogamy. Certainly Jubilees is novel in the emphasis on the issue, but the issue is not new (Ezra 9–10; Neh 13:27), and the punishment is probably derived from the interpretation of giving a child to Molech as exogamy (Lev 18:21; 20:2–5). This is not as tendentious an interpretation as it may first appear, since the context in Lev 18 concerns sexual relationships, and Lev 20:5 uses the verb זנה ("to commit sexual impropriety").[67] Any image of Molech as a demon would only reinforce the interpretation as a prohibition of exogamy, due to the association of Gentiles with demons.[68] Again, for Jubilees, narrative example is an authority right along with explicit legal formulae. The context here is explicitly Levi's slaughter of Shechem, and Phinehas's violent zeal against intermarriage is present in all but name. The divine approval of the latter in particular (Num 25:11–13) leads easily to the conclusion that exogamy is to be punished by death. This is another example of tendentious interpretation and emphasis, but the law is very much derivative of familiar authorities.

The sixth and final example is the law of tithes, including a second tithe, in Jub. 32:10–15. This is not the place to resolve all the issues related to tithing laws in ancient Judaism.[69] Suffice it to say that, whether the author of Jubilees received or developed the solution, the problem was certainly received. Jubilees differs from the rabbinic solution,[70] but any

---

67. The basic shift is interpreting "Molech" in Lev 20:2 as "an idolater" or "a marriage that will lead to idolatry," rather than the historical-critical interpretation of "a demon who feeds on child immolation." Rabbinic sources give a similar interpretation, as a prohibition of impregnating a foreign woman. See m. Meg. 4:9, b. Meg. 25a; Kugel, "Interpolations in *Jubilees*," 268; Géza Vermès, "Leviticus 18:21 in Ancient Jewish Bible Exegesis," in *Studies in Aggadah, Targum and Jewish Liturgy in Memory of Joseph Heinemann* (מחקרים באגדה תרגומים ותפלות ישראל לזכר יוסף היינמן) (ed. Jakob J. Petuchowski and Ezra Fleischer; Jerusalem: Magnes, 1981), 108–24. For more detailed analysis, see Hayes, *Gentile Impurities and Jewish Identities*, 73–81.

68. Cf. Jub. 1:11. See the chapter on the spatial axis. See also VanderKam, "The Demons in the *Book of Jubilees*," 339–64; Hanneken, "Angels and Demons," 11–25; Reed, "Enochic and Mosaic Traditions in Jubilees," 353–68.

69. García Martínez, "The Heavenly Tablets in the Book of Jubilees," 258; Finkelstein, "Jubilees and the Rabbinic Halaka," 52–53; Albeck, *Das Buch der Jubiläen und die Halacha*, 30–32.

70. Finkelstein, "Jubilees and the Rabbinic Halaka," 52.

solution short of source criticism is likely to conclude that at least two distinct tithes must be taking place. Among the "contradictions" are whether the tithe is given to a priest or a Levite (Deut 26:3–4; Num 18:21) and, similarly, whether it is "holy to the LORD" or can be eaten by resident aliens, orphans, and widows (Lev 27:30; Deut 14:29). The second tithe is most directly related to the מַעֲשֵׂר מִן־הַמַּעֲשֵׂר, "tithe of the tithe" (Num 18:26). To be sure, the heavenly tablets authorize one solution to the exclusion of others. Even with this qualification, however, it is significant that Jubilees works with the materials of received authority, as creative as it may be in doing so.[71] Any good solution to problems and ambiguities in received authority derives a certain authority. Recourse to a higher authority by way of the genre "apocalypse" raises the possibility of conspicuous overkill.

Although these six examples exhaust the category García Martínez calls "new halakot," there are other examples that are somewhat new.[72] The examples above give a fair, though not exhaustive, sample of the use of the "heavenly tablets" authority in Jubilees. These are not just random examples of not-so-novel interpretations in Jubilees. Although the heavenly tablets are neither fundamental to all the apocalypses nor limited to apocalypses, heavenly tablets are one manifestation of the pattern in apocalypses of asserting direct recourse to heavenly authority.[73] It would be one thing if Jubilees simply used both authorizing mechanisms in different places. The literary discord comes in the fact that Jubilees frames derivative interpretation as an apocalypse, not only in the general framework of the book, but in specific passages with reference to the heavenly tablets.

A few examples will help illustrate the typical association of "heavenly tablets." As much as the contents vary, there is never a case, besides Jubilees, when information is asserted to come from the heavenly tablets when it could just as easily have been derived from a known earthly authority.

---

71. García Martínez comments, "It is interesting here that the appropriate halakah on tithes is legitimated through recourse to the H[eavenly]T[ablets], which justify the exegesis that has been made upon a biblical basis" ("The Heavenly Tablets in the Book of Jubilees," 258).

72. See note 61 above.

73. The "master paradigm" of *Semeia* 14 (1.4) lists "a written document, usually a heavenly book" (Collins, "Apocalypse: The Morphology of a Genre," 6). Baynes attributes greater significance to the heavenly tablets as a constituent element that, among others, determines the genre "apocalypse" ("My Life Is Written Before You," 166).

Even when the information is not described as a "secret" or "mystery," it is novel and otherwise unavailable. In 1 En. 103:1–2 the heavenly tablets are the source of knowledge of a "mystery" concerning future events. The Apocalypse of Weeks is likewise introduced with the heavenly tablets as the source (93:2).[74] While verses 3–8 could be considered derivative, these verses are mere background for verses 9–17.[75] One can speak of traditional motifs and allusions, but on the scale of new and derived, the main part of the Apocalypse of Weeks is thoroughly new. In other sources, especially earlier sources, and sometimes in Jubilees, the tablets are not so much a source of revelation as a record of deeds to be used for assigning reward and punishment.[76] Still, it is safe to say that the ideas of mysterious revelation available only in heaven, and heavenly tablets in particular, were associated with the apocalypses.[77]

4.1.3.2. Departures from Genesis and Exodus

As indicated by the foregoing, Jubilees persistently weaves other received authorities into its retelling of Genesis–Exodus. Although the vast majority of Jubilees follows Gen 1 through Exod 24, there are some noteworthy excurses. Significantly, however, even when Jubilees departs from the narrative of Genesis–Exodus, it works with received authorities. Rather than defining and surveying all the excurses, we will focus on one salient example.[78] Jubilees 23 is of vital interest because it concentrates use of the genre

---

74. There may be room to doubt that the introduction was written at the same time as the apocalypse, but the correlation between 93:2 and 93:10 makes clear that it is meant as an introduction to the Apocalypse of Weeks, and not the entire Epistle of Enoch (Stuckenbruck, *1 Enoch 91–108*, 66–67).

75. Indeed, the subject of the vision, as posted in the introduction, is not introduced until verse 10: "concerning the sons of righteousness, and concerning the chosen of eternity, and concerning the plant of truth" (93:2).

76. For example, 1 En. 81:1–2; Dan 12:1. García Martínez counts two such uses in Jubilees (19:9; 30:19–22) but also discusses the ambiguity and possible overlap with the six passages he classifies "the Book of Destiny" ("The Heavenly Tablets in the Book of Jubilees," 246–50).

77. For more on the ancient question of whether revealed wisdom was readily available on earth or required some sort of heavenly journey, see Argall, *1 Enoch and Sirach*, 92–94.

78. For further examples and discussion, see Brooke, "Exegetical Strategies in Jubilees 1–2," 39–57. Brooke rightly emphasizes the integration of Deuteronomy and

"apocalypse" of the historical type. Jubilees 23 departs from the flow of the narrative in Genesis but continues to depend on received authorities. The chapter begins with the record of the longevity of Abraham in Genesis, then molds Ps 90, Isa 65, and the covenant curses (Deut 28 especially, also Lev 26) into a historical apocalypse. James Kugel has shown how the use of Ps 90 is even greater than previously thought.[79] The use of Third Isaiah and Isa 65 in particular is rather clear and is especially interesting for our purposes because it demonstrates how a text can be received and used as part of the tradition even if a basic tension exists at the level of ideas. Even if some texts are used more (or in more ways) than others, the concept of received traditions must be understood broadly. There was no such thing as a canon that defined which works were supremely authoritative and which could not be used at all. The dependence on the covenant curses has also been long recognized, although it is striking that the thematic parallels do not mimic the exact wording. These three areas do not exhaust the use of received authorities in Jub. 23, much less the book as a whole, but they do give a good sample of the flexibility and persistence with which Jubilees uses various traditions. Jubilees is almost always creative, but almost always has some familiar, received authority at the core.

Psalm 90 in Jubilees 23. The relationship between Ps 90 and Jub. 23 is not a mere case of thematic or linguistic parallel. Verse after verse influences Jub. 23 on point after point. Kugel is careful to be clear that Jub. 23 weaves in Ps 90 but does not simply reword it. The effect is to derive authority from the received psalm for an interpretation that ultimately goes back to Gen 25:7 (the life span of Abraham): "By weaving these other themes in with a few obvious references to Psalm 90, the author of Jubilees could provide the whole chapter with a certain legitimacy."[80] Although the dependence on Psalm 90 does not compare to the overall dependence on Genesis–Exodus, the continuity of use of verse after verse

---

the prophetic texts, among others, into Genesis–Exodus to create a portrait of overall consistency. On the production of an apocalyptic revelatory framework by weaving together Exod 24 and Deut 31 in Jub. 1, see Hanneken, "The Book of Jubilees among the Apocalypses," 462–65.

79. Kugel, "The Jubilees Apocalypse," 322–37.

80. Ibid., 336. For additional discussion of the authority conferred by weaving accepted authorities into new compositions, see Najman, "Interpretation as Primordial Writing," 408; Levinson, *Legal Revsion and Religious Renewal*; Daniel K. Falk, *The Parabiblical Texts: Strategies for Extending the Scriptures among the Dead Sea Scrolls* (Companion to the Qumran Scrolls 8; New York: T&T Clark, 2007).

distinguishes even this excursus in Jubilees from the tangential allusions typical of the apocalypses.

Psalm 90 itself can be understood as an interpretation of the problem of longevity, such that the first parallel is natural and might not even be counted as a dependence if not for the continuation.

כִּי אֶלֶף שָׁנִים בְּעֵינֶיךָ כְּיוֹם אֶתְמוֹל כִּי יַעֲבֹר וְאַשְׁמוּרָה בַלָּיְלָה׃

> For a thousand years in your eyes are like yesterday gone by, or a watch in the night. (Psalm 90:4)

Jubilees had already made this familiar interpretation with respect to the death of Adam, "He lacked seventy years from a thousand years because a thousand years are one day in the testimony of heaven" (Jub. 4:30). The decline of life span from a day to a portion of a day (אַשְׁמוּרָה), or a millennium to a portion thereof, is taken up in Jubilees: "For the times of the ancients were nineteen jubilees for their lifetimes. After the flood they started to decrease from nineteen jubilees" (Jub. 23:9). The image of grass withering and drying in the twilight of life, לָעֶרֶב יְמוֹלֵל וְיָבֵשׁ (Ps 90:6), flows into Jub. 23:9, 10. Verse 7, as so often in the Psalms, sounds vague at first but actually fuels a specific point in Jubilees, that suffering comes as punishment from God, not an independent force of evil (Jub. 23:22–23):

כִּי־כָלִינוּ בְאַפֶּךָ וּבַחֲמָתְךָ נִבְהָלְנוּ׃

> For we are consumed in your anger, terrorized by your wrath. (Psalm 90:7)

The most direct parallel comes from Ps 90:10:

יְמֵי־שְׁנוֹתֵינוּ בָהֶם שִׁבְעִים שָׁנָה וְאִם בִּגְבוּרֹת ׀ שְׁמוֹנִים שָׁנָה
וְרָהְבָּם עָמָל וָאָוֶן כִּי־גָז חִישׁ וַנָּעֻפָה׃

> The days of our years are within seventy, or eighty at best,
> but still a rush of stress and affliction, as it passes quickly and is gone. (Ps 90:10)

Together with Isa 65 (below), this forms Jub. 23:15:

Then it will be said: "The days of the ancients were numerous—as many as a thousand years—and good. But now the days of our lives, if a man has lived for a long time, are seventy years, and, if he is strong, eighty years." All are evil, and there is no peace during the days of that evil generation. (Jub. 23:15)

Even more significantly, Ps 90 provides support for the idea of calendrical rectitude as key to repentance and restoration:

לִמְנוֹת יָמֵינוּ כֵּן הוֹדַע וְנָבִא לְבַב חָכְמָה:

Teach us to count our days properly, that we may come to a wise heart. (Ps 90:12)

As we shall see in the next section, Jubilees avoids any suggestion that one needs to be a sage to keep the calendrical and other commandments, but the idea that improper counting of days is part of the problem goes into Jub. 23:19, and the idea that studying the laws properly brings restoration forms Jub. 23:26. As one might expect, restoration of length and quality of life are found both in Ps 90:14 and Jub. 23:27–29. Kugel also shows how Ps 90:15 is understood in Jub. 23:27.[81]

שַׂמְּחֵנוּ כִּימוֹת עִנִּיתָנוּ שְׁנוֹת רָאִינוּ רָעָה:

Gladden us (by giving back) the days you took away, the years we saw suffering. (Ps 90:15)

In Jub. 23:27 life span will be restored to a thousand years and, literally, "to many more years than many days," or as VanderKam provides, "to more years than the number of days (had been)."

On the one hand, Jubilees avoids verbal recycling. On the other hand, Ps 90 finds more than a passing tangential allusion in Jub. 23. The psalm is not the sole foundation of the chapter, but several points in the psalm appear at several points throughout Jub. 23. Moreover, most of the parallels had not been noted before Kugel's 1994 article, causing one to wonder how many other passages in Jubilees are infused with the authority of familiarity just below the horizon of modern scholarship. The closer one

---

81. Kugel, "The Jubilees Apocalypse," 334.

looks, the more it becomes apparent that Jubilees packs scripture with more scripture.

Third Isaiah in Jubilees 23. The treatment of Isa 65 is slightly more complicated due to tension at the level of ideas. Although Third Isaiah does not consistently fall on one side of the different positions in Jubilees and the typical apocalypses, we have encountered a good number of cases where Jubilees seems to disagree with Third Isaiah.[82] It is important to distinguish reference to received scriptures from endorsement of the ideas most apparently implied. Indeed, as a body of authoritative writings began to take shape out of heterogeneous components, it was inevitable that for any one thinker a preferred set of ideas would dominate and inform the reading of other texts. Writings were not approached with a "love it or burn it" mentality, and authority could be accepted at different levels and degrees. Thus, it should not surprise us if Jubilees uses Third Isaiah as an authority and takes up the issues while offering interpretations that seem to go against the plain sense. Although a certain degree of looseness with sources, as just seen with Ps 90, is expected, previous chapters showed some subtle ways in which Jubilees inverts Isa 65. Jubilees 23 more than alludes to Isa 65, but that does not mean the message is imported without revision.

Third Isaiah in general makes a number of "appearances" in Jubilees and chapter 23 in particular, but Isa 65–66 most intersects with the restoration account in Jub. 23:28–31.[83] The first example is something of a variation in that the description of the restoration in Isaiah is adapted to describe the decline of history in Jubilees.

לֹא־יִהְיֶה מִשָּׁם עוֹד עוּל יָמִים וְזָקֵן
אֲשֶׁר לֹא־יְמַלֵּא אֶת־יָמָיו
כִּי הַנַּעַר בֶּן־מֵאָה שָׁנָה יָמוּת
וְהַחוֹטֶא בֶּן־מֵאָה שָׁנָה יְקֻלָּל:

---

82. This is hardly surprising, as the relationship between Third Isaiah and the apocalypses has long been recognized. See especially Hanson, *The Dawn of Apocalyptic*.

83. Nickelsburg and Endres have discussed the parallels between Third Isaiah and Jub. 23. Nickelsburg argues that the cry in Jub. 23:24–25 relates to Isaiah 63:15–64:1, whereas Endres prefers to describe a more general influence of Third Isaiah. The examples considered here may not be exhaustive but are the most direct parallels. See George W. E. Nickelsburg, *Resurrection, Immortality, and Eternal Life in Intertestamental Judaism* (Harvard Theological Studies 26; Cambridge: Harvard University Press, 1972), 21–22; Endres, *Biblical Interpretation in the Book of Jubilees*, 58 (= 1982, 86).

> There will no longer be an infant or an elder
> who does not fill out its days.
> One who dies at a hundred years old will be considered a youth,
> and one who falls short of one hundred will be considered cursed. (Isa 65:20)

This verse influences two verses in Jubilees, the second of which was already mentioned in connection with Ps 90:10.

> At that time, if a man lives a jubilee and one-half of years, it will be said about him: "He has lived for a long time." But the greater part of his time will be (characterized by) difficulties, toil, and distress without peace. (Jub. 23:12)

> Then it will be said: "The days of the ancients were numerous—as many as a thousand years—and good. But now the days of our lives, if a man has lived for a long time, are seventy years, and, if he is strong, eighty years." All are evil, and there is no peace during the days of that evil generation. (Jub. 23:15)

In chapter 3, on the temporal axis, we considered the significance of the fact that Jubilees pieces together sources to establish an emphatically gradual decline and how anything gradual contrasts with the typical view of history in the apocalypses. Here the main point is that Jubilees works with the material of Third Isaiah, which can safely be counted as received authority. A lesser point may also fit a pattern. Notice that Jubilees inverts the analogy: rather than one being reckoned accursed in the restoration, one is reckoned blessed in the decline.

Another fairly clear parallel, with another twist, is found in Jub. 23:28. Here it is worth comparing the translations of VanderKam and Charles (1902), as well as the pertinent words from Isa 65:20.

> ወአልቦ ፡ ልሂቀ ፡
> ወአልቦ ፡ ዘይጸግብ ፡ መዋዕለ ፡
> እስመ ፡ ኵሎሙ ፡ ሕፃናት ፡ ወደቂቀ ፡ ይከውኑ

> There will be no old man,
> nor anyone who has lived out his lifetime,
> because all of them will be infants and children. (Jub. 23:28, VanderKam)

> And there will be no old man

nor one who is [not] satisfied with his days,
for all will be (as) children and youths. (Jub. 23:28, Charles)

לֹא־יִהְיֶה מִשָּׁם עוֹד עוּל יָמִים וְזָקֵן
אֲשֶׁר לֹא־יְמַלֵּא אֶת־יָמָיו
כִּי הַנַּעַר...

There will no longer be an infant or an elder
who does not fill out its days.
for the youth… (Isa 65:20)

Line breaks are added to VanderKam's texts to aid comparison, and brackets are added to indicate Charles's emendation, which he mentions only in a footnote: "I have added the negative form from a comparison of Is. lxv. 20." VanderKam's translation is certainly acceptable and probably goes back to שבע ימים, as he suggests.[84] Nevertheless, Charles is right to notice a parallel and right to notice a discord. Scholars, apparently including Charles himself in 1917, rejected the option of adding a "not" to make the text say what one would like it to say.[85] Without emending, the discord presumably goes back to the original work. The original audience, like Charles, might have expected the exact opposite. More explicably, Jubilees makes simpler sense of "infant" by moving it to an example of what there will be, not what there will not be. The net meaning is not very different, but it might seem that Jubilees develops discord for the sake of discord, to undermine or at least "correct" Third Isaiah. It is difficult to establish the intent of the distortion, since Jubilees regularly reworks formulations. At any rate, it is at least clear that Jubilees is building from familiar authoritative texts.

Nickelsburg also brings some looser parallels.[86]

---

84. The phrase appears in Gen 35:29; 1 Chr 23:1; 29:28; 2 Chr 24:15; and Job 42:17 as a way of referring to dying of old age.

85. See VanderKam's note *ad loc.* and R. H. Charles and G. H. Box, *The Book of Jubilees; or The Little Genesis* (London: Society for Promoting Christian Knowledge; New York: Macmillan, 1917).

86. Nickelsburg, *Resurrection, Immortality, and Eternal Life*, 21–22. See also the discussion in Endres, *Biblical Interpretation in the Book of Jubilees*, 59–60 (= 1982, 88–89).

> The wolf and the lamb shall graze together,
> and the lion will eat grass like an ox.
> But the serpent's food is dust!
> They will not do harm, and they will not destroy anywhere on my holy
> mountain, says the LORD. (Isa 65:25)

> They will complete and live their entire lifetimes peacefully and joyfully.
> There will be neither a satan nor any evil one who will destroy. For their
> entire lifetimes will be times of blessing and healing. (Jub. 23:29)

We cannot be too confident that the audience would have made the comparison, but if they did, the implied differences are as striking as the similarities. Here the variations are not linguistic twists but implications at the level of ideas. First, if the wolf is read to represent a foreigner and the lamb an ethnic Jew (as in the Animal Apocalypse), then Third Isaiah says they will co-exist in Jerusalem, whereas Jubilees says God will remove foreigners from the land of Israel (Jub. 23:30). The possible connection between "serpent" and "satan" is more complicated; suffice it to recall from chapter 2 that Jubilees has a low view of the activity of contra-divine cosmic forces, at least as far as Israel is concerned. Consequently, there is no satan to punish, only to be absent.

There are still more suggested parallels, but the remaining can be mentioned only briefly. The parallel with Isa 65:13 (good Jews will be radically rewarded; bad Jews will be radically tortured) seems, if anything, an anti-parallel with Jub. 23:30. The only overlap is the language of servants, contrasted with enemies. In Third Isaiah the vindication of the elect includes the punishment of other Jews. Jubilees avoids or condemns any suggestion of division within Judaism (see ch. 2) and gives no weight to vindictive judgment in the eschatological sequence (the nations are excluded from restoration, not tortured; see ch. 3). There is a similar (anti-)parallel of reward and punishment between Isa 66:14 and Jub. 23:31. Here, however, there is also a specific verbal parallel, again inverted. In Isaiah "bones will sprout like grass," but in Jubilees "bones will rest in the earth."

All these parallels are possible, but even if several of them are dismissed, we can still make the basic point that is relevant here: Jubilees works with Third Isaiah as material even when it wanders off from Genesis–Exodus. Jubilees, at its moments of least "rewrittenness," follows received texts more closely than the average apocalypse at its most derivative. Jubilees resonates with Third Isaiah and in a way absorbs its authority, even while making other claims to authority. The use of a received authority may invite comparison, but it does not answer the question of whether the basic positions are consonant. One can receive an aspect of a tradition less enthusiastically than another aspect of the tradition. Jubilees 23, for example, draws from the apocalypses in genre, Third Isaiah (just discussed), and Deuteronomy (next discussed). As we have seen in the preceding chapters, Jubilees develops its ideas from Deuteronomy far more than Third Isaiah and the apocalypses.

The covenant curses in Jubilees 23. Finally, Jub. 23 fills the place of "final woes" in a historical apocalypse with the covenant curses of Deut 28 (and perhaps Lev 26). Although the thematic similarities are unmistakable and a number of images overlap, the dependence is not word for word. The closest point of contact is between Deut 28:49–50 and Jub. 23:23:

> The Lord will bring against you a nation from far away, from the end of the earth, like an eagle swooping down—a nation whose language you do not understand—an ominous nation that will neither respect old age nor have compassion for a child. (Deut 28:49–50)

> He will arouse against them the sinful nations who will have no mercy or kindness for them and who will show partiality to no one, whether old or young, or anyone at all, because they are evil and strong so that they are more evil than all mankind. (Jub. 23:23; cf. 4Q176 frag. 20)

The description of the foreign invader(s) is certainly similar, but the more significant parallels between the chapters are thematic. Chapter 3 already demonstrated how Jubilees both uses and adapts the covenant curses. The basic theological similarity is the claim that the "woes" of sickness, famine, and invasion are punishments from God intended to prompt sinners to repentance. The main adaptation is to place the covenant curses in the form of the final woes of a historical apocalypse. Unlike the typical apocalypses, the woes are covenantal punishment; more strikingly, they are adapted such that they can be understood to have been fulfilled in the past. Somewhat in language and imagery but more so in theology, Jub. 23 aligns itself with the authority of Deut 28.

Psalm 90, Third Isaiah, and Deut 28 do not exhaust the extent to which Jub. 23 uses received authorities. The allusion to Ps 79:2–3 in Jub. 23:23 will be discussed in chapter 5. Davenport argues for use of Jer 6:23 in the same verse,[87] and Wintermute finds a number of other parallels worthy of mar-

---

87. Davenport, *The Eschatology of the Book of Jubilees*, 34 n. 3.

ginal note.[88] The examples discussed suffice to give a fair evaluation of the use of received authorities in Jub. 23. Without downplaying the extent to which Jubilees creatively molds its materials, Jubilees is persistently derivative. Derivative does not mean slavishly deferential, but it does mean that the contents, however rearranged, come from publicly received authority. Even when emphasis is shifted, a degree of authority is derived when the building blocks are derived. Even when Jubilees departs from "rewriting" Genesis–Exodus, Jubilees remains a "rewriting" of received authorities.

Jubilees 23 is a particularly salient example, but only one example, of an excursus from Genesis–Exodus that continues to adhere to received traditions. Other examples would lead to interesting questions, such as the existence of a single written "Book of Noah,"[89] the subtleties of manner of use of the Book of Watchers,[90] the state of patriarch and priest Levi traditions before Jubilees,[91] or a nontextual but written map of the world.[92] The excursuses are important for establishing the limits of derivation, but we should not lose sight of the fact that the vast majority of Jubilees retells and interprets in a very direct way Genesis through Exod 24.[93] One must also take into account that the text that became known as the Samaritan Penta-

---

88. O. S. Wintermute, "Jubilees," in *The Old Testament Pseudepigrapha* (ed. James H. Charlesworth; 2 vols.; Garden City, N.Y.: Doubleday, 1983–1985), 2:99–102. The theme of declining longevity depends in a more general way on Genesis through Joshua.

89. See ch. 2 n. 25.

90. J. T. A. G. M. van Ruiten emphasizes the very close verbal adherence to Genesis–Exodus but finds the connection to the Book of the Watchers so loose that it should not be thought of as a literary dependence. See his *Primaeval History Interpreted*, 212; idem, "A Literary Dependency of Jubilees on 1 Enoch?" in Boccaccini, *Enoch and Qumran Origins*, 93. Segal (*The Book of Jubilees*, 115–18), on the other hand, counts Jub. 5:1–12 as so dependent on the Book of the Watchers that it cannot be considered authored by the person responsible for producing the book. See also James C. VanderKam, "Enoch Traditions in Jubilees and Other Second-Century Sources," *Society of Biblical Literature 1978 Seminar Papers* (SBLSP 13; 2 vols.; Missoula, Mont.: Scholars Press, 1978): 1:229–51; idem, *Enoch and the Growth*, 179–88; idem, *Enoch, a Man for All Generations* (Studies on Personalities of the Old Testament; Columbia: University of South Carolina Press, 1995), 110–21.

91. See n. 7 above.

92. Daniel Machiela, "From Enoch to Abram: The Text and Character of the Genesis Apocryphon (1Q20) in Light of Related Second Temple Jewish Literature," (Ph.D. dissertation, University of Notre Dame, 2007).

93. See n. 58 above.

teuch is no less received than that which became known as the Masoretic Text and that even the interpretations, direct as they may be, were often received orally or in texts no longer known to us. All things considered, Jubilees is persistently derivative of received authority. Alexander can plausibly suggest that the author of Jubilees "was the recipient of certain traditions which he honestly supposed went back to Moses himself."[94] Jubilees is creative in ways more analogous to *objet trouvé* than to sculpture from raw clay.[95] Jubilees might be best understood as a reconstruction, based on scattered evidence, of heavenly tablets that must exist in order to explain the authority of the received tradition. Jubilees reconciles authorities and postulates a unity in the source of authorities that appear to be disparate, but Jubilees does not unveil new revelation.[96]

The point, however, is not simply that Jubilees differs from contemporary apocalypses in that it can be described as rewritten scripture or that Jubilees differs from other examples of rewritten scripture in that it claims to be an apocalypse. Jubilees makes claims and cues the reader to expect that something new is going to be revealed. If we distinguish the claims from the actual contents, we arrive at a clear discord.

Jubilees claims to be an independent revelation from the highest authority, on par with the Pentateuch itself. It is important to temper this statement with the fact that Jubilees seems to acknowledge the Pentateuch as "first" (Jub. 6.22) and handed to Moses already written, whereas Jubilees is nominally secondary in that it was dictated.[97] The independence is also tempered by the fact that the first law and Jubilees are revealed from the same source to the same person in the same place at roughly the same time.[98] Still, scholars are on the right track to observe that the claim to revelation from the heavenly tablets in the form of an apocalypse is a claim to be on par with, not derived from, the Pentateuch.[99] The ancient

---

94. Alexander, "Retelling the Old Testament," 101. See Jub. 45:16 for the idea that the Levites preserved all the ancestral teaching in a broad sense.

95. The analogy should not be taken too far, however. Authorship in antiquity fills the spectrum of "originality." Creative reworking based on a large number of sources and traditions is better characterized as authorship than redaction. For a different view, see Segal, *The Book of Jubilees*.

96. For the theological claim that the received traditions, and writings in particular, are unitary and consistent, see Kugel, *Traditions of the Bible*, 17.

97. See n. 54.

98. VanderKam, "Scriptural Setting," 61–72.

99. Nickelsburg, "Scripture in 1 Enoch and 1 Enoch as Scripture," 347; Him-

audience, like modern scholars, would expect such a claim to introduce a new revelation that qualifies, rather than builds upon, the authority of the "first" revelation.[100] As we have seen, however, those expectations are not met. The claim does not concord with the actual content.

4.2. The Dependence of Revelation on Wisdom

This section considers simultaneously two strands of one basic observation. (1) The basic observation is that revelation is closely aligned with wisdom in the typical early apocalypses but not in Jubilees. (2) The first strand concerns wisdom per se, particularly the use of the term or a near equivalent,[101] in the context of a prerequisite to, result of, or identification with receipt of revelation. Jubilees avoids the term almost completely and qualifies the concept. (3) The second strand concerns the view of revelation as coded or otherwise inaccessible. Jubilees has a concept of "seeking" the laws, but it does not convey meaning in allegorical or symbolic codes, it does not read Genesis as if coded, and it diminishes codes that do appear in Genesis. (4) The important point for the present work is that Jubilees uses the genre "apocalypse" to frame a revelation that differs in its view of revelation from what a reader would expect from an apocalypse. (5) One might speculate further that what concerns Jubilees is not opposition to wisdom as a general virtue but as a form of elitism. Jubilees seems to suggest that the laws by which covenantal fidelity and blessings can be achieved are accessible to all of Israel, regardless of intelligence, profession, esoteric initiation, or other form of elitism. The subsections will consider the Enochic apocalypses, the Danielic apocalypses,

---

melfarb, "Torah, Testimony, and Heavenly Tablets," 27–28; Najman, "Interpretation as Primordial Writing," 388; Boccaccini, *Beyond the Essene Hypothesis*, 90. It is also important to be aware that these comments are partly in reaction to the assertion that Jubilees claims to supplant the Pentateuch, particularly by Ben Zion Wacholder, "*Jubilees* as the Super Canon: Torah-Admonition versus Torah-Commandment," in *Legal Texts and Legal Issues: Proceedings of the Second Meeting of the International Organization for Qumran Studies, Cambridge 1995* (ed. Moshe J. Bernstein, Florentino García Martínez, and John Kampen; STDJ 23; Leiden: Brill, 1997), 195–211.

100. See, for example, Nickelsburg, "Scripture in 1 Enoch and 1 Enoch as Scripture," 347.

101. We will not ignore the distinction Daniel makes between wisdom and enlightenment, but, for the present consideration of a view of revelation as restricted to an elite, they function the same way.

and Jubilees. First, each of the preceding introductory points should be explained further.

(1) The history of scholarship on the categories of "wisdom" and "prophecy" is as complex as that of "apocalyptic."[102] The important development for the present purpose is that "wisdom" can include "revealed wisdom," along with the types of wisdom associated with the canonical wisdom literature. Not only are the genres "wisdom" and "apocalypse" compatible; the early apocalypses tend to identify wisdom and revelation. Revealed wisdom is not the only kind of wisdom, nor is it limited to the apocalypses, but it is typical of the early apocalypses. Jubilees exhibits a kind of revelation independent of wisdom.

(2) Although there is much more to revealed wisdom than use of the term "wisdom" and the distribution of the term is not even, terminology provides a quick way of assessing different views of revelation. In the Enochic and Danielic apocalypses, wisdom is an all-encompassing category for that which is received when revelation is received and that

---

102. Among the milestones, Gerhard von Rad challenged the tendency to view "apocalyptic" as the child of prophecy by arguing that the view of history makes it the child of wisdom (*Old Testament Theology* [2 vols.; New York: Harper & Row, 1965], 2:306). Hans-Peter Müller refined von Rad's point by specifying mantic wisdom ("Mantische Weisheit und Apokalyptik," in *Congress Volume: Uppsala, 1971* [ed. P. A. H. de Boer; VTSup 22; Leiden: Brill, 1972], 268–93). See further on mantic wisdom, VanderKam, *Enoch and the Growth*; idem, "The Prophetic-Sapiential Origins of Apocalyptic Thought," in *A Word in Season: Essays in Honour of William McKane* (ed. James D. Martin and Philip R Davies; JSOTSup 42; Sheffield: JSOT Press, 1986), 163–76. Martin Hengel developed the category of "higher wisdom through revelation" in *Judaism and Hellenism: Studies in Their Encounter in Palestine during the Early Hellenistic Period* (Philadelphia: Fortress, 1974), 210–18. Smith ("Wisdom and Apocalyptic," 131–56) and Stone ("Lists of Revealed Things," 414–52) advanced the study of the distinctive form of wisdom associated with the apocalypses. For discussion on the issues in Q scholarship (especially Kloppenborg and Mack), and as a significant contribution in its own right, see Collins, "Wisdom, Apocalypticism, and Generic Compatibility," 165–85. Matthew J. Goff has worked extensively on the overlap of wisdom and apocalyptic elements, most recently in *Discerning Wisdom: The Sapiential Literature of the Dead Sea Scrolls* (VTSup 116; Leiden: Brill, 2007). For a recent review of scholarship, see Macaskill, *Revealed Wisdom and Inaugurated Eschatology*, 1–24. See also Torleif Elgvin, "Wisdom with and without Apocalyptic," in *Sapiential, Liturgical, and Poetical Texts from Qumran: Proceedings of the Third Meeting of the International Organization for Qumran Studies, Oslo, 1998* (ed. Daniel K. Falk, Florentino García Martínez, and Eileen M. Schuller; STDJ 35; Leiden: Brill, 2000), 15–38; Andreas Bedenbender, "Jewish Apocalypticism: A Child of Mantic Wisdom?" *Henoch* 24 (2002): 189–96.

which defines the righteous. Jubilees, however, divorces revelation from wisdom. Jubilees uses the term twice, once to describe Enoch and once in connection with Joseph, but never to describe that which is revealed from the heavenly tablets, that which one must have in order to receive revelation, or that which one gains as a result of revelation. Jubilees elevates the intelligence of Abraham, Isaac, and Jacob but avoids the terminology of wisdom and even attributes the rejection of a form of wisdom to the intelligence of Abram.

(3) The typical identification of apocalyptic revelation with revealed wisdom is related to the tendency to describe revelation as a mystery or to convey it in codes. The issue is not how easily the revelation might be decoded but the assertion that revelation is mysterious, not easily grasped, or hidden from the ordinary mind. This view of limited access to revelation can be expressed in many forms. Lange has already shown how Jubilees differs from the typical apocalypses in that it rejects allegorical dreams.[103] Jubilees does not communicate in code, it does not read Genesis as if a code, and it downplays coded revelation within Genesis. More generally, Jubilees disambiguates the revelation that is necessary to be righteous and rewarded under the covenant. Jubilees presents the revelation received by Moses as if completely transparent. The laws should be studied in order to be observed, but without the expectation of a new revelation that will supersede the plain sense of the original (as in Dan 9).

(4) The important point is that the view of revelation in Jubilees is different from the view that is typically conveyed by the genre "apocalypse." When a reader encounters the literary features of heavenly tablets revealed through an angelic intermediary to an exemplary human on matters of the cosmic realm and the meaning of history, the reader expects a certain view to be expressed about each of those things. In this case, the reader expects an apocalypse to convey a view of revelation as coded, mysterious, and accessible only to the wise. Jubilees subverts that expectation. The discord between the ideas cued by the literary framework and the ideas sustained accentuates the rejection of the expected ideas.

(5) Even without speculating on social context, it is not difficult to imagine what the concern might have been. The issue here seems to be related to the issue discussed in chapter 2, that Jubilees addresses all of Israel without singling out a group for eschatological reward. "Wisdom" is

---

103. Lange, "Divinatorische Träume," 25–38.

often not just a general virtue attainable by anyone but a set of learned skills that define an elite scribal class.[104] Jubilees presumably aims to emphasize that the covenant between God and Israel is accessible to and incumbent on all of Israel, even those who do not have the luxury of devoting themselves to the life of a sage,[105] even those who do not meditate on enigmas, and even those who are not particularly bright. Deuteronomy 30:11–14 illustrates the issue and the basic position taken by Jubilees:

> For this commandment that I command you today is not too mysterious for you or far away. It is not in the heavens, such that one might say, "Who will go up to the heavens to get it for us, such that we could observe and do it?" Nor is it across the sea, such that one might say, "Who will cross the sea to get it for us, such that we could observe and do it?" On the contrary, it is very close to you! In your mouth! In your mind! Do it!

Although one should not conclude direct cause and effect, one could imagine the author of an Enochic apocalypse reading Deut 30 and wondering what in the heavens is so interesting or the author of a Danielic apocalypse what this mysterious thing over the waters is.[106] Regardless of whether the author of Jubilees thought of the issue in terms of Deut 30, it is

---

104. Karel van der Toorn reconstructs the development of wisdom as scribal elitism, as opposed to the practical wisdom of elders: "The comparison between Old Babylonian and the Standard Babylonian versions of Gilgamesh reveals a fundamental change. Where wisdom used to be a spoken counsel by someone with experience, it turned into knowledge of secrets from distant days. Such knowledge could be obtained only through disclosure by some god or an exceptional human being. Since it had been committed to writing—by Gilgamesh and others—it was accessible to the scribal elite. Wisdom became scribal wisdom—knowledge of mysteries that had little to do with the practical realities of everyday life" ("Why Wisdom Became a Secret: On Wisdom as a Written Genre," in *Wisdom Literature in Mesopotamia and Israel* [ed. Richard J. Clifford; Atlanta: Society of Biblical Literature, 2007], 28–29).

105. The present work does not endeavor to include Ben Sira in the comparison, but the reader might occasionally notice that Jubilees seems to be more proximate to Ben Sira than the apocalypses on some fundamental positions. Jubilees and Ben Sira might agree that one should travel to the temple, not the cosmos, to find appropriate instruction (Sir 24:23; Argall, *1 Enoch and Sirach*, 55), but Jubilees does not share Ben Sira's elitism (see especially Sir 38:24).

106. Bodies of water are a recurring locus of revelation in the Danielic apocalypses (7:2; 8:2; 10:4).

an apt description of the difference between the view of revelation typical of the apocalypses and that of Jubilees. In contrast to the view of revelation typically found in the apocalypses, Jubilees presents the law and testimony revealed to Moses at Sinai and, consequently, the requirements for righteousness and reward under the covenant, as foolproof.

4.2.1. THE ENOCHIC APOCALYPSES

The Enochic apocalypses tie revelation to wisdom (best described as revealed wisdom) and view revelation as coded or otherwise accessible only by way of wisdom. The apocalypses vary in the frequency with which the word "wisdom" is used to describe that which is revealed and in the ways in which the inaccessibility of revelation is expressed. Among the variations, however, one can identify a common perspective that sees revelation as distant and restricted to an elite.

The most numerous explicit identifications of Enoch's revelation with wisdom occur in the Epistle of Enoch and the Parables.[107] Even if the Epistle (other than the Apocalypse of Weeks) is dated after Jubilees, the numerous explicit references to Enoch's revelation as wisdom indicate patterns that had been implicit in the earlier apocalypses and especially indicate how they were read close to the time of Jubilees. Thus, the Book of the Watchers uses the word "wisdom" rarely (that which will be given to the chosen in 5:8; the fruit that nourishes the holy ones in 32:3, 6; cf. the አእምሮ, "knowledge," that humans are destined to understand in 14:3). Be that as it may, Nickelsburg, Argall, and Knibb point to language and motifs that show wisdom to be a "comprehensive category" that designates the Book of the Watchers and Enochic literature in general, as well as that which defines the chosen. Among these are the wisdom term "parable" in 1:2, the list of contents in 2:1–5:3, and the pursuit of knowing everything in 25:2.[108] Argall uses 5:8 to argue that "[t]he phrase 'to give wisdom' is a technical expression for Enoch's revelation."[109] Knibb discusses motifs such as sapiential admonition based on natural order (1 En. 2:1—5:4) and

---

107. 1 En. 92:1 (cf. 4Q212 frag. 1, col. 2, line 23, אנושא כ[וח]בים); 1 En. 37; 42; 48:1; 49:1, 3; 51:3; 61:7, 11; 63:2; 94:5; 98:1, 3, 9; 99:10; 100:6; 101:8; 104:12; 105:1.

108. Nickelsburg, *1 Enoch: A Commentary*, 52. See also the observation illustrated from later examples in Stone, "Lists of Revealed Things," 416–18.

109. Argall, *1 Enoch and Sirach*, 20.

places of mystery outside the human realm (1 En. 17–19).[110] Especially in light of later developments, one can safely conclude that the Book of the Watchers was viewed as a book of revealed wisdom at the time of Jubilees.

Although the Book of the Watchers has been read as an allegory for priestly marriage purity,[111] the view of revelation as accessible only to a wise elite is better seen in the treatment of the tree-of-wisdom motif. In general, it is important not to conclude from the view of revelation as coded that the meaning is exhausted by the substitution of decoded equivalents.[112] The Book of the Watchers is a good example of an apocalypse the meaning of which is not exhausted by coded equivalents, in this case understanding the watchers as priests. By means of comparison with Sirach, Argall has demonstrated how the Book of the Watchers uses the tree-of-wisdom motif to emphasize the remoteness and inaccessibility of wisdom, other than by way of a certain esoteric chain of transmission.[113] Although the Book of the Watchers does not develop the idea of stages of revelation to the same extent as the Danielic apocalypses, the role of the interpreting angel functions within the same cluster of ideas. Even when revelation is right before one's eyes, one still requires interpretation from an authorized figure (e.g., 1 En. 18:14).

The Apocalypse of Weeks explicitly defines "wisdom" as that which is given (one might say revealed) to the chosen (93:10; see also 91:10), and it defines the chosen as a group apart from those who stray from wisdom (93:8). The apocalypse itself is part of that wisdom and exemplifies the view of revelation as cryptic. The point is not that the code is particularly difficult to crack but that revelation is presented as if cryptic and only understood by a chosen few at a chosen time. Regardless of disputed social realities and the ease of cracking the code, the Apocalypse of Weeks uses

---

110. Knibb, "Enoch in Light of Qumran Wisdom," 206–10.

111. Suter, "Fallen Angel, Fallen Priest," 115–35; Nickelsburg, "Enoch, Levi, and Peter," 575–600. The work can also be read as allegorical in the sense that at least part of what is said of the judgment and restoration in the days of Noah refers rather to a future judgment and restoration.

112. Advanced by Gunkel and emphasized by Collins, *Apocalyptic Imagination*, 16–17.

113. "In *1 Enoch*, the great wisdom represented by the Tree is inaccessible to ordinary mortals. It is made known to angels and they, in turn, communicate it to Enoch through interpretations of his visions. Enoch then brings this wisdom from heaven to the chosen and righteous, who 'eat' it (82:3b)" (Argall, *1 Enoch and Sirach*, 94).

the literary motif of esotericism.¹¹⁴ Regardless of how elaborate a chronology might (or might not) be implied in the system of weeks, a week certainly represents something other than a week. The identification of the man who will be saved as Noah and the man who will be taken up as Elijah, for example, may not have been too difficult for the intended audience, but the references are presented as cryptic in the narrative setting. Again, revelation is presented as a code accessible only to the wise.

The Animal Apocalypse does not use a word for "wisdom" in its allegory, but the opening of eyes (90:6 and more frequently the absence thereof) functions the same way as does the revelation of wisdom in the Apocalypse of Weeks. The Animal Apocalypse is also a prime example of coded revelation. Again, the issue is not how many ancient Jews could have actually cracked the code but that revelation is presented as if if is a code that is fully understandable only at a special time by an audience that is made to feel special. Wisdom is required to decipher the revelation, and further wisdom regarding current events results from the revelation. Wisdom is not a general virtue that describes all of Israel; it marks the boundaries of an elite group.¹¹⁵

4.2.2. The Danielic Apocalypses

The Danielic apocalypses vary from the Enochic apocalypses in some details but share the same basic view of revelation. Revelation is cryptic and accessible only to an enlightened elite. The elitism is moderated in that greater allowance is made for the "masses" to receive instruction from the enlightened. The masses might become righteous if they heed the enlightened, but they do not themselves become enlightened (Dan 12:3). The elite are not isolated, but they remain exclusive. The elite are not distinguished by a skill set that can be taught but by access to ongoing revelation. Revela-

---

114. For more on separating the literary motif from social reality, see Adler, "Introduction," 13-16; Stone, "Apocalyptic Literature," 431-32; Collins, *Apocalyptic Imagination*, 39; idem, *Daniel: A Commentary*, 339-40.

115. See further, Nickelsburg, *1 Enoch: A Commentary*, 52-53. If the discussion is extended to include the Epistle of Enoch, one finds an intermediate group comparable to the multitude in Daniel. In the Epistle, 1 En. 99:10, one finds an opportunity to become blessed, even if one cannot oneself become wise, by listening to the words of the wise. The dominant emphasis in the Epistle is on the wise themselves (see especially 104:12 and n. 108 above).

tion continues to be cryptic, as in the Enochic apocalypses, but the "code" moves further beyond the human realm of decipherment.¹¹⁶ The decoding of revelation is not a matter of wisdom in the sense of human skill but enlightenment in a purely revealed sense.

Thus, the first variation is the avoidance of the root חכם, "wise," in favor of שכל (for lack of a better alternative), "enlightened." For the purposes of comparing views of the elite accessibility of revelation, enlightenment is every bit as elite as wisdom and more so. "Wisdom" comes off almost badly, as a human skill vastly inferior to the access to heavenly revelation associated with enlightenment. Or rather, true wisdom is a trait that humans cannot fully possess, but only God, who reveals it as God wishes (Dan 2:20–21).¹¹⁷ Thus, in the book as a whole,¹¹⁸ the root חכם usually refers to the Babylonian professionals whose skill is markedly inferior to the revelation of an enlightened person. Wisdom is still a part of Daniel's mortal skill set (Dan 1:4, 17, 20), but Daniel denies the sufficiency of mortal wisdom.

> As for me, this mystery was not revealed to me by means of my own wisdom (superior as it is to all mortals), but in order to make known to the king the fact of the interpretation, so that you can know your own thoughts. (Dan 2:30)

---

116. Carmignac ("Qu'est-ce que l'Apocalyptique," 10, 20–21) held the revelation of secrets that are normally hidden from human intelligence to be essential to the apocalypses. He distinguishes the apocalypses from rabbinic literature according to the means employed to excavate secrets from the Torah.

117. The idea that wisdom and knowledge come from God is not new. What is striking is the emphatic contrast between learned human skill and revealed enlightenment. See Alexander Rofé, "Revealed Wisdom: From the Bible to Qumran," in *Sapiential Perspectives: Wisdom Literature in Light of the Dead Sea Scrolls* (ed. Ruth Clements, John J. Collins, and Gregory E. Sterling; STDJ 51; Leiden: Brill, 2004), 1–11.

118. We are justified in not limiting the consideration to the apocalypses because the court tales establish the view of revelation that is used in the apocalypses. To an extent the authors of the apocalypses may have cast their view of revelation into the court tales (particularly in Dan 1–2 and occasional redactional glue). To a further extent the view of revelation in the court tales may have attracted the authors of the apocalypses to attach the apocalypses to the court tales. The court tales cannot be the only basis for establishing the view of revelation in the apocalypses, but they are foundational.

Although the orthodoxy of the queen may be suspect, she, too, seems to recognize a difference between mortal wisdom and access to divine wisdom:

> There is a man in your kingdom who has a divine holy spirit. In the days of your father he was found to have illumination, enlightenment, and wisdom like the wisdom of the gods. (Dan 5:11)

Again in Dan 5:14, Daniel's wisdom needs to be qualified as different from ordinary wisdom, but "enlightenment" requires no qualification.

Apparently building on the view of wisdom as a human skill, the apocalypses never use the root חכם, "wise." The root שכל, "enlightened," can be used rather loosely (Antiochus Epiphanes has it in the sense of "cunning" in 8:25; it seems to reflect a human activity in 9:13), but usually it refers to a specific group and the (mediated) divine action that defines them. The near identification of enlightenment with revelation appears in Dan 9:22:

> He explained it to me, saying, "Daniel, I have just now come out to enlighten your understanding."

In Dan 1:17 enlightenment is given by God to Daniel, with a scribal connotation (cf. 9:1). Access to this enlightenment defines Daniel himself as an "enlightened one" in 1:4 and also a latter-day group of "enlightened ones" to be identified as the circle of composition (Dan 11:33, 35; 12:3, 10). The latter-day enlightened ones show no humility in identifying themselves with Daniel, as the most significant difference is that they understand even more than Daniel himself did (12:8, 10).

Thus we come to an additional perspective on the view of revelation in stages already raised in the previous section. In Daniel, revelation is not a deposit left behind in the distant past to be preserved and passively studied. Rather, revelation is ongoing and cumulative, such that understanding improves with new revelation. The revelation at Sinai was not complete (cf. Jub. 1:26[119]), the prophecy of Jeremiah was not final (Dan 9:24), and even the vision of Daniel was not immediately understood (12:8). The latter-day enlightened ones concern themselves with former prophecies and visions,

---

119. "First and last" in Jub. 1:26 indicates completeness, not necessarily eschatology, as is frequently found in Chronicles: הָרִאשֹׁנִים וְהָאַחרֹנִים (1 Chr 29:29; 2 Chr 9:29; 12:15; 16:11; 20:34; 25:26; 26:22; 28:26; 35:27).

but they reserve for themselves the final stage of revelation. Like Daniel, they have access to divine revelation, and they have the further advantage of seeing the events unfold in their own days.

Chapter 2 already considered the view of divisions of humanity for purposes of restoration (i.e., Daniel holds the enlightened up for special reward, while Jubilees admits no eschatological divisions within Israel). The point here is that Daniel views revelation as accessible only to an enlightened elite, comparable to the identification of wisdom and revelation in the Enochic apocalypses. To a certain extent Daniel opens up the elitism by allowing the multitude to be instructed by the enlightened, but allowing the public to obey is hardly a democratic reform. The enlightened distinguish themselves from the masses not by teachable skills or knowledge but by access to ongoing revelation. God reveals wisdom and enlightenment to the wise and the enlightened, not to all of Israel (see again Dan 2:21).

Another implication of the view of multiple stages of revelation is that all revelation becomes cryptic, regardless of whether it had seemed cryptic. The writing on Belshazzar's wall offers a particularly cryptic first stage of revelation (Dan 5), and Dan 2 emphasizes the independence of the second stage so much so that it occurs without knowledge of the first stage of Nebuchadnezzar's dream. Daniel 2 also uses the language of secrets (רָזִין, 2:18, 19, 27, 28, 29, 30, 47) and mysteries (מְסָתְרָתָא, 2:22) for that which God reveals. Curiously, however, cognate language is not found in the apocalypses, even though the contents could be called mysterious to Daniel even after they are revealed (8:27; 12:8). The apocalypses are persistently cryptic, whether they are "deliberately elusive" (especially Dan 7)[120] or use roundabout ways of referring to things such as units of time (time, times, half a time; 2,300 mornings and evenings). The most significant implication comes from Dan 9. Jeremiah's prophecy had seemed anything but cryptic, but the meaning turned out to be other than what it appeared to mean. The received prophecy is decoded "like a symbol in a dream."[121] By extension, all of received scripture can be treated as a first stage of revelation subject to amendment.[122]

---

120. Collins, *Daniel: A Commentary*, 296.
121. Ibid., 359.
122. In the words of Fishbane, "Prophetic words are no longer predominantly living speech, but rather inscribed and inscrutable data whose true meanings are an

It is common for ancient interpreters to treat received scripture as "cryptic" to an extent. Kugel uses the word to describe a common assumption among ancient interpreters, and Jubilees both describes and exhibits a process of "seeking out" the commands.[123] As we shall see, however, Jubilees draws the line with allegorical codes. It may never be clear how the author of Jubilees justified certain modifications of the received texts of Genesis and Exodus, but it is at least clear that Jubilees never makes the move Daniel makes. Daniel treats all revelation, whether in received scriptures or in visions, as a code that can be amended with further revelation, showing relatively little regard for the original.

Daniel differs from the Enochic apocalypses in significant ways but shares use of the literary genre "apocalypse" and the basic view of revelation as cryptic and accessible only to a wise elite. The genre necessarily raises the issue of revelation and typically presents that which is revealed as mysterious, ambiguous, esoteric, and elite, reserved for a particular group at a particular time.[124] Jubilees, however, uses the genre to frame what it claims was revealed clearly at Sinai for all Israel to understand and obey.

4.2.3. Jubilees

In Jubilees revelation is fully accessible to all of Israel. This is most striking in what it does not say but also in some positive emphases. Jubilees never uses the language of "secret" or "mystery" and uses the word "wisdom" only twice, neither of which compares to the "comprehensive category" of wisdom in the Enochic apocalypses or enlightenment in Daniel. Only in a very general sense are "sapiential motifs" used. Jubilees does not use codes, symbols, or allegories and downplays them where they appear in Genesis. The contrast also comes out in some positive emphases. Most generally, the revelation of the heavenly tablets at Sinai is presented as public instruction for all Israel for all time. Jubilees elevates the intelligence of Abraham, for example, in a way that effectively critiques a kind of wisdom. In general, Jubilees pursues a course of disambiguation, not reveling in enigmas.

---

esoteric mystery revealed by God to a special adept and his pious circle (cf. Daniel 9:22–23, 10:14–21, 11:33–5, 12:9–13)" (*Biblical Interpretation in Ancient Israel*, 484).

123. Kugel, *Traditions of the Bible*, 15; Jub. 23:26.

124. The idea that the Danielic apocalypses are intended for a time other than the time of Daniel is emphasized in 7:28; 8:19, 26; 10:14; 12:4, 9.

The differences are at times dramatic and at times subtle. The claims Jubilees makes seem to leave some problems unresolved, especially from a modern perspective. It may be difficult to get past the perspective of Jubilees as a pseudepigraphon that inherently implies the inadequacy of former revelation, invents "new" revelation, or views former revelation as an inaccessible secret code. Yet, as Alexander and Kugel have already suggested, the author of Jubilees claims and appears to believe that the book of Jubilees sets down the instructions and clarifications that were revealed to Israel at Sinai.[125]

4.2.3.1. Revelation without the Elitism of Wisdom

Jubilees strikingly avoids the distinctive language and motifs of "wisdom," particularly in the context of access to revelation. In more subtle ways, Jubilees elevates the intelligence of biblical heroes without, or even in opposition to, certain aspects of "scribal" or "mantic" wisdom. The net effect is to emphasize the claim that the heavenly tablets were made clearly accessible to all of Israel. This emphasis is not unique in Jewish thought in antiquity, but it contrasts sharply with the view of revelation typical of the apocalypses.

Jubilees does not often appear in scholarly discussion of wisdom and the apocalypses. When Benjamin Wright set out to study wisdom in Jubi-

---

125. Alexander writes: "The likeliest explanation is, however, that he was the recipient of certain traditions which he honestly supposed went back to Moses himself. ... The author of Jubilees may have felt that he was simply collecting and editing the esoteric traditions that had been faithfully passed down in priestly circles from the time of Moses to his own day" ("Retelling the Old Testament," 101). Kugel explains: "Suppose we were to be able to talk to the author of Jubilees and say, 'Come on, what's all this with the heavenly tablets and the angel of the presence? You made this up!' The author could reply in all seriousness, 'not a word'" (18 March 2004, Liss Lecture, University of Notre Dame; confirmed by correspondence 21 August 2007). Kugel's point had more to do with the phenomenon of pseudepigraphy in general—how an author can assume an identity to such an extent that the imagined or reconstructed conversations take on a reality of their own. This point would not distinguish Jubilees from contemporary apocalypses, but it remains significant that Jubilees is a prime example of a pseudepigraphon in which it is relatively easy to see how the author found the basis to reconstruct or imagine content.

The word "clarifications" reflects the Damascus Document, מדוקדק (CD 16.3). Finally, see also Najman, *Seconding Sinai*.

lees for the 2007 Enoch Seminar, which was mostly dedicated to Jubilees, he confirmed the lack of distinctive sapiential features in Jubilees.[126] Although he went on to discuss less-distinctive motifs, such as parent-child instruction, the most striking observation is the initial observation, the absence of wisdom features. Indeed, the words "mystery" and "secret" never appear,[127] and the word "wisdom" appears only twice.[128] One of these is merely a variation of Gen 41:39 on the lips of Pharaoh about Joseph: "We will not find a man as wise and knowledgeable as this man, for the spirit of the Lord is with him" (Jub. 40:5).[129] This verse is also the closest Jubilees comes to a sapiential usage of አእምሮ, "knowledge."[130] The other mention of wisdom does not come from Genesis directly but the received expansions about the figure of Enoch.

---

126. Benjamin G. Wright, "Jubilees, Sirach, and Sapiential Tradition," in Boccaccini and Ibba, *Enoch and the Mosaic Torah*, 116–30.

127. Samuel I. Thomas includes Jubilees in the cluster of texts reflecting the idea of antediluvian transmission of knowledge, but otherwise Jubilees is remarkably absent from his study of mysteries and secrets at Qumran (*The "Mysteries" of Qumran: Mystery, Secrecy, and Esotericism in the Dead Sea Scrolls* [SBLEJL 25; Atlanta: Society of Biblical Literature, 2009]).

128. This was determined by searching an electronic copy of VanderKam's translation. The translation is so literal that it seems safe to conclude that the Ethiopic term ጥበብ is not otherwise used. Margin of error remains possible in circuitous phraseology for the concept of wisdom, text variants not used in the translation, and the usual remote possibility that a word or passage was lost to the Ethiopic manuscript tradition.

For later examples of the view of scripture study as a means for unveiling נסתרות, "secrets," see the discussion of the Damascus Document and Community Rule in Gary A. Anderson, "The Status of the Torah before Sinai: The Retelling of the Bible in the Damascus Document and the Book of Jubilees," *DSD* 1 (1994): 10–19. Jubilees may have a concept of not-yet revealed laws in Jub. 33:16, but nothing remains unrevealed after Sinai.

129. Jub. 42:2 omits the detail in Gen 44:5 about Joseph performing divination with a cup, an activity that could be linked to mantic wisdom. See further, page 271 below.

130. God has knowledge in Jub. 2:2. The tree of knowledge (not wisdom) appears not where one would expect it in Jub. 3 but later in Jub. 4:30. As for humans, knowledge is never mentioned positively. It is evil in Jub. 5:2 and departs in 23:11. Although Rofé ("Revealed Wisdom," 3–4) found in this a movement of opposition to the idea that wisdom comes with age, the term here need not have any sapiential connotation, polemical or otherwise.

> He was the first of mankind who were born on the earth who learned (the art of) writing, instruction, and wisdom and who wrote down in a book the signs of the sky in accord with the fixed patterns of their months so that mankind would know the seasons of the years according to the fixed patterns of each of their months. (Jub. 4:17; cf. 11QJub frag. 3 line 2)

This is a fair description of the figure of Enoch developed in the received traditions, plus some emphasis on calendrical rectitude. Jubilees is not opposed to understanding the figure of Enoch as a wisdom hero from the chosen line, but Enoch's wisdom is not a paradigm that all subsequent recipients of revelation (ultimately all of Israel) must follow.[131]

As has long been recognized, Jubilees receives Jewish traditions that develop the figure of Enoch in the paradigm of the Eastern sage, making him the first of scribes whose wisdom includes astronomy and a body of learning well beyond literacy.[132] Again, Enoch's wisdom is not a general virtue attainable by all but a set of learned skills that define the "scribal" profession. Jubilees does not polemicize for or against the figure of Enoch or a certain kind of professional wisdom. The issue is more subtle: How does the perspective of the author shape the portrayal of Enoch? What is developed, and what is adapted or left behind? If we focus on the issue of revelation, three emphases stand out. First, the lessons Enoch learns about calendar are transmitted to all the children of Eve, not an elite school of professional sages or esoteric "chosen righteous." Second, Enoch's astronomical learning is carefully limited to calendrical rectitude. Observing the signs of heaven for any other purpose is strictly forbidden. Third,

---

131. There are, however, those who hold the figure of Enoch and the Enochic literature as foundational to the view of revelation in Jubilees. See Helge S. Kvanvig, "Jubilees—Between Enoch and Moses: A Narrative Reading," *JSJ* 35 (2004): 246–61. In recent works Boccaccini moderates the claim that Jubilees develops directly out of Enochic Judaism. See "From a Movement of Dissent," 193–210. Cf. idem, *Beyond the Essene Hypothesis*, 86–98.

132. VanderKam, *Enoch and the Growth*, 180–85; Kvanvig, *Roots of Apocalyptic*, 263–69. The fact that Enoch also offers incense points to the connection between Babylonian scribal curriculum and Jewish priestly curriculum, on which see Henryk Drawnel, "Priestly Education in the *Aramaic Levi Document* (*Visions of Levi*) and *Aramaic Astronomical Book* (4Q208–211)," *RevQ* 22 (2006): 547–74. More recently, idem, "Some Notes on Scribal Craft and the Origins of the Enochic Literature," *Henoch* 31 (2009): 66–77.

Jubilees embraces writtenness as a means of ensuring accuracy but leaves behind the associated activities of sages. Writing is a device for guaranteeing public record, not an elite or cryptic channel of secret wisdom. Though somewhat adapted, Enoch is still allowed to be Enoch, the originator of wisdom in the mode of Eastern sages, and he fits into Jubilees' account of revelation history. Enoch is a sage who receives revelation, but not all who receive revelation are sages. Wisdom and the figure of Enoch have their place in Jubilees, but they do not define the view of revelation. Other recipients of revelation are taught to write but are not otherwise associated with the term "wisdom" or the activities of the sages.

For example, Abraham is literate (Jub. 11:16; 12:27), intelligent (11:23–24), and a teacher (11:23; 21:1; 25:7) but not a sage. Abraham's realization of God's absolute sovereignty would have had the potential to take the form of "revealed wisdom." In fact, Jubilees crafts Abraham's intellect in such a way that avoids revealed and mantic wisdom and carefully limits the legitimacy of astronomical wisdom (Jub. 12:16–18).[133] Along with the insights Abraham makes on his own, the knowledge revealed to Abraham is more quotidian (for the audience) than esoteric. For example, with the help of an angelic teaching assistant, God teaches Abraham Hebrew (12:25–27). Whatever implications the Hebrew language may have had as the language of creation or as a national language,[134] for the Jewish audi-

---

133. Enoch may have known the proper use of observing the signs of the sky (fixing a calendar), but the Eastern sages err in attempting to fix the *character* of the year. Jubilees limits Enoch's licit astronomical observation to calendar (Jub. 4:17) and traces the illicit kind of astronomical observation to the watchers, by way of Kainan (Jub. 8:3; cf. 1 En. 8:3).

134. Karlheinz Müller discusses the significance of the revelation of the Hebrew language to Abraham in Jub. 12:25–27 in "Die Hebräische Sprache der Halacha als Textur der Schöpfung: Beobachtungen zum Verhältnis von Tora und Halacha im Buch der Jubiläen," in *Bibel in jüdischer und christlicher Tradition: Festschrift für Johann Maier zum 60. Geburtstag* (ed. Helmut Merklein, Karlheinz Müller, and Günter Stemberger; Athenäums Monografien. Theologie 88; Frankfurt am Main: Hain, 1993), 157–76. For Müller, since Hebrew is the language of creation, any attempt to understand the wisdom of creation, or the creator through the created, depends on understanding Hebrew. It might be noted that, however common the idea of divine wisdom embedded in creation may be in the second century B.C.E. (see especially Sir 1:8 but also 24:8), Jubilees does not quite make this concern explicit. If Jubilees does engage in this line of thought, the distinctive feature remains, as Müller indicates, that Jubilees claims the divine will is clearly articulated in the book of Jubilees ("in eine verständliche Mitteilung," 166). Müller also makes the point that Hebrew is the language of

ence of a book in Hebrew (likely in Jerusalem), this kind of revelation was neither mysterious nor, perhaps more importantly, elite.

Revelation in Jubilees is elite only in that it is limited to the chosen line; the receipt of revelation is not a special skill limited to a sagely elite. Jubilees avoids not only the language of "wisdom" but any trace of the elitism of the משכילים, "enlightened ones," over the רבים, "multitude," or the chosen righteous who consume wisdom like fruit. The issue can be illustrated with an example outside the apocalypses. Ben Sira denies that one can become wise if occupied with tending herds (Sir 38:25), but for Jubilees this kind of wisdom is of little use to the herdsmen Abraham, Isaac, and Jacob. In the next subsection we will consider some of the individual revelations received by the patriarchs for how they disambiguate allegory and vague meaning. To conclude this subsection we will consider the prime example of radically nonelite revelation: the Sinaitic revelation of law and testimony to all of Israel.

It is easy to think of Jubilees as revelation involving heavenly tablets, the angel of the presence, and Moses and to forget about the people of Israel at the base of the mountain. Jubilees does not vary from Exodus in the point that the revelation is for all of Israel. The point only stands out

---

halakah, which, as generally in Jubilees, is fixed from the beginning of creation. Thus the audience understood their halakah as unmediated by the ambiguities of idiom and translation, in line with the following point that Jubilees avoids any view of revelation as cryptic or ambiguous.

Müller's elaborate discussion of the re-revelation of Hebrew to Abraham does not include whether the language implicitly rejected is Greek or Aramaic. Certainly it would fit the view of the Gentiles in Jubilees to imply that the most particularly Jewish language, Hebrew, is the one true language and all Gentile languages are babbled, making the true order of creation and God's law inaccessible to Gentiles (cf. Jub. 15:31). Jubilees does make clear that the language of the books of Enoch and Noah was Hebrew (Jub. 12:27), so the most proximate alternative was Aramaic (1 Enoch was written in Aramaic; presumably the tablets Enoch reads are in Aramaic; Gen 31:47 suggests Abraham's extended family spoke Aramaic). If Jubilees is arguing that Hebrew, not Aramaic, is the language of law and creation (and divine wisdom, as Müller takes as implicit), this would put Jubilees into additional conflict with all early Enochic literature and part of Daniel. However, the fact that Daniel "switches" to Hebrew prohibits making too much of a possible Hebrew versus Aramaic tension at a time when both languages were well understood in Jerusalem. This issue does seem to warrant further investigation. For the present purposes, language is not a feature of the apocalyptic literary genre.

For reference to Hebrew as a national language, see 2 Macc 7:8, 21, 27; 12:37.

in comparison with the apocalypses. The revelation contained in Jubilees is not intended only for a later generation, is not limited to a chosen few, and is not sealed up or kept secret. It is instruction on how to keep the covenant that is binding on all of Israel. Jubilees both asserts that it is for all Israel and carries out the program of accessibility throughout the book.

From the first verse after the prologue, Jubilees introduces itself as revelation received by Moses "so that you may teach them" (Jub. 1:1). Jubilees provides frequent reminders of the ultimate recipients of the revelation, "Now you [Moses] command the Israelites…" (2:26, 29; 6:13, 20, 32; 15:28; 28:7; 30:11, 17, 21; 33:13, 18; 41:26; 49:15, 22). Other explicit statements include: "This law and testimony were given to the Israelites as an eternal law throughout their generations" (2:33; 3:14; 49:8).[135] Jubilees also provides for continuity of the teaching office: "He [Jacob] gave all his books and the books of his fathers to his son Levi so that he could preserve them and renew them for his sons until today" (45:16).[136] The concern for continuous written transmission also relates to the assertion of reliable, distortion-free transmission, which brings us to the next subsection. By itself, there is nothing shocking about the idea that revelation was given at Sinai to all of Israel with no distinction of an esoteric group, not hidden away for a distant time or requiring special wisdom skills. The discord comes as this thoroughly public, foolproof revelation is framed as an apocalypse.

4.2.3.2. Revelation Made Unambiguous and Accessible

Dramatically different from the apocalypses, and even compared to the base text of Genesis, Jubilees disambiguates revelation. Jubilees avoids allegorical symbolism and potentially ambiguous visions. Jubilees does not communicate in code, does not read Genesis as if a code, and downplays codes that do appear in Genesis. Jubilees introduces angelic teachers not as interpretive guides of fantastic visions but as tutors for language

---

135. Like Deut 29:21, Jub. 1:5 refers to a future generation who will suffer divine punishment before realizing their errors. From a historical-critical perspective, this may be the actual original audience (still like Deuteronomy), but Jubilees claims to have been instructed to all of Israel for all time.

136. See chapter 2 on the spatial axis for the lack of sectarian division of Israel. The distinction of the Levites is traditional and public, not comparable to the groups singled out in the Enochic and Danielic apocalypses.

and memory skills, guaranteeing the clarity and accuracy of the laws and testimony.

We begin with the observation of Armin Lange that Jubilees rejects the allegorical dreams typical of apocalyptic literature.[137] The issue is not whether God communicates in dreams but the allegorical nature of the dreams.[138] Lange follows Artemidorus in distinguishing allegorical dreams from theorematic dreams, which are understandable without interpretation. Jubilees adds only theorematic dreams, minimizes the allegorical aspect of the dreams of Joseph, and recasts Enoch's dream vision as theorematic.

Among the examples of dreams added, but conspicuously unlike the apocalypses in directness and objectivity, is Levi's dream:

> That night he stayed at Bethel. Levi dreamed that he—he and his sons—had been appointed and made into the priesthood of the most high God forever. When he awakened, he blessed the Lord. (Jub. 32:1)

Another unambiguous dream in addition to the base text is also found in Jub. 41:24, where Judah is told that he is forgiven. The heavenly tablets appear in dreams, but these are not symbols of anything other than tablets, and the message is never ambiguous (see Jub. 32:21).

Lange finds allegorical dreams in Jubilees only in the retelling of the Joseph story, and even then downplayed. Joseph's dreams of the sheaves and the stars are simply omitted (Gen 37:5-9). Jubilees mentions that Joseph correctly interpreted the dreams of the butler and baker but does not recount the dreams themselves (Jub. 39:16-17; Gen 40:8-23). The

---

137. Lange, "Divinatorische Träume," 25–38. Lange also deals with the Genesis Apocryphon and concludes, "Allegorical dreams were used at the time of the composition of Jubilees almost exclusively in works that are close to the apocalyptic movement or originate from it" (35: "allegorische Träume zur Abfassungszeit des Jubiläenbuches positiv fast ausschließlich in Werken verwendet wurden, die der apokalyptischen Bewegung nahestehen oder aus ihr stammen"). The present argument approaches exclusivity differently because of the distinction of literary genre, ideas, and religiosocial movement. If the cluster of ideas is typical and distinctive of the apocalypses, it is apocalyptic even when found outside the literary genre. The movement of origin is irrelevant for the present discussion. For a broader discussion, see Flannery-Dailey, *Dreamers, Scribes, and Priests*.

138. Jubilees seems to interchange dreams and visions. Compare Gen 15:1 (vision) and Jub. 14:1 (dream).

dreams of the pharaoh are also assumed as necessary to advance the story, but, not only are the contents omitted, any dramatic tension about the interpretation is spoiled from the first sentence: "At that time the pharaoh had two dreams in one night about the subject of the famine that would come on the whole land" (Jub. 40:1).[139] Jubilees is not trying to replace Genesis or polemicizing against the legitimacy of allegorical dreams in Genesis, but Jubilees does present its own revelation according to its "no nonsense" view of revelation. Whatever complex and ambiguous stories may have been received by Israel, the bottom line of covenantal fidelity, the law, and the testimony is completely unambiguous.

Similarly, Lange continues, Jub. 4:19 refers to a dream vision of Enoch (presumably the Animal Apocalypse or the entire Book of Dreams) with no mention of any symbolism. We might add that there is also some variation in the response of Enoch and the audience. The Animal Apocalypse concludes with Enoch disturbed and weeping (90:41–42), while Jub. 4:19 emphasizes the objective clarity: "He saw everything and understood." The Enochic apocalypses are not always clear on whether Enoch's revelation was made public or kept esoteric, but Jubilees emphasizes the public nature of Enoch's testimony, "He wrote a testimony for himself and placed it upon the earth against all mankind and for their history" (Jub. 4:19).[140]

Lange's study advances the present argument, even though his conclusion operates with slightly different categories. Lange concludes that Jubilees opposed the apocalyptic movement and cannot be called apocalyptic, but he does not separate literary genre, typical ideas, and social movement.[141] The view of revelation as cryptic is part of the typical ideas, not the morphology of the literary genre. The view of Jubilees on this issue is not the view typically found in apocalypses, but that does not necessarily indicate the literary genre used (or the social origin of the work).

In addition to the allegorical dreams considered by Lange, there are other examples of disambiguation in Jubilees. For example, Gen 49 was a hotbed of ambiguous meaning, particularly the prediction of the royal destiny of Judah.

---

139. Cana Werman studies the tendency in Jubilees to diminish dramatic tension in "היחס לגויים בספר היובלים ובספרות קומראן בהשוואה להלכה התנאית הקדומה ולספרות חיצונית בת התקופה" (Ph.D. dissertation, Hebrew University, 1995).

140. Literally, "against all the children of Eve and for their generations."

141. Lange, "Divinatorische Träume," 35.

לֹא־יָסוּר שֵׁבֶט מִיהוּדָה וּמְחֹקֵק מִבֵּין רַגְלָיו עַד כִּי־יָבֹא שִׁילֹה[142] וְלוֹ יִקְּהַת עַמִּים:

> The scepter shall not depart from Judah, nor the ruler's staff from between his feet, until tribute comes to him; and the obedience of the peoples is his. (Gen 49:10, NRSV)

Jubilees makes only a brief mention of the deathbed blessings of Jacob at that particular place in the story.

> Israel blessed his sons before he died. He told them what would happen to them in later days in the land of Egypt. He blessed them and blessed Joseph with double territory. (Jub. 45:14)[143]

It is not the case, however, that Jubilees gives no further account of Jacob's prediction. The first change is that Jubilees moves the revelation to explain how Jacob knew all this. Genesis 49 gives no indication of how or even that Jacob's oracle was divine revelation, but Jubilees attaches it to an elaborated revelation event at Bethel. The second change is that the revelation is not oracular in the sense of poetic ambiguity but becomes a matter-of-fact statement.

Interestingly, however, Jacob is not the first to receive revelation about the future role of Judah. Earlier, a spirit of prophecy had descended into Isaac's mouth:

> Then he said to Judah: "May the Lord give you the power and strength to trample on all who hate you. Be a prince—you and one of your sons—for Jacob's sons." (Jub. 31:18)

---

142. Qere: שִׁילוֹ.

143. Although it does not matter for the present purposes, this translation comes from the Latin, rather than VanderKam's preferred reading from the Ethiopic, as discussed in ch. 3 n. 85. The issue there is whether Jubilees reads בְּאַחֲרִית הַיָּמִים, "in later days," from Gen 49:1 to mean the future relative to Jacob but not the second century or future in a sense of unrealized eschatology. Even if one favors the Ethiopic text over the Latin, there is an additional, if not absolute, emphasis that Jacob foretells what will happen *in Egypt*. The word order in Ethiopic and Latin makes it unlikely, but not impossible, that "in Egypt" indicates where Jacob told them what would happen, not where it would happen. Ethiopic manuscripts 21, 35, and 63 (from the first, third, and fifth best families), like the Latin, lack a conjunction between "in the land of Egypt" and "in later days."

256   THE SUBVERSION OF THE APOCALYPSES IN JUBILEES

Jacob also received at Bethel a revelation that overlaps in content with Gen 49:10:

> He spoke to him a second time: "I am the Lord who created heaven and earth. I will increase your numbers and multiply you very much. Kings will come from you, and they will rule wherever they set foot against anyone." (Jub. 32:18)[144]

A more general connection is made between Gen 49 and Jub. 32.

> Jacob called his sons and said, "Gather around so I can tell you what will happen to you in later days." (Gen 49:1)

> In a night vision he saw an angel coming down from heaven with seven tablets in his hands. He gave (them) to Jacob, and he read them. He read everything that was written in them—what would happen to him and his sons throughout all ages. (Jub. 32:21)

Jubilees is not at all opposed to the idea that Jacob received revelation about the destiny of Judah. The striking shift, for the present purpose,[145] is that Gen 49 was an ambiguous oracle with no mention of how Jacob gained his knowledge, and Jubilees turns it into a matter-of-fact, perfectly clear revelation with all the authority of God, the heavenly tablets, the angel of the presence, and continuous written transmission. This same revelatory sequence brings us to an additional point: the transformation of angelic teaching from interpretive guide of the wonders of the cosmos to a tutor in language and memory skills.

There are subtle but noteworthy differences in the way angels teach in Jubilees compared to the typical apocalypses. In addition to what was said in chapter 2 about angelic agency, the point relevant to the view of revelation is that, in the apocalypses, angels typically provide explanations of otherwise ungraspable wonders, and even their interpretations often

---

    144. Again, this translation follows a reading defended elsewhere. The problem is not relevant to the present issue. See page 189 above.

    145. There are, of course, other interesting issues in these texts, including the formulation of the royal prophecy with respect to a single figure, not a dynasty, and the tendency (or complete replacement, depending on the manuscript) toward fulfilling the prediction in the past (relative to the second century) history of Israel rather than the eschatological future.

leave an enigma or two. The authority of their revelation is often taken for granted or conveyed indirectly as a general divine commission.

In Jubilees, the angels have less autonomy in that they transmit revelation from the heavenly tablets, not their own voices (Jub. 6:35).[146] When angels are not simply delivering or dictating tablets, they are tutoring the skills required to guarantee reliable written transmission. They may offer an occasional aside about what should be obvious from the heavenly tablets (e.g., the chosen place for the temple is Jerusalem, not Bethel; Jub. 32:22), but they do not provide independent interpretations of ungraspable mysteries. Thus, in the revelation to Jacob at Bethel just discussed, the angel facilitates the revelation by delivering the heavenly tablets and guaranteeing an accurate copy.

> Then Jacob said: "Lord, how shall I remember everything just as I have read and seen?" He said to him: "I will remind you of everything." When he had gone from him, he awakened and remembered everything that he had read and seen. He wrote down all the things that he had read and seen. (Jub. 32:25–26)

In the case of Abram, an angel is assigned the relatively mundane job of language tutoring (Jub. 12:25–27). The overall trend suggests an underlying view of revelation. Revelation is not an angelic interpretation of cosmic mysteries to a bewildered recipient, followed by an esoteric chain of transmission. Rather, revelation consists of clear and direct instructions through a passive angelic messenger to a well-trained and supervised copyist, passed down (or re-revealed) in a continuous line. The ultimate source of revelation is the heavenly tablets, and they were completely revealed to all Israel at Sinai. This revelation was foolproof and need only be preserved and studied, not amended.

The individual points considered in this chapter constitute various perspectives on the core issue of revelation. The accessibility of revelation relates to the public reception of revelation, which relates to the familiarity

---

146. "For I know and from now on will inform you—not from my own mind because this is the way the book is written in front of me." If one takes it as a contradiction that the angel seems to offer occasional asides, then it is an ancient contradiction. Jubilees, consistently or not, presents the revealing angel as a zero-interference transmitter.

of authority. Like Deut 30, Jubilees emphasizes that there are no excuses for covenantal infidelity. Everything that one needs to know can be easily known and, indeed, is already known from the received tradition. In a sense, Jubilees may inherently be a work of creativity and "decoding," or at least searching, of tradition. Nevertheless, Jubilees does obey its own rules. Revelation has a single source and so must be consistent with and derived from received revelation. The traditions of Israel attributed to Sinai are sufficient for all time, including both before Sinai and beyond the eschatological turning point to eternity. The revealed covenant is incumbent on, and hence accessible to, all of Israel. Jubilees testifies to the sufficiency of the tradition far more than it challenges it.

The view of revelation conveyed in Jubilees is not particularly surprising in the general context of Judaism in antiquity, nor is it surprising that one text would differ in ideas from other texts. The surprise is that one view of revelation is conveyed through a literary genre that typically conveys a contrary worldview. From the first chapter of Jubilees, and in frequent reminders throughout the text, Jubilees presents itself as a revelation of heavenly tablets through an angel to an exemplary ancient figure. Jubilees uses the genre as defined in *Semeia* 14 and exemplified by prior works such as the early Enochic apocalypses and Daniel. The use of the genre creates reader expectations. These expectations come from observation of prior examples, as well as the basic assumption that literature introduces elements because they are necessary and relevant. A reader expects an apocalypse to convey new, mysterious, and elite revelation partially because that is what other apocalypses convey and partially because such a claim lends itself to authorizing revelation that cannot be authorized by more mundane means. The use of a genre itself conveys meaning, and the decision to frame Jubilees as an apocalypse bears special significance. The genre raises issues and suggests a set of positions on those issues. Jubilees raises the issues but rejects the positions typically, almost inherently, conveyed by the genre. Indeed, consideration of authorial intent and related questions in the following chapter will support a conclusion that the author raises the issues *in order to* reject the typical ideas.

5
Explanation

The preceding chapters show that Jubilees conforms to the apocalyptic genre at the level of literary morphology but radically departs at the level of the ideas raised by the genre. Careful sifting of the data supports an observation of a clear pattern. This chapter attempts to explain the observation. What meaning does the pattern convey? The discussion thus far has not relied on reconstruction of authorial intent, audience response, or particulars of historical and cultural context. Such considerations operate at an inherently lesser level of certainty than the comparison of literary features. In order to explain the significance of the pattern it will be necessary to venture into more speculative territory. Well-established theory and carefully examined assumptions will provide guidance on the journey.

The pattern of adoption of literary morphology and subversion of ideas is qualitatively significant. Jubilees is not a sporadic mixture of apocalyptic and anti-apocalyptic elements or a midpoint on a spectrum from apocalyptic to nonapocalyptic literature. The use of the literary morphology establishes a dialogical relationship with apocalypses, or rather an imaginary dialogue that becomes a one-sided argument. The similarities suffice to evoke comparison but are superficial and give way to a contrary sustained meaning. The discord enhances the contrast and dramatizes the "realization" of the actual message for the intended audience. The subversion is meaningful in literary structure and cultural context.

From the outset, it is important to consider the alternative, that Jubilees is different only in the usual ways that make every text unique. It is true that synchronic variation and diachronic development occur regularly without constituting subversion. What distinguishes Jubilees is not merely the quantitative measure of similarities and differences but the pattern in the layers of abstraction. The separation of layers of abstraction is not unique by itself. It has long been observed that the sectarian literature from Qumran and the Pauline corpus reflect the ideas typical of apocalypses but do not use the literary morphology.[1] This pattern does not constitute a subversion of the literary morphology. The logic does not work in both directions. One pattern of similarity and difference does not simply have the opposite meaning as its converse.

Even within a common literary morphology, a certain amount of synchronic variation and innovation is expected. One might even imagine that the author sampled indiscriminately from the literary elements current in Judaism and produced a hybrid that is odd but random, or if not completely random, based on no more meaningful a method than comprehensiveness. Thus, perhaps the author includes, at the expense of context, everything deemed relevant to retelling Genesis–Exodus, which happens to include literary elements related to revelation, angelic agency, explanations of suffering, and protology/eschatology. "Overkill" and unusual combinations do not constitute subversion.

Diachronic development could also explain a degree of difference without subversion. Genres regularly change and develop; some scholars even believe genres develop in regular cycles of "life and death."[2] Even if later apocalypses rejected most of the "innovations" in Jubilees, that could be an accident of history. Certain differences might be explicable if one text was written in the middle of a civil war and another with a few years of retrospect. Historical context might suggest a purpose of harmonizing or diplomatically combining previously divisive elements in the interest of a new (perhaps forced and artificial) unity. Indeed, such a purpose would be consistent with other indicators in Jubilees.

The above explanations of synchronic variation or diachronic development might suffice if there were not a clear pattern of similarities and differences or if the pattern were other than what it is. The previous chapters show that Jubilees is not a mixture of continuities and discontinui-

---

1. Collins, "Apocalypticism and Literary Genre," 428; Stegemann, "Die Bedeutung der Qumranfunde," 496.

2. Alastair Fowler, "The Life and Death of Literary Forms," *New Literary History* 2 (1971): 199–216. See also, idem, *Kinds of Literature*, 42–43. Hans Robert Jauss, discussed below, is also concerned with changes in the reader's horizons of expectations based on new works that expand or shift the horizons. Certainly if Jubilees were written later than 4 Ezra, for example, the discussion would be different. However, the most proximate antecedents of Jubilees, the Apocalypse of Weeks and the Animal Apocalypse, mark the sharpest contrast.

ties and various levels or random similarities and differences. Jubilees includes more than the minimum requisite elements of literary morphology, including structural framework, but radically inverts all the ideas implied. The changes in ideas are not incremental reforms or developments. The superficial mention of demons in Jubilees would not have diplomatically appeased one who thought that demons explain the suffering of the righteous if everything said about demons, and all apocalyptic issues, runs in the other direction. Historical circumstance may illuminate why the author held certain positions, but it does not explain why the author used a literary genre that implies radically opposite positions.

The genre is not an indiscriminate list of literary and conceptual features measured by counting instances of conformity and divergence. Non-prototypical apocalypses such as Jubilees cannot be described adequately in terms of a single spectrum of more-like or less-like the prototype. The layers of abstraction have a meaningful relationship, and the manipulation of that relationship is meaningful. The literary morphology raises issues. Jubilees is not diplomatic on those issues but clear in expressing different ideas. Even in the interest of unity, the author would not want to suggest that the author's ideas are compatible with the opposite ideas. The author does not use the literary morphology to create an illusion of compatibility but to illustrate the author's own points by accentuating the contrast. The effect can also be seen from the perspective of the audience, which forms expectations based on superficial indicators of the apocalyptic genre. Discord follows when the sustained ideas subvert those expectations. Dramatic internalized "realization" results from the resolution of the discord. The following two sections will explore the processes of the author and audience, respectively. The third section will turn to the date of Jubilees and the historical context, particularly the Maccabean revolt. A fourth section will examine the cultural significance of the symbols and issues on which Jubilees clashes with the apocalypses. Although the debate is not comparable to the rift over Hellenistic assimilation, the conflict touches on important and enduring issues. We should not attribute Jubilees to the same intellectual circle, social circle, or form of Judaism as texts that maintain typical apocalyptic ideas.

5.1. Literary Insights into the Author's Process

The communication of meaning involves use and adaptation of borrowed elements at all levels.³ The difficulty is becoming aware of and naming the many unconscious processes involved. Mikhail Bakhtin contributed some key concepts that will aid analysis of the relationship between Jubilees and prior apocalypses. Bakhtin studies the fluid space of "metalinguistics" between the more rigid structures of linguistics and genre formalism. Bakhtin does not deny the existence of rigid, stable categories but explores the variety of complex relationships. This section will use Bakhtin's study of three varieties of ways in which participation in a genre implies dialogical relationships with previous examples of a genre.⁴ Bakhtin allows us to talk about the author's conscious or subconscious choices and intent in engaging the apocalypses, without falling into simplistic explanations. It would be too simplistic to say the purpose of Jubilees (or the author's intent) is to attack the apocalypses. It would be too simplistic to call Jubilees a parody of the apocalypses. Subversion is more subtle.

First, it is not necessary to imagine that the author set out to write an apocalypse or to subvert an apocalypse. The purpose of addressing a set of issues naturally leads to the "dialogic overtones"⁵ of the genre, in our case apocalyptic literary morphology. Once the author chose to address

---

3. Systems of shared conventions are required for all communication of meaning, although these conventions can be subverted or expanded (see the following section). Several layers of systems of shared conventions, or codes, have been described along a hierarchy of layers of abstraction. For example, Fokkema describes the linguistic code, the literary code, the generic code, the sociocode, and the author's idiolect. Of particular interest for the next section, the generic code "instructs the reader to activate certain expectations and to suppress others, depending on the genre" (Bert Cozijnsen, "A Critical Contribution to the *Corpus Hellenisticum Novi Testamenti*: Jude and Hesiod," in *The Use of Sacred Books in the Ancient World* (ed. L. V. Rutgers et al.; CBET 22; Leuven: Peeters, 1998), 90. See also Douwe Wessel Fokkema, *Literary History, Modernism, and Postmodernism* (Utrecht Publications in General and Comparative Literature 19; Amsterdam: Benjamins, 1984), 8–12.

4. A recent collection of essays illustrates many ways in which Bakhtin's ideas can contribute to biblical studies: Roland Boer, ed., *Bakhtin and Genre Theory in Biblical Studies* (SemeiaSt 63; Atlanta: Society of Biblical Literature, 2007). For dialogical relationships, see especially Carleen Mandolfo, "Dialogic Form Criticism: An Intertextual Reading of Lamentations and Psalms of Lament," in Boer, *Bakhtin and Genre Theory*, 69–90. The volume also includes a reprint of Newsom, "Spying out the Land," 437–50. See also idem, "Bakhtin," in *Handbook of Postmodern Biblical Interpretation* (ed. A. K. M. Adam; St. Louis: Chalice, 2000), 20–27; idem, *The Book of Job: A Contest of Moral Imaginations* (Oxford: Oxford University Press, 2003), 11–31.

5. Mikhail M. Bakhtin, *Speech Genres and Other Late Essays* (ed. Caryl Emerson

contemporary issues of revelation, transcendent agents on the spatial axis, and the structure of history, it was natural for the literary genre to come into play to at least some extent. That does not diminish the significance of Jubilees' dialogical relationship with the apocalypses. Every utterance is a response to preceding utterances in a given sphere. "Very frequently the expression of our utterance is determined not only—and sometimes not so much—by the referentially semantic content of this utterance; but also by others' utterances on the same topic to which we are responding or with which we are polemicizing."[6] Jubilees can be thought of as a dialogue with prior apocalypses on certain issues. Their utterances are acknowledged through the use of the literary genre. The external comparison with the apocalypses becomes internalized within Jubilees in the dialogue between borrowed and rejected layers of the genre. In that sense, at least, Jubilees is what Bakhtin calls "double-voiced."[7]

Once we think of Jubilees' use of the apocalyptic genre as dialogue with prior apocalypses, the question becomes how we characterize the dialogue. Bakhtin describes three nonexhaustive varieties: stylization of the other's word to a common purpose, parody of the other's word to a cross-purpose, and hidden polemic. All three are worth considering for how they might apply to Jubilees, but the third variety is the most useful for characterizing the relationship of Jubilees to the apocalypses in general.

Stylization to a common purpose requires a basic agreement between the two voices. Though not necessarily imitated, the ideas and authority of the former voice are summoned by the second voice to further the same interest. "Having penetrated into another person's word and having made itself at home in it, the author's idea does not collide with the other person's idea, but rather follows the direction of that idea."[8] The present work

---

and Michael Holquist, trans. Vern W. McGee; University of Texas Press Slavic Series 8; Austin: University of Texas Press, 1986), 92.

6. Ibid., 91.

7. Bakhtin is also concerned with other senses that do not apply to Jubilees. The author of Jubilees does not truly allow the different voices to speak for themselves, as Bakhtin believes Dostoevsky does. The dialogue in Jubilees is more of a one-sided confrontation that simulates dialogue in the aim of monological claims; see Bakhtin, *Problems of Dostoevsky's Poetics* (trans. William Rotsel; Ann Arbor, Mich.: Ardis, 1973), 150–69; idem, *Problems of Dostoevsky's Poetics* (trans. Caryl Emerson; Theory and History of Literature 8; Minneapolis: University of Minnesota Press, 1984), 181–204.

8. Bakhtin, *Problems of Dostoevsky's Poetics*, 1973, 160; 1984, 193.

should eliminate this possibility as a comprehensive solution. Jubilees is generally at cross-purposes with the apocalypses at the level of ideas. However, it would be difficult to rule out the possibility that specific instances in Jubilees can be understood in this way, that is, instances in which Jubilees uses an apocalyptic technique without subverting the direct implication. For example, even if Jubilees *generally* relies on publicly received authority and seriously qualifies the legitimacy of new esoteric revelation, it remains possible that the author adapted the apocalyptic authorization technique without completely rejecting it. Thus the author might share a small instance of similar purpose—to add authority—among many disagreements in what is authorized. It may not necessarily be the case that the author opposes everything apocalyptic for the sake of opposing everything apocalyptic.

The second variety, parody, occupies the opposite extreme. Parody not only opposes the direction of the other's words; it opposes the other's words directly. Interestingly, Bakhtin's discussion of parody does not include elements of humor or any reference to his previous discussion of laughter, carnival, and Menippean satire. The second and third varieties differ from the first variety in that they oppose the other's words. Two issues distinguish the second variety from the third: direct use and direct opposition. The question of direct use is more ambiguous. On the one hand, Jubilees does not quote at length or sustain reference to any one apocalypse. On the other hand, Bakhtin's sense of "word" is not as narrow as verbatim quotation.[9] The use of the other's literary morphology could constitute direct use sufficient to meet Bakhtin's criterion: "the deliberate perceptibility of the other person's word in the parody must be particularly sharp and distinct."[10] The apocalyptic framework may not suffice to make this generally the case with Jubilees, but smaller instances might still be considered. For example, recontextualized phrases and images such as "righteous plant," "great day of judgment," and the white children might still qualify as Bakhtinian parody even if parody does not serve as a comprehensive explanation. Direct use may be difficult to assess. The more important distinction between the second and third varieties concerns the object of speech.

---

9. Emerson translates "discourse" where Rotsel translates "word" (ibid., 1973, 150, 167; 1984, 181, 202).

10. Ibid., 1973, 160; 1984, 193.

The third variety, hidden polemic, is like the second variety in that the second voice runs counter to the first voice. It differs from the second variety in that the second voice need not make direct use of the first voice. The clearer difference, for our purposes, is that in parody the object of the second voice is the first voice. The second is basically attacking the first directly. In hidden polemic, the second voice is addressing a separate object, with awareness of the difference in what the first voice has already said about the object. The first voice can be attacked with "swipes" and "jabs,"[11] but indirectly or secondarily while the primary object of speech is something else. Thus, for Jubilees we can say the objects of speech include things such as esoteric revelation, demons, angelic agents, and the timing of judgment and restoration. The author conveys certain ideas about these objects, but does so in a way that reflects awareness that the apocalypses say different things about the same objects. Thus Bakhtin's description of the third variety of double-voiced speech describes Jubilees remarkably well:

> In the hidden polemic the author's word is directed toward its object, as in any other word, but in addition, every statement about the object is so constructed that, besides expressing its object oriented meaning, it strikes a blow at the other person's word about the same topic and at the other person's statement about the same object.[12]

In Bakhtin's terms, the subversion of the apocalypses is a secondary meaning, but secondary does not imply unimportant.

> Alongside its object-oriented meaning there appears a second meaning—the directedness toward the other person's word. It is impossible to fully and fundamentally understand such a word if only its direct, object-oriented significance is taken into consideration.[13]

It is not enough to say Jubilees differs from the typical apocalyptic ideas. Jubilees expresses its ideas through the apocalyptic literary genre to strike an additional blow at the typical apocalyptic ideas.

---

11. Ibid., 1973, 162–63; 1984, 196.
12. Ibid., 1973, 162; 1984, 195.
13. Ibid., 1973, 162; 1984, 196.

Bakhtin's approach to authorial process presents an appropriately nuanced explanation of Jubilees. Jubilees departs from the genre beyond the usual "stylization" of a genre but does not parody or attack the apocalypses directly (at least for the most part).[14] Jubilees has many purposes, among which is the subversion of the ideas associated with the apocalypses. The conflict in ideas is primary and leads to the subversive use of the literary genre. The literary morphology casts a knowing glance at the apocalypses and sets up a dialogue, or at least a comparison between a caricatured position and a developed set of ideas. In order to appreciate more fully how the superficial use of the literary genre "strikes a blow at the other person's word," it will be helpful to shift focus from the author's process in communicating meaning to the audience's process in determining meaning.

5.2. Literary Insights into the Audience's Process

Literary theorist Hans Robert Jauss developed the analysis of the reader's "horizons of expectations" as part of his proposal of literary history based on an aesthetics of reception.[15] His concerns were fundamentally diachronic, but he tied his diachronic analysis to a series of synchronic analyses, starting with the original audience. The original audience encountered

---

14. This category should be useful in describing other instances of subversion that otherwise might be mistaken for direct polemic. Recently, with reference to the Epistle of Enoch, Loren Stuckenbruck ("The Epistle of Enoch," 411–13) described a variety of manners of engagement that help move past the simplistic extremes of adoption or polemic. Of course, simple dependence and rejection still exist, as in the case of the Epistle's rejection of Qoheleth. Stuckenbruck does not place the treatment of Deuteronomy in the same category. The Epistle does not reject Deuteronomy but an interpretation of it. The Epistle accepts Deuteronomy, with the crucial (and typically apocalyptic) distinction that it will apply to the future, not the present. The same reshaping applied to Deuteronomy also applies to the Book of the Watchers in the often discussed verse about human responsibility for sin (1 En. 98:4). Stuckenbruck calls this "shift in emphasis," not direct polemic. Such attention to subtle degrees of qualified acceptance and partial rejection is necessary also to describe the relationship between Dan 9 and Deuteronomy or Jubilees and Third Isaiah or the Book of the Watchers.

15. Hans Robert Jauss, *Toward an Aesthetic of Reception* (Theory and History of Literature 2; Minneapolis: University of Minnesota Press, 1982). Jauss's theory is put to use for the analysis of parallels in ancient literature (beyond the basic categories of influence or analogy) by Cozijnsen, "Jude and Hesiod," 79–109. Jauss is also invoked by Robert A. Kugler, "Hearing 4Q225: A Case Study in Reconstructing the Religious Imagination of the Qumran Community," *DSD* 10 (2003): 81–103.

a new work with expectations based on conventional similarities with familiar works, particularly genre.[16] A work could satisfy those expectations or challenge them.[17] Jauss did not discuss ancient literature, but Jubilees could fit in his description of the poetic effect Cervantes achieves by evoking and then challenging the horizon of expectations of knight tales in *Don Quixote*.[18] Jauss is especially helpful to scholars of early Jewish literature in describing the restoration of the horizon of expectations of the original readers, which naturally changes for later readers, partially because of the influence of the work itself.[19] Especially when the identity, intent, and influences of the author are not known, the treatment of the "horizon of expectations" can be established through comparison with works known to the intended audience.[20]

The audience's experience of literature begins with morphology. Generic morphology cues reader expectations of generic meaning. Reader expectations can be built on association with other known examples of a genre. There is also an inner logic that connects morphology and ideas. For example, one might automatically assume that angelic agents are introduced because they are relevant or that a revelation of heavenly sources will reveal information not already known on earth. There is a typical but not absolute relationship between literary morphology and ideas. The preliminary meaning based on reader expectations is subject

---

16. Jauss, *Toward an Aesthetic of Reception*, 23.

17. "A literary work, even when it appears to be new, does not present itself as something absolutely new in an informational vacuum, but predisposes its audience to a very specific kind of reception by announcements, overt and covert signals, familiar characteristics, or implicit allusions. It awakens memories of that which was already read, brings the reader to a specific emotional attitude, and with its beginning arouses expectations for the 'middle and end,' which can then be maintained intact or altered, reoriented, or even fulfilled ironically in the course of the reading according to specific rules of the genre or type of text" (ibid.).

18. Ibid., 24.

19. Ibid., 25. Although the present work is not concerned with reception history following the original author and audience, the reception history of Jubilees is particularly interesting. Jubilees was accepted as authoritative among the sectarians known from Qumran, who, on one hand, integrated Jubilees with apocalyptic ideas and, on the other hand, produced no apocalypses and seem to have lost interest in the books of Enoch. Perhaps partially through the influence of Jubilees, the horizon of expectations for the apocalypses changed, and centuries later 4 Ezra and 2 Baruch would use the genre in ways unlike the pre-Jubilees apocalypses.

20. Ibid., 28.

to constant revision. The revised meaning can differ from the preliminary in several ways. At the most basic level, a superficial meaning may derive from a term such as "great day of judgment," and a revision could come from the attached verb being in the past tense. The next more cerebral level would be if a phrase such as "righteous plant" appears in context such that the elite group is all of Israel rather than a group within Israel. The revision can occur on broader levels of plot, such as ominous literary elements (e.g., demons and Mastema) proving ultimately ineffective and harmless. In some cases, conspicuous omission, once noticed, can prompt a revision of preliminary meaning, such as the absence of cosmic agents and fixed dates from the eschatological sequence. At any rate, the audience recognizes apocalyptic literary morphology, which cues associations and expectations of apocalyptic ideas and meaning. The sustained meaning discords with the preliminary meaning.

The intended audience resolves the discord by recognizing the sustained, less superficial meaning as the "real" meaning. The audience engages in an artificial process of discovery. The audience's resolution of the discord dramatizes the "joy of discovery" and internalizes the "real" meaning. The incongruity between literary morphology and sustained ideas not only sets up a direct contrast between ideas; it shifts the evaluation of the competing ideas from the author's claims to the audience's discernment. Potentially, the discovery of an idea as being more sustainable in the text creates the illusion that the idea is more sustainable in reality. The subversion of reader expectations, through subversion of the literary genre, communicates meaning far more dramatically than a more direct argument.

By many definitions, the term "irony" would well describe such a manipulation of generic expectations, an incongruity of meaning, a discord that is not merely ambiguous but resolvable by higher analysis, a pair of normative and ignorant audiences (real or imagined). Carolyn Sharp's recent book, *Irony and Meaning in the Hebrew Bible*, argues that no one method suffices to identify all irony; she gives as the first example of many possibilities the following:

> Genre analysis is often needed, particularly to understand ways in which the medium of communication may be being subverted by content inappropriate to that medium, based on expectations about what the genre is normally intended to signal.[21]

---

21. Carolyn J. Sharp, *Irony and Meaning in the Hebrew Bible* (Bloomington: Indi-

Thus far Jubilees fits well. Sharp goes on to discuss several approaches based primarily on incongruities, discords, misdirection, and audience pairs.[22] Such features are important, Sharp explains, but not all discord and misdirection constitutes irony. On a case-by-case basis, we might argue that Jubilees is not ordinary discord because the discord is resolved by a higher order of reasoning, or the misdirection differs from plot twists because the conflicting directions come from different layers of abstraction, or the incongruity functions more like a riddle than an open ambiguity. It is much more difficult to offer a comprehensive definition of irony. Sharp maintains that irony resists definition, but her working definition qualifies the "misdirection" with a contrast between "said" and "unsaid":

> Irony is a performance of misdirection that generates aporetic interactions between an unreliable "said" and a truer "unsaid" so as to persuade us of something that is subtler, more complex, or more profound than the apparent meaning. Irony disrupts cultural assumptions about the narrative coherence that seems to ground tropological and epistemological transactions, inviting us to an experience of alterity that moves us toward a new insight by problematizing false understandings.

One might wonder if the truer meaning need always be more subtle, complex, or profound. The more important qualifier, which may exclude Jubilees, is the contrast between "said" and "unsaid." In Jubilees, one might say that the literary morphology misdirects and suggests an unreliable meaning that could be called "said." In *some* cases the truer meaning is not quite said, such as "esoteric or coded revelation is not legitimate or necessary." In some cases the truer meaning is, eventually, said outright, as in "there is no injustice" (Jub. 5:13) or "God made no angel to rule over Israel" (15:32). One could argue that the unreliable "said" in Jubilees is the superficial appearance from generic cues, and the "unsaid" is said in more subtle ways or at a higher level of reasoning. One would soon question the payoff of making such arguments.

We need not conclude that Jubilees does or does not constitute irony, only that the term does not appear to be helpful in describing Jubilees. If all subversion of literary genre is irony, then Jubilees is irony, but the general

---

ana University Press, 2009), 28. Similarly, she notes that irony "usually plays on culturally conditioned differences between audience expectations and results" (27).

22. Ibid., 10–35.

term does not help us more than the precise term. Scholarly approaches to irony differ, and some definitions might exclude Jubilees as misdirection but not irony. Furthermore, popular associations with irony, such as "sarcastic," "satirical," and "unfortunate," introduce more confusion. For the present purposes, "subversion of literary genre" will be more helpful than "irony."

Another set of descriptors merit discussion, even if the present scope disallows an adequate foundation of methodology, evidence, and argumentation to make a firm conclusion. Humor is difficult to explain within one culture, much more so across cultural space and time. However, terms such as "ridicule," "satire," or "parody" (in the usual sense, not Bakhtin's) would require some consideration of humor in Jubilees. The above discussion of Bakhtin's sense of parody introduces the scope of possibilities.[23] One would not want to say that humor is the primary, direct, or pervasive interest of Jubilees. We can look for moments of humor in Jubilees' sideways attacks, but not on such a scale that would negate the serious claims.[24] With such qualifications in mind, we can consider two categories of humor that may be operative in Jubilees and point to a third category that depends on the discussion of cultural symbols below.

Demotion is making light of something in the specific sense. Demotion takes something that is serious or threatening and turns it or its function into something frivolous and harmless. For example, in the latter chapters of Jubilees, Mastema becomes more a bungling stooge than an enemy of God and leader of cosmic evil.[25] Mastema is bound at will and

---

23. See also Erich S. Gruen (*Diaspora: Jews amidst Greeks and Romans* [Cambridge: Harvard University Press, 2002], 135–201), who discussed humor in the diaspora. Gruen presents a positive side of Jewish life in foreign lands, not just laughing through the tears. Gruen emphasizes the difficulty of definition but illustrates the variety of humor with numerous examples, including 2 Maccabees, in which Gruen finds subversion of seriousness even though the primary purpose is not comedy.

24. Gruen emphasizes this point: "The comic vein by no means undermines the serious intent. … Comedy is rarely more effective than when it is serious" (ibid., 137).

25. Gruen's discussion of the demotion of Satan in the Testament of Job demonstrates some analogies with Jubilees in which Mastema is even less effective. Gruen compares the Testament of Job to a comic drama and points out that "Satan emerges as a deft master of disguises that avail him nothing." Further analogies appear when Gruen asserts, "the author is evidently playing with the [testament] genre" and mocks apocalyptic speculation on the functions of the cosmos by those who do not understand their own bodily functions (ibid., 193–201, 211).

unbound only long enough to create more trouble for the Egyptians ostensibly being helped. In the eschatological sequence, the apocalyptic "final woes" are partially demoted to woes that are not very final or woeful: "stomach pains, snow, hail, frost, fever, cold, and numbness" (Jub. 23:13). Another demotion occurs relative to the Joseph story in Genesis, which the audience presumably knew well. In Gen 44, Joseph has a divination cup. The serious point in Jubilees is that the patriarchs did not practice divination of any sort. In many instances Jubilees simply avoids paraphrasing or very loosely paraphrases the relevant passages in Genesis. Jubilees 43:10, however, addresses the parallel directly but demotes the significance of the cup: "the cup with which I drink" (Jub. 42:25). Joseph then becomes excessively emotional about his silverware: "Do you not know that a man takes pleasure in his cup, as I do in this cup?" (43:10). This sentence parallels Gen 44:15: "Do you not know that a man such as I practices divination?" It would be different if Jubilees avoided the issue or shifted the emphasis to the value of silver. Keeping the same dramatic response while radically demoting the significance of the object sounds funny. The purpose may be to accentuate the point (patriarchs did not practice divination) by summoning comparison with Genesis, rather than to entertain, but the process involves demotion nonetheless. Whether the author intended these demotions to be humorous, even secondarily, is not readily knowable.

Another type of humor is hyperbole. Not all "overkill" is humorous, and Jubilees certainly had a serious concern to justify the authority of the Levites. Within that serious purpose, however, the account of Levi's election is hyperbolic in quantity and subversive in resolution. No less than six independent sources justify the election of Levi: (1) merit for killing exogamists (Jub. 30:18–20; parallels Phinehas); (2) Isaac's prophecy (31:14–15); (3) Jacob's vision of the heavenly tablets (31:32); (4) the testimony of the angel of the presence (31:32); (5) Levi's dream (32:1); and (6) reapplication of the law of tithes (32:2–3). Even if the quantity of justification would not have seemed excessive, the logical structure is striking. Reasons 2–5 involve some form of revelation, but after all this Jacob still does not put the priestly clothes on Levi and ordain him. As if all the above were inadequate, Jacob seems to be finally convinced by legal interpretation, namely, the law of tithes. Jubilees is certainly serious in its concern for Levitical authority, legal interpretation, and testing claims of revelation. A serious point may nevertheless be illustrated with humorous hyperbole. Similarly, Jubilees can be quite serious on the point that all necessary revelation became public to all Israel long ago and was preserved by the Levites.

Throughout Jubilees a tension builds around the unfulfilled expectation that hidden things would be revealed. With only a partial exception in Jub. 23, Jubilees reveals the past.[26] This tension builds to a climax, perhaps ridiculously so, when the angel reveals to Moses his own embarrassing past: "Then you were afraid and ran away because of this matter" (47:12).

Evaluating humor purely within the realm of texts may be impossibly subjective. Demotion and hyperbole are far more likely to be humorous when they make light of or exaggerate icons of groups, issues, and tensions. This will bring us to the following sections on historical and cultural context. Some examples to be discussed below warrant mention here because they may constitute moments of humor. For example the "white children" in Jub. 23 seem to demote the white children glorified in the Animal Apocalypse and perhaps in other sources such as Daniel and the Birth of Noah. If Enoch and Noah were sources of tension as cultural symbols, it may be humorous that their books are identified with the legal material associated with Moses or that Enoch's final destination seems to be demoted from heaven to Eden. Certainly the temple and priesthood were hot topics. Jubilees' description of the Levitical cult renewing the cosmos displaces some examples of apocalyptic eschatology that link cosmic renewal to replacement of the temple and priesthood.

These examples may suggest some possibilities to be considered by the reader or future studies. The present discussion does not warrant conclusions about humor in Jubilees. Subversion of literary genre does not necessarily entail humor. Bold claims in terms of parody, ridicule, satire, or humor face formidable methodological obstacles.

5.3. Historical Context

A number of factors indicate that Jubilees was composed in the middle of the second century B.C.E. Correlation with events described in 1 Maccabees and other sources supports a date in the 150s, likely shortly after 159 B.C.E. Not only does Jubilees reflect awareness of the Maccabean revolt up through the death of Alcimus and retreat of Bacchides; it reflects a negative evaluation of the revolt itself. Jubilees views *all* the militant groups involved as hypocritical and fratricidal. It stands to reason that apocalyptic

---

26. Historical apocalypses sometimes reveal the past to authorize the claim about the future, which dominates. Jub. 23 makes a small prediction relative to the time of Moses, but most of that is past relative to the audience.

ideas and texts, particularly the Animal Apocalypse and Danielic apocalypses, were associated with violent resistance in the 160s B.C.E.[27] Jubilees' negative evaluation of the revolt illuminates the historical context of Jubilees' subversion of the apocalypses. The next section will turn to a number of additional issues and reforms that dominated the cultural context of the revolt besides the violence itself.

The book of Jubilees as we know it can be treated as a coherent composition. Most of the book is known only from an Ethiopic translation of a Greek translation of a Hebrew original.[28] The fourteen copies of the book partially preserved at Qumran generally support the reliability of the Ethiopic manuscripts.[29] Translation and scribal error introduce some corruption, but there is no evidence of a systematic theological or other tendency in the process of translation and transmission. There are no Christian interpolations. Various units of a few verses have been suspected as possible interpolations by Qumran sectarians or others, but no manuscript evidence or scholarly consensus has supported any such suggestion.[30] In the other direction, Jubilees certainly draws from many written and oral (legal and narrative) traditions besides the Pentateuch, but it reproduces none of them.[31] Among ancient texts, Jubilees is a remarkably well-preserved example of a coherent composition by a single author at a single time.

---

27. For detailed analysis of the forms of resistance, see Portier-Young, *Apocalypse against Empire*.

28. VanderKam's 1989 critical edition and DJD 13 provide adequate textual information. Only a few traces of additional textual evidence have been suggested subsequently. See Hanneken, "The Book of Jubilees among the Apocalypses," 112–20. VanderKam; *The Book of Jubilees*; James C. VanderKam and Jozef T. Milik, "Jubilees," in *Qumran Cave 4: Parabiblical Texts Part 1* (ed. Harold W. Attridge et al., DJD 13; Oxford: Clarendon, 1994), 1–185.

29. VanderKam and Milik, "Jubilees," 4.

30. Most recently, Kugel identified twenty-nine interpolations based on rhetorical seams or tensions. For more on Kugel, Berner, Ravid, and others who postulated multiple authorship to explain tensions in the work, see ch. 1 nn. 19 and 21. Note that Kugel concedes that the author and interpolator were substantially like-minded. The present study finds distinctive patterns throughout the book of Jubilees, which would be consistent with unity of authorship but could also apply to the final form of the book, however one imagines it came about.

31. Segal (*The Book of Jubilees*, 35) argues for calling the person responsible for producing the book the redactor rather than the author, mainly because of the dependence on earlier ideas. However, received ideas are so thoroughly reworked that the

The case for dating the composition of Jubilees depends on evidence from Qumran, the compositions that depend on Jubilees and on which it depends, and its knowledge of events through 159 B.C.E. but apparently not 152 or later.[32] The case for a date no earlier than 159 depends on correlation of events described in 1 Maccabees with the description of the wars of Jacob and more so the "predictions" in Jub. 23 (discussed below). Also, Jub. 4:19 apparently refers to the Animal Apocalypse (a dream of Enoch that encompasses human history), dated to 165–160 B.C.E.[33] The firm limit for the latest date of composition is established by the Qumran evidence. The oldest copy of Jubilees has been dated from paleography to the last quarter of the second century B.C.E., although Milik suggests a date closer to the middle of the century.[34] Jubilees is also interpreted as an authority in the Damascus Document, which is usually dated to around 100 B.C.E.[35] Since Jubilees is not itself a sectarian composition, it stands

---

final product is distinctive and "original" by ancient standards. See further ch. 1 nn. 20 and 21.

32. I offer a more detailed discussion and a review of the history of scholarship in Hanneken, "The Book of Jubilees among the Apocalypses," 141–80.

33. VanderKam, *Enoch, a Man for All Generations*, 114, 119; Nickelsburg, *1 Enoch: A Commentary*, 72; Michael A. Knibb, "Which Parts of 1 Enoch Were Known to Jubilees? A Note on the Interpretation of *Jubilees* 4.16–25," in *Reading from Right to Left: Essays on the Hebrew Bible in Honour of David J. A. Clines* (ed. J. Cheryl Exum and H. G. M. Williamson; JSOTSup 373; London: Sheffield Academic Press, 2003), 260. For the date of the Animal Apocalypse, see Milik and Black, *The Books of Enoch*, 44; Tiller, *Commentary on the Animal Apocalypse*, 61–79; Nickelsburg, *1 Enoch: A Commentary*, 360–61. Note the difficulty regarding the unity of the composition of the Animal Apocalypse. If it is not unified, Jubilees does not necessarily know the final form. For an argument that Jubilees knows the tradition but not the text itself, see van Ruiten, "A Literary Dependency of Jubilees on 1 Enoch," 90–93.

34. 4Q216, VanderKam and Milik, "Jubilees," 2.

35. Devorah Dimant, however, has challenged the consensus that the Damascus Document cites Jubilees in "Two 'Scientific' Fictions: The So-Called Book of Noah and the Alleged Quotation of Jubilees in CD 16:3–4," in *Studies in the Hebrew Bible, Qumran, and the Septuagint: Essays Presented to Eugene Ulrich on the Occasion of His Sixty-Fifth Birthday* (ed. Peter W. Flint, James C. VanderKam, and Emanuel Tov; VTSup 101; Leiden: Brill, 2003), 242–48. Further discussion of the authoritative status of Jubilees at Qumran can be found in Aharon Shemesh, "4Q265 and the Authoritative Status of Jubilees at Qumran," in Boccaccini and Ibba, *Enoch and the Mosaic Torah*, 247–60; VanderKam, "Authoritative Literature," 399; idem, "Questions of Canon," 106; idem, *The Dead Sea Scrolls Today* (Grand Rapids: Eerdmans, 1994); 154; Joseph M. Baumgarten, "Purification after Childbirth and the Sacred Garden in

to reason that some time must have passed before it was accepted, copied, and interpreted by the sectarians known from Qumran.³⁶

The less firm limit on the latest date of composition follows from the unlikelihood that Jubilees could have been written during the Hasmonean dynasty, starting with Jonathan's claim of the high priesthood in 152 B.C.E. Not only does Jubilees not reflect details from the Hasmonean dynasty, but the historical "prediction" in Jub. 23 is not compatible with the resumption of war after the relatively peaceful intersacerdotium. Jubilees' naïve opposition to sectarianism and optimism about the high priesthood would have been difficult to maintain as the Hasmonean dynasty established calendar and policies in direct opposition to Jubilees.³⁷ Although the status of Esau and sons, intermarriage, and the borders of Jewish identity were also issues in the 150s B.C.E., a case can be made for a later date if these were bigger issues later in the century.³⁸ A date in the 130s or later is less probable but still compatible with the basic claim that the historical context of Jubilees is the aftermath of the Maccabean revolt.

Numerous correlations between Jubilees and the events described in 1 Maccabees (as well as 2 Maccabees, Daniel, and Josephus) suggest a date in the 150s B.C.E. It is necessary to keep in mind the bias of 1 Maccabees in order to read critically for the historical reality, which Jubilees views very differently. First Maccabees attempts to portray Judah Maccabee (and family) as the beloved leader of a united Israel in resistance to for-

---

4Q265 and *Jubilees*," in *New Qumran Texts and Studies: Proceedings of the First Meeting of the International Organization for Qumran Studies, Paris 1992* (ed. George J. Brooke and Florentino García Martínez; Leiden: Brill, 1994), 3–10; Todd R. Hanneken, "The Use of Jubilees in 4Q390," in *A Teacher for All Generations: Essays in Honor of James C. VanderKam* (ed. Eric F. Mason; JSJSup 153.1; Leiden: Brill, 2011), 407–27.

36. Cana Werman ("ספר היובלים ועדת קומרן," 38–39) argues that Jubilees as we have it is a Qumran sectarian composition. She addresses the absence of distinctive language of the sect as the difference between writings for internal or external audiences. However, §2.2.1.4 made the case for seeing Jubilees as rejecting sectarian divisions in general (similarly Himmelfarb). Also, if Jubilees originated within the Qumran sects, it would be the only sectarian composition translated in antiquity into Greek, Latin, Syriac, and Ethiopic. See further VanderKam, "Recent Scholarship on Jubilees," 209.

37. VanderKam, *Textual and Historical Studies*, 249–52, 281; Finkelstein, "Pre-Maccabean Documents in the Passover Haggadah (Concluded)," 23; Solomon Zeitlin, "The Book of Jubilees: Its Character and Its Significance," *JQR* 30 (1939): 1–31.

38. Himmelfarb, *A Kingdom of Priests*, 72–78.

eign aggression and a handful of traitors. A critical read of 1 Maccabees, together with 2 Maccabees and Josephus, suggests that the revolt is better characterized as a civil conflict into which foreign powers were drawn by various parties at various times.[39] There may have been a major rift over cultural assimilation, but on both sides of that rift there were multiple groups with conflicts and tenuous alliances. We should be cautious before identifying the groups described in one text with the groups described in another text, especially if they are described generally as righteous and wicked. Even terms such as "pietists" (חסידים) and "the enlightened" (משכילים) may be more social descriptors than technical terms for well-defined groups. Finally, Judah Maccabee was a controversial figure even among those who opposed Menelaus and Antiochus Epiphanes. Opposition to Hellenistic assimilation does not automatically entail support of Judah Maccabee. Even before we come to more elaborate discussion, the fact that Jubilees prohibits fighting on the Sabbath (Jub. 50:12) suggests a fundamental disagreement with Mattathias and Judah Maccabee (1 Macc 2:41).

The most specific correlation between Jubilees and the events of the 160s B.C.E. appears in the "historical apocalypse" of Jub. 23. First, it is worth considering two major concerns in Jubilees that are known to have been hotly contested during the time of Antiochus Epiphanes (175–164 B.C.E.) and the Maccabean revolt (167–160 B.C.E.), even if they could have been relevant at other times. The supporters of Hellenistic assimilation opposed circumcision and promoted a Greek gymnasium in Jerusalem (1 Macc 1:14–15). Jubilees 15 argues emphatically that circumcision is nonnegotiable and cannot even be delayed.[40] In particular, Jub. 15:33 uses

---

39. Josephus certainly had his own bias in retelling 1 Maccabees as though Antiochus was unfortunate enough to have been drawn in by the wicked side of a civil conflict (see, e.g., *B.J.* 1.31). Be that as it may, he reverses the bias in 1 Maccabees in ways echoed by modern scholars. See Louis H. Feldman, "Josephus' Portrayal of the Hasmoneans Compared with 1 Maccabees," in *Josephus and the History of the Greco-Roman Period: Essays in Memory of Morton Smith* (ed. Fausto Parente and Joseph Sievers; Leiden: Brill, 1994), 41–42; Isaiah Gafni, "Josephus and I Maccabees," in *Josephus, the Bible, and History* (ed. Louis H. Feldman and Gohei Hata; Detroit: Wayne State University Press, 1989), 116–31.

40. Menachem Kister ("לתולדות כת האיסיים," 6–7 n. 26) points out that the emphasis on the particular day would not fit a debate with those who rejected circumcision outright. Jubilees emphasizes both the importance of circumcision and its timing. The former emphasis would address those who rejected circumcision out-

the term "sons of Beliar" (ውሉደ ፡ ቢልአር) to describe those who reject circumcision, which parallels the "lawless sons" (υἱοὶ παράνομοι)[41] who do the same in 1 Macc 1:11–15.[42] According to 1 Macc 1:14 and 2 Macc 4:9–12, Jason built a gymnasium in Jerusalem near the beginning of the reign of Antiochus Epiphanes. As the Greek name suggests, the gymnasium involved nakedness, which Jubilees twice prohibits (3:30–31; 7:20). In the first instance, the connection to Gentile practice is explicit: "as the nations uncover themselves" (3:31). These issues could have been discussed at other times, but we know they were particularly discussed during the reign of Antiochus Epiphanes and the Maccabean revolt.

It is also possible to correlate Jubilees with specific events described in 1 Maccabees up through 159 B.C.E. James VanderKam discussed extensive parallels in geographic details between the wars of Jacob in Jubilees and the wars of Judah Maccabee up through 161 B.C.E.[43] Further correlations

---

right, the latter those who accepted it under normal circumstances but in times of persecution would have been tempted to delay or compromise the law.

Martha Himmelfarb (*A Kingdom of Priests*, 72–77) links the emphasis on circumcision to adult conversion and intermarriage, particularly with respect to Idumeans. She presents evidence that this became more of an issue under Hasmonean expansion, which would suggest a late date of composition, closer to the date of the earliest manuscript. However, membership in God's people could have been debated earlier, and the possibility of an additional concern with conversion does not diminish the concern with foregoing circumcision entirely, as was particularly an issue under Antiochus Epiphanes. For more discussion on whether the debates in Jubilees fits in the reign of Hyrcanus, see n. 44 below. For more on halakic debates concerning circumcision, see ch. 2 n. 99.

41. Forms of παράνομος translate בליעל twelve times in the Septuagint.

42. The issue also appears in 1 Macc 1:60–61 and 2 Macc 6:10, where circumcised babies and their mothers are killed, and again in 1 Macc 2:46, where boys in Israel are forcibly circumcised.

43. VanderKam, *Textual and Historical Studies*, 217–46. Robert Doran challenged the certainty of details of the argument but did not provide a more certain alternative. Rather, he argues unconvincingly that Jub. 34–38 has a literary function and therefore cannot tell us about the historical context of the author. See "The Non-dating of Jubilees: Jub 34–38; 23:14–32 in Narrative Context," *JSJ* 20 (1989): 1–11. The attempt to find echoes of historical context in the descriptions of Jacob's wars began with F. Bohn, "Die Bedeutung des Buches der Jubiläen: Zum 50jährigen Jubiläum der ersten, deutschen Übersetzung," *Theologische Studien und Kritiken* 73 (1900): 167–84, who was followed by Charles, *Jubilees*, lxiii–lxvi. Doron Mendels followed Charles in identifying the wars as those of Hyrcanus, not Judah. Mendels (*Land of Israel as a Political Concept*, 57–88) takes the concern with Esau and the Edomites in Jubilees as mandat-

with events described in 1 Maccabees emerge from analysis of the "historical apocalypse" in Jub. 23. Jubilees accurately "predicts" the struggle for the high priesthood leading to civil war, famine, and foreign invasion, eventually followed by nonmilitary resolution in the death of Alcimus and retreat of the Seleucid general Bacchides (159 B.C.E.). The claim of peace and gradual restoration would have been tenable for as long as seven years, as far as we know, although earlier in this range may be more likely. Jubilees seems not to be aware of Jonathan's claim to royal and high-priestly offices in 152 B.C.E.[44]

The first major correlation is the description of a conflict over religious

---

ing the conquest of Idumea, which fits in his larger historical structure to the 120s B.C.E. Mendels is not aware of the paleography of 4Q216. He goes to the extreme of taking anything in Jubilees beyond Genesis as political manifesto. Although his reading of Jacob's wars is no more likely than VanderKam's, he does make a good point that calls for humility in assessing our certainty: he points out the imbalance of sources from different periods, such that a large number of parallels from one period over another may be misleading. Be that as it may, the parallels in Jub. 23 are more specific than the parallels in Jacob's wars.

44. The events of 152 would contradict the prediction of return to unity, peace, and prosperity through study of the law. Jonathan's high priesthood would have challenged Jubilees' optimism about the high priesthood, other than the interruption of the civil war (Jub. 31:13–17; 45:16; 49:21; 23:21). See VanderKam, *Textual and Historical Studies*, 249–52. Albert Baumgarten's (*Flourishing of Jewish Sects*, 86) social history of sectarianism in the second and first centuries B.C.E. suggests that sectarianism flourished after the consolidation of the Hasmonean dynasty, starting with Jonathan in 152 B.C.E. Jubilees itself represents an earlier, presectarian stage that later fueled sectarianism when the Hasmonean dynasty did not meet the expectations of radical separation of Jews from Gentiles. Especially if one accepts the additional arguments in §2.2.1.4 that Jubilees is not sectarian, Baumgarten's model supports composition before 152. However, Martha Himmelfarb (*A Kingdom of Priests*, 81) argues that Jubilees is not presectarian but antisectarian and is written in response to the rise or Jewish sectarianism during the Hasmonean dynasty. Jubilees is nonsectarian, but I believe it is naïvely presectarian. Once sectarianism flourished and the Hasmoneans established a lunar calendar and other practices strongly rejected in Jubilees, emphasis on "all Israel" and omission of sectarian election would not have been enough to counter sectarianism. Jubilees reflects the particular time period of power vacuum and reconstruction in the 150s when one could be so naïve as to imagine that Jews would be reunited around strict adherence to a particular interpretation of the law. By the time of Hyrcanus, uncompromising adherence to the principles of Jubilees would inevitably have led to sectarianism (as later becomes clear in the Damascus Document and 4Q390). For another way in which Jubilees fueled sectarianism, see ch. 2 n. 99.

authority that leads to violence between Jews and false claims to the high priesthood. The rebels use violence but succeed only in shedding blood, not bringing anyone back to the right way. All sides are characterized by violence, cheating, and greed. Some or all invoke the name of God falsely and defile the holy of holies. This tumult over religious authority generally describes the entire time from the high priesthood of Jason through the death of Alcimus. Physical violence began as early as the riot of Lysimachus in 2 Macc 5:5–7. However, if one reads past the differing evaluations, the same pattern continues just as much through Judah Maccabee. Judah's violence went well beyond conspiracy and a riot to sustained guerilla warfare. First Maccabees spins Judah and family as resisting foreign aggression, but it is still clear that they kill many Jews (e.g., 1 Macc 2:44). Judah claimed to act on behalf of God and the ancestral laws, but Jubilees disagreed on at least one point: fighting on the Sabbath (1 Macc 2:41; Jub. 50:12).[45] The sources are mixed on whether Judah claimed the high priesthood, but it is not likely that Judah stopped short of rededicating the holy of holies or respected Alcimus's claim to high priesthood.[46] If 2 Maccabees describes Judah as confiscating goods and giving a tenth to the poor, an opponent could describe the same action as "elevat[ing] themselves for (the purpose of) cheating and through wealth so that one takes everything that belongs to another" (2 Macc 8:28; Jub. 23:21). The phrase "those who escape" fits Judah's guerilla tactics particularly well (Jub. 23:21; 1 Macc 5:24; 7:11, 30; but see also Menelaus in 2 Macc 5:5 and Jason in 2 Macc 5:7).

The next major correlation is the description of foreign invasion. Some have suggested an earlier date for the composition of Jubilees, claiming that Antiochus does not appear in Jub. 23. However, Jubilees has theologi-

---

45. Lutz Doering ("The Concept of the Sabbath in the Book of Jubilees," 201–2) noted the difference of opinion but thought the lack of polemical tone in Jub. 50:12 reduces the probability that the verse is reacting directly to Mattathias's decision as described in 1 Macc 2:41. It is perfectly plausible that the idea and even the list of prohibitions existed earlier. Regardless of the sequence, a fundamental disagreement exists on a life-or-death issue. On other conflicting legal rulings, Jubilees is not short of polemical tone. We may not have certain evidence that Judah himself took a position on calendar debates, but his successors went on to use the lunar calendar that Jubilees hated (see 1 Macc 4:52; 2 Macc 1:18; 10:5).

46. First Maccabees sets up a wall of propriety around Judah's rededication of the temple. Josephus (A.J. 12.414) makes use of a source that includes Judah as high priest. See James C. VanderKam, *From Joshua to Caiaphas: High Priests after the Exile* (Minneapolis: Fortress, 2004), 241–44.

cal reasons for emphasizing Jewish sin as the primary problem and reducing the Seleucid armies to divine punishment sent by God.[47] In Jub. 23, the sinful nations kill indiscriminately and extensively. This could be metonymy for the general time in which Seleucid forces were present in Judea, throughout the 160s (1 Macc 1:29–36; 2 Macc 5:11; 6:1; Dan 11:25–29). However, the invasions of Bacchides and Alcimus in 161–160 B.C.E. stand out from the others in 1 Maccabees as the most violent of all the invasions. Of course, such an evaluation could only be made with retrospect, but another link connects Jub. 23:22–23 with 1 Macc 7:16–17. Both use Ps 79 to describe a massacre:

> A psalm of Asaph.
> O God, the nations have entered your domain,
> defiled your holy temple, and made Jerusalem into ruins.
> They have left the bodies of your servants as food for the birds of the sky,
> the flesh of your pious ones [חֲסִידֶיךָ] to the beasts of the earth.
> They shed their blood like water around Jerusalem,
> and there was none to bury them. (Ps 79:1–3)

Jubilees 23 echoes the psalm in the images of the nations plundering Jerusalem and slaughter such than none are left to bury the dead.

> [God] will deliver them to the sword, judgment, captivity, plundering, and devouring. He will arouse against them the sinful nations. … Much blood will be shed on the earth, and there will be no one who gathers up (corpses) or who buries (them). (Jub. 23:22–23)

First Maccabees 7:16–17 refers directly to the third verse of the psalm, and the context fits as well.

> But [Alcimus] arrested sixty of them [οἱ Ἀσιδαῖοι] and killed them in one day, according to the text of scripture: "The flesh of your pious ones and their blood they have shed around Jerusalem, and there was no one to bury them." (1 Macc 7:16–17)

---

47. Jub. 15:34; 23:22–23; cf. 2 Macc 5:17; 6:12; Finkelstein, "Pre-Maccabean Documents in the Passover Haggadah (Concluded)," 23–24; Rowley, *The Relevance of Apocalyptic*, 90; Nickelsburg, *Jewish Literature* (2nd ed.), 73–74; Jonathan A. Goldstein, "The Date of the Book of Jubilees," in *Semites, Iranians, Greeks, and Romans: Studies in Their Interactions* (Atlanta: Scholars Press, 1990), 161–80.

The most obvious connection pertains to killing with none left to bury. The second connection is the object, the "pietists" (חסידים, οἱ Ἀσιδαῖοι; in Jub. 23:23 Israelites are slaughtered indiscriminately). The word was becoming something of a technical term, though not a well-defined group.[48] The third connection may pertain to defiling and ruining. Although a number of moments in the 160s could have been thought of as defiling the temple and ruining Jerusalem, the most proximate and literal parallel is Alcimus's attempt to tear down the wall of the inner court of the temple (1 Macc 9:54). Even if Alcimus himself was not a Gentile, his henchmen were. He certainly entered God's domain, the holy of holies. It may not necessarily be the case that this event was widely understood as "The Psalm 79 Massacre" (*mutatis mutandis*), but the psalm is not used to describe any other massacres in the second century B.C.E. It would be quite a coincidence if Jub. 23:23 used the psalm to refer to an unrelated massacre in the same period.

Brief mention can be made of the famines described in both works. Jubilees 23:18 describes a severe famine as follows:

> There will be no produce from the vine and no oil. … All will be destroyed together—animals, cattle, birds, and all fish of the sea. (Jub. 23:18)

Similarly, 1 Maccabees describes a famine in 162 B.C.E. (1 Macc 6:54) and another in 160 B.C.E. (9:24).[49] A famine is not a unique event, but it fits in a list of historical parallels.

---

48. Collins, *Apocalyptic Imagination*, 78–79. Philip R. Davies strongly rejects the claim that the pietists were a group in "Ḥasidim in the Maccabean Period," *JJS* 28 (1977): 127–40. Richard A. Horsley refers to them as groups (plural) of intellectuals who resist Hellenistic assimilation (*Jesus and the Spiral of Violence: Popular Jewish Resistance in Roman Palestine* [San Francisco: Harper & Row, 1987], 66–68). John Kampen (*The Hasideans and the Origin of Pharisaism: A Study in 1 and 2 Maccabees* [SBLSCS 24; Atlanta: Scholars Press, 1988]) takes the later transliteration of the term into Greek as indicative of a distinct group but notes the difficulty of deriving from the early sources much about them beyond that they are leading citizens.

49. First Maccabees dubiously attributes the famine to the sabbatical year, and Jubilees is more concerned with fitting a theological explanation than conveying accurate history. Jack Pastor defends the historical reliability of the event itself in "The Famine in 1 Maccabees: History or Apology?" in *The Books of the Maccabees: History, Theology, Ideology: Papers of the Second International Conference on the Deuteronomical Books, Pápa, Hungary, 9–11 June, 2005* (ed. Géza G. Xeravits and József Zsengellér; JSJSup 118; Leiden: Brill, 2007), 31–43.

The last major correlation between Jub. 23 and 1 Maccabees is sudden peace in 159 B.C.E. The revolt, now led by Jonathan following the death of Judah in 160, was going badly, and Bacchides and Alcimus were secure. Then Alcimus died suddenly of natural causes, and "seeing that Alcimus was dead, Bacchides returned to the king, and the land of Judah was quiet for two years" (1 Macc 9:57). In fact, the next seven years could be described as peaceful. The conspiracy and battle at Bethbasi two years later, in 157, may not have interrupted the perception of peace. After years of valiant battles and bloody rivalries for the high priesthood, the death of Alcimus and retreat of Bacchides were remarkably bloodless. They were followed by a lack of conflict until 152, other than the incident in 157 (1 Macc 9:73). Although it is difficult to imagine that no one claimed the high priesthood for seven years, no such claim survived in the permanent record;[50] 1 Macc 10:21 reports that Jonathan did not claim the high priesthood until 152.

Jubilees 23 seems to know and interpret this bloodless peace and gradual restoration: "In those days the children will begin to study the laws, to seek out the commands, and to return to the right way" (Jub. 23:26). The result is a gradual return to longevity ("generation by generation"), the beginnings of which could have been perceived in the sudden absence of war and famine. Jubilees gives a theological explanation for the retreat of Bacchides under no military pressure: God withdraws punishment in response to repentance ("he will expel his enemies," Jub. 23:30). Jubilees' claims could be maintained as long as peace and piety were proceeding without human violence, and longevity could be perceived to be gradually increasing. If the incident at Bethbasi in 157 could have been ignored, this would permit a date of composition any time between 159 and 152. Within that range, an earlier date may be preferred. Such optimism of gradual but steady return to piety and prosperity may have been difficult to sustain, even if we do not know specific details that would have challenged it.

The correlation between Jubilees and the events of the Maccabean revolt establishes the historical context of composition. Jubilees does not merely reflect knowledge of the revolt; it judges it harshly as a fratricidal and hypocritical civil war. It views the invading forces as agents of God's chastisement, such that resisting foreign armies amounts to resisting God. Based on analogy with other apocalypses, one might at first imagine that

---

50. VanderKam, *Joshua to Caiaphas*, 244–50.

Jubilees takes sides in its description of the civil war. It is important to recognize that Jubilees says that "all have acted wickedly" and condemns the bloodshed "by each group." Neither side succeeds in doing anything except replacing the wickedness of one group with the wickedness of another group. The most decisive point is the divine reaction. God does not intervene to support one side of the other but sends in foreign nations to punish both sides equally. None of the Jews killing other Jews in the civil war gains divine approval. Repentance, the only good solution, is described in Jub. 23:26 as beginning to study the laws. Here it is particularly relevant that one of the laws, according to Jub. 50:12, is a prohibition of fighting on the Sabbath (*contra* 1 Macc 2:41).

The Animal Apocalypse is an easy example of an apocalypse that was written or revised to encourage joining a military resistance, with promises of imminent divine vindication and reward.[51] It might be tempting to say only that Jubilees responds to the Animal Apocalypse in particular on this point. However, the subversion of the apocalypses in Jubilees is much more comprehensive. Jubilees maintains an attack on apocalyptic ideas, not any one text. The other major data set from the period, the Danielic apocalypses, differs from the Animal Apocalypse substantially but illustrates the deeper level at which apocalyptic ideas cast a light on the Maccabean revolt. The idea of a final battle between forces of good and evil encourages participation in violence, even if the participation is viewed as symbolic of allegiance more than practically efficacious within a cosmic conflict.[52] Even apocalypses not contemporary with the revolt convey ideas that would easily, or even automatically, encourage violence. The apocalypses are not uniform in the precise action they encourage in the face of hardship and suffering, such as the events of the 160s. At a general level, however, they all reject the explanation of suffering as chastisement from God, they all contribute to demonizing opponents, and they all glamorize violent struggle, even if they did not have the same (or any) actual war in mind. It is easy to imagine how the author's opposition to the Maccabean revolt would have contributed to opposition to the apocalypses.

---

51. See ch. 3 n. 15 for discussion of Assefa's contrary opinion. Portier-Young (*Apocalypse against Empire*, 363–81) describes the Animal Apocalypse as "a synergistic understanding of war" in which military resistance joins other forms of resistance.

52. The "enlightened ones" encourage "those who know their God" to "stand firm and take action." The book of Daniel emphasizes theological meaning in military struggle and defeat, but does not oppose military action. See §2.2.2.2.

Violent resistance was a concrete issue that affected every Judean at the time. The ideas in Jubilees certainly would have been controversial, and the conflict in ideas could not have been missed or dismissed as minor. These ideas fundamentally conflict with the apocalypses. There is not an exclusive correlation between apocalyptic ideas and the revolt—certainly other ideas also contributed to militancy.[53] Even a loose association between apocalyptic ideas and militancy would help explain the historical context of the subversion of the apocalypses. If the author perceived the apocalypses as contributing to tearing Israel apart, encouraging violence against other Jews and resistance to divine chastisement, we find one clear reason (among others) why the author would want to subvert the apocalypses.

5.4. Cultural Context

The Maccabean revolt was the dominant issue in the historical context. Jubilees' position on the war would have been noticed at the time, not as a matter of friendly disagreement, but as a major social issue. We can also consider some additional issues from the cultural context that may cast light on the significance or motivation of the subversion of the apocalypses. It is one thing if Jubilees suggests an alternative view on something that was not a major issue in the cultural context. If Jubilees subverts a cultural symbol, we can be sure the subversion would have been noticed at the time, and we have a good idea that the differences were not friendly disagreements or minor reforms. We may also gain insight into the reasons the author of Jubilees would have subverted the apocalypses.

There are two difficulties in establishing the cultural context of the subversion of the apocalypses. First, it is not always clear what was a cultural symbol at the time. For example, scholars differ on whether the figure of Enoch was a cultural symbol that defined a competing form of Judaism. Even when we have evidence of running debates, the question remains whether the debates existed as disagreements within groups or functioned to organize distinct identity. Second, it is not always clear how closely a particular position is aligned with the apocalypses. Thus far we have con-

---

53. First Maccabees describes the deeds and motivations behind the revolt in terms of virtue, with hardly a trace of theology, apocalyptic or otherwise. Second Maccabees gives a theological interpretation of the revolt more proximate to Jubilees than the apocalypses, in that the weal and woe of Israel is explained as the consequence of the piety and sin of Israel.

sidered many issues that are inherent in the literary genre and distinctive of the apocalypses. Other issues may also be relevant to the cultural context of the subversion of the apocalypses, even if a certain position is neither exclusive to nor pervasive among the apocalypses. Consequently, the suggestions of cultural context in this section merit consideration only as possibilities that may or may not combine with external or future evidence and argumentation. The core argument is that Jubilees subverts the apocalypses. The explanation of why Jubilees subverts the apocalypses cannot be exhausted with certainty. Many of the issues inherent in the genre discussed in the preceding chapters have cultural significance. The following considers a sample of issues, closely or loosely associated with the apocalypses, with a particular view to the cultural context of Jubilees.

Chapter 4 considered the issue of revelation inherent in the literary genre. More can be said about the cultural context of allegorical dreams by incorporating comparison with Sirach. Several decades before Jubilees, the validity of allegorical dreams was debated. It stands to reason that Jubilees' positions on the issue would have been recognized as participating in the debate and opposing the position of the apocalypses. Previous scholarship on the relationship between Sirach and 1 Enoch offers terminological distinctions that will be helpful for characterizing Jubilees as well. The relationship between Sirach and 1 Enoch has been described as direct polemic, indirect polemic, and rivalry.[54] Randall Argall uses the term "rivalry" to emphasize that the differences were tokens distinguishing otherwise very similar alternatives competing for the same space. Specifically, according to Argall, both texts represent wisdom schools competing for the same students.[55] This point is worth keeping in mind while characterizing the relationship between Jubilees and the apocalypses. The differences between Jubilees and the apocalypses may be numerous and substantial, but the conflict is so heated precisely because they are competing for the same limited space for theological interpretations of traditions and current situations. The analogous relationships should not suggest that Jubilees and Sirach come from the same group, even if they agree in disagreeing with some apocalyptic ideas.

---

54. According to Boccaccini (*Middle Judaism*, 80), Ben Sira directly confronts the apocalyptic movement. Wright ("Fear the Lord," 218–22) prefers to characterize the conflict as indirect. Argall (*1 Enoch and Sirach*, 97, 247) emphasizes rivalry on a few issues in the context of close proximity in competition for the same social space.

55. Argall, *1 Enoch and Sirach*, 250–51.

Sirach seems to know and deliberately reject the view of allegorical dreams associated with the apocalypses. Particularly striking is Sir 34:1–8 (Argall's translation):

> Empty and false are the hopes of stupid men,
>   and fools are sent winging by dreams.
> Like one grasping at shadows and chasing the wind
>   is the one who attends to dreams.
> The dream-vision is "this thing" means "that thing,"
>   what compares to some person means that person.
> From the unclean, what will be [made] clean?
>   And from liars, what will be true?
> Divinations and omens and dreams are foolish,
>   and like a woman in labor, the heart fantasizes.
> Unless from the Most High it is sent as a visitation,
>   do not give your heart to them.
> For dreams have led many astray,
>   and those who hoped in them perished.
> Without deceit the Law will be fulfilled,
>   and perfect wisdom is in the mouth of the faithful.

The passage goes well beyond Deut 13 in condemning omens and seems to be motivated by response to the view of revelation associated with the apocalypses (see also Sir 3:21–24). Argall, who dates the Epistle of Enoch early, suggests 104:10 may be a response of sorts to Ben Sira, "And I know this mystery, that sinners will ... compose writings in their own names."[56] Meanwhile, apocalypses continued to be written with the claim that the wise must decode symbols in dreams in order to understand the present. When Jubilees expresses the opposite view, it is not suggesting a reform or compromise but defending an established position in an old debate. Even though Jubilees uses the literary morphology of the apocalypses, the original audience would have grasped that Jubilees sustains ideas opposite the apocalypses.

Scholars continue to dispute the significance of Enoch, Moses, and the law as cultural symbols, as well as the relationships between them.[57]

---

56. Ibid., 97. Stuckenbruck (*1 Enoch 91–108*, 589–93; idem, "The *Epistle of Enoch*," 415–16) discusses the textual difficulties and favors the view that 1 En. 104:9 castigates writings such as Ben Sira and Jubilees for appealing to the figure of Enoch without adopting the Enochic tradition.

57. See most recently, Paul Heger, "*1 Enoch*—Complementary or Alternative to

The evidence does not support a bold claim that Enoch and Moses were emblems of competing forms of Judaism that fundamentally differed on the necessity of legal observance. Nevertheless, these figures and the law deserve consideration among the cultural symbols that may have been recognized as significant, though not exclusively definitive, at the time of Jubilees. Jubilees treats Enoch, Noah, and Moses as positive figures and expands them beyond the simple sense of Genesis and Exodus. At least in Jubilees, the issue is not a matter of rejecting one or another. Various general proposals have been made that Jubilees subsumes the authority of one into another or domesticates one to fit another basic framework.[58]

Mosaic Torah?" *JSJ* 41 (2010): 29–62. For the view of the law in 1 Enoch, see ch. 4 n. 12. Eventually the controversy over ideas associated with Enoch led to rejection of the figure of Enoch, but the time of Jubilees is a different matter. Sirach, for example, speaks positively of the figure of Enoch while rejecting several ideas associated with Enochic literature. See Wright, "Fear the Lord," 214–17; Randal A. Argall, "Reflections on 1 Enoch and Sirach: A Comparative Literary and Conceptual Analysis of the Themes of Revelation, Creation and Judgment," in *Society of Biblical Literature 1995 Seminar Papers* (SBLS: 34; Atlanta: Scholars Press, 1995), 337–51. For a radical proposal that the rift between Enochic and Mosaic Judaism spanned the Second Temple Period, see Margaret Barker, *The Lost Prophet: The Book of Enoch and Its Influence on Christianity* (Nashville: Abingdon, 1989). In rabbinic literature, the reticence toward Enoch is supported by Targum Onqelos on Gen 5:24 (God killed him) and according to Ginzberg is true of Tannaitic and most Amoraic rabbinic literature, although Himmelfarb calls for moderation. See Louis Ginzberg, *The Legends of the Jews* (7 vols.; Philadelphia: Jewish Publication Society of America, 1909–1928), 5:163; idem, "Some Observations on the Attitude of the Synagogue towards the Apocalyptic-Eschatological Writings," *JBL* 41 (1922): 115–36; Martha Himmelfarb, "A Report on Enoch in Rabbinic Literature," in *Society of Biblical Literature 1978 Seminar Papers* (SBLSP 13; 2 vols.; Missoula, Mont.: Scholars Press, 1978): 1:259–69.

58. Boccaccini, "From a Movement of Dissent," 196–200; idem, *Beyond the Essene Hypothesis*, 90; Kvanvig, "Jubilees—Between Enoch and Moses," 260; Paolo Sacchi, "History of the Earliest Enochic Texts," in *Enoch and Qumran Origins: New Light on a Forgotten Connection* (ed. Gabriele Boccaccini; Grand Rapids: Eerdmans, 2005), 404; John Sietze Bergsma, "The Relationship between Jubilees and the Early Enochic Books (Astronomical Book and Book of the Watchers)," in Boccaccini and Ibba, *Enoch and the Mosaic Torah*, 50–51; Reed, "Enochic and Mosaic Traditions in Jubilees," 366–68; Dorothy M. Peters, *Noah Traditions in the Dead Sea Scrolls: Conversations and Controversies of Antiquity* (SBLEJL 26; Atlanta: Society of Biblical Literature, 2008), 88–91; Philip S. Alexander, "The Enochic Literature and the Bible: Intertextuality and Its Implications," in *The Bible as Book* (ed. Edward D. Herbert and Emanuel Tov; London: British Library, 2002), 57.

Rather than rehearsing and adjudicating all the previous arguments, a new argument can be made based on a passage that has not been considered in this regard.

As discussed in chapter 4, Jubilees generally follows a principle of the unity and consistency of all revelation. In particular, Jub. 21:10 does not reject the figures or writings of Enoch and Noah but insists that their books contained the exact same law known to us only in Lev 19:5–8:

> Eat its meat during that day and on the next day; but the sun is not to set on it on the next day until it is eaten. It is not to be left over for the third day because it is not acceptable to him. For it was not pleasing and is not therefore commanded. All who eat it will bring guilt on themselves because this is the way I [Abraham] found (it) written in the book of my ancestors, in the words of Enoch and the words of Noah. (Jub. 21:10)

Of course, we would like to know what the author had in mind when speaking of the books of Enoch and Noah.[59] No ancient, intact Book of Noah is known to us. Such a book, real or imagined, could easily have included teachings on blood and sacrifice, based on Gen 9, but duplication of Mosaic law from Leviticus should be at least somewhat surprising.[60] It is all the more striking that the laws of Leviticus are attributed to Enoch. Based on the Enochic literature known to us, any legal material, let alone temple practice, contrasts with the type of material expected from Enochic books. Jubilees claims that Enoch and Noah taught the exact same laws as

---

59. See ch. 2 n. 24.

60. Genesis Apocryphon 10.17 projects additional details onto the sacrifice of Noah, and 5.29 mentions a book of Noah. Aramaic Levi 10:10 (Mount Athos) asserts that Abraham read in the "Book of Noah concerning the Blood" regulations about handling blood. Both are more closely connected to Gen 9. Both of these documents are difficult to date and may depend on Jubilees, or all three may depend on an actual Book of Noah. See James L. Kugel, *The Ladder of Jacob: Ancient Interpretations of the Biblical Story of Jacob and His Children* (Princeton: Princeton University Press, 2006), 155; Robert A. Kugler, *From Patriarch to Priest: The Levi-Priestly Tradition from Aramaic Levi to Testament of Levi* (SBLEJL 9; Atlanta: Scholars Press, 1996); Joseph A. Fitzmyer, *The Genesis Apocryphon of Qumran Cave 1 (1Q20): A Commentary* (3rd ed.; BO 18B; Rome: Pontifical Biblical Institute, 2004), 26–28; Jonas C. Greenfield, Michael E. Stone, and Esther Eshel, *The Aramaic Levi Document: Edition, Translation, Commentary* (SVTP 19; Leiden: Brill, 2004), 180; Esther Eshel, "The Noah Cycle in the Genesis Apocryphon," in *Noah and His Book(s)* (ed. Michael E. Stone, Aryey Amihay, and Vered Hillel; SBLEJL 28; Atlanta: Society of Biblical Literature, 2010), 77–95.

Moses and that the heavenly tablets were not fully revealed until Moses (Jub. 33:16; 1:29; 50:13). The possibility remains that Enoch and Moses were not competing cultural symbols to any significant degree, and the eternality of the Mosaic covenant and law was not widely contested.[61] At least to a moderate degree, however, it stands to reason that Jubilees' assertion that Enoch and Noah taught the same temple regulations as Moses stakes a claim in the cultural context surrounding the Enochic apocalypses. This point does not include the Danielic apocalypses.[62]

The temple and priesthood were cultural symbols in any period, and all the more so in the 160s B.C.E. Unless they happen to come up as part of the spatial axis, these are not necessary elements of the literary genre, nor does a common cluster of ideas about them span the Enochic and Danielic apocalypses. Nevertheless, a generally negative attitude toward the temple and priesthood is found in the early Enochic apocalypses, while an emphatically positive attitude pervades Jubilees. The issue merits inclusion in the cultural context of the subversion of the genre. The ideas in which Jubilees differed from the apocalypses, some more than others, were unmistakable cultural symbols of central importance to Judean society at the time.

Finally, the most obvious cultural symbol of all is the name given to the normative group. As discussed in §2.2.1.4, Jubilees maintains the principal group description of "Israel" or "sons of Jacob," frequently with emphasis, "all Israel." The matter is not reducible to different revelatory settings. Even from the first week of creation, according to Jubilees, God chooses the Israelites for eternal distinction. Jubilees avoids terms such as "the wise" or "the enlightened" and uses "righteous plant" only in reference to all of

---

61. This does not include the lawless ones described in 1 Macc 1:11 as rejecting laws and covenants that separate Jews from Greeks. They were outside this debate. One would still have to account for what appears to be a distinctive lack of emphasis on the Sinai covenant in the Animal Apocalypse and the "new law" in the Apocalypse of Weeks.

62. Jubilees does not mention the figure of Daniel. It would be no simple matter to suggest that the figure of Moses as a cultural symbol is subordinated or demoted in Dan 9. It may be the case that Dan 9 presents the law of Moses, or a simple reading thereof, as an insufficient explanation of and proposed response to the present moment. This hardly constitutes a rejection of the law of Moses or Moses as a figure. See also Stuckenbruck's discussion of how the Epistle of Enoch subverts an opposing interpretation of Deuteronomy without opposing Deuteronomy itself ("The *Epistle of Enoch*," 411–13).

Israel. At least within the text, the primary symbol that organizes identity is descent from Jacob. Of course, we would like to know more about those who began to study the laws properly in Jub. 23:26, presumably from the author of Jubilees. We would like to know what happened to them and how Jubilees came to be interpreted in sectarian ways (e.g., 4Q390). We would like to know if the author identified as a "pietist" (חסיד) and what that would have meant. What we do know is that Jewish identity was in crisis in the decade preceding the composition of Jubilees. The apocalypses were associated with the claim that not all, or not only, descendants of Jacob constituted the normative group. Jubilees says the opposite.

Not only does Jubilees subvert the ideas inherently raised by the apocalyptic literary genre; in the process it argues against some apocalypses concerning several major cultural symbols that were hotly contested at the time. The distinctive ideas in Jubilees cannot be attributed to literary flourishes and variations within a genre or minor reforms in the same basic movement as the apocalypses. In historical and cultural context, Jubilees clashes strongly with the typical apocalypses. The fact that Jubilees uses the literary genre of the apocalypses can best be explained as a deliberate subversion of the apocalypses.

5.5. Conclusion

The relationship between Jubilees and the apocalypses has defied explanation since the beginning of the modern study of Jubilees in the nineteenth century. Some scholars treat Jubilees with the apocalypses as another example of the genre, set of ideas, or social movement. Others disregard any generic association between Jubilees and the apocalypses. The best assessments have been to identify Jubilees as a fuzzy case of the apocalyptic genre. Closer analysis shows that Jubilees is like the apocalypses in some specific ways but not others. By distinguishing layers of abstraction we see that Jubilees fits the apocalypses fully at the level of literary morphology but not at all at the level of ideas typically conveyed about the elements of the literary morphology. In fact, the ideas in Jubilees are the perfect opposite of the typical ideas.

On the spatial axis, all apocalypses describe an invisible world, particularly evil supernatural powers. Typically, evil supernatural powers explain suffering in the present, and good supernatural powers promise vindication and reward in the future. In Jubilees, the "bad" forces have no relevance for the righteous; they only maintain God's transcendence while carrying out God's justice against the sinful nations. They do not interfere in the relationship between God and Israel, they do not violate the will of God, and they certainly do not explain injustice. Rather, Jubilees denies the existence of injustice by maintaining that all sin is perfectly punished without delay. Also related to the spatial axis, the God's-eye view includes a classification of human beings. Typically the apocalypses dissolve the boundaries between Jews and Gentiles, both by excluding Jews from among God's righteous people and including non-Jews, especially in the future. Jubilees emphatically asserts the eternal immutability of the categories "Jew" and "Gentile." Furthermore, the apocalypses address the impact of invisible agents on the visible groups of humans and the proper response of humans. Typically, cosmic violence in the invisible realm is tied to political violence in the visible realm, and humans participate in that violence (sometimes by fighting with hope of God-assisted victory but also as victims or martyrs with hope of victory in an afterlife). Jubilees categorically condemns fratricidal violence, which it identifies as the root cause of the struggle for the high priesthood in the days of Antiochus Epiphanes (starting with Jason and Menelaus, through Judah Maccabee). The primary permeation of the boundary between the invisible and visible realms is the revelation of the heavenly tablets as the law and testimony of Israel. There is no glorification of violence in the present or future. Study and practice of the law is the only action required of the sons of Israel.

In all apocalypses, the God's-eye view of the visible and invisible realms (spatial axis) closely relates to the God's-eye view of the meaning of history (temporal axis). The present fundamentally contrasts with the future, which is often modeled by the distant past. In the typical apocalypse, the pattern of history is one of exponential decline through the present moment. History has reached its nadir with the climax of evil (unjust suffering). Justice is deferred for a collective judgment, usually predetermined in the near future and including the entire cosmos, human and nonhuman. Subsequently, a fundamentally new creation will replace the familiar creation, or at least social order. Jubilees replaces the "apocalyptic" pattern of decline, crisis, judgment, and restoration with a "Deuteronomistic" pattern of sin-punishment-repentance-restoration. Jubilees presents a fundamentally different view of, first, the recent past, second, the overall structure, and third, the future. First, Jubilees demotes the "final woes" from horrific to quotidian problems. The departure from God's plan for separation and longevity is not recent. The recent surge of punishment was a response to a recent surge of sin, not a crisis or challenge to God's control over history. Second, Jubilees does account for the broader pattern of decline, but Israel is not waiting for intervention and new creation from God. God's work was completed in creation, which unfolded over the jubilee of jubilees and climaxed with release from slavery, return to the land, and construction of the sanctuary of Aaron. Subsequently, there is no determined date for which to wait. The fulfillment of God's plan for creation depends only on the Israelites studying the laws and establishing purity, particularly separation from the Gentiles. Therefore, third, the future has already begun with a change as simple as study of the laws. Perhaps the most radical difference is that the future fulfills but does not reform the traditional institutions of Israel, particularly the boundaries of territory and people, priesthood, temple, and law.

Most fundamental to what makes an apocalypse an apocalypse is the manner of revelation. An apocalypse reveals knowledge from a heavenly source to an exemplary human for transmission to an implied audience. Typically an apocalypse reveals hidden things that are otherwise unknowable. They resonate with familiar traditions but build to something fundamentally new. On this point, Jubilees differs by degree along a spectrum. Jubilees has the same features of "new" and "familiar" but reverses the balance. Jubilees dwells on the familiar and suggests a new understanding of the familiar. The implication is that there is no legitimate new revelation, only study and exposition of what was already known. Jubilees denies its own novelty not only within the narrative but for the audience. The first audience of Jubilees would have thought it all sounded familiar, even if it was brought together like never before (the first narrative audience, Moses the Levite, should have heard most of it before). The audience of the typical apocalypse was made to feel that a secret had been revealed. The typical apocalypses also make a narrative claim to antiquity but often acknowledge the implied later audience for which understanding is expected. This relates to another fundamental difference in the view of revelation. In the typical apocalypse, revelation is transmitted to an elite audience. An elite form of wisdom is tied to revelation as the prerequisite of revelation, the consequence of revelation, or is identified with the revelation itself. In Jubilees, the implied audience is all of Israel. This is explicit in the narrative, as Moses is instructed to convey the revelation to all of Israel, and in allusion to the later audience, all of Israel, which the Levites are expected to teach continuously in every generation. Whatever the social reality may have been, Jubilees presents itself as instruction for Israelites of all times and all classes.

Thus Jubilees ceases to be a fuzzy case among the apocalypses. It uses the basic structure and elements of the literary morphology but expresses ideas at odds with the typical apocalypses. There are other works that express the ideas of Jubilees without the literary morphology. There are other works that express the ideas of the typical apocalypses without the literary morphology. There are other works that present an opposing set of ideas for the purposes of rejecting it. There are many combinations of literary elements and ideas in the ancient world. The pattern in Jubilees, however, is not a random combination but a highly effective rhetorical device. By using the literary morphology, the author establishes a comparison with other apocalypses. The result of that comparison is atypical but clear. Jubilees rejects the ideas typical of the apocalypses. The genre creates expectations in the audience. The ideas sustained discord with the preliminary expectations. The audience resolves the discord by concluding that the sustained ideas are more correct—indeed, sustainable—than the expected ideas. The audience experiences this resolution as a discovery, as though it were arrived at independently. The effect is to attack the ideas of the apocalypses without appearing to attack the works themselves. Indeed, Jubilees makes room for the legitimacy of books of Enoch and other ancestors, but only with the proper, revised meaning. Jubilees "revises" non-apocalypses as well, but with the apocalypses the revised meaning is opposite the former meaning. Jubilees subverts the apocalypses by using their literary morphology, summoning the audience's understanding about their meaning, and replacing it with an opposite meaning.

It is possible for a text to be subversive without the author intending it to be subversive. It is possible that the final pattern came about without having been planned. It is even possible that the author intended to integrate disparate elements diplomatically and tried awkwardly to integrate ideas in Judaism that the author fundamentally failed to appreciate. When we include in the discussion what we know about the historical and cultural context of Judea in the 150s B.C.E., it becomes probable that the author knew exactly what was happening and even set out to subvert the apocalypses, among other purposes in the book. The issues of theodicy, eschatology, temple, priests, law, revelation, the evaluation of the Maccabean revolt and Judah's family, the boundaries of God's people, and all the other issues addressed were unmistakable hot topics. Context suggests that the author of Jubilees deliberately subverted the apocalypses.

Bibliography

Adler, William. "Introduction." Pages 1-31 in *The Jewish Apocalyptic Heritage in Early Christianity*. Edited by James C. VanderKam and William Adler. Minneapolis: Fortress, 1996.

Albeck, Chanoch. *Das Buch der Jubiläen und die Halacha*. Bericht der Hochschule für die Wissenschaft des Judentums 47. Berlin: Berlin-Schöneberg, 1930.

Alexander, Philip S. "The Enochic Literature and the Bible: Intertextuality and Its Implications." Pages 57-69 in *The Bible as Book*. Edited by Edward D. Herbert and Emanuel Tov. London: British Library, 2002.

———. "Retelling the Old Testament." Pages 99-121 in *It Is Written: Scripture Citing Scripture: Essays in Honour of Barnabas Lindars, SSF*. Edited by Donald A. Carson and H. G. M. Williamson. Cambridge: Cambridge University Press, 1988.

Allison, Dale C. *The End of the Ages Has Come: An Early Interpretation of the Passion and Resurrection of Jesus*. Philadelphia: Fortress, 1985.

Anderson, Gary A. *The Genesis of Perfection: Adam and Eve in Jewish and Christian Imagination*. Louisville: Westminster John Knox, 2001.

———. "The Status of the Torah Before Sinai: The Retelling of the Bible in the Damascus Document and the Book of Jubilees." *DSD* 1 (1994): 1-29.

Argall, Randal A. *1 Enoch and Sirach: A Comparative Literary and Conceptual Analysis of the Themes of Revelation, Creation and Judgment*. SBLEJL 8. Atlanta: Scholars Press, 1995.

———. "Reflections on 1 Enoch and Sirach: A Comparative Literary and Conceptual Analysis of the Themes of Revelation, Creation and Judgment." Pages 337-51 in *Society of Biblical Literature 1995 Seminar Papers*. SBLSP 34. Atlanta: Scholars Press, 1995.

Assefa, Daniel. *L'Apocalypse des animaux (1 Hen 85-90): Une propagande militaire? Approches narrative, historico-critique, perspectives théologiques*. JSJSup 120. Leiden: Brill, 2007.

Aune, David E. "The Apocalypse of John and the Problem of Genre." *Semeia* 36 (1986): 65-96.

Bakhtin, M. M. *Problems of Dostoevsky's Poetics*. Translated by Caryl Emerson. Theory and History of Literature 8. Minneapolis: University of Minnesota Press, 1984.

———. *Problems of Dostoevsky's Poetics*. Translated by William Rotsel. Ann Arbor, Mich.: Ardis, 1973.

———. *Speech Genres and Other Late Essays*. Translated by Vern W. McGee. Edited by

Caryl Emerson and Michael Holquist. University of Texas Press Slavic Series 8. Austin: University of Texas Press, 1986.

Baldick, Chris. *The Oxford Dictionary of Literary Terms*. 3rd ed. Oxford: Oxford University Press, 2008.

Barker, Margaret. "Beyond the Veil of the Temple: The High Priestly Origins of the Apocalypses." *SJT* 51 (1998): 1–21.

———. *The Lost Prophet: The Book of Enoch and Its Influence on Christianity*. Nashville: Abingdon, 1989.

Barr, James. "Jewish Apocalyptic in Recent Scholarly Study." *BJRL* 58 (1975): 9–35.

Barton, John. "The Significance of a Fixed Canon of the Hebrew Bible." Pages 67–83 in *Hebrew Bible/Old Testament: The History of Its Interpretation*. Edited by Magne Sæbø. Göttingen: Vandenhoeck & Ruprecht, 1996.

Baumgarten, Albert I. *The Flourishing of Jewish Sects in the Maccabean Era: An Interpretation*. JSJSup 55. Leiden: Brill, 1997.

Baumgarten, Joseph M. "Purification after Childbirth and the Sacred Garden in 4Q265 and *Jubilees*." Pages 3–10 in *New Qumran Texts and Studies: Proceedings of the First Meeting of the International Organization for Qumran Studies, Paris 1992*. Edited by George J. Brooke and Florentino García Martínez. Leiden: Brill, 1994.

Baynes, Leslie. "'My Life Is Written Before You': The Function of the Motif 'Heavenly Book' in Judeo-Christian Apocalypses, 200 B.C.E.–200 C.E." Ph.D. dissertation, University of Notre Dame, 2004.

Bedenbender, Andreas. *Der Gott der Welt tritt auf den Sinai: Entstehung, Entwicklung und Funktionsweise der frühjüdischen Apokalyptik*. ANTZ 8. Berlin: Institut Kirche und Judentum, 2000.

———. "Jewish Apocalypticism: A Child of Mantic Wisdom?" *Henoch* 24 (2002): 189–96.

———. "The Place of the Torah in the Early Enoch Literature." Pages 65–79 in *The Early Enoch Literature*. Edited by Gabriele Boccaccini and John J. Collins. Leiden: Brill, 2007.

Beentjes, Pancratius C. *The Book of Ben Sira in Hebrew: A Text Edition of All Extant Hebrew Manuscripts and a Synopsis of All Parallel Hebrew Ben Sira Texts*. VTSup 68. Leiden: Brill, 1997.

Ben-Dov, Jonathan. "Tradition and Innovation in the Calendar of Jubilees." Pages 276–93 in *Enoch and the Mosaic Torah: The Evidence of Jubilees*. Edited by Gabriele Boccaccini and Giovanni Ibba. Grand Rapids: Eerdmans, 2009.

Bergsma, John Sietze. "The Relationship between Jubilees and the Early Enochic Books (Astronomical Book and Book of the Watchers)." Pages 36–51 in *Enoch and the Mosaic Torah: The Evidence of Jubilees*. Edited by Gabriele Boccaccini and Giovanni Ibba. Grand Rapids: Eerdmans, 2009.

Berner, Christoph. *Jahre, Jahrwochen und Jubiläen: Heptadische Geschichtskonzeptionen im antiken Judentum*. BZAW 363. Berlin: de Gruyter, 2006.

Bernstein, Moshe J. "'Rewritten Bible': A Generic Category Which Has Outlived Its Usefulness?" *Textus* 22 (2005): 169–96.

Betz, Hans D. "On the Problem of the Religio-Historical Understanding of Apocalyptic." *JTC* 6 (1969): 134–56.

Blenkinsopp, Joseph. "The Judaean Priesthood during the Neo-Babylonian and Achaemenid Periods: A Hypothetical Reconstruction." *CBQ* 60 (1998): 25–43.

Blum, Erhard. "Formgeschichte—A Misleading Category? Some Critical Remarks." Pages 32–45 in *The Changing Face of Form Criticism for the Twenty-First Century*. Edited by Ehud Ben Zvi and Marvin A. Sweeney. Grand Rapids: Eerdmans, 2003.

Boccaccini, Gabriele. *Beyond the Essene Hypothesis: The Parting of the Ways between Qumran and Enochic Judaism*. Grand Rapids: Eerdmans, 1998.

———. "From a Movement of Dissent to a Distinct Form of Judaism: The Heavenly Tablets in Jubilees as the Foundation of a Competing Halakah." Pages 193–210 in *Enoch and the Mosaic Torah: The Evidence of Jubilees*. Edited by Gabriele Boccaccini and Giovanni Ibba. Grand Rapids: Eerdmans, 2009.

———. "Jewish Apocalyptic Tradition: The Contribution of Italian Scholarship." Pages 33–50 in *Mysteries and Revelations: Apocalyptic Studies since the Uppsala Colloquium*. Edited by John J. Collins and James H. Charlesworth. Sheffield: JSOT Press, 1991.

———. *Middle Judaism: Jewish Thought, 300 B.C.E. to 200 C.E.* Minneapolis: Fortress, 1991.

———. "Qumran and the Enoch Groups: Revisiting the Enochic-Essene Hypothesis." Pages 37–66 in *The Bible and the Dead Sea Scrolls: The Second Princeton Symposium on Judaism and Christian Origins*. Edited by James H. Charlesworth. Waco, Tex.: Baylor, 2006.

———. "The Solar Calendars of Daniel and Enoch." Pages 311–28 in *The Book of Daniel: Composition and Reception*. Edited by John J. Collins, Peter W. Flint, and Cameron VanEpps. Leiden: Brill, 2001.

Boer, Roland. *Bakhtin and Genre Theory in Biblical Studies*. SemeiaSt 63. Atlanta: Society of Biblical Literature, 2007.

Bohn, F. "Die Bedeutung des Buches der Jubiläen: Zum 50jährigen Jubiläum der ersten, deutschen Übersetzung." *Theologische Studien und Kritiken; eine Zeitschrift für das gesamte Gebiet der Theologie* 73 (1900): 167–184.

Brooke, George J. "Exegetical Strategies in Jubilees 1–2: New Light from 4QJubilees[a]." Pages 39–57 in *Studies in the Book of Jubilees*. Edited by Matthias Albani, Jörg Frey, and Armin Lange. Tübingen: Mohr Siebeck, 1997.

———. "Genre Theory, Rewritten Bible and Pesher." *DSD* 17 (2010): 332–57.

Buss, Martin J. *Biblical Form Criticism in Its Context*. JSOTSup 274. Sheffield: Sheffield Academic Press, 1999.

Caquot, André. "Les enfants aux cheveux blancs: Réflexions sur un motif." Pages 161–72 in *Mélanges d'histoire des religions offerts à Henri-Charles Puech*. Paris: Presses Universitaires de France, 1974.

Carmignac, Jean. "Description du phénomène de l'Apocalyptique dans l'Ancien Testament." Pages 163–70 in *Apocalypticism in the Mediterranean World and the Near East: Proceedings of the International Colloquium on Apocalypticism, Uppsala, August 12–17, 1979*. Edited by David Hellholm. Tübingen: Mohr Siebeck, 1983.

———. "Qu'est-ce que l'Apocalyptique: Son emploi à Qumrân." *RevQ* 10 (1979): 3–33.

Charles, R. H. *The Book of Jubilees: or The Little Genesis*. London: Black, 1902.

Charles, R. H., and G. H. Box. *The Book of Jubilees; or The Little Genesis*. London: Society for Promoting Christian Knowledge; New York: Macmillan, 1917.
Charlesworth, James H. "What Is an Apocalyptic Text, and How Do We Know That? Seeking the Provenience of the Book of the Watchers." *Henoch* 30 (2008): 37–41.
Clarke, Ernest G. *Targum Pseudo-Jonathan: Deuteronomy*. ArBib 5B. Collegeville, Minn.: Liturgical Press, 1998.
Coblentz Bautch, Kelley. "What Becomes of the Angels' 'Wives'? A Text-Critical Study of 1 Enoch 19:2." *JBL* 125 (2006): 766–80.
Cody, Aelred. *A History of Old Testament Priesthood*. Rome: Pontifical Biblical Institute, 1969.
Collins, Adela Yarbro. "Introduction." *Semeia* 36 (1986): 1–11.
Collins, John J. "Apocalypse: The Morphology of a Genre." *Semeia* 14 (1979): 1–19.
———. *The Apocalyptic Imagination: An Introduction to Jewish Apocalyptic Literature*. 2nd ed. Grand Rapids: Eerdmans, 1998.
———. "Apocalypticism and Literary Genre in the Dead Sea Scrolls." Pages 403–30 in *The Dead Sea Scrolls after Fifty Years: A Comprehensive Assessment*. Edited by Peter W. Flint and James C. VanderKam. Leiden: Brill, 1998.
———. *Apocalypticism in the Dead Sea Scrolls*. Literature of the Dead Sea Scrolls. London: Routledge, 1997.
———. "The Court-Tales in Daniel and the Development of Apocalyptic." *JBL* 94 (1975): 218–34.
———. *Daniel: A Commentary on the Book of Daniel*. Hermeneia. Minneapolis: Fortress, 1993.
———. "Epilogue: Genre Analysis and the Dead Sea Scrolls." *DSD* 17 (2010): 389–401.
———. "Ethos and Identity in Jewish Apocalyptic Literature." Pages 51–65 in *Ethos und Identität: Einheit und Vielfalt des Judentums in hellenistisch-römischer Zeit*. Edited by Matthias Konradt and Ulrike Steinert. Paderborn: Schöningh, 2002.
———. "From Prophecy to Apocalypticism: The Expectation of the End." Pages 129–61 in *The Origins of Apocalypticism in Judaism and Christianity*. Vol. 1 of *The Encyclopedia of Apocalypticism*. Edited by John J. Collins. New York: Continuum, 1998.
———. "Genre, Ideology, and Social Movements in Jewish Apocalypticism." Pages 11–32 in *Mysteries and Revelations: Apocalyptic Studies since the Uppsala Colloquium*. Edited by John J. Collins and James H. Charlesworth. Sheffield: JSOT Press, 1991.
———. "The Legacy of Apocalypticism." Pages 155–66 in *Encounters with Biblical Theology*. Minneapolis: Fortress, 2005.
———. "Pseudepigraphy and Group Formation in Second Temple Judaism." Pages 43–58 in *Pseudepigraphic Perspectives: The Apocrypha and Pseudepigrapha in Light of the Dead Sea Scrolls*. Edited by Esther G. Chazon, Avital Pinnick, and Michael E. Stone. Leiden: Brill, 1999.
———. "Wisdom, Apocalypticism, and Generic Compatibility." Pages 165–85 in *In Search of Wisdom: Essays in Memory of John G. Gammie*. Edited by Leo G. Perdue. Philadelphia: Westminster John Knox, 1993. Repr. as pages 385–404 in *Seers, Sybils and Sages in Hellenistic-Roman Judaism*. Leiden: Brill, 1997.

Cozijnsen, Bert. "A Critical Contribution to the *Corpus Hellenisticum Novi Testamenti*: Jude and Hesiod." Pages 79–109 in *The Use of Sacred Books in the Ancient World*. Edited by L. V. Rutgers et al. CBET 22. Leuven: Peeters, 1998.

Cross, Frank Moore. *Canaanite Myth and Hebrew Epic: Essays in the History of the Religion of Israel*. Cambridge: Harvard University Press, 1973.

Davenport, Gene L. *The Eschatology of the Book of Jubilees*. StPB 20. Leiden: Brill, 1971.

Davies, Graham I. "Apocalyptic and Historiography." *JSOT* 5 (1978): 15–28.

Davies, Philip R. "Ḥasidim in the Maccabean Period." *JJS* 28 (1977): 127–40.

Dibelius, Martin. "Zur Formgeschichte der Evangelien." *TRu* NS 1 (1929): 185–216.

Dillmann, August. "Das Buch der Jubiläen oder die kleine Genesis." *Jahrbücher der Biblischen Wissenschaft* 2–3 (1850–1851): 230–56, 1–96.

Dimant, Devorah. "The Biography of Enoch and the Books of Enoch." *VT* 33 (1983): 14–29.

———. "Two 'Scientific' Fictions: The So-Called Book of Noah and the Alleged Quotation of Jubilees in CD 16:3–4." Pages 230–49 in *Studies in the Hebrew Bible, Qumran, and the Septuagint: Essays Presented to Eugene Ulrich on the Occasion of his Sixty-Fifth Birthday*. Edited by Peter W. Flint, James C. VanderKam, and Emanuel Tov. Leiden: Brill, 2003.

DiTommaso, Lorenzo. "Apocalypses and Apocalypticism in Antiquity (Part I)." *CurBR* 5 (2007): 235–86.

———. "Apocalypses and Apocalypticism in Antiquity (Part II)." *CurBR* 5 (2007): 367–432.

Dix, G. H. "The Enochic Pentateuch." *JTS* 27 (1925–1926): 29–42.

Doering, Lutz. "The Concept of the Sabbath in the Book of Jubilees." Pages 179–205 in *Studies in the Book of Jubilees*. Edited by Matthias Albani, Jörg Frey, and Armin Lange. Tübingen: Mohr Siebeck, 1997.

———. "Jub 50:6–13 als Schlussabschnitt des Jubiläenbuchs—Nachtrag aus Qumran oder ursprünglicher Bestandteil des Werks?" *RevQ* 20 (2002): 359–87.

Doran, Robert. "The Non-dating of Jubilees: Jub 34–38; 23:14–32 in Narrative Context." *JSJ* 20 (1989): 1–11.

Drawnel, Henryk. "Priestly Education in the *Aramaic Levi Document* (*Visions of Levi*) and *Aramaic Astronomical Book* (4Q208–211)." *RevQ* 22 (2006): 547–74.

———. "Some Notes on Scribal Craft and the Origins of the Enochic Literature." *Henoch* 31 (2009): 66–77.

Dubis, Mark. *Messianic Woes in First Peter: Suffering and Eschatology in 1 Peter 4:12–19*. Studies in Biblical Literature 33. New York: Lang, 2002.

Elgvin, Torleif. "Wisdom with and without Apocalyptic." Pages 15–38 in *Sapiential, Liturgical, and Poetical Texts from Qumran: Proceedings of the Third Meeting of the International Organization for Qumran Studies, Oslo, 1998*. Edited by Daniel K. Falk, Florentino García Martínez, and Eileen M. Schuller. Leiden: Brill, 2000.

Endres, John C. *Biblical Interpretation in the Book of Jubilees*. CBQMS 18. Washington, D.C.: Catholic Biblical Association of America, 1987.

Eshel, Esther. "The Noah Cycle in the Genesis Apocryphon." Pages 77–95 in *Noah and His Book(s)*. Edited by Michael E. Stone, Aryey Amihay, and Vered Hillel. SBLEJL 28. Atlanta: Society of Biblical Literature, 2010.

Falk, Daniel K. *The Parabiblical Texts: Strategies for Extending the Scriptures among the Dead Sea Scrolls*. Companion to the Qumran Scrolls 8. New York: T&T Clark, 2007.
Feldman, Louis H. "Josephus' Portrayal of the Hasmoneans Compared with 1 Maccabees." Pages 41–68 in *Josephus and the History of the Greco-Roman Period: Essays in Memory of Morton Smith*. Edited by Fausto Parente and Joseph Sievers. Leiden: Brill, 1994.
Finkelstein, Louis. "The Book of Jubilees and the Rabbinic Halaka." *HTR* 16 (1923): 39–61.
———. "Pre-Maccabean Documents in the Passover Haggadah (Concluded)." *HTR* 36 (1943): 1–38.
———. "Some Examples of the Maccabean Halaka." *JBL* 49 (1930): 20–42.
Fishbane, Michael A. *Biblical Interpretation in Ancient Israel*. Oxford: Oxford University Press, 1985.
Fishelov, David. *Metaphors of Genre: The Role of Analogies in Genre Theory*. University Park: Pennsylvania State University Press, 1993.
Fitzmyer, Joseph A. *The Genesis Apocryphon of Qumran Cave 1 (1Q20): A Commentary*. 3rd ed. BibOr 18B. Rome: Pontifical Biblical Institute, 2004.
Flannery-Dailey, Frances. *Dreamers, Scribes, and Priests: Jewish Dreams in the Hellenistic and Roman Eras*. JSJSup 90. Leiden: Brill, 2004.
———. "Lessons on Early Jewish Apocalypticism and Mysticism from Dream Literature." Pages 231–47 in *Paradise Now: Essays on Early Jewish and Christian Mysticism*. Edited by April D. DeConick. SBLSymS 11. Atlanta: Society of Biblical Literature, 2006.
Fletcher-Louis, Crispin. "Jesus and Apocalypticism." Pages 2877–2909 in *The Historical Jesus*. Vol. 3 of *Handbook for the Study of the Historical Jesus*. Edited by Tom Holmén and Stanley E. Porter. 4 vols. Leiden: Brill, 2011.
———. "Jewish Apocalyptic and Apocalypticism." Pages 1569–1607 in *The Study of Jesus*. Vol. 2 of *Handbook for the Study of the Historical Jesus*. Edited by Tom Holmén and Stanley E. Porter. 4 vols. Leiden: Brill, 2011.
Fokkema, Douwe Wessel. *Literary History, Modernism, and Postmodernism*, Utrecht Publications in General and Comparative Literature 19. Amsterdam: Benjamins, 1984.
Forsyth, Neil. *The Old Enemy: Satan and the Combat Myth*. Princeton: Princeton University Press, 1987.
Fowler, Alastair. *Kinds of Literature: An Introduction to the Theory of Genres and Modes*. Cambridge: Harvard University Press, 1982.
———. "The Life and Death of Literary Forms." *New Literary History* 2 (1971): 199–216.
Frow, John. *Genre*. Edited by John Drakakis. The New Critical Idiom. London: Routledge, 2006.
Gafni, Isaiah. "Josephus and I Maccabees." Pages 116–31 in *Josephus, the Bible, and History*. Edited by Louis H. Feldman and Gohei Hata. Detroit: Wayne State University Press, 1989.
García Martínez, Florentino. *The Dead Sea Scrolls Translated: The Qumran Texts in English*. 2nd ed. Leiden: Brill; Grand Rapids: Eerdmans, 1996.
———. "Encore l'apocalyptique." *JSJ* 17 (1986): 224–32.

---. "The Heavenly Tablets in the Book of Jubilees." Pages 243–60 in *Studies in the Book of Jubilees*. Edited by Matthias Albani, Jörg Frey, and Armin Lange. Tübingen: Mohr Siebeck, 1997.
García Martínez, Florentino, and Eibert Tigchelaar. *The Dead Sea Scrolls Study Edition*. Leiden: Brill, 1999.
Ginzberg, Louis. *The Legends of the Jews*. 7 vols. Philadelphia: Jewish Publication Society of America, 1909–1928.
---. "Some Observations on the Attitude of the Synagogue towards the Apocalyptic-Eschatological Writings." *JBL* 41 (1922): 115–36.
Goff, Matthew J. *Discerning Wisdom: The Sapiential Literature of the Dead Sea Scrolls*. VTSup 116. Leiden: Brill, 2007.
---. "Qumran Wisdom Literature and the Problem of Genre." *DSD* 17 (2010): 286–306.
Goldstein, Jonathan A. "The Date of the Book of Jubilees." Pages 161–80 in *Semites, Iranians, Greeks, and Romans: Studies in Their Interactions*. BJS 217. Atlanta: Scholars Press, 1990.
Grabbe, Lester L. "Prophetic and Apocalyptic: Time for New Definitions—and New Thinking." Pages 107–33 in *Knowing the End from the Beginning: The Prophetic, the Apocalyptic and Their Relationships*. Edited by Lester L. Grabbe and Robert D. Haak. London: T&T Clark, 2003.
Greenfield, Jonas C., and Michael E. Stone. "The Enochic Pentateuch and the Date of the Similitudes." *HTR* 70 (1977): 51–65.
Greenfield, Jonas C., Michael E. Stone, and Esther Eshel. *The Aramaic Levi Document: Edition, Translation, Commentary*. SVTP 19. Leiden: Brill, 2004.
Gruen, Erich S. *Diaspora: Jews amidst Greeks and Romans*. Cambridge: Harvard University Press, 2002.
Gunkel, Hermann. "Jesaia 33, eine prophetische Liturgie: Ein Vortrag." *ZAW* 42 (1924): 177–208.
Halpern-Amaru, Betsy. *The Empowerment of Women in the Book of Jubilees*. JSJSup 60. Leiden: Brill, 1999.
---. "The Festivals of Pesaḥ and Massot in the Book of Jubilees." Pages 309–22 in *Enoch and the Mosaic Torah: The Evidence of Jubilees*. Edited by Gabriele Boccaccini and Giovanni Ibba. Grand Rapids: Eerdmans, 2009.
---. *Rewriting the Bible: Land and Covenant in Post-biblical Jewish Literature*. Valley Forge, Pa.: Trinity Press International, 1994.
Hanneken, Todd R. "Angels and Demons in the Book of Jubilees and Contemporary Apocalypses." *Henoch* 28 (2006): 11–25.
---. "The Book of Jubilees among the Apocalypses." Ph.D. dissertation, University of Notre Dame, 2008.
---. "Creation and New Creation in the Hebrew Bible and Early Jewish Literature." Pages 79–93 in *God, Grace, and Creation*. Edited by Philip Rossi. Maryknoll, N.Y.: Orbis, 2010.
---. "The Status and Interpretation of Jubilees in 4Q390." Pages 407–28 in *A Teacher for All Generations: Essays in Honor of James C. VanderKam*. Edited by Eric F. Mason. JSJSup 153.1. Leiden: Brill, 2011.

Hanson, Paul D. "Apocalypse, Genre and Apocalypticism." *IDBSup*, 27–34.
———. *The Dawn of Apocalyptic*. Philadelphia: Fortress, 1975.
———. "Jewish Apocalyptic against Its Near Eastern Environment." *RB* 78 (1971): 31–58.
———. "Prolegomena to the Study of Jewish Apocalyptic." Pages 389–413 in *Magnalia Dei, the Mighty Acts of God: Essays on the Bible and Archaeology in Memory of G. Ernest Wright*. Edited by Werner E. Lemke, Patrick D. Miller, and Frank Moore Cross. Garden City, N.Y.: Doubleday, 1976.
Hartman, Lars. *Asking for a Meaning: A Study of 1 Enoch 1–5*. ConBNT 12. Lund: Gleerup, 1979.
———. "An Early Example of Jewish Exegesis: *1 Enoch* 10:16—11:2." *Neot* 17 (1983): 16–27.
———. "Survey of the Problem of Apocalyptic Genre." Pages 329–43 in *Apocalypticism in the Mediterranean World and the Near East: Proceedings of the International Colloquium on Apocalypticism, Uppsala, August 12–17, 1979*. Edited by David Hellholm. Tübingen: Mohr Siebeck, 1983.
Hayes, Christine Elizabeth. *Gentile Impurities and Jewish Identities: Intermarriage and Conversion from the Bible to the Talmud*. Oxford: Oxford University Press, 2002.
Heger, Paul. "*1 Enoch*—Complementary or Alternative to Mosaic Torah?" *JSJ* 41 (2010): 29–62.
Hellholm, David. "Introduction." Pages 1–6 in *Apocalypticism in the Mediterranean World and the Near East: Proceedings of the International Colloquium on Apocalypticism, Uppsala, August 12–17, 1979*. Edited by David Hellholm. Tübingen: Mohr Siebeck, 1983.
———. "The Problem of Apocalyptic Genre and the Apocalypse of John." *Semeia* 36 (1986): 13–64.
Hengel, Martin. *Judaism and Hellenism: Studies in Their Encounter in Palestine during the Early Hellenistic Period*. Philadelphia: Fortress, 1974.
Himmelfarb, Martha. "The Book of Jubilees and Early Jewish Mysticism." Pages 384–94 in *Enoch and the Mosaic Torah: The Evidence of Jubilees*. Edited by Gabriele Boccaccini and Giovanni Ibba. Grand Rapids: Eerdmans, 2009.
———. "Jubilees and Sectarianism." Pages 129–31 in *Enoch and Qumran Origins: New Light on a Forgotten Connection*. Edited by Gabriele Boccaccini. Grand Rapids: Eerdmans, 2005.
———. *A Kingdom of Priests: Ancestry and Merit in Ancient Judaism*. Jewish Culture and Contexts. Philadelphia: University of Pennsylvania Press, 2006.
———. "A Report on Enoch in Rabbinic Literature." Pages 259–69 in vol. 1 of *Society of Biblical Literature 1978 Seminar Papers*. 2 vols. SBLSP 13. Missoula, Mont.: Scholars Press, 1978.
———. "Some Echoes of *Jubilees* in Medieval Hebrew Literature." Pages 115–41 in *Tracing the Threads: Studies in the Vitality of Jewish Pseudepigrapha*. Edited by John C. Reeves. SBLEJL 6. Atlanta: Scholars Press, 1994.
———. "Torah, Testimony, and Heavenly Tablets: The Claim to Authority of the *Book of Jubilees*." Pages 19–29 in *A Multiform Heritage: Studies on Early Judaism and*

Christianity in Honor of Robert A. Kraft. Edited by Benjamin G. Wright. Scholars Press Homage Series 24. Atlanta: Scholars Press, 1999.

Horsley, Richard A. *Jesus and the Spiral of Violence: Popular Jewish Resistance in Roman Palestine.* San Francisco: Harper & Row, 1987.

Jauss, Hans Robert. *Toward an Aesthetic of Reception.* Theory and History of Literature 2. Minneapolis: University of Minnesota Press, 1982.

Jellinek, Adolph. "ספר נח." Pages 155–60 in בית המדרש. Yerushalayim: Sifre Vahrmann, 1967.

Kampen, John. *The Hasideans and the Origin of Pharisaism: A Study in 1 and 2 Maccabees.* SBLSCS 24. Atlanta: Scholars Press, 1988.

Kelly, Henry Ansgar. *Satan: A Biography.* Cambridge: Cambridge University Press, 2006.

Kister, Menahem. "לתולדות כת האיסיים: עיונים בחזון החיות, ספר היובלים וברית דמשק." *Tarbiz* 56 (1986): 1–18.

———. "על שני מטבעות לשון בספר היובלים." *Tarbiz* 70 (2001): 289–300.

Klawans, Jonathan. *Impurity and Sin in Ancient Judaism.* Oxford: Oxford University Press, 2000.

Knibb, Michael A. "The Book of Enoch in the Light of the Qumran Wisdom Literature." Pages 193–210 in *Wisdom and Apocalypticism in the Dead Sea Scrolls and in the Biblical Tradition.* Edited by Florentino García Martínez. Leuven: Peeters, 2003.

———. "The Use of Scripture in *1 Enoch* 17–19." Pages 165–78 in *Jerusalem, Alexandria, Rome: Studies in Ancient Cultural Interaction in Honour of A. Hilhorst.* Edited by Florentino García Martínez and Gerard P. Luttikhuizen. Leiden: Brill, 2003.

———. "Which Parts of 1 Enoch Were Known to Jubilees? A Note on the Interpretation of *Jubilees* 4.16–25." Pages 254–62 in *Reading from Right to Left: Essays on the Hebrew Bible in Honour of David J. A. Clines.* Edited by J. Cheryl Exum and H. G. M. Williamson. London: Sheffield Academic Press, 2003.

Knoppers, Gary N. "Hierodules, Priests, or Janitors? The Levites in Chronicles and the History of the Israelite Priesthood." *JBL* 118 (1999): 49–72.

Koch, Klaus. *The Growth of the Biblical Tradition: The Form-Critical Method.* Translated by S. M. Cupitt. New York: Scribner, 1969.

———. "History as a Battlefield of Two Antagonistic Powers in the Apocalypse of Weeks and in the Rule of the Community." Pages 185–99 in *Enoch and Qumran Origins: New Light on a Forgotten Connection.* Edited by Gabriele Boccaccini. Grand Rapids: Eerdmans, 2005.

———. *Ratlos vor der Apokalyptik: Eine Streitschrift über ein vernachlässigtes Gebiet der Bibelwissenschaft und die schädlichen Auswirkungen auf Theologie und Philosophie.* Gütersloh: Mohn, 1970.

———. *The Rediscovery of Apocalyptic: A Polemical Work on a Neglected Area of Biblical Studies and Its Damaging Effects on Theology and Philosophy.* Translated by Margaret Kohl. Naperville, Ill.: Allenson, 1972.

Kugel, James L. "The Jubilees Apocalypse." *DSD* 1 (1994): 322–37.

——. *The Ladder of Jacob: Ancient Interpretations of the Biblical Story of Jacob and His Children*. Princeton: Princeton University Press, 2006.

——. "On the Interpolations in the *Book of Jubilees*." *RevQ* 24 (2009): 215–72.

——. *Traditions of the Bible: A Guide to the Bible as It Was at the Start of the Common Era*. Cambridge: Harvard University Press, 1998.

Kugler, Robert A. *From Patriarch to Priest: The Levi-Priestly Tradition from Aramaic Levi to Testament of Levi*. SBLEJL 9. Atlanta: Scholars Press, 1996.

——. "Hearing 4Q225: A Case Study in Reconstructing the Religious Imagination of the Qumran Community." *DSD* 10 (2003): 81–103.

Kvanvig, Helge S. "Jubilees—Between Enoch and Moses: A Narrative Reading." *JSJ* 35 (2004): 243–61.

——. *Roots of Apocalyptic: The Mesopotamian Background of the Enoch Figure and of the Son of Man*. WMANT 61. Neukirchen-Vluyn: Neukirchener, 1988.

Lakoff, George. *Women, Fire, and Dangerous Things: What Categories Reveal about the Mind*. Chicago: University of Chicago Press, 1987.

Lambdin, Thomas Oden. *Introduction to Classical Ethiopic (Geʻez)*. HSS 24. Missoula, Mont.: Scholars Press, 1978.

Lambert, David. "Did Israel Believe That Redemption Awaited Its Repentance? The Case of Jubilees 1." *CBQ* 68 (2006): 631–50.

Lange, Armin. "Divinatorische Träume und Apokalyptik im Jubiläenbuch." Pages 25–38 in *Studies in the Book of Jubilees*. Edited by Matthias Albani, Jörg Frey, and Armin Lange. Tubingen: Mohr Siebeck, 1997.

——. "Interpretation als Offenbarung: Zum Verhältnis von Schriftauslegung und Offenbarung in apokalyptischer und nichtapokalyptischer Literatur." Pages 17–33 in *Wisdom and Apocalypticism in the Dead Sea Scrolls and in the Biblical Tradition*. Edited by Florentino García Martínez. Leuven: Peeters, 2003.

Leslau, Wolf. *Comparative Dictionary of Geʻez (Classical Ethiopic): Geʻez-English, English-Geʻez, with an Index of the Semitic Roots*. Wiesbaden: Harrassowitz, 1987.

Levinson, Bernard M. *Legal Revision and Religious Renewal in Ancient Israel*. Cambridge: Cambridge University Press, 2008.

Lieber, Elinor. "Asaf's 'Book of Medicines': A Hebrew Encyclopedia of Greek and Jewish Medicine, Possibly Compiled in Byzantium on an Indian Model." *Dumbarton Oaks Papers* 38 (1984): 233–49.

Macaskill, Grant. *Revealed Wisdom and Inaugurated Eschatology in Ancient Judaism and Early Christianity*. JSJSup 115. Leiden: Brill, 2007.

Mach, Michael. "Demons." *EDSS* 1:176–78.

Machiela, Daniel. "From Enoch to Abram: The Text and Character of the Genesis Apocryphon (1Q20) in Light of Related Second Temple Jewish Literature." Ph.D. dissertation, University of Notre Dame, 2007.

Mandolfo, Carleen. "Dialogic Form Criticism: An Intertextual Reading of Lamentations and Psalms of Lament." Pages 69–90 in *Bakhtin and Genre Theory in Biblical Studies*. Edited by Roland Boer. SemeiaSt 63. Atlanta: Society of Biblical Literature, 2007.

Matlock, R. Barry. *Unveiling the Apocalyptic Paul: Paul's Interpreters and the Rhetoric of Criticism*. JSNTSup 127. Sheffield: Sheffield Academic Press, 1996.

Mendels, Doron. *The Land of Israel as a Political Concept in Hasmonean Literature: Recourse to History in Second Century B.C. Claims to the Holy Land.* TSAJ 15. Tübingen: Mohr Siebeck, 1987.

Milik, Jozef T., and Matthew Black. *The Books of Enoch: Aramaic Fragments of Qumrân Cave 4.* Oxford: Clarendon, 1976.

Müller, Hans-Peter. "Mantische Weisheit und Apokalyptik." Pages 268–93 in *Congress Volume: Uppsala, 1971.* Edited by P. A. H. de Boer. Leiden: Brill, 1972.

Müller, Karlheinz. "Die Hebräische Sprache der Halacha als Textur der Schöpfung: Beobachtungen zum Verhältnis von Tora und Halacha im Buch der Jubiläen." Pages 157–76 in *Bibel in jüdischer und christlicher Tradition: Festschrift für Johann Maier zum 60. Geburtstag.* Edited by Helmut Merklein, Karlheinz Müller, and Günter Stemberger. Frankfurt am Main: Hain, 1993.

Najman, Hindy. "Interpretation as Primordial Writing: Jubilees and Its Authority Conferring Strategies." *JSJ* 30 (1999): 379–410.

———. *Seconding Sinai: The Development of Mosaic Discourse in Second Temple Judaism.* JSJSup 77. Leiden: Brill, 2003.

Newsom, Carol A. "Bakhtin." Pages 20–27 in *Handbook of Postmodern Biblical Interpretation.* Edited by A. K. M. Adam. St. Louis: Chalice, 2000.

———. *The Book of Job: A Contest of Moral Imaginations.* Oxford: Oxford University Press, 2003.

———. "Pairing Research Questions and Theories of Genre: A Case Study of the Hodayot." *DSD* 17 (2010): 241–59.

———. "Spying Out the Land: A Report from Genology." Pages 437–50 in *Seeking Out the Wisdom of the Ancients: Essays Offered to Honor Michael V. Fox on the Occasion of His Sixty-Fifth Birthday.* Edited by Ronald L. Troxel, Kelvin G. Friebel, and Dennis Robert Magary. Winona Lake, Ind.: Eisenbrauns, 2005.

Nickelsburg, George W. E. *1 Enoch: A Commentary on the Book of 1 Enoch.* Hermeneia. Minneapolis: Fortress, 2001.

———. "Enoch, Levi, and Peter: Recipients of Revelation in Upper Galilee." *JBL* 100 (1981): 575–600.

———. "Enochic Wisdom and Its Relationship to the Mosaic Torah." Pages 81–94 in *The Early Enoch Literature.* Edited by Gabriele Boccaccini and John J. Collins. Leiden: Brill, 2007.

———. "Enochic Wisdom: An Alternative to the Mosaic Torah?" Pages 123–32 in *Hesed Ve-Emet: Studies in Honor of Ernest S. Frerichs.* Edited by Jodi Magness and Seymour Gitin. BJS 320. Atlanta: Scholars Press, 1998.

———. *Jewish Literature between the Bible and the Mishnah: A Historical and Literary Introduction.* 2nd ed. Minneapolis: Fortress, 2005.

———. "The Nature and Function of Revelation in 1 Enoch, Jubilees, and Some Qumran Fragments." Pages 91–119 in *Pseudepigraphic Perspectives: The Apocrypha and Pseudepigrapha in Light of the Dead Sea Scrolls.* Edited by Esther G. Chazon, Avital Pinnick, and Michael E. Stone. Leiden: Brill, 1999.

———. *Resurrection, Immortality, and Eternal Life in Intertestamental Judaism.* Harvard Theological Studies 26. Cambridge: Harvard University Press, 1972.

———. "Scripture in 1 Enoch and 1 Enoch as Scripture." Pages 333–54 in *Texts and Contexts: Biblical Texts in Their Textual and Situational Contexts: Essays in Honor of Lars Hartman*. Edited by Tord Fornberg and David Hellholm. Oslo: Scandanavian University Press, 1995.

———. "Wisdom and Apocalypticism in Early Judaism: Some Points for Discussion." Pages 17–37 in *Conflicted Boundaries in Wisdom and Apocalypticism*. Edited by Benjamin G. Wright and Lawrence M. Wills. SBLSymS 35. Atlanta: Society of Biblical Literature, 2005. First published as pages 715–32 in *Society of Biblical Literature 1994 Seminar Papers*. SBLSP 33. Atlanta: Scholars Press, 1994.

Nickelsburg, George W. E., and James C. VanderKam. *1 Enoch 2: A Commentary on the Book of 1 Enoch, Chapters 37–82*. Hermeneia. Minneapolis: Fortress, 2011.

Olyan, Saul M. "Ben Sira's Relationship to the Priesthood." *HTR* 80 (1987): 261–86.

———. "Zadok's Origins and the Tribal Politics of David." *JBL* 101 (1982): 177–93.

Pagels, Elaine. *The Origin of Satan*. New York: Random House, 1995.

Pastor, Jack. "The Famine in 1 Maccabees: History or Apology?" Pages 31–43 in *The Books of the Maccabees: History, Theology, Ideology: Papers of the Second International Conference on the Deuteronomical Books, Pápa, Hungary, 9–11 June, 2005*. Edited by Géza G. Xeravits and József Zsengellér. Leiden: Brill, 2007.

Paul, Shalom M. "Heavenly Tablets and the Book of Life." Pages 345–53 in *The Gaster Festschrift*. Edited by David Marcus. New York: ANE Society, 1974.

Peters, Dorothy M. *Noah Traditions in the Dead Sea Scrolls: Conversations and Controversies of Antiquity*. SBLEJL 26. Atlanta: Society of Biblical Literature, 2008.

Philonenko, Marc. "L'apocalyptique qoumrânienne." Pages 211–18 in *Apocalypticism in the Mediterranean World and the Near East: Proceedings of the International Colloquium on Apocalypticism, Uppsala, August 12–17, 1979*. Edited by David Hellholm. Tübingen: Mohr Siebeck, 1983.

Pitre, Brant. *Jesus, the Tribulation, and the End of the Exile: Restoration Eschatology and the Origin of the Atonement*. WUNT 2/204. Tübingen: Mohr Siebeck, 2005.

Portier-Young, Anathea. *Apocalypse against Empire: Theologies of Resistance in Early Judaism*. Grand Rapids: Eerdmans, 2011.

Rad, Gerhard von. *Old Testament Theology*. 2 vols. New York: Harper & Row, 1965.

Ravid, Leora. "The Book of Jubilees and Its Calendar—A Reexamination." *DSD* 10 (2003): 371–94.

———. "הלכות השבת בספר היובלים נ 13-6." *Tarbiz* 69 (2000): 161–66.

———. "המינוח המיוחד של לוחות השמים בספר היובלים." *Tarbiz* 68 (1999): 463–71.

Reed, Annette Yoshiko. "Enochic and Mosaic Traditions in Jubilees: The Evidence of Angelology and Demonology." Pages 353–68 in *Enoch and the Mosaic Torah: The Evidence of Jubilees*. Edited by Gabriele Boccaccini and Giovanni Ibba. Grand Rapids: Eerdmans, 2009.

———. *Fallen Angels and the History of Judaism and Christianity: The Reception of Enochic Literature*. New York: Cambridge University Press, 2005.

Regev, Eyal. "Jubilees, Qumran, and the Essenes." Pages 426–40 in *Enoch and the Mosaic Torah: The Evidence of Jubilees*. Edited by Gabriele Boccaccini and Giovanni Ibba. Grand Rapids: Eerdmans, 2009.

Rofé, Alexander. "Revealed Wisdom: From the Bible to Qumran." Pages 1–11 in *Sapiential Perspectives: Wisdom Literature in Light of the Dead Sea Scrolls*. Edited by Ruth Clements, John J. Collins, and Gregory E. Sterling. Leiden: Brill, 2004.

Rowland, Christopher. *The Open Heaven: A Study of Apocalyptic in Judaism and Early Christianity*. New York: Crossroad, 1982.

———. "Review of: *The Apocalyptic Imagination: An Introduction to the Jewish Matrix of Christianity*, by John J. Collins; and *Jewish Writings of the Second Temple Period*. Edited by Michael E. Stone." *JTS* 37 (1986): 484–90.

Rowley, H. H. *The Relevance of Apocalyptic: A Study of Jewish and Christian Apocalypses from Daniel to the Revelation*. 3rd ed. Greenwood, N.C.: Attic, 1980.

Ruiten, J. T. A. G. M. van. "A Literary Dependency of Jubilees on 1 Enoch?" Pages 90–93 in *Enoch and Qumran Origins: New Light on a Forgotten Connection*. Edited by Gabriele Boccaccini. Grand Rapids: Eerdmans, 2005.

———. *Primaeval History Interpreted: The Rewriting of Genesis 1–11 in the Book of Jubilees*. JSJSup 66. Leiden: Brill, 2000.

Russell, D. S. *The Method and Message of Jewish Apocalyptic, 200 BC–AD 100*. OTL. Philadelphia: Westminster, 1964.

Russell, Jeffrey Burton. *The Devil: Perceptions of Evil from Antiquity to Primitive Christianity*. Ithaca, N.Y.: Cornell University Press, 1977.

Sacchi, Paolo. "The Book of the Watchers as an Apocalyptic and Apocryphal Text." *Henoch* 30 (2008): 9–26.

———. "History of the Earliest Enochic Texts." Pages 401–7 in *Enoch and Qumran Origins: New Light on a Forgotten Connection*. Edited by Gabriele Boccaccini. Grand Rapids: Eerdmans, 2005.

———. *Jewish Apocalyptic and Its History*. Translated by William J. Short. JSPSup 20. Sheffield: Sheffield Academic Press, 1990.

———. "The Theology of Early Enochism and Apocalyptic: The Problem of the Relation between Form and Content of the Apocalypses; the Worldview of Apocalypses." *Henoch* 24 (2002): 77–85.

Sanders, E. P. "The Genre of Palestinian Jewish Apocalypses." Pages 447–59 in *Apocalypticism in the Mediterranean World and the Near East: Proceedings of the International Colloquium on Apocalypticism, Uppsala, August 12–17, 1979*. Edited by David Hellholm. Tübingen: Mohr Siebeck, 1983.

———. *Paul and Palestinian Judaism: A Comparison of Patterns of Religion*. Philadelphia: Fortress, 1977.

Schmidt, Johann Michael. *Die jüdische Apokalyptik*. Neukirchen-Vluyn: Neukirchener, 1969.

Schmithals, Walter. *The Apocalyptic Movement: Introduction and Interpretation*. Translated by John E. Steely. Nashville: Abingdon, 1975.

Schubert, Friedemann. *Tradition und Erneuerung: Studien zum Jubiläenbuch und seinem Trägerkreis*, Europäische Hochschulschriften 3, Geschichte und ihre Hilfswissenschaften 771. Frankfurt am Main; New York: Lang, 1998.

Schürer, Emil. *Geschichte des jüdischen Volkes im Zeitalter Jesu Christi*. Leipzig: Hinrichs, 1886.

Scott, James M. *On Earth as in Heaven: The Restoration of Sacred Time and Sacred Space in the Book of Jubilees*. JSJSup 91. Leiden: Brill, 2005.
Seeligmann, Isac Leo. *The Septuagint Version of Isaiah: A Discussion of Its Problems*. Leiden: Brill, 1948.
Segal, Michael. "Between Bible and Rewritten Bible." Pages 10–28 in *Biblical Interpretation at Qumran*. Edited by Matthias Henze. Grand Rapids: Eerdmans, 2005.
———. *The Book of Jubilees: Rewritten Bible, Redaction, Ideology and Theology*. JSJSup 117. Leiden: Brill, 2007.
Sharp, Carolyn J. *Irony and Meaning in the Hebrew Bible*. Bloomington: Indiana University Press, 2009.
Shemesh, Aharon. "4Q265 and the Authoritative Status of Jubilees at Qumran." Pages 247–60 in *Enoch and the Mosaic Torah: The Evidence of Jubilees*. Edited by Gabriele Boccaccini and Giovanni Ibba. Grand Rapids: Eerdmans, 2009.
Sinding, Michael. "After Definitions: Genre, Categories, and Cognitive Science." *Genre* 35 (2002): 181–220.
Smith, Jonathan Z. "Wisdom and Apocalyptic." Pages 131–56 in *Religious Syncretism in Antiquity: Essays in Conversation with Geo Widengren*. Edited by Birger Albert Pearson. Missoula, Mont.: Scholars Press, 1975.
Stegemann, Hartmut. "Die Bedeutung der Qumranfunde für die Erforschung der Apokalyptik." Pages 496–530 in *Apocalypticism in the Mediterranean World and the Near East: Proceedings of the International Colloquium on Apocalypticism, Uppsala, August 12–17, 1979*. Edited by David Hellholm. Tübingen: Mohr Siebeck, 1983.
Stone, Michael E. "Apocalyptic Literature." Pages 383–441 in *Jewish Writings of the Second Temple Period: Apocrypha, Pseudepigrapha, Qumran, Sectarian Writings, Philo, Josephus*. Edited by Michael E. Stone. Assen: Van Gorcum; Philadelphia: Fortress, 1984.
———. "The Book(s) Attributed to Noah." *DSD* 13 (2006): 4–23.
———. "Lists of Revealed Things in the Apocalyptic Literature." Pages 414–52 in *Magnalia Dei, the Mighty Acts of God: Essays on the Bible and Archaeology in Memory of G. Ernest Wright*. Edited by Werner E. Lemke, Patrick D. Miller, and Frank Moore Cross. Garden City, N.Y.: Doubleday, 1976.
Stone, Michael E., Aryey Amihay, and Vered Hillel, eds. *Noah and His Book(s)*. SBLEJL 28. Atlanta: Society of Biblical Literature, 2010.
Stuckenbruck, Loren T. *1 Enoch 91–108*. CEJL. Berlin: de Gruyter, 2007.
———. "The Book of Jubilees and the Origin of Evil." Pages 294–308 in *Enoch and the Mosaic Torah: The Evidence of Jubilees*. Edited by Gabriele Boccaccini and Giovanni Ibba. Grand Rapids: Eerdmans, 2009.
———. "The *Epistle of Enoch*: Genre and Authorial Presentation." *DSD* 17 (2010): 358–88.
———. "The Origins of Evil in Jewish Apocalyptic Tradition: The Interpretation of Genesis 6:1–4 in the Second and Third Centuries B.C.E." Pages 87–118 in *The Fall of the Angels*. Edited by Christoph Auffarth and Loren T. Stuckenbruck. Leiden: Brill, 2004.
Sturm, Richard E. "Defining the Word 'Apocalyptic': A Problem in Biblical Criti-

cism." Pages 17–48 in *Apocalyptic and the New Testament: Essays in Honor of J. Louis Martyn*. Edited by Joel Marcus and Marion L. Soards. Sheffield: JSOT Press, 1989.
Suter, David Winston. "Fallen Angel, Fallen Priest: The Problem of Family Purity in 1 Enoch 6–16." *HUCA* 50 (1979): 115–35.
———. "Why Galilee? Galilean Regionalism in the Interpretation of 1 Enoch 6–16." *Henoch* 25 (2003): 167–212.
Swales, John. *Genre Analysis: English in Academic and Research Settings*, Cambridge Applied Linguistics Series. Cambridge: Cambridge University Press, 1990.
Talmon, Shemaryahu. "The Crystallization of the 'Canon of Hebrew Scriptures' in the Light of Biblical Scrolls from Qumran." Pages 5–20 in *The Bible as Book*. Edited by Edward D. Herbert and Emanuel Tov. London: British Library, 2002.
Tcherikover, Victor. *Hellenistic Civilization and the Jews*. Philadelphia: Jewish Publication Society of America, 1959.
Testuz, Michel. *Les idées religieuses du Livre des Jubilés*. Genève: Droz, 1960.
Thomas, Samuel I. *The "Mysteries" of Qumran: Mystery, Secrecy, and Esotericism in the Dead Sea Scrolls*. SBLEJL 25. Atlanta: Society of Biblical Literature, 2009.
Tigchelaar, Eibert. "More on Apocalyptic and Apocalypses." *JSJ* 18 (1987): 137–44.
Tiller, Patrick A. *A Commentary on the Animal Apocalypse of I Enoch*. SBLEJL 4. Atlanta: Scholars Press, 1993.
———. "The 'Eternal Planting' in the Dead Sea Scrolls." *DSD* 4 (1997): 312–35.
Toorn, Karel van der. "Why Wisdom Became a Secret: On Wisdom as a Written Genre." Pages 21–29 in *Wisdom Literature in Mesopotamia and Israel*. Edited by Richard J. Clifford. SBLSymS 36. Atlanta: Society of Biblical Literature, 2007.
Ulrich, Eugene. "From Literature to Scripture: Reflections on the Growth of a Text's Authoritativeness." *DSD* 10 (2003): 3–25.
———. "The Notion and Definition of Canon." Pages 21–35 in *The Canon Debate*. Edited by Lee Martin McDonald and James A. Sanders. Peabody, Mass.: Hendrickson, 2002.
Ulrich, Eugene, and Frank Moore Cross. *Qumran Cave 4.IX: Deuteronomy, Joshua, Judges, Kings*. DJD 14. Oxford: Clarendon, 1995.
VanderKam, James C. "The Angel Story in the Book of Jubilees." Pages 151–70 in *Pseudepigraphic Perspectives: The Apocrypha and Pseudepigrapha in Light of the Dead Sea Scrolls*. Edited by Esther G. Chazon, Avital Pinnick, and Michael E. Stone. Leiden: Brill, 1999.
———. "Authoritative Literature in the Dead Sea Scrolls." *DSD* 5 (1998): 382–402.
———. "Biblical Interpretation in *1 Enoch* and *Jubilees*." Pages 96–125 in *The Pseudepigrapha and Early Biblical Interpretation*. Edited by James H. Charlesworth and Craig A. Evans. Sheffield: JSOT Press, 1993.
———. *The Book of Jubilees*. Guides to Apocrypha and Pseudepigrapha. Sheffield: Sheffield Academic Press, 2001.
———. *The Book of Jubilees: A Critical Text*. 2 vols. CSCO 510–511. Leuven: Peeters, 1989.
———. *The Dead Sea Scrolls Today*. Grand Rapids: Eerdmans, 1994.
———. "The Demons in the *Book of Jubilees*." Pages 339–64 in *Die Dämonen: Die*

Dämonologie der israelitisch-jüdischen und frühchristlichen Literatur im Kontext ihrer Umwelt. Edited by Armin Lange, Hermann Lichtenberger, and Diethard Römheld. Tübingen: Mohr Siebeck, 2003.

———. "The End of the Matter? Jubilees 50:6–13 and the Unity of the Book." Pages 267–84 in *Heavenly Tablets: Interpretation, Identity and Tradition in Ancient Judaism*. Edited by Lynn LiDonnici and Andrea Lieber. Leiden: Brill, 2007.

———. *Enoch and the Growth of an Apocalyptic Tradition*. Washington, D.C.: Catholic Biblical Association of America, 1984.

———. "Enoch Traditions in Jubilees and Other Second-Century Sources." Pages 229–51 in vol. 1 of *Society of Biblical Literature 1978 Seminar Papers*. 2 vols. SBLSP 13. Missoula, Mont.: Scholars Press, 1978.

———. *Enoch, a Man for All Generations*. Studies on Personalities of the Old Testament. Columbia: University of South Carolina Press, 1995.

———. *From Joshua to Caiaphas: High Priests after the Exile*. Minneapolis: Fortress, 2004.

———. "Genesis 1 in Jubilees 2." *DSD* 1 (1994): 300–321.

———. "The Origins and Purposes of the Book of Jubilees." Pages 3–24 in *Studies in the Book of Jubilees*. Edited by Matthias Albani, Jörg Frey and Armin Lange. Tübingen: Mohr Siebeck, 1997.

———. "The Prophetic-Sapiential Origins of Apocalyptic Thought." Pages 163–76 in *A Word in Season: Essays in Honour of William McKane*. Edited by James D. Martin and Philip R Davies. Sheffield: JSOT Press, 1986.

———. "The Putative Author of the Book of Jubilees." *JSS* 26 (1981): 209–17.

———. "Questions of Canon Viewed through the Dead Sea Scrolls." Pages 91–109 in *The Canon Debate*. Edited by Lee Martin McDonald and James A. Sanders. Peabody, Mass.: Hendrickson, 2002.

———. "Recent Scholarship in the Book of Jubilees." *CurBR* 6 (2008): 405–31.

———. "Review of Michael Segal, *The Book of Jubilees*." *JSP* 20 (2010): 154–57.

———. "The Scriptural Setting of the Book of Jubilees." *DSD* 13 (2006): 61–72.

———. "Studies in the Apocalypse of Weeks (1 Enoch 93:1–10; 91:11–17)." Pages 366–79 in idem, *From Revelation to Canon: Studies in the Hebrew Bible and Second Temple Literature*. Leiden: Brill, 2000.

———. "Studies in the Chronology of the Book of Jubilees." Pages 522–44 in idem, *From Revelation to Canon: Studies in the Hebrew Bible and Second Temple Literature*. Leiden: Brill, 2000.

———. "Studies on the Prologue and Jub. 1." Pages 266–79 in *For a Later Generation: The Transformation of Tradition in Israel, Early Judaism, and Early Christianity*. Edited by Randal A. Argall, Beverly Bow, and Rodney Alan Werline. Harrisburg, Pa.: Trinity Press International, 2000.

———. *Textual and Historical Studies in the Book of Jubilees*. Missoula, Mont.: Scholars Press, 1977.

VanderKam, James C., and Jozef T. Milik. "Jubilees." Pages 1–185 in *Qumran Cave 4: Parabiblical Texts Part 1*. Edited by Harold W. Attridge et al. Oxford: Clarendon, 1994.

VanderKam, James C., and George W. E. Nickelsburg. *1 Enoch: A New Translation, Based on the Hermeneia Commentary*. Minneapolis: Fortress, 2004.

Vermès, Géza. *The Complete Dead Sea Scrolls in English*. New York: Allen Lane/Penguin, 1997.

———. "Leviticus 18:21 in Ancient Jewish Bible Exegesis." Pages 108–24 in *Studies in Aggadah, Targum and Jewish Liturgy in Memory of Joseph Heinemann* (מחקרים באגדה תרגומים ותפלות ישראל לזכר יוסף היינימן). Edited by Jakob J. Petuchowski and Ezra Fleischer. Jerusalem: Magnes, 1981.

Vielhauer, Philipp. "Apocalypses and Related Subjects." Pages 581–607 in *New Testament Apocrypha*. Edited by E. Hennecke and W. Schneemelcher. Philadelphia: Westminster, 1965.

Volz, Paul. *Die Eschatologie der jüdischen Gemeinde im neutestamentlichen Zeitalter, nach den Quellen der rabbinischen, apokalyptischen und apokryphen Literatur dargestellt*. Tübingen: Mohr Siebeck, 1934.

Wacholder, Ben Zion. "*Jubilees* as the Super Canon: Torah-Admonition versus Torah-Commandment." Pages 195–211 in *Legal Texts and Legal Issues: Proceedings of the Second Meeting of the International Organization for Qumran Studies, Cambridge 1995*. Edited by Moshe J. Bernstein, Florentino García Martínez, and John Kampen. Leiden: Brill, 1997.

Wellhausen, Julius. *Prolegomena to the History of Israel*. Edinburgh Black, 1885. Repr., Atlanta: Scholars Press, 1994.

Werman, Cana. "*Jubilees* 30: Building a Paradigm for the Ban on Intermarriage." *HTR* 90 (1997): 1–22.

———. "היחס לגויים בספר היובלים ובספרות קומראן בהשוואה להלכה התנאית הקדומה ולספרות חיצונית בת התקופה." Ph.D. dissertation, Hebrew University, 1995.

———. "ספר היובלים ועדת קומרן: לשאלת היחס בין השניים." *Meghillot* 2 (2004): 37–55.

———. "The תורה and the תעודה Engraved on the Tablets." *DSD* 9 (2002): 75–103.

Wiesenberg, Ernest. "The Jubilee of Jubilees." *RevQ* 9 (1961–1962): 3–40.

Williamson, Robert, Jr. "Pesher: A Cognitive Model of the Genre." *DSD* 17 (2010): 307–31.

Wintermute, O. S. "Jubilees." Pages 35–142 in vol. 2 of *The Old Testament Pseudepigrapha*. Edited by James H. Charlesworth. 2 vols. Garden City, N.Y.: Doubleday, 1983–1985.

Wray, T. J., and Gregory Mobley. *The Birth of Satan: Tracing the Devil's Biblical Roots*. New York: Palgrave Macmillan, 2005.

Wright, Benjamin G., III. "'Fear the Lord and Honor the Priest': Ben Sira as Defender of the Jerusalem Priesthood." Pages 189–222 in *The Book of Ben Sira in Modern Research: Proceedings of the First International Ben Sira Conference, 28–31 July 1996, Soesterberg, Netherlands*. Edited by Pancratius C. Beentjes. Berlin: de Gruyter, 1997.

———. "Joining the Club: A Suggestion about Genre in Early Jewish Texts." *DSD* 17 (2010): 260–85.

———. "Jubilees, Sirach, and Sapiential Tradition." Pages 116–30 in *Enoch and the Mosaic Torah: The Evidence of Jubilees*. Edited by Gabriele Boccaccini and Giovanni Ibba. Grand Rapids: Eerdmans, 2009.

Zeitlin, Solomon. "The Book of Jubilees: Its Character and Its Significance." *JQR* 30 (1939): 1–31.

Zerbe, Gordon. "'Pacifism' and 'Passive Resistance' in Apocalyptic Writings: A Critical Evaluation." Pages 65–95 in *The Pseudepigrapha and Early Biblical Interpretation*. Edited by James H. Charlesworth and Craig A. Evans. Sheffield: JSOT Press, 1993.

Zimmerli, Walther. *Ezekiel: A Commentary on the Book of the Prophet Ezekiel*. Hermeneia. Philadelphia: Fortress, 1979.

Index of Ancient Sources

Hebrew Bible

Genesis
1	174, 176–78, 225
2–3	33 n. 92
3	32, 54 n. 5, 55
3:21	221
4:7	33
4:15	161 n. 57
5–6	205
5:24	287 n. 57
6	54 n. 5, 57
6:1–4	59 n. 19
6:5	31 n. 90, 33
9	288
9:6	115 n. 127, 161 n. 57
15:1	60 n. 20, 253 n. 138
15:16	153, 216
17:1	60 n. 20
17:12	222
17:14	222
18	67 n. 38
18:1–2	60 n. 20
19:24–25	161
22	78–79
22:11	60 n. 20
22:12	78
25:7	226
26:2	60 n. 20
26:24	60 n. 20
26:28	162
28:14	188 n. 117
31:47	251 n. 134
32	60 n. 20
35:9	60 n. 20
35:29	231
37:5–9	253
40:8–23	253
41:39	248
44	271
44:5	248 n. 129
44:15	271
46:24	60 n. 20
49	175 n. 85, 254–56
49:1	175 n. 85, 255 n. 143, 256
49:10	255–56

Exodus
4:6	147
4:24	80
4:24–26	79 n. 61
11:4	79 n. 63
12:12–13	79 n. 63
12:23	67 n. 38, 80 n. 63
12:27	79 n. 63
12:29	79 n. 63
15:6	84
23:32	163 n. 60
24	27, 174–75, 179, 206 n. 26, 225, 226 n. 78, 234
25	174, 176
25:8	175 n. 84
29:45	175 n. 84

Leviticus
9	174–76
12:3	222
13	46
13:3	147
18	223

Leviticus (cont.)		28:26	143
18:18	222	28:27–28	138
18:21	223	28:29	47
19:5–8	36 n. 100, 288	28:31	47
20:2	223 n. 67	28:35	138–39
20:2–5	223	28:38–40	140
20:5	223	28:48	144
24	222	28:49–50	233
24:19–20	222	28:50	143
25	191–92	28:51	141 n. 24
25:1	191	28:53–57	143
25:10	190	28:59–61	138–39
25:18	193	29:21	252
26	136, 138, 141, 214 n. 42, 226, 233	29:25	65, 66, 178 n. 91
27:30	224	30	239, 258
		30:11–14	239
Numbers		31	226 n. 78
5:3	175 n. 84	31:17	70 n. 39
12:10	46	32:8	64–65, 67–68, 70, 75, 178 n. 91
12:12	147	33	205
18:21	224		
18:26	224	Joshua	
20:16	66 n. 35	1:3	189
22	75, 205	24:29	126
25	100 n. 99, 112		
25:11–13	223	Judges	
35:33	161 n. 57	1:8	161 n. 58
35:34	175 n. 84		
36:4	192 n. 126	2 Samuel	
		24	76 n. 55
Deuteronomy		24:1	76
4:19	66, 178 n. 91		
7:9	182	2 Kings	
11:24	189	6:16–17	83, 105 n. 113
13	286		
13:14	73	1 Chronicles	
14:29	224	21	76 n. 55
15:9	73, 87	21:1	75–76
21	42	23:1	231 n. 84
23:15	16:44	29:28	231 n. 84
26:3–4	224	29:29	176 n. 86, 244 n. 119
28	41, 136, 138–44, 198, 226, 233		
28:21–22	138	2 Chronicles	
28:22–24	140	7:3	176
28:24	139 n. 23	9:29	176 n. 86, 244 n. 119

12:15	176 n. 86, 244 n. 119	Isaiah	
16:11	176 n. 86, 244 n. 119	4:5	179 n. 94
20:34	176 n. 86, 244 n. 119	14:12–15	212 n. 40
24:15	231 n. 84	24:21	67 n. 38
25:26	176 n. 86, 244 n. 119	41:4	176 n. 86
26:22	176 n. 86, 244 n. 119	44:6	176 n. 86
28:26	176 n. 86, 244 n. 119	48:12	176 n. 86
35:27	176 n. 86, 244 n. 119	51:9–10	83 n. 68
36	214 n. 42	52:12–13	105 n. 113
36:20–22	214	61:6	166
		63:3	105 n. 113
Ezra		63:5	83 n. 69
1:1	214	63:9	66, 70, 83 n. 69
9–10	223	63:15–64:1	229 n. 83
		63:19–64:1	166
Nehemiah		65	182, 226–27, 229–33
13:27	223	65–66	205
		65:9	90
Job		65:13	232
1–2	75, 79	65:15	48, 166 n. 68
26:7	83 n. 68	65:17–25	166
26:12–13	83 n. 68	65:20	45, 47, 125, 146, 229–31
33:23	67 n. 38	65:25	232
42:17	231 n. 84	66:14	232
		66:16	83 n. 69, 105 n. 113, 161 n. 58
Psalms			
51:9	147	66:18	90
79	143, 280	66:21	90, 166
79:1–3	280	66:22	166 n. 67
79:2–3	233		
90	182, 226–29, 233	Jeremiah	
90:4	33, 227	6:23	233
90:6	227	25:11	213–14
90:7	227	25:12	213–14
90:10	125, 227, 230	29:10	213–14
90:12	228	31:31	181 n. 100
90:14	228		
90:14–15	172 n. 81	Ezekiel	
90:15	228	1–2	205, 243 n. 118
96:5	62	34	203, 205–6
106:35	62	36:26	62 n. 22
109:6	75		
		Daniel	
Proverbs		1–6	208 n. 33
8:22	177 n. 87	1:4	95 n. 91, 243

Daniel (cont.)

1:6	97 n. 92
1:17	243–44
1:20	243
2	109, 124, 151–52, 170, 207–8, 210, 245
2:18	245
2:19	210, 245
2:20–21	243
2:21	210, 245
2:22	245
2:27	245
2:28	245
2:29	245
2:30	243, 245
2:34	108
2:35	170
2:43	124
2:44	170
2:45	108
2:47	245
3–6	207
3:11	208 n. 33
4	210
4:5	210
4:10	208
4:14	208
4:15	210
4:22	208
4:26	208
4:32	208
5	210, 245
5:11	210, 244
5:14	210, 244
5:18–21	209
5:25	208 n. 31
5:26–28	208, 210
6:10	110
7	57, 83, 84 n. 72, 109, 124, 152, 170, 208, 212 n. 40, 245
7:2	239 n. 106
7:7	124
7:9	46, 147 n. 31
7:10	68, 152
7:11	108, 208 n. 33
7:12	152, 214
7:13	83, 147 n. 31
7:18	83
7:20	124
7:21	81
7:22	83
7:25	68, 81
7:27	83
8	124, 135, 153
8:1	209 n. 34
8:2	239 n. 106
8:7	153
8:10	212 n. 40
8:10–12	81
8:16	72 n. 41
8:25	84, 108
8:27	209 n. 34, 245
9	38, 47, 57, 84, 124, 135, 153, 171–72, 197, 207, 207, 209, 211–16, 238, 245, 266, 289 n. 62
9:2	213
9:11	144, 215
9:13	215
9:21	72 n. 41, 209 n. 34
9:22	244
9:22–23	246 n. 122
9:23	84 n. 73
9:24	213, 216, 244
9:26	124, 135
9:27	84, 163 n. 60
10–11	124
10–12	96, 111, 153, 211, 212 n. 40
10:1	211 n. 39
10:4	239 n. 106
10:12	109 n. 34
10:13	57, 72 n. 41
10:14–21	246 n. 122
10:21	68, 72 n. 41
11	44, 46–47, 85, 109
11:14	96, 109
11:24	124
11:25–29	280
11:30	95
11:32	95
11:32–33	95–96

INDEX OF ANCIENT SOURCES

11:32–35	84 n. 73, 108–9	2	110, 114
11:33	96, 244	2:26	113
11:33–35	96, 246 n. 122	2:27–43	132 n. 15
11:34	145	2:41	276, 279, 283
11:34–35	46	2:44	279
11:35	146, 244	2:46	277 n. 42
11:36	81	2:54	113
11:36–45	84 n. 73	4:52	279 n. 45
11:45	84 n. 72, 108	5:24	279
12	83, 96, 135, 170	6:54	281
12:1	68, 72 n. 41, 96, 135, 225 n. 76	7:11	279
12:1–3	96	7:16–17	280
12:2	95, 111, 153	7:17	143
12:2–3	96	7:30	279
12:3	96, 242, 244	9	156
12:4	96	9:24	281
12:8	244–45	9:54	281
12:8–10	211	9:57	282
12:9–13	246 n. 122	9:73	282
12:10	96, 244	10:21	282
12:12	135		
		2 Maccabees	
Hosea		1:18	279 n. 45
4:3	43, 141	3:25	109
9	72	4:9–12	277
		5:5	279
Zephaniah		5:5–7	279
1:3	141	5:7	279
		5:11	280
Zechariah		5:17	280 n. 47
1–6	212 n. 40	6:1	280
1:12	67 n. 38, 214	6:10	277 n. 42
3	75–76	6:12	280 n. 47
11	205 n. 25	7:8	251 n. 134
		7:21	251 n. 134
Deuterocanonical Books		7:27	251 n. 134
		8:28	279
1 Maccabees		10:5	279 n. 45
1:11	163, 218, 289	11:8	109
1:11–15	277	12:37	251 n. 134
1:14	277		
1:14–15	276	Sirach	
1:15	99 n. 97	1:8	250 n. 134
1:29–36	280	1:12–13 (10–11)	104 n. 110
1:60–61	277 n. 42	3:21–24	286

Sirach (cont.)		20:1–8	72 n. 41
11:26–28	104 n. 110	20:15	68
17:17	67, 70	22:4	150 n. 36
24:8	250 n. 134	25:4–6	167 nn. 71–72
24:23	239 n. 105	32:6	54
30:4–6	104 n. 110	37	240 n. 107
34:1–8	286	42	240 n. 107
38:24	239 n. 105	46:1	247 n. 31
38:25	251	48:1	240 n. 107
40:1–13	104 n. 110	49:1	240 n. 107
		49:3	240 n. 107
Pseudepigrapha		51:3	240 n. 107
		61:7	240 n. 107
1 Enoch		61:11	240 n. 107
1	205	63:2	240 n. 107
1–36	54	69:2	53 n. 2
1:1	150 n. 36	72:1	168, 190
1:2	121	80	121, 130, 134
1:7–8	129 n. 11	80:2	130
2:1–5:4	240	80:4	130
5:9	167 n. 71	80:6	55
6:3	54	80:8	130
6:7	53 n. 2, 72 n. 41	81:1–2	225 n. 76
8:3	250 n. 133	81:2	168
9:1	72 n. 41	81:8	92
9:1–4	68	82:1	168
9:7	54 n. 4	82:2	92
10:3	129	82:3	92
10:5	131 n. 14	82:4	92
10:8	54, 129	86:1–89:1	202
10:12	88	87:4	158
10:16	91	88:2	129 n. 10
10:16–11:2	167	88:3	131
10:20–21	91	89:6	145
13:8	107 n. 115	89:10	145
14	205, 212 n. 40	89:11	145
15:2	87 n. 77	89:12	170
15:7	54	89:13	145
15:8–16:1	61	89:41	122
16:1	88, 150	89:54–58	151
16:3	54	89:55	144 n. 26
17–19	202 n. 14, 205 n. 23, 241	89:59	68
18:14	241	89:59–72	206
19:2	58:17	89:60	137
20–36	202 n. 14	89:65	122, 144 n. 26

INDEX OF ANCIENT SOURCES

89:65–90:13	81	93:9–17	225
89:71	68	93:10	241
89:74	122	94:5	240 n. 107
89:77	151	94:9	133, 151 n. 39
90:3	122	94:11–95:1	133 n. 18
90:6	197, 242	96:2	133 n. 18
90:6–7	42	96:8	151 n. 39
90:6–10	94	98:1	240 n. 107
90:7	94, 122	98:3	240 n. 107
90:12–16	85	98:4	266 n. 14
90:13	122	98:8	151 n. 39
90:13–14	83, 133	98:9	240 n. 107
90:13–15	131 n. 15	98:12	108
90:13–18	132	99:4–6	134
90:14	109	99:10	240 n. 107, 242 n. 115
90:17	122	99:16	134
90:18	133	99:16–100:6	134
90:20–27	83, 151	100:4	84, 134, 151 n. 39
90:28–29	170	100:5	67 n. 38, 133 n. 18
90:30	94	100:6	134, 240 n. 107
90:31	131 n. 15	100:11–13	134
90:32	146	100:13	134
90:33	170	101:2	134 n. 20
90:36	95	101:8	240 n. 107
90:38	95, 131 n. 15, 170	102:1–3	134, 151 n. 39
90	132 n. 16	103:1–2	225
91:1	240 n. 107	103:3	133 n. 18
91:5–7	123	103:8	151 n. 39
91:7	134	103:9–15	133 n. 18, 134
91:7–9	151 n. 39	104:5	133 n. 18
91:7–10	123	104:9	286 n. 56
91:10	241	104:12	240 n. 107, 242 n. 115
91:11–13	93	104:13	93
91:14	93, 168	105:1	93, 240 n. 107
91:15	151 n. 38	106:2	46, 146
91	122		
92:1	240 n. 107	2 Enoch	
92:4–5	151 n. 39	29–31	71
93:1	202		
93:2	225	Jubilees	
93:3	202	Prologue	182 n. 102
93:3–8	225	1	27, 28, 37, 87, 143, 171, 174 n. 82, 226
93:4	121		
93:6	169	1:1	27, 252
93:8	241	1:3	37

Jubilees (cont.)

1:5–28	9 n. 19
1:5	27, 252 n. 135
1:5–6	69 n. 39
1:5–28	174 n. 82
1:7	27
1:9	28
1:10	87
1:11	62, 87, 223 n. 68
1:15	127 n. 7
1:16	98
1:18	69 n. 39
1:19–21	27
1:20	73
1:22–25	116, 185
1:23	127 n. 7
1:25	99
1:26	27, 174–75, 244
1:26–28	174
1:26–29	174–180
1:27	176, 186
1:28	99
1:28–29	52
1:29	29, 97–98, 148 n. 33, 174, 176–80, 192, 289
2	80 n. 65, 184, 187 n. 112
2:1	27
2:20	98
2:26	252
2:29	252
2:33	182 n. 102, 185, 252
3	248 n. 130
3:14	182 n. 102, 252
3:15–16	33 n. 92, 55 n. 5
3:17–31	55 n. 5
3:31	55 n. 5, 221
4:6	70, 79 n. 60
4:15	59
4:17	249–50
4:19	58, 159, 254, 274
4:20	53 n. 2
4:23	58, 159
4:23–24	79 n. 60
4:24	159
4:26	29, 52, 190
4:30	248 n. 130, 33, 173 n. 81, 227, 248 n. 130
4:31	33, 161
4:32	222
5	28, 33, 129, 157–58
5:1	98 n. 96
5:1–12	234 n. 90
5:2	31 n. 90, 33, 192, 248 n. 130
5:3	33, 193
5:6–11	28
5:10	33, 157
5:10–11	157
5:10–12	62 n. 22
5:11–15	34
5:12	55, 62, 148 n. 33, 178
5:13	32, 34, 54 n. 5, 115, 158, 269
5:15	158
5:17	127 n. 7
5:17–18	63
6:2	190
6:8	115 n. 127
6:13	252
6:14	182
6:18–19	63 n. 26
6:20	252
6:22	206 n. 26, 218, 235
6:32	252
6:34	28
6:35	37, 59 n. 20, 257
7:20	221
7:21	98 n. 96
7:33	161
7:39	159
8	188
8:3	36 n. 101, 59, 250 n. 133
8:10	60 n. 20, 188
8:12	188
8:17	188
8:18	188
8:19	52
8:20	60 n. 20, 188
8:21	188
9	103, 161 n. 58
9:15	161 n. 58, 188
10	35

10:1	35, 64	15:32	37, 269
10:3	69	15:33	28, 73, 276
10:7	35	15:34	280 n. 47
10:8	28, 35, 62, 69, 77 n. 58	16	161
10:9	61	16:1	60
10:11	72, 74, 75 n. 51, 86	16:5	161
10:13	63	16:6	161
10:13–14	36	16:9	88
10:17	159, 160	16:17–18	69, 70
10:23	88	16:23	98 n. 96
11:2–5	114	16:26	98, 185
11:4	62	16:30	182
11:5	78	18:9	60 n. 20
11:11	78	18:13	52
11:16	250	18:14	60 n. 20
11:23	250	19:2	180
11:23–24	250	19:18	98
12:16–18	36 n. 101, 250	19:25	29, 87, 116, 180
12:19	98 n. 96	19:28	69, 78
12:20	69, 75	19:28–29	69
12:25–27	37, 60 n. 20, 250, 257	19:29	70
12:27	250, 251 n. 134	20:2	115
13	161	20:3	127 n. 7
13:16–21	39	20:5–6	161
13:20	188 n. 116	20:6	127 n. 7
13:25	112, 182 n. 102	21:1	250
13:26	182	21:3	127 n. 7
14:1	60 n. 20, 253 n. 138	21:10	36, 288
14:7	188 n. 116	21:20	69
14:14	162	21:24	98–99
14:20	63 n. 26	22:9–10	98
15	80 n. 65, 276	22:11	103 n. 108
15:1	60 n. 20	22:22	161
15:9	185	22:23	185
15:10	188 n. 116	22:27	188 n. 116
15:19	185	23	28, 38, 40–41, 74 n. 49, 82, 85–87, 99, 101, 103, 105–6, 112, 114, 116, 119, 125, 126 n. 4, 127, 136–39, 142–44, 146, 148–49, 154–57, 163–65, 171–73, 182, 185–87, 193–94, 197, 225–29, 233–36, 272, 274–76, 278–80, 282
15:25	182		
15:26	99 n. 97		
15:27	186		
15:28	252		
15:30	98		
15:30–31	98		
15:30–32	37, 185	23:9	161, 227
15:31	62, 75, 77, 87, 187, 251 n. 134	23:10	227, 23:11, 28, 126 n. 4, 154
15:31–32	69	23:11	248 n. 130

Jubilees (cont.)

23:12	10 n. 19, 138, 230	28:7	252
23:13	136 n. 21, 138–39, 142, 271	29:11	113
23:14–31	9 n. 19, 127 n. 6, 174 n. 82	30:7–16	112 n. 123
23:15	227–28, 230	30:8	185
23:16–21	102, 137, 146	30:9	223
23:16	42, 102 n. 104, 137	30:10	73, 182
23:17	42	30:11	252
23:18	140–41, 281	30:14–15	185–86
23:19	228	30:17	252
23:20	115 n. 127, 116	30:17–18	112
23:21	137, 278–79	30:18	98, 178 n. 92, 186
23:22	28, 85	30:18–20	271
23:22–23	142, 144, 155, 227, 280	30:21	252
23:23	38, 233, 281	30:22	127 n. 7
23:24–25	145, 229 n. 83	30	100 n. 99
23:24	47, 145	31:12	60 n. 20
23:25	126 n. 4, 146–47	31:13–17	278
23:26	42, 63, 102, 127 n. 7, 148, 182, 228, 246, 281, 283, 290	31:14	186, 187 n. 112
		31:14–15	271
		31:18	255–56
23:26–31	28, 179	31:32	271
23:26–27	28, 172	32	256
23:27–29	228	32:1	186, 253, 271
23:27	55, 228	32:2–3	271
23:28–31	229	32:10	98 n. 96, 182
23:28	230–31	32:10–15	223
23:29	29, 74, 86, 232	32:18–19	189
23:30	86, 148 n. 32, 155, 160 n. 56, 179, 189, 232, 282	32:19	189 n. 119
		32:20	60 n. 20
23:30–31	29	32:21	253, 256
23:31	160 n. 56, 232	32:22	257
24	113, 163	32:25–26	257
24:9	60 n. 20	33:11	98
24:22	60 n. 20	33:13	252
24:28	114 n. 126	33:16	182 n. 102, 248, 289
24:28–30	163	33:16–17	183
24:29	113	33:18	252
25:7	250	34–38	277 n. 43
25:11	185	34:19	127 n. 7
25:15	60 n. 20	35:14	164
25:17	188 n. 116	35:17	70
25:18	99	36:6	98
26:20	185	36:10	161–62, 164
27:23	189 n. 117	36:20	183 n. 105
28:6	222	37:6–14	98

INDEX OF ANCIENT SOURCES   323

38:11–12	115	Testament of Dan	
38:14	28, 103 n. 108, 163	6:2	68 n. 38
39:16–17	253		
40:1	254	Testament of Levi	
40:5	248	3:5	68 n. 38
40:9	29, 74		
41:24	253	Testament of Reuben	
41:26	127 n. 7, 252	5:6	58 n. 17
42:2	248 n. 129		
42:25	271	Testament of Moses	
43:10	271	10:2–3	84 n. 71
44:5	60 n. 20		
45:14	175 n. 85, 255	DEAD SEA SCROLLS	
45:16	36, 63, 200 n. 11, 235 n. 94, 252, 278	Genesis Apocryphon	
46:2	29, 74	10.17	288 n. 60
48	80 n. 65		
48:3	81	Pesher Habakkuk	
48:3–4	80	2.3	181
48:5	85 n. 74	7.1–2	209
48:10	79 n. 62		
48:11	79 n. 62	War Scroll	
48:13	28, 66	vii, 6–7	16 n. 44
48:15	79 n. 60	13:4	72 n. 44
48:15 18	81	13:11	72 n. 44
48:18	81		
49	80 n. 65	1QS Rule of the Community	
49:2	79 n. 63	A 3.23	72 n. 44
49:4	53, 81, 88	A 4.12–13	80 n. 64
49:8	182, 252	B 3.26	181 n. 100
49:15	63, 252	B 5.5	181 n. 100
49:17	182 n. 102	B 5.21	181 n. 100
49:21	278		
49:22	252	Damascus Document	
50	28, 87	6.19	181 n. 100
50:2–5	190, 192	8.21	181 n. 100
50:3	193	16.3	247 n. 125
50:4	181 n. 99	16.5	72 n. 44, 73 n. 45
50:4–5	27	20.12	181 n. 100
50:5	28–29, 74, 86, 116, 127 n. 7, 186, 189, 193	Cave 4	
50:6	27	4Q37 Deut^j	65
50:6–13	9 n. 19	4Q176	233
50:12	27, 276, 279, 283	4Q177 Catena A	72 n. 44
50:13	27, 289	4Q197 Tob^b	169 n. 74

Cave 4 (cont.)

4Q205 Enoch[d]	169 n. 74
4Q212 Enoch[g]	131 n. 13, 151 n. 38, 240 n. 107
4Q213a Levi[b]	169 n. 74
4Q216 Jub[a]	98, 176, 184, 274 n. 34, 278 n. 43
4Q217 papJub[h]	70, 189 n. 118
4Q221 Jub[f]	99
4Q246	169 n. 74
4Q252	191
4Q286 Ber[a]	72 n. 44
4Q390	72 n. 44, 278 n. 44, 290
11Q12 Jub	249

Josephus, *Antiquities*

12.414	279 n. 46
13.297	221 n. 62

Josephus, *War*

1.31	276 n. 39
1.31–32	163 n. 60
2.142	6, 16 n. 44, 53, 71–72

NEW TESTAMENT

1 Corinthians

11:10	16 n. 44

1 Timothy

2:5	68 n. 38

2 Peter

2:9	34 n. 94
3:7	34 n. 94

Jude

1:6	34 n. 94

RABBINIC

Mishnah

m. Šabb. 19:5	100 n. 97
m. Meg. 4:9	223 n. 67

Babylonian Talmud

b. Meg. 25a	223 n. 67

Targum Onqelos

Gen 5:24	287 n. 57

Targum Pseudo-Jonathan

Deut 32:8	65

Other

Book of Asaph the Physician	62, 72, 74

Index of Modern Authors

Adler, William   32 n. 88, 242 n. 114
Albeck, Chanoch   221 n. 63, 223 n. 69
Alexander, Philip S.   201, 205, 218 n. 54, 235, 247, 287
Allison, Dale C.   127 n. 8
Amihay, Aryey   36 n. 100, 63 n. 25
Anderson, Gary A.   ix, 55 n. 6, 248 n. 128
Argall, Randal A.   67 n. 36, 149 n. 34, 150 n. 37, 158 n. 51, 225 n. 77, 239 n. 105, 240–41, 285–87
Assefa, Daniel.   107 n. 116, 131–32 n. 15, 283 n. 51
Aune, David E.   19 n. 59, 23 n. 75, 24, 30 n. 87
Bakhtin, M. M.   262–266, 270
Baldick, Chris   145 n. 27
Barker, Margaret   22 n. 72, 287 n. 57
Barr, James   12 n. 22, 21 n. 65
Barton, John   199 n. 9
Baumgarten, Albert I.   89 n. 80, 100 n. 97, 278 n. 44
Baumgarten, Joseph M.   274 n. 35
Baynes, Leslie   220 n. 59, 224 n. 73
Beaton, Rhodora E.   x
Bedenbender, Andreas   144 n. 26, 201 n. 12, 215 n. 45, 237 n. 102
Beentjes, Pancratius C.   67 nn. 36–37
Ben-Dov, Jonathan   5 n. 6, 191 n. 123
Bergsma, John Sietze   287 n. 58
Berner, Christoph   9 n. 19, 126 n. 4, 127 n. 6, 174 n. 82, 192 n. 124, 273 n. 30
Bernstein, Moshe J.   196 n. 1
Betz, Hans D.   200 n. 11
Black, Matthew   201 n. 12, 274 n. 33
Blenkinsopp, Joseph   101 n. 100
Blum, Erhard   7 n. 14
Boccaccini, Gabriele   5 n. 6, 6, 21 n. 67, 67 n. 36, 201 n. 12, 236 n. 99, 249 n. 131, 285 n. 54, 287 n. 58
Boer, Roland   262 n. 4
Bohn, F.   277 n. 43
Box, G. H.   231 n. 85
Brooke, George J.   15 n. 41, 219 n. 58, 225 n. 78
Buss, Martin J.   7 n. 14, 13 n. 29
Caquot, André   146 n. 28
Carmignac, Jean   13 n. 30, 17 n. 47, 19–21, 243 n. 116
Charles, R. H.   34, 47 n. 111, 72 n. 43, 74 n. 48, 113 n. 126, 148, 157 n. 50, 160 n. 56, 172, 187 n. 114, 230–31, 277 n. 43
Charlesworth, James H.   21 n. 69
Clarke, Ernest G.   65 n. 30
Coblentz Bautch, Kelley   58 n. 17
Cody, Aelred   101 n. 100
Collins, Adela Yarbro   16 n. 45, 23 n. 75
Collins, John J.   ix, xi, 2 n. 2, 4–5, 12 n. 22, 28, 13 n. 31, 14 nn. 34, 36, 15 n. 39, 16 n. 45, 17 nn. 47–48, 18 nn. 50–53, 19, 20 nn. 60–61, 21 nn. 66, 68, 23, 24 n. 78, 25 n. 80, 26 n. 84, 39 n. 105, 83 n. 70, 91 n. 84, 93 n. 88, 102 n. 104–105, 104, 109, 124, 144 n. 26, 145, 152, 197 n. 5, 200 nn. 9, 11, 207 n. 27, 208, 211 n. 38, 212 n. 40, 213, 214 n. 41, 215 nn. 43, 45, 47, 216 n. 49, 224 n. 73, 237 n. 102, 241 n. 112, 242 n. 114, 245 nn. 120–121, 260 n. 1, 281 n. 48

Cozijnsen, Bert 262 n. 3, 266 n. 15
Cross, Frank Moore 65 n. 29, 101 n. 100
Davenport, Gene L. 9, 10 n. 21, 148 n. 32, 233
Davies, Graham I. 19 n. 55
Davies, Philip R. 218 n. 48
DiTommaso, Lorenzo 12 n. 22
Dibelius, Martin 7 n. 14
Dillmann, August 4
Dimant, Devorah 10 n. 20, 38 n. 102, 274 n. 35
Dix, G. H. 201 n. 12
Doak, Mary ix
Doering, Lutz 10 n. 20, 184 n. 109, 279 n. 45
Doran, Robert 277 n. 43
Drawnel, Henryk 249 n. 132
Dubis, Mark 127 n. 8
Elgvin, Torleif 237 n. 102
Endres, John C. 219 n. 58, 229 n. 83, 231 n. 86
Eshel, Esther 288 n. 60
Eshel, Hanan ix
Falk, Daniel K. 226 n. 80
Feldman, Louis H. 276 n. 39
Finkelstein, Louis 221 n. 63, 223 n. 69–70, 275 n. 37, 280 n. 47
Fishbane, Michael A. ix, 212 n. 40, 214 n. 42, 245 n. 122
Fishelov, David 15 nn. 39–40
Fitzmyer, Joseph A. 288 n. 60
Flannery-Dailey, Frances 22 n. 71, 253 n. 137
Fletcher-Louis, Crispin 20 nn. 60, 62, 22 n. 72, 31 n. 89, 180 n. 98
Fokkema, Douwe Wessel 262 n. 3
Foreman, J. Wesley x
Forsyth, Neil 75 n. 52
Fowler, Alastair 14–15 nn. 37–38, 260 n. 2
Frow, John 15 n. 37
Gafni, Isaiah 276 n. 39
García Martínez, Florentino 21 n. 68, 73 n. 45, 220–225
Ginzberg, Louis 287 n. 57

Goff, Matthew J. 15 n. 41, 237 n. 102
Goldstein, Jonathan A. 280 n.47
Grabbe, Lester L. 20 n. 60
Greenfield, Jonas C. 201 n. 12, 288 n. 60
Gruen, Erich S. 270 nn. 23–25
Gunkel, Hermann 7 n. 14, 13 n. 29, 241 n. 112
Halpern-Amaru, Betsy 80 n. 63, 143 n. 25, 185 n. 110, 188 nn. 115, 117
Hanneken, Todd R. 7 n. 14, 11 nn. 21–22, 18 n. 54, 19 n. 58, 24 n. 78, 57 n. 14, 64 n. 28, 137 n. 22, 165 n. 65, 187 n. 114, 189 n. 119, 193 n. 127, 223 n. 68, 226 n. 78, 273 n. 28, 274 n. 32, 275 n. 35
Hanson, Paul D. 5, 12, 13 n. 29, 17 n. 48, 19 n. 56, 23, 45 n. 110, 66 n. 34, 91 n. 82, 105 n. 113, 229 n. 82
Hartman, Lars 13 n. 31, 201 n. 12, 204 n. 19, 205 n. 23
Hayes, Christine Elizabeth 185 n. 110, 223 n. 67
Heger, Paul 286 n. 57
Hellholm, David 12, 13 n. 31, 17 n. 50, 23 n. 75, 24
Hengel, Martin 6, 237 n. 102
Hillel, Vered 36 n. 100, 63 n. 25
Himmelfarb, Martha 6 n. 9, 39 n. 106, 62 n. 24, 74 n. 49, 100 n. 97, 127 n. 6, 185 n. 110, 187 n. 113, 220 nn. 59, 61, 275 n. 36, 275 n. 38, 277 n. 40, 278 n. 44, 287 n. 57
Horsley, Richard A. 281 n. 48
Jauss, Hans Robert 260 n. 2, 266–67
Jellinek, Adolph 62 n. 24, 74 n. 48
Kampen, John 281 n. 48
Kelly, Henry Ansgar 75 n. 52
Kister, Menahem 10 n. 19, 42 n. 108, 147 n. 30, 221 nn. 61–62, 276 n. 40
Klawans, Jonathan 185 n. 110
Knibb, Michael A. 202 n. 14, 205 n. 23, 240, 241 n. 110, 274 n. 33
Knoppers, Gary N. 101 n. 100
Koch, Klaus 5, 7 n. 14, 12, 13 nn. 29, 32, 17 n. 48, 21 n. 65, 201 n. 11

Kugel, James L.　　ix, 9 n. 19, 78 n. 59, 164 n. 63, 172 n. 81, 177 n. 87, 219 n. 58, 220 n. 59, 223 n. 67, 226, 228, 235 n. 96, 246–247, 273 n. 30, 288 n. 60
Kugler, Robert A.　　266 n. 15, 288 n. 60
Kvanvig, Helge S.　　200 n. 11, 249 nn. 131–132, 287 n. 58
Lakoff, George　　24 n. 79, 25 nn. 80–81
Lambdin, Thomas Oden　　178 n. 89
Lambert, David　　127 n. 7
Lange, Armin　8, 209 n. 36, 238, 253–54
Leslau, Wolf　　139
Levinson, Bernard M.　　199 n. 8, 200 n. 10, 226 n. 80
Lieber, Elinor　　62 n. 24
Macaskill, Grant　　167 n. 69, 237 n. 102
Mach, Michael　　80 n. 64
Machiela, Daniel　　234 n. 92
Mandolfo, Carleen　　262 n. 4
Matlock, R. Barry　　15, 20 nn. 60, 63
Mendels, Doron　　115 n. 128, 163 n. 62, 277 nn. 43
Milik, Jozef T.　　184, 201 n. 12, 273 nn. 28–29, 274
Mobley, Gregory　　75 n. 52, 81 n. 67, 86 n. 75
Müller, Hans-Peter　　237 n. 102
Müller, Karlheinz　　250 n. 134
Najman, Hindy　　ix, 196 n. 2, 218 n. 51, 219, 220 n. 59, 226 n. 80, 236 n. 99, 247 n. 125
Newsom, Carol A.　　14, 22 n. 70, 25 n. 79, 262 n. 4
Nickelsburg, George W. E.　　14 n. 33, 38 n. 104, 42, 55 n. 7, 56 nn. 10–11, 94, 97 n. 93, 108, 123, 130 n. 12, 131 nn. 13–14, 133 n. 17, 134 n. 19, 150, 151 n. 38, 158, 168–169, 196 n. 3, 201 n. 12, 202 n. 17, 203–204, 205 nn. 24–25, 209, 229 n. 83, 231 n. 235, 99, 236 n. 100, 240, 241 n. 111, 242 n. 115, 274 n. 33, 280 n. 47
Olyan, Saul M.　　67 n. 36, 101 n. 100

Pagels, Elaine　　75 n. 52, 81 n. 67
Pastor, Jack　　281 n. 49
Paul, Shalom M.　　220 n. 59
Peters, Dorothy M.　　287 n. 58
Philonenko, Marc　　20–21 n. 64
Pitre, Brant　　127 n. 8
Portier-Young, Anathea　　44 n. 109, 108 n. 117, 273 n. 27, 283 n. 51
Rad, Gerhard von　　237 n. 102
Ravid, Leora　5 n. 6, 9 n. 19, 10 n. 21, 220 n. 59, 273 n. 30
Reed, Annette Yoshiko　　xi, 55 n. 9, 60 n. 20, 223 n. 68, 287 n. 58
Regev, Eyal　　179 n. 94
Rofé, Alexander　　243 n. 117, 248 n. 130
Rowland, Christopher　　7 n. 12, 15, 19 n. 60, 20 n. 62, 217 n. 50
Rowley, H. H.　　12 n. 23, 19 n. 56, 111 n. 122, 148 n. 32, 160 n. 56, 172 n. 78, 280 n. 47
Ruiten, J. T. A. G. M. van　219 n. 58, 234 n. 90, 274 n. 33
Russell, D. S.　　7 n. 12, 12 n. 24, 17 n. 48, 65 n. 31, 81 n. 67, 148 n. 32, 172
Russell, Jeffrey Burton　75 n. 52, 81 n. 67
Sacchi, Paolo　　6, 21 n. 67, 55, 56 n. 12, 201 n. 12, 287 n. 58
Sanders, E. P.　　17 n. 47, 201 n. 12
Schmidt, Johann Michael　　11 n. 22
Schmithals, Walter　　12 n. 24
Schubert, Friedemann　　5–6
Schürer, Emil　　12 n. 23
Scott, James M.　　126 n. 4, 154 n. 47, 191–92 n. 124
Seeligmann, Isac Leo　　66 n. 33
Segal, Michael　8 n. 16, 10 nn. 20–21, 32 n. 91, 33 n. 93, 58 nn. 16, 18, 62 n. 22, 66 n. 35, 73 n. 47, 75 n. 51, 76 n. 55, 77 n. 58, 80 n. 65, 99 n. 97, 157 n. 48, 182 n. 104, 210 n. 36, 218 n. 53, 220 n. 59, 221 n. 61, 234 n. 90, 235 n. 95, 273 n. 31
Sharp, Carolyn J.　　268–269
Shemesh, Aharon　　274 n. 35
Sinding, Michael　　17 n. 48, 24 n. 79

Smith, Jonathan Z. 200 n. 11, 237 n. 102
Stegemann, Hartmut 5, 13 n. 30, 17 n. 47, 19, 20 n. 64, 30 n. 87, 260 n. 1
Stone, Michael E. 8 n. 16, 12, 17 n. 48, 20 n. 60, 36 n. 100, 63 n. 25, 136 n. 21, 197 n. 5, 200 n. 11, 201 n. 12, 237 n. 102, 240 n. 108, 242 n. 114, 288 n. 60
Stuckenbruck, Loren T. 56 nn. 11, 13, 59 n. 19, 93 nn. 87–88, 121 n. 1, 131 n. 13, 151 n. 38, 168 n. 72, 169 n. 74, 200 n. 10, 202 n. 15, 225 n. 74, 266 n. 14, 286 n. 56, 289 n. 62
Sturm, Richard E. 18 n. 51, 20 n. 63
Suter, David Winston 55 n. 7, 201 n. 11, 241 n. 111
Swales, John 15 n. 39, 24 n. 79
Talmon, Shemaryahu 199 n. 9
Tcherikover, Victor 111 n. 121
Teeter, D. Andrew x
Testuz, Michel 6, 10 nn. 19, 21, 61 n. 21, 73 n. 46, 97, 101 n. 102, 104, 148 n. 32, 154 n. 47, 191 n. 124
Thomas, Samuel I. 248 n. 127
Tigchelaar, Eibert 17 n. 50, 21 n. 68, 73 n. 45
Tiller, Patrick A. 91 n. 83, 94–95, 131 n. 14, 132 n. 16, 205 n. 25, 274 n. 33
Toorn, K. van der 239 n. 104
Ulrich, Eugene ix–x, 65 n. 29, 199 n. 9
VanderKam, James C. ix–xi, 1 n. 1, 8 n. 16, 10 n. 21, 27, 28 n. 85, 34 nn. 94, 96, 97, 35 nn. 98–99, 56 nn. 10–11, 58 n. 19, 62 n. 23, 65 n. 31, 71 n. 40, 94 n. 89, 98 n. 96, 130 n. 12, 140, 142, 157 nn. 49–50, 159 n. 53, 163, 168 n. 73, 174 n. 82, 175 n. 83, 177 nn. 88, 178, 180 n. 96, 182, 183 n. 106, 184, 189, 191 n. 122, 192 nn. 124–125, 197 n. 4, 199 n. 9, 200 n. 11, 218 nn. 53–54, 219 n. 58, 220 n. 59, 223 n. 68, 228, 230–231, 234 n. 90, 235 n. 98, 237 n. 102, 248 n. 128, 249 n. 132, 255 n. 143, 273 nn. 28–29, 274 nn. 33–35, 275 nn. 36–37, 277, 278 nn. 43–44, 279 n. 46, 282 n. 50
Vermès, Géza 73 n. 45, 223 n. 67
Vielhauer, Philipp 12 n. 24, 17 n. 48, 19 n. 56
Volz, Paul 160 n. 56
Wacholder, Ben Zion 236 n. 99
Wellhausen, Julius 100–101 n. 100
Werman, Cana 10 n. 20, 101 n. 102, 137 n. 22, 185 n. 110, 220 n. 59, 254 n. 139, 275 n. 36
Wiesenberg, Ernest 10 nn. 20–21
Williamson, Robert, Jr. 14 n. 35
Wintermute, O. S. 233–234
Wray, T. J. 75 n. 52, 81 n. 67, 86 n. 75
Wright, Benjamin G., III 14 n. 35, 15 n. 41, 67 n. 36, 247–248, 285 n. 54, 287 n. 57
Zahn, Molly x
Zeitlin, Solomon 275 n. 37
Zerbe, Gordon 110 n. 120
Zimmerli, Walther 101 n. 100

Index of Subjects

Abraham, 37, 39–40, 60, 78–81, 91–92, 98–99, 112, 115, 125, 155, 164, 188, 226, 238, 246, 250–51, 257, 288
afterlife, 29, 104, 114, 160, 291
Alcimus, 272, 278–82
angels, 32–39, 53–88, 186–87, 257
Antiochus, 5, 111, 114, 124, 132, 135, 163, 244, 276–77, 279, 291
apocalypticism, 7, 13, 16–18, 23
audience, 8, 16, 19, 24–25, 27, 30–31, 38, 43, 47, 53, 81, 125, 141, 147–48, 156, 172–79, 198–99, 211–13, 218–20, 231–32, 242, 266–72, 292–93
authorial intent, 19, 178, 266–72, 293
authorship of Jubilees, 9–11, 273
Bacchides, 156, 272, 278, 280, 282
Beliar, 29, 72–73, 87, 277
biblical interpretation, 196–236
Book of Noah, 62, 146, 234, 274, 288
calendar, 5–6, 28, 89, 92, 181, 190–93, 220–21, 275, 278–79
centripetal interpretation, 201, 205
chastisement, 39, 43, 47, 57, 61, 126–27, 129, 136–38, 149, 155, 193, 282–84
circumcision, 28, 50, 52, 79, 99–100, 182–83, 186–87, 222, 276–77
coded revelation, 236–48, 252
cosmic catastrophe, 43, 48, 120, 125–26, 128, 130–31, 133–34, 136, 142
cultural symbols, 284–90
date of composition of Jubilees, 272–84
deferred judgment, 148–161, 216, 291
demons, 53–88
demotion, 270–72
determinism, 9, 105, 127, 291–92

Deuteronomistic ideas, 38–39, 43, 62, 119, 145, 155, 181, 187, 194, 215–16, 291
discord, 25, 30–31, 145, 175, 178, 208, 215, 217, 219, 224, 231, 235, 238, 252, 259, 261, 268–69, 293
dreams, 253–54, 285–86
dualism, 32, 49, 91
elitism, esotericism, 30, 97–104, 236–58
enlightened ones, 46, 95, 108–10, 146, 211, 236, 242–46, 251, 276, 289
Enoch, 6–7, 92, 107, 202–3, 248–50, 284–287
eschatology, 19–21, 38–49, 165–93, 272, 293
Essenes, 6, 16, 53, 71, 97
evil. *See* theodicy
exogamy, 33, 58, 89, 112, 117, 182, 185–86, 223, 271, 275, 277
exponential decline, 120–26, 291
family resemblance model, 15, 17
final woes, 41, 127–48
flood, 35, 43, 107, 129, 134, 141–42, 157–61
function of genre, 8, 12–13, 20, 23–24, 201
genre, 11–22, 260–72
Gentiles, 35, 39, 59–60, 69–70, 91–97, 251, 277–78, 291–92
gymnasium, 50, 55, 221, 276–77
halaka. *See* law
hasidim. *See* pietists
Hasmoneans, 89, 113, 275, 277–78
heavenly tablets, 3, 9, 11, 16, 27–29, 52, 63, 175, 177–83, 191–93, 219–25, 235, 238, 256–58

-329-

horizon of expectations. *See* reader expectations
humor, 41, 81, 145, 264, 270–72
injustice. *See* theodicy
irony, 25–26, 268–70
Jacob, 27–28, 38, 70, 87, 89, 92, 98–99, 112, 115–17, 163–64, 175, 185, 189, 222, 238, 251–52, 255–57, 271, 274, 277–78, 289–90
Judah Maccabee, 46, 93–94, 111, 132–33, 275–77, 279, 282, 291, 293
judgment day(s), 16, 28, 33–34, 38, 40, 88, 133, 149–61, 165, 178, 264, 268
law, 3, 4, 28, 32, 36, 38, 40–42, 63, 77, 79, 85, 87, 90, 92, 102–3, 105, 114, 116, 126, 148, 155–56, 168–69, 171–72, 174–75, 177, 181–83, 186, 190, 192, 194–96, 216, 218, 220–25, 235–36, 238, 240, 248, 251, 253–54, 271–73, 277, 279, 283, 286–93
Levi, Levites. *See* priesthood
literary morphology, 2–3, 11–31, 259–69, 293
longevity, 29, 40, 55, 103, 125–26, 137, 142, 146–47, 154–55, 166–67, 170, 173, 181, 193, 226–28, 234, 282, 291
Maccabean Revolt. *See* war
maskilim. *See* enlightened ones
Mastema, 28–30, 35–36, 53, 59, 62–63, 69–82, 270
master paradigm, 14, 17, 26–31, 224
Molech, 72–73, 223
morphology. *See* literary morphology
Moses, 4, 9, 27, 34, 36, 63, 79–80, 82, 85, 87, 125–126, 147, 157, 159, 162, 168–69, 171, 174, 176–79, 181–83, 186, 193, 198, 201, 204, 212–13, 215–16, 218–19, 235, 238, 240, 247, 249, 251–52, 272, 286–89, 292
new creation. *See* eschatology
Noah, 33, 35–36, 46, 59–65, 91–92, 107, 121, 129, 133, 146, 161, 167, 188, 190, 221, 234, 241–42, 251, 272, 287–89
parody, 262–66, 270, 272
Paul, 18, 20–21, 54, 126, 260

Philistines, 113, 162–163
pietists, 93–95, 102, 132, 276, 280–81, 290
plant, 9, 16, 91–92, 98–99, 225, 264, 268, 289
polemic, 67, 69, 100, 103, 180, 186, 212, 216, 248–49, 254, 263, 265–66, 279, 285
priesthood, 6, 38, 48, 52, 55, 58, 63, 89–90, 92, 97, 100–101, 112–13, 165–67, 170–72, 175–76, 178–82, 186–87, 194, 197–98, 223–24, 234, 241, 253, 271–72, 275, 278–79, 282, 289, 291–93
prototype theory, 9, 14, 24–25
Qumran, 4, 6, 18, 20–21, 32, 72, 248, 260, 273–75
reader expectations, 8, 11, 23–25, 41–42, 50, 81, 125, 130, 136, 144, 147–49, 156, 179, 195–99, 219, 221, 236, 238, 258, 261–62, 266–72, 293
redactor. *See* authorship of Jubilees
repentance, 3, 28, 39–40, 42–43, 47, 57, 62, 78, 84, 87, 112, 116, 119, 126–27, 129, 136–38, 144, 149, 153, 155–56, 164, 172, 174, 194, 215–16, 228, 233, 282–83, 291
resurrection, 29, 48, 85, 96, 103, 110, 114, 133, 160, 170
revelatory framework, 3–4, 19, 22, 27, 30, 49, 198
sabbath, 32, 52, 100, 110, 114–15, 117, 184–87, 220, 222, 276, 279, 283
sanctuary. *See* temple
satans, 29, 36, 48, 70–77, 81–82, 86, 115, 232, 270
satire, 25–26, 145, 264, 270, 272
sectarianism, 6, 88–104, 148, 278, 290
sin. *See* theodicy
Sodom, 106, 113–14, 149, 153, 161–62
stages of revelation, 207–16, 241, 244–45
subversion, 39–50, 259–270, 290, 293
temple, sanctuary, 28, 167–69, 171, 174–80, 186, 272, 281, 288–89, 292
territory, 187–189
theodicy, 31–38, 54–64, 157–65

Urzeit typology, 91, 121–22, 203
violence, 44–47, 101–17, 146, 223, 272–73, 279–84, 291
war, Maccabean Revolt, 44–47, 93–94, 101–7, 114–17, 134–137, 186, 272–77, 282–84

watchers, 28, 33–35, 54–59, 71, 129, 157–58, 202, 241, 250
white children, 46, 144–48, 264, 272
wisdom, 40, 92, 110–11, 210, 236–58
worldview, 21–23

www.ingramcontent.com/pod-product-compliance
Lightning Source LLC
Chambersburg PA
CBHW021818300426
44114CB00009BA/225